CRITICAL PREFACES
OF THE
FRENCH RENAISSANCE

CRITICAL PREFACES
OF THE
FRENCH RENAISSANCE

BY
BERNARD WEINBERG

NORTHWESTERN UNIVERSITY PRESS
EVANSTON, ILLINOIS
1950

NORTHWESTERN UNIVERSITY STUDIES

Virgil B. Heltzel, *Editor*

Humanities Series Number Twenty

Open access edition funded by the National Endowment for the Humanities/Andrew W. Mellon Foundation Humanities Open Book Program.

Bernard Weinberg. Critical Prefaces of the French Renaissance.
Evanston, Ill.: Northwestern University Press, 1950.

ISBN 978-0-8101-3876-6 (paper)
ISBN 978-0-8101-3877-3 (ebook)

TO MY
MOTHER AND FATHER

FOREWORD

The purpose of the present volume is to provide a collection of representative critical prefaces of the French Renaissance in an accurate and readable text. This collection is intended not chiefly for the specialist in Middle French, but rather for those concerned with the critical ideas of the sixteenth century. Both the nature of the Introduction and the selection and presentation of the representative texts have been determined by this aim.

The Introduction. In the Introduction, five major texts of the sixteenth century in France are analyzed in considerable detail: Sebillet's *Art poétique françoys* (1548), Du Bellay's *Deffence et Illustration de la langue françoyse* (1549), Jacques Peletier du Mans's *Art poétique* (1555), Pierre Delaudun's *Art poétique* (1597), and Vauquelin de la Fresnaye's *Art poétique français* (1605). None of these texts is included in the collection. They have been studied in the Introduction for two main purposes: first, to supplement the texts published here in order to give the reader a more adequate conception of the total critical production of the century; and second, to emphasize through the analysis the principal critical problems and topics of the century, in the light of which the prefaces themselves may be better understood. Other critical documents (such as Fabri's *Art de pleine rhétorique*) have not been discussed; once again, the Introduction is selective rather than all-inclusive, and is not meant to be a history of critical theory in the Renaissance.

The Prefaces. The prefaces printed here were published between 1525 and 1611, and are arranged chronologically in order of their publication.[1] They have been selected as representative expressions of the ideas current with respect to the various genres practiced in the century: tragedy, comedy, epic, lyric, satire, romance of chivalry, history, short story, translation, and with respect to the nature of the poetic art in general. Some of them are well known and have been reprinted since the sixteenth century; others are less famous and have never been reprinted. It should be emphasized that this is a choice of prefaces, not a complete collection. The choice was influenced in part at least by considerations of availability of materials, since the project was undertaken and completed during the wartime years when complete access to European materials was not possible. Two of the texts are not prefaces, Estienne Dolet's *La Manière de bien traduire* (1540) and Ronsard's *Abrégé de l'art poétique* (1565); the first is included because it contains ideas on a Renaissance genre not otherwise separately treated in the prefaces, the second because it rounds out

[1] In a few cases, rearrangements have been made of texts within a given year, in order to bring together texts which were closely related in idea.

the presentation of Ronsard's critical ideas. All of the texts are not equally important; but it is hoped that each one will make some contribution to the totality of ideas on the genre which it treats or on the poetic art as a whole.

The Texts. In all but a few cases, the text printed here is that of the first edition. First editions are used in order to present the earliest expressions of the critical ideas, with subsequent changes in those expressions reflected in the variants. For purposes of making these texts more readily accessible to the reader interested primarily in criticism, the following editorial practices have been followed:

Paragraphing—In most cases, no paragraphing was found in the original text. I have introduced paragraph divisions freely according to what seemed to be the divisions of ideas of the text. This implies an interpretation of the text, and may be a source of deformation. But the advantages of breaking up the solid mass of the original are such that it is worth while running the risk. The reader will understand that all paragraphing is my own.

Punctuation—In a similar way, the texts have been completely repunctuated. In the originals, punctuation often depended on the caprice of the printer and even on the type faces available to him; it is impossible to tell to what extent it represented the wishes of the author. Hence I have not hesitated to divide or combine sentences, to introduce commas and semicolons, parentheses and dashes, quotation marks and italics, in accordance with what seemed to me to be the logical and grammatical exigencies of the text. This again involves interpretation and the risk of deformation, and the reader should keep it in mind when studying the texts. It does, however, result in a considerable clarification of many of the texts and in a much greater ease in reading.

Spelling—The spelling of the original texts has at all times been scrupulously retained. The following practices, now current in the edition of sixteenth-century texts, have been followed:

u and *v*, *i* and *j* have been distinguished;

the overstroke and other orthographic abbreviations have been solved; "&" and "⁊" have been written "et"; "ę" representing Greek "αι" or Latin "ae" has been transcribed as "e";

the apostrophe has been deleted or added in accordance with modern usage, e.g. to give such combinations as *qu'elle*, *n'y*, *s'en*, and *davantage*;

ligature or non-ligature of *oe*, *ae* follows the original text;

capital letters, indiscriminately used in the originals, have been removed except from proper names; they have been used uniformly for adjectives formed on proper names and for certain titles of respect when used for specific persons;

hyphens have been added in such combinations as *ont-ils*, *ceux-là*, and removed from such combinations as *gentilz-hommes;*

words such as *tresillustre, pour ce que* have been written *très illustre, pource que,* in accordance with the modern conventions of division (but *pour ce* when *ce* is the strong postpositive demonstrative has of course not been combined);

the practice in combining such words as *à fin* has varied, depending upon the spelling and accentuation in the original text and upon the apparent meaning of the words;

obvious typographical errors have been corrected, and the original form has been given among the variants.

Accents—the accentuation of the original texts has been respected, except that:

the acute accent has been added to indicate final stressed *e* or *ee;*

the grave accent has been added to such words as *après, très, près, à, là, ès, dès, où,* and has been substituted for the acute when it appeared on the same words, e.g. *lá, és, dés;*

the diaeresis has been printed as in the originals, but it has been added to the word *païs* and to such words as *obeïssant* when, in verse passages, the *i* counts as a syllable;

the cedilla has been retained or added in all forms of *sçavoir* requiring it, but it has been removed from such forms as *sceu;* it has been added elsewhere in accordance with modern usage.

Citations—since citations of Greek and Latin texts in the originals are frequently faulty, words and passages have been quoted as they now appear in the Loeb editions or in other standard modern texts.

The result of these editorial practices is a text which represents faithfully the spelling and word order of the original, but which takes certain liberties with paragraphing, punctuation, and accentuation. The philologist who wishes to use the texts exactly as originally printed now has access to photostats and microfilms for his special investigations; and the general reader, interested in the ideas of the texts, is spared the many idiosyncrasies, accidents, and confusing characteristics of the originals.

Collations and Variants. Many of the prefaces printed here were published in one edition only, and the problem of variants does not exist. For the rest, I have not attempted to collate all existing editions. It became apparent, from a study of the texts printed here, that the variants in these materials are very largely orthographic. In other cases, they are such variants as might have been introduced by the printer rather than by the author. Moreover, a collation of all editions of all texts was impossible during the years when the texts were established; even had it been possible, it would not have yielded results commensurate with the effort involved. I have therefore tried to collate with the first edition as many contemporary editions as were available and at least one posthumous edition. Any significant variants introduced during the lifetime of the author thus stand a fair chance of being represented here, although they may not always be shown in the very first edition in which they appeared. The general practice with respect to variants has been as follows:

> purely orthographic variants are not given; if the word is the same tense, number, gender, no account is taken of divergencies of spelling;
>
> variant readings from collated editions are given in diplomatic transcription, except for the solution of over-strokes and other common abbreviations; the general editorial practices used for the texts are not applied to the variants;
>
> italics in the original texts are not always reflected in the variants, especially where they would be confused with my own italicized indications;
>
> printer's errors in the basic text, corrected in the present text, are reflected in the variants, where they appear with the date of the basic text.

Bibliographical Materials. A short bibliographical note precedes each text. It gives in detail information about the edition used as the basic text and about the editions collated, and sources from which additional information may be derived. The discussions following are limited to matters of authorship, date of composition, circumstances of composition, and available modern editions. No attempt is made to interpret or comment upon the texts themselves.

Notes. In the notes, I have tried to identify all references, allusions, or citations involving other works, ancient or modern, and to clarify other allusions of a biographical or historical character. This has not always been possible, and there are a number of passages or persons upon which I have been able to throw no light. I have not attempted to trace sources of the ideas expressed in the texts, since this would be the subject for an independent investigation of great complexity. Unless otherwise stated, references in the notes to Greek and Latin works are to the editions in the Loeb Classics.

Glossary. The glossary, which has been kept to a minimum, includes only such words as the general reader, using a standard dictionary, might not be able to find; the *Dictionnaire général* of Hatzfeld, Darmesteter, and Thomas has been used as the standard. It is assumed that this "general reader" will have some notions of the forms and spellings peculiar to sixteenth-century French and will be able to recognize equivalents of modern words even when the spelling is confusingly different.

Index. The index lists critical terms and names of authors and critics.

Work on this collection of prefaces was begun in 1941, interrupted for over three years by the war, completed in large part without the possibility of final checking and collating in European libraries. Materials for it had to be restricted, with few exceptions, to those available in libraries in the United States and those obtainable on microfilm from the Bibliothèque Nationale. In this connection, I am indebted to my brother, Dr. Saul S. Weinberg, and to Professor Louis Robert of the Collège de France, who secured French materials for me almost immediately after the liberation. I am especially grateful to the staffs of the Bibliothèque Nationale, the Library of Congress, Harvard College Library, the Newberry Library, and the Pierpont Morgan Library (as well as to the staffs of other libraries where original materials were obtained or consulted) for their splendid cooperation. For much sound advice on the procedures to be followed in the establishment of the texts, I owe a debt of gratitude to an expert in such matters, my friend William J. Roach of the University of Pennsylvania. Finally, I should like to express my appreciation to Professor Virgil B. Heltzel, editor of the "Northwestern University Studies," for his expeditious and sympathetic handling of all editorial matters.

B. W.

Evanston, Illinois, October 15, 1949

TABLE OF CONTENTS

INTRODUCTION

To the short critical statements afforded by the prefaces of this collection must be added, if we wish to understand the development of literary theory in the French Renaissance, the longer expressions found in the formal *arts poétiques*. These *arts poétiques* themselves are supplemented by a number of works on language, prosody, and rhetoric. The works which are analyzed in this Introduction give a representation of the principal methods of approach to the problem of literature in the sixteenth century. Although they all belong to the second half of the century (the earliest is Sebillet's of 1548), they contain enough of the traditional material inherited from the earlier years of the century to indicate the persistence of traditional elements and approaches beside the new points of view which appeared about 1550. In the analyses, methods and points of view have been sought rather than a census of details. The method of analysis itself may be found useful in the reading of the critical prefaces.

1. Thomas Sebillet

Thomas Sebillet's *Art poétique françoys*, 1548,[1] is not a completely systematic treatise. It represents a combination of such elements as the traditional rules for the handling of the verse genres, the Platonic notion of the divine source of poetry, the Horatian statement of the ends of poetry, and rhetorical teachings from Cicero, Quintilian, and Aristotle's *Rhetoric*. In spite of the fact that these elements are never completely synthesized, a kind of pattern does emerge for the whole work; and although Books I and II, on poetry in general and on the specific genres, respectively, are largely separate, enough of the theory stated in the first finds entry into the second to establish a thread at least of connection. However, there are various incomplete developments, lacunae in argument, and unrelated notions which make a completely satisfactory explanation of the text impossible.

For Sebillet's theory of poetry in general, the concept at the source of all other ideas is that of the divinity of poetry. From God spring science ("mere ... et nourrice de l'œuvre vertueus," I, i, 8) and art (in which is found "ceste divine perfection que nous appellons Vertu," I, i, 7); but these are so close to each other as to be practically indistinguishable. In all of the arts is visible something of the "feu divin," but in none so much as in the poetic art ("ce que plus proprement j'appelleroie divine inspiration," I, i, 8–9). For on the one hand the poet writes only when "inspiré de quelque divine afflation," and on the other hand poetry alone is characterized by "lés nombres ... la perfection et divinité desquelz soutient et entretient

[1] Ed. Félix Gaiffe, "Société des Textes français modernes," Paris: Librairie E. Droz, 1932.

l'admirable machine de cest univers, et tout ce qu'elle clost et contient" (I, i, 9–10).

It must follow then that the poet himself is of divine filiation. Plato, indeed, has called the poets "enfans dés dieuz" (I, i, 9); they are gifted with "quelque don divin, et céleste prérogative" (I, i, 10). The first manifestations of poetry were connected with religion; the Hebrew prophets were "asseuréz de divinité," the Greek oracles had at least a "grande apparence" of divinity, the Roman priests dedicated themselves to "louenges et supplications auz dieuz," and modern Christian liturgy celebrates in verse the "vrai charactére de la divinité" (I, i, 12–13).

Something at least of this divinity shows through in the poem itself. For the most important part of the poem is the invention, "[ce] qu'il [the poet] puisse proprement dire et commodément adapter au subjét qu'il veut déduire en son Pöéme" (I, iii, 23). It is invention which distinguishes the poet from the rimester (I, ii, 20) and which is the primary determinant of the success of the poem (II, i, 114). Now this invention (quoting Horace) is a product of the "entendement et esprit divin" of the poet (I, iii, 23). It springs from "la subtilité et sagacité de l'esprit: laquéle si Dieu a déniée a l'homme, pour neant se travaillera-il de dire ou faire en despit de Minerve: singuliérement en l'art de pöésie" (I, iii, 24). It is invention, finally, which represents the part of "nature" in poetry as against that of "art," an opinion in which both Horace and Quintilian concur (I, iii, 25).

Thus God is the source of the arts in general, of the poetic art in particular, of the nature of the poet, and of that within the poem which constitutes its particular excellence, invention. At the same time, there are elements, at each stage in this descending chain, for which God is not responsible. These are the elements ascribable to "art," in the special sense of technique or skill. The primary source here is the philosophers and rhetoricians, "qui en ont escrit livres propres et particuliers" (I, iii, 25–26). In each of the arts, presumably, the divine fire would be supplemented by a special knowledge, derived from human sources, which would direct the practice of the art. In poetry, this special knowledge consists of what is generally called the "art of poetry" (in a secondary sense), i.e. the technique of versification, and is derived from such treatises as the one which Sebillet is now writing: "Car ce qu'en Pöésie est nommé art, et que nous traitons comme art en cest opuscule, n'est rien que la nue escorce de Pöésie, qui couvre artificiélement sa naturéle séve, et son ame naturélement divine" (I, i, 10)—a statement which is clarified by another, "je m'en vay montrer ... tout ce qui fait a l'art de ce qu'on appelle Ryme" (I, i, 15).[2]

[2] It is evident from Bk. I, Chap. II that by "ryme" is meant the whole art of versification.

In a similar way, the poet's divine gift must be supplemented by study, doctrine, and precept (I, i, 10), which again relate especially to versification. It is to be noted that such study provides the artifice which is added to nature, but is never a substitute for nature. Rime is but a "nue escorce" covering "la séve et le boys" of invention and eloquence (I, ii, 20); it produces only "le vide son des vocables," which is never a substitute for solid invention (I, iii, 22). As for the poem itself, its principal component of invention is completed by two others, disposition and elocution; these are not specifically ascribed either to nature or to artifice, but it seems more likely from the general treatment in the text that they belong rather to nature (cf. I, iii, 27–28, I, iv, 29–33, where both seem to be learned from models rather than from precepts, although some precepts are applicable). Finally, all of the graces of rime and of versification in general are the products of artifice.

This general conception of poetry gives rise to two of the main characteristics of Sebillet's treatment in subsequent parts of the *Art poëtique françoys*. In the first place, since invention comes from God and is hence ineffable, and since the art of versification comes from man and is hence teachable, Sebillet will concentrate his attention on the latter. He will discuss rhythm in general and the various rules of language which affect rhythm, rime in general and the various characteristics of language which affect rime, and the traditions and rules governing the kinds of verses and rime schemes to be used in each of the current poetic genres. In the second place, since the art of poetry (in the broader sense) does not reduce exclusively to such precepts, since the poet must be aided with respect to such things as invention, language, style, Sebillet will call extensively upon the example of models. If he cannot teach these aspects of poetry, he can at least point out to the poet examples of successful achievement; the assumption is that the poet, by following these examples, will himself be successful. Various passages of general import indicate this intention:

> l'invention, et le jugement compris soubz elle se conferment et enrichissent par la lecture des bons et classiques pöétes françois comme sont entre les vieux Alain Chartier, et Jan de Meun: mais plus lui profiteront les jeunes comme imbus de la pure source françoise ... entre lesquelz lira le novice dés muses françoises, Marot, Saingelais, Salel, Heroet, Scéve, et telz autres bons espris ... et autrement les suivre pas a pas comme l'enfant la nourrice, partout ou il vouldra cheminer par dedans le pré de Pöésie (I, iii, 26–27).

> mais encor pourra-il grandement locupléter et l'invention et l'économie, de la lecture et intelligence des plus nobles Pöétes Grecz et Latins (I, iii, 28).

Moreover, for each of the genres one or several models are proposed, and the process becomes so general that even on matters of versification Sebillet sometimes limits himself to pointing out a model.[3]

These generalizations on the poetic art raise a number of questions, the answers to which should throw additional light on Sebillet's theory. How is poetry distinguished from the other arts involving language? If such traditionally rhetorical terms as invention, disposition, and elocution are used in connection with poetry, what is the relationship of rhetoric to poetry? Do considerations of the audience distinguish rhetoric from poetic? What is the end of poetic composition? To all of these, fairly clear solutions may be found.

Poetry is distinguished from the other arts involving language exclusively by its use of rhythm or "numbers." Early in the text we are told of the excellence that belongs to the poetic art because of its use of "lés nombres dont les Poétes mesurent leurs carmes" (I, i, 10). Throughout, it is apparent that measured discourse and poetry are synonymous. The Hebrew prophets sang "en vers pöétiquement mesuréz," "en mesure versifiée" (I, i, 11); the Greek oracles "estoient en vers" and the Roman priests addressed the gods in praise and entreaties "mesurées en carmes pöétiques"; Christian prayers are "en vers et carmes mesuréz" (I, i, 12–13). Rime is of secondary importance, and should be considered only as an ornament to meter (I, ii, 18). Sebillet offers no definition of poetry; were he to do so, it would probably be defined as "a composition of words in measured or rhythmical form."

Indeed, it is only the presence of numbers which separates poetry from rhetoric. "Car la Rhétorique est autant bien espandue par tout le pöéme, comme par toute l'oraison. Et sont l'Orateur et le Poëte tant proches et conjoinz, que semblables et égauz en plusieurs choses, différent principalement en ce, que l'un est plus contraint de nombres que l'autre" (I, iii, 21–22). Numerous other passages confirm this initial statement. Invention is the first part of both arts (I, iii, 21 ff.). Nature is prior to art in both disciplines, as Horace and Quintilian demonstrate (I, iii, 25). The poet may learn his "art" from such rhetoricians as Cicero, Quintilian, and Aristotle, although he will take other poets as his models (I, iii, 25–26, 28). Both poets and rhetoricians are sources for elocution (I, iv, 29). And so forth. Hence poetry is a kind of rhetoric, sharing with rhetoric the three parts of invention, disposition, and elocution, learning about language from the same preceptors, differing from rhetoric only in the use of meter.

If this is the case, then it is pertinent to ask whether the audience, which

[3] For example, "Je ne m'amuseray ne toy a te spécifier l'usage de la ryme [in the rondeau]: car te proposant l'exemple, tu ne saurois faillir a l'imiter" (II, iii, 122).

in traditional rhetoric is an important element in the determination of the form, has a like function with respect to poetry. For Sebillet, it does so only in a very limited sense. There are some fifteen passages which might be construed as referring to an audience, and in each case it is merely an audience whose ear would be pleased or offended by proper or improper handling of harmony, meter, and rime. Thus rime in French verse is a "consonance portant par l'organe de l'ouye délectation à l'esprit" (I, ii, 19). One must be careful in innovation of words lest "l'asprété du mot nouveau n'égratigne et ride lés aureilles rondes" (I, iv, 32). The equivocal rime "fait cest unison et resemblance plus égale et de ce plus poignante l'ouye" (I, vii, 63). And all rimes, regardless of spelling, must be "soustenuz par le son de aureille, que je te dy encor estre le principal du collége de la ryme" (I, viii, 88). Except in this manner, the audience need not be taken into consideration in the writing of the poem. It is not possessed of standards, prejudices, or expectations which have to be met in the poem; in a sense, it is without character.[4] Thus in so far as poetry, for Sebillet, is a part of rhetoric, it is a part of an incomplete rhetoric, one in which the poet-rhetorician operates practically without regard for the character of his audience.

If the poet does not write for a specific audience which influences his writing, what ends does he propose for the poetic art? Sebillet gives several alternative and unrelated solutions. For one thing, the French poet will work for the greater glory of French verse: "l'exaltation de ceste françoise pöésie" (I, iii, 27). He will follow the lead of those young poets who have worked so well that "l'esperance est grande de la voir dedans peu d'ans autant sainte et autant auguste que elle fut soubz le Cesar Auguste" (I, i, 15). In a word, he will work for "l'illustration et augmentation de notre langue françoise" (I, iv, 31–32). Or again, his own glory may be the end which he seeks; just as the Greek poets enjoyed "admiration et louenge de leur divine versification" (I, i, 13), he may obtain from the well made poem "faveur et applaudissement" (I, v, 41). If he writes in the dramatic genres, he may seek to "ensemble profiter et resjouïr," following the precept of Horace (II, viii, 164); tragedy, for example, presents "ce que fait a l'information de nos mœurs et vie" (II, viii, 162), and allegory similarly seeks "l'instruction dés mœurs" (II, viii, 163).[5] Finally, he may strive only to

[4] This statement will have to be modified later in the light of the criteria that Sebillet offers for poetry, since some of these are related to the audience.

[5] The *cantique* also has a special end, since it is addressed to the gods "a fin de destourner le mal, ou continuer le bien" (II, vi, 143). The introduction of the *utile dulci* principle of Horace seems merely to be an echoing of a tradition, and does not fit into the general scheme of the work. As a matter of fact, the remainder of the passage in which it is mentioned shows clearly that it is completely misunderstood.

make himself perfect in his art, to produce poems which attain perfection in their respective genres; this is the goal which Sebillet envisages in his treatment of the genres:

> Car je m'en vay te montrer en ce second livre toutes lés formes et differences dés Pöémes usurpées en l'art Poétique François, et au passé, et au présent: a fin qu'entendant quéle matiére se traite mieus en cestuy cy, ou en cestuy la, et quéle forme de ryme y est plus souvent et plus proprement usurpée, tu n'ays rien que souhaitter pour t'eslever a la perfection du Pöéte (II, Preface, 102).

Of the various ends proposed, it is this last one which seems to be the most effectively operative in Sebillet's work. For in the treatment of the individual genres, the precepts and remarks are directed to the achievement of the special perfection (or "vertu") proper to each genre. The poet is to work primarily toward the creation of the "perfect" poem in its genre (even if the "perfection" may reside only in correct prosodic form or in a clever turn of phrase); if he achieves it, one or more of the other ends indicated may also be served.

In the light of these general concepts of poetry, Sebillet's treatment of the genres becomes more than a hackneyed repetition of the traditional rules and regulations for the writing of each of the kinds. That treatment occupies about one-half of the total work. Part of it at least is informed by the more general theory, although much of the time we have little more than unimaginative retailing of rules. For each of the genres, Sebillet treats the following subjects: the matter, the form, the "vertu" or special excellence, the model or models to be imitated, the rime scheme, and the kind of verse. The genres studied are the epigram, sonnet, rondeau, ballade, chant royal, cantique (including the ode), epistle, elegy, dialogue (including eclogue, morality, tragedy, farce, comedy), coq-à-l'âne, blason, enigma, complaint, lay, translation (including the "grand œuvre" or epic), and derivative forms of each of these.

The *matière* of the poem consists of all those elements of the poem which are contributed by invention, disposition, and elocution—of the things treated, the words used, and the arrangement of things and words. Negatively stated, it consists of everything except meter, rime scheme, and rime. Thus after Sebillet has discussed invention, disposition, and elocution (Bk. I, Chaps. III–IV), he inquires, with respect to the entire structure, "quéle en restera la forme?" (I, v, 34) and goes on to an analysis of the various line lengths. Introducing Book II, he speaks of "quéle matiére se traite ... et quéle forme de ryme" (II, Preface, 102). The sonnet and the epigram, he says, are similar "et de matiére, et de mesure" (II, ii, 115). This is in line with his earlier distinction between the contributions of nature and of art to the poem: nature, supplying the poet with his divine gift of invention, is responsible for the matter of the poem, whereas art (in the narrower sense of artifice) directs its versification, or form. Once again, and for the same reasons as before, Sebillet's indications with respect to matter will be extremely sketchy (these things coming to the poet by birth or being learned by him from the work of others equally gifted), while his sections on form will be lengthy and detailed. This same distinction accounts for the supremacy of matter over form. Sebillet insists that, in spite of certain rules and traditions governing the use of different verses, "l'éspéce du carme n'empesche point le Pöéme autrement bien fait de rencontrer faveur et applaudissement" (I, v, 41). What is meant by "autrement bien fait" is explained in a second passage: "l'espéce du carme ne diminue ny augmente gueres la grace du pöéme du quel l'invention et élocution sont autrement ingenieuses" (II, i, 114). Thus the principal factor in the excellence of the poem is the nature and handling of the matter, not the versification. Matter determines form; such details as the length of the poem, the type of verse, and the rime scheme depend upon the matter. The form is "Diverse, selon l'entreprise de l'œuvre, et la commodité de l'assiette" (I, v, 34); there is no limit for the length of the epigram, "mais le alongeons tant que le requiert la matiére prise" (II, i, 104); if you write a *chant*, it will be "de la forme que tu penseras la plus commode et propre a la matiére dont tu l'entreprendras bastir" (II, v, 141–42); since the ode is about lovers, it is "aussy peu constant qu'ilz sont, et autant prompt a changer de son, de vers, et de Ryme" (II, vi, 147–48). Grave and serious matters require longer verses, Alexandrines or decasyllables, while light and humorous subjects permit the shorter octosyllable (pp. 41, 113, 118, 122, 127 and *passim*).

As for the various genres, they are assigned *matières* of different kinds. Some have no fixed or delimited subject matter. The epistle contains anything that may be contained in a letter, "soit bien, soit mal: soit plaisir, soit desplaisir: soit amour, soit haine" (II, vii, 153–54); the epigram is merely a "titre ou superscription d'œuvre que ce soit" (II, i, 103). Other genres are restricted only in so far as they may treat serious or light subjects. The ballade, for example, may treat anything the author wishes; "Si est elle néantmoins moins propre a facécies et légéretéz" (II, iv, 131). A third group contains such matter—still largely unspecified—as is proper to a special end. The chant royal is "une allégorie obscure envelopant soubz son voile louenge de Dieu ou Déesse, Roy ou royne, Seigneur ou Dame" (II, v, 137); the cantique contains "priére ou detestation" (II, vi, 143); the farce or sotie is made up of "badineries, nigauderies, et toutes sotties esmouvantes à ris et plaisir" (II, viii, 165); and the coq-à-l'âne treats "lés vices de chacun, qui y sont repris librement" (II, ix, 167). In a fourth category are those genres devoted to the various passions. The sonnet is proper to "affections et passions gréves" (II, ii, 116), the ode, to love—"lés affections et passions ou tristes, ou joieuses, ou creintives, ou esperantes, desquéles ce petit Dieu ... tourmente et augmente lés esperis dés Amoureus" (II, vi, 147), the elegy also to love, "et déclare sés desirs, ou plaisirs, et tristesses a celle qui en est la cause et l'obgét" (II, vii, 155); the chanson to love and drinking (II, vi, 150–51). Finally, there are those genres which present a certain type of personage and action. The eclogue is defined as follows:

> un Dialogue, auquel sont introduis Bergers et gardeurs de bestes, traittans soubz propos et termes pastoraus, mortz de Princes, calamitéz de temps, mutations de Republiques, joyeus succés et evenemens de fortune, louenges Pöétiques, et téles choses ou pareilles (II, viii, 159).

The morality (like Greek and Latin tragedy) deals with "narrations de fais illustres, magnanimes et vertueus, ou vrays, ou au moins vraysemblables" (II, viii, 162), and the complaint with "la matiére déplorable: qui est le plussouvent mort facheuse et importune: par fois amoureuse deffortune, c'est a dire desplaisir ou dommage receu de l'amour" (II, xii, 179).

The notion of *matière* thus expands and becomes somewhat clearer as we examine it in connection with the various genres. But except for the larger ones, it still remains rather tenuous; little help is given to the aspiring poet on this all-important element. In most cases, indeed, discussion of *matière* boils down to the simple assertion that it is "grave et sérieuse" on the one hand or "légère et facécieuse" on the other. In so far as matter determines type of verse, this simple assertion will be followed by another indicating use of a long or a short line. The real concern with respect to *forme* is not verse length but rime scheme and riming, and here the tradition is called upon for the careful explanations which Sebillet gives, and which he clarifies by quotation of numerous poems. It is here that the models enter conspicuously, largely in demonstration of rules for versification rather than as exemplars of proper handling of matter or of good invention. Indeed in the treatment of the genres, riming and rime schemes are paramount; the other aspects (which have been emphasized in this analysis because of their philosophical interest) are secondary.

For most of the genres discussed, Sebillet gives suggestions with respect to what he calls the "vertu" of the specific genre. The term is not defined, but it is apparent from the context that it means some special excellence belonging to that genre only. It is possible that here again there is some connection with the more general theory of poetry. For at the very beginning of the *Art poétique françoys* he had spoken of "ceste divine perfection que nous appellons Vertu," of the "vertueuse appellation" of the arts (I, i, 7), and of the "œuvre vertueus" (I, i, 8). The context indicates a connection between "vertu," perfection, and divinity. If each kind of poem has its own "vertu," then this should be its perfection in kind and it should be related to the invention of the poem, to the *matière.* This supposition is borne out by some of the discussions of "vertu." In the chant royal, for example, "l'élégance et pertinente déduction de l'allégorie est la premiére vertu ... : La seconde, la cohérence du refrain a chaque couplet" (II, v, 140). In all forms of the dialogue it is "le Décore dés personnes observé a l'ongle, et la convenante et apte reddition du Moral et allégorie" (II, viii, 163). In the enigma it is "l'obscurité tant dilucide que le bon esprit la puisse ésclercir aprés s'y estre quelque peu appliqué" (II, xi, 176). For other genres, the "vertu" seems to spring rather from the handling of the materials; but it is still something superior to mere versification. In the rondeau, "leur vertu premiére est de faire rentrer ou le vers ou l'hémistiche tant proprement et tant a propos, qu'il ne semble pas répété du commencement: mais tant cohérent a la fin de son couplet en suite de propos et sentence, comme si là fut son siége propre et particulier" (II, iii, 130). For the ballade, "sa premiére vertu et perfection est, quand le refrain n'est point tiré par lés cheveus pour rentrer en fin de couplet: mais y est répété de mesme grace et connéxion [as in the rondeau]" (II, iv, 135). If this interpretation of "vertu" as a special quality of invention, disposition, or elocution (rather than of versification) be correct, then Sebillet is consistent with his general principle that the *matière,* not the *forme,* is the important part of the poem.

Regardless of the genre, there are certain criteria applicable to any poem; and although these are vague and not adequately described, they throw a little further light on Sebillet's theories in general. Among the terms used in praise of poems, *doux* and its derivative forms are very frequent. From the context, it appears that at times *doux* refers to the sound of the poem, at times to its general effect or tone. Rime produces "douz et parfaiz accords" (I, ii, 19), repetition in the rondeau gives it its "douceur et grace" (II, iii, 119); on the other hand, Saint-Gelais is an "Autheur tant dous que divin" (II, vi, 148). A closely related term is *grâce,* with its derivatives; this seems usually to mean the general turn of the idea and the phrasing in the poem, although it sometimes refers to sound. Thus "les épigrammes qui ont plus de vers, sont ceus aussy qui ont moins de grace" (II, i, 104); in the rondeau, the repetition of the hemistich "n'ha moins de grace, que si le demy ou l'entier premier couplet fut repris et repété" (II, iii, 126). Related terms of praise are *élégant* (pp. 63, 171, 176), *savoureux* (p. 31), *plaisant* (pp. 86, 165), *harmonie* (p. 135), all of which have a similar reference to sound, turn of phrase, and general tone or effect. Their contraries are usually *rude* and *âpre:* "tant qu'il [the poet] trouvera mos dous et propres, ne se charge dés rudes et aspres" (I, iv, 30); "la rudesse de beaucoup de mos nouveaus" (I, iv, 33). The criterion for the *matière,* for invention, disposition, and elocution, even for the relationship of form to matter, is found in a whole group of words related to the idea of propriety or appropriateness: *propre, proportion, analogie, propos, décore.* For invention: "Trouve donc le Pöéte avant toute autre chose, qu'il puisse proprement dire et commodément adapter au subjét qu'il veut déduire en son Pöéme, tant soit grand, ou tant soit petit" (I, iii, 23). For disposition: "il regardera aussy songneusement a joindre les unes choses auz autres proprement au progrés de son pöéme: et y mettre lés fins et lés commencemens ... bien-séans" (I, iii, 27). For elocution: "les dictions, mos ou vocables: entre lesquelz a autant bien chois et élection, comme entre lés choses, pour en rejetter lés mal convenantes et aptes, et retenir les propres et bienséantes" (I, iv, 29). The poet may invent new rime schemes, but he must be careful that "l'analogie y soit toujours gardée, et qu'il n'y ait ryme sans raison" (I, vii, 70). Similarly, "l'autheur peut a sa phantasie asseoir lés vers symbolisans, maisque il le face avec analogie et raison" (II, i, 112). He may invent new forms of the *chant:*

> Pourtant voulant faire chant autre que Royal, fay-le de la forme que tu penseras la plus commode et propre a la matiére dont tu l'entreprendras bastir: et tu n'y feras faute digne de reprehension, maisque tu te proposes l'analogie par tout recommandée par moy icy dedans, et ce decore tant inculqué par Horace au discours de son Art Pöétique (II, v, 141–42).

The eclogue must be so written that "lés propos et personnes constituantes le narré sentent, avec leur decore gardé, la Bergerie" (II, viii, 160–61), and the "vertu" of the morality is "le Décore dés personnes observé a l'ongle" (II, viii, 163). There are numerous other passages which might be cited to the same effect. From all passages, it becomes apparent that some such scheme as this is in operation: for each kind of poem, there is a particular subject matter or at least a particular intention; to the subject or intention must be properly fitted the things or materials to be used, the arrangement of these materials, the words in which they are expressed, the rimes and sounds and rhythms which decorate them. When such a proper adaptation is made, the poem is perfect and the poet's immediate end is achieved.

But when is everything in the poem chosen, arranged, contrived in the proper manner? We are not told. There remain, however, three possibilities which may be derived from the nature of the argument in the text as a whole. (1) Propriety or appropriateness is something which the poet judges for himself as a result of his divine gift. The general relationship of his "entendement et esprit divin" to the three major parts of poetic and rhetoric, and to *matière* in general, makes this supposition plausible. (2) The poet may improve his understanding of this propriety by the study of the models. Here the text is more helpful, since all three treatments of invention, disposition, and elocution (Bk. I, Chaps. III and IV) refer the poet specifically to the models for assistance. (3) The audience itself, although unspecified, may be considered as a kind of judge of appropriateness and of the consequent perfection. For if it grants "faveur et applaudissement," "admiration et louenge" to the successful poet, it does so in the light of the perfection of the work—perfection towards which the poet strives and which is a function of the proper assemblage of all the elements of the poem. In this interpretation, the audience comes to have a somewhat more important role than that previously assigned to it in this analysis, as the judge of sound and rime alone.

Sebillet's *Art Poëtique françoys* is thus of greater interest to the historian of literary ideas than were the works of the type included in the *arts de seconde rhétorique*. It shares with these works a concern with matters of prosody, with the rules for versifying the various kinds of poems. But it superimposes upon these rules a philosophy of poetry which comes to inform at least in part the conception of the rules themselves. Where the work remains traditional is in its failure to achieve a subordination of the rules to the broader principles, or a reconception of the rules in the light of those principles. This state of affairs is found again in other works of the century; to a certain degree at least, the prosodic tradition of the *arts de seconde rhétorique* persists alongside of the new theory of poetry, to which it is never completely assimilated.

2. Joachim du Bellay

As its title indicates, Joachim du Bellay's *Deffence et Illustration de la langue françoise* (1549)[6] is a treatise primarily concerned with the improvement of the French language, and hence with problems of a linguistic character. But since the writing of poetry in French is one of the principal means for rendering the language illustrious, and since the problems of poetry and the problems of language are at many points inseparable for Du Bellay, many ideas of interest for the history of poetic theory in the century emerge from the document. These do not constitute a fully for-

[6] Ed. Henri Chamard, Paris: Fontemoing, 1904; new edition, Paris: Didier, 1948 ("Société des Textes français modernes"). My references give first the pages for the 1904 ed. and then, in brackets, the pages for the 1948 ed. The text is that of the 1948 ed.

mulated theory of poetry, since many aspects of the subject are willfully excluded and others enter only accidentally. They do, however, make a distinctive contribution because of their emphasis on matters of diction.

The specific intention of the work, to defend French against its detractors and against those who prefer Greek and Latin to it, and to indicate ways in which French may be raised to the level of excellence of the classical languages, is clearly stated and constantly reiterated. This intention itself results from a more general purpose, that of bringing fame and glory to France. It is a patriotic motive; Du Bellay writes out of "affection naturelle envers ma Patrie" (Dedication, p. 35 [6]). He hopes that some day France will rule over other nations: "Le tens viendra (peut estre), & je l'espere moyennant la bonne destinée Francoyse, que ce noble & puyssant Royaume obtiendra à son tour les resnes de la monarchie" (I, iii, 73 [27]). But what is the relationship between the greater destiny of France and the improvement of its language? The answer is found in two assumptions. First, the surest source of everlasting glory for a nation is in its literary products; the example of Rome is cited:

> La gloire du peuple Romain n'est moindre (comme a dit quelqu'un) en l'amplification de son langaige que de ses limites. Car la plus haulte excellence de leur republique, voire du tens d'Auguste, n'etoit assez forte pour se deffendre contre l'injure du tens, par le moyen de son Capitole, de ses thermes & magnifiques palaiz, sans le benefice de leur Langue, pour la quele seulement nous les louons, nous les admirons (II, xii, 320–21 [183–84]).

All perishes, the written word alone survives:

> sans la divine Muse d'Homere, le mesme tumbeau qui couvroit le corps d'Achille, eust aussi accablé son renom. Ce qu'avient à tous ceux qui mettent l'asseurance de leur immortalité au marbre, au cuyvre, aux collosses, aux pyramides, aux laborieux edifices, & autres choses non moins subjectes aux injures du ciel et du tens, de la flamme & du fer, que de fraiz excessifz & perpetuelle sollicitude (II, v, 242–43 [134–35]).

Second, the development of a satisfactory language is a prior step to the production of a great literature. This assumption is implicit throughout the work; it becomes explicit in such statements as the following:

> nostre Langue ... s'elevera en telle hauteur & grosseur, qu'elle se poura egaler aux mesmes Grecz & Romains, produysant comme eux des Homeres, Demosthenes, Virgiles & Cicerons (I, iii, 73–74 [27–28]).

> Je ne veux pas donner si hault loz à notre Langue, pour ce qu'elle n'a point encores ses Cicerons & Virgiles: mais j'ose bien asseurer que si les scavans hommes de notre nation la daignoint autant estimer que les Romains faisoint la leur, elle pouroit quelquesfoys & bien tost se mettre au ranc des plus fameuses (I, xii, 160 [84–85]).

This dominant place of language in the ultimate greatness of French literature and even of the French nation results from a special conception of the place of diction in literary composition. Du Bellay starts with the Ciceronian division of the "cinq parties de bien dire," in which it is apparent from the context that *bien dire* must be extended from rhetoric to all forms of composition. The five parts are listed as "l'invention, l'eloquution, la disposition, la memoire & la pronuntiation" (I, v, 82–83 [32]). Of these five, the last two are non-linguistic in character: "ces deux dernieres ne se aprennent tant par le benefice des Langues, comme elles sont données à chacun selon la felicité de sa nature, augmentées & entretenues par studieux exercice & continuelle diligence" (*loc. cit.*). Similarly the third, disposition, is outside the realm of rule and precept, and is therefore eliminated: "la disposition gist plus en la discretion & bon jugement de l'orateur qu'en certaines reigles & preceptes" (*loc. cit.*). Only two parts of rhetoric remain for discussion, invention and elocution. If invention is retained at all, it is because it is equated with "l'intelligence parfaite des Sciences," and because the writer can attain such knowledge only from ancient authors, either in Greek and Latin or in translation. In so far as the translator of classical treatises makes a contribution to the growth of his language, he enters into the special field of Du Bellay's treatise; but such translation is specifically characterized as a secondary and an insufficient means of "illustration" (I, v, 90 [38]).

What Du Bellay is really interested in, then, is diction. "Elocution" is characterized as the "partie certes la plus difficile, & sans la quelle toutes autres choses restent comme inutiles." It is the part which makes it possible to judge one orator as more excellent than another; moreover, and this is extremely significant, it is in terms of this element that we will estimate "un genre de dire meilleur que l'autre" (I, v, 85 [34]). This makes it possible to foresee that when Du Bellay later comes to make distinctions among literary genres, he will place in the highest rank that genre which is capable of supporting the most elegant diction. It also explains why, in the linguistic sections of the treatise, the emphasis is constantly on matters of vocabulary and of the sound of words.

The same priority of matters of diction accounts for the extraordinary position of poetry in the treatise. Both poetry and oratory are considered, for purposes of the discussion, as subordinate to language: "le poëte & l'orateur sont comme les deux piliers qui soutiennent l'edifice de chacune Langue" (II, i, 167–69 [87]); this must mean that through their efforts as creators both poet and orator contribute the desired qualities to the language in which they write. Diction becomes, rather than a contributing element towards the excellence of poetry, an end which is served in part by poetry itself. Thus when he comes to treat poetry, in Book II, Du Bellay will exclude from the treatment all matters which are not linguistic in character; he will not speak of the Platonic "idea" of the poet (II, i, 170 [89]), he will omit all such subjects as prosodic details, the kinds of verses, the "vertuz & vices du poëme," the figures of thought and of speech, the commonplaces (II, ix, 282–83 [159]). Instead, he will discuss those qualities of diction which will conform to the standards that he establishes. Certain other more general and more philosophical considerations will appear, as we shall see, but they will not constitute the major interest of the work. As for oratory, the other "pillar of the edifice of language," it is omitted from discussion altogether since Estienne Dolet has treated it completely in his *Orateur françois* (I, xii, 162 [86]), a work which was never published.

With these general features of the work in mind, we may now proceed to a statement of Du Bellay's views on language before going on to a more detailed analysis of his concept of poetry. These views range from the broadest philosophical conceptions of the nature of language to the most detailed suggestions for the improvement of the French language. Du Bellay distinguishes the end of language, which was invented "à nostre bien & utilité: affin que presens, absens, vyfz & mors, manifestans l'un à l'autre le secret de notz cœurs, plus facilement parvenions à notre propre felicité, qui gist en l'intelligence des Sciences, non point au son des paroles" (I, x, 132 [64]); the end, restated, is to "signifier entre nous les conceptions & intelligences de l'esprit" (I, i, 48 [13]). As a means to this end, language was invented by man, and all of its progress—or lack of progress—is attributable to man alone. Its origin is the "vouloir & arbitre des mortelz" (I, i, 47 [12]); "toutes Langues sont d'une mesme valeur, & des mortelz à une mesme fin d'un mesme jugement formées" (I, x, 128 [61]). If any language fails to develop to the same extent as another, it is the fault of the men who use it, not of nature (I, iii, 69 [23]). Thus it is within the power and the volition of any group of men to improve the language which their ancestors have invented. No language is by nature doomed to inferiority, to a secondary place among languages; any one is susceptible of increased powers of expression: "je croy qu'à un chacun sa Langue puysse competemment communiquer toute doctrine" (I, x, 128 [61]).

Only two factors might prevent a modern language such as French from equaling Greek and Latin in its qualities: one, if the general cultural level of the French were below that of the Greeks and Romans; the other, if nature had endowed the French with less wit than their predecessors—with insufficient wit to "illustrate" their language. That either of these conditions exists is denied vehemently and repeatedly throughout the work. With respect to the first: "en civilité de meurs, equité de loix, magnanimité de couraiges, bref en toutes formes & manieres de vivre non moins louables que profitables, nous ne sommes rien moins qu'eux" (I, ii,

58 [17–18]). In a later passage, where the virtues of France are specifically compared to those of Rome, and after an enthusiastic listing of France's beauties, Du Bellay goes on to remark:

> je ne parleray de tant de metiers, arz & sciences, qui florissent entre nous, comme la musique, peinture, statuaire, architecture & autres, non gueres moins que jadis entre les Grecz & Romains. ... quand à la pieté, religion, integrité de meurs, magnanimité de couraiges, & toutes ces vertuz rares & antiques (qui est la vraye & solide louange), la France a tousjours obtenu sans controverse le premier lieu (II, xii, 324–25 [185–86]).

With respect to the second argument, he insists that nature is unimpaired in her fecundity, that she is as generous to men in modern times as to the ancients, that the French are just as capable of producing great works as the Greeks and the Romans. To prove this he lists printing, gunpowder, "avecques tant d'autres non antiques inventions, qui montrent veritablement que par le long cours des siecles les espris des hommes ne sont point si abatardiz qu'on voudroit bien dire" (I, ix, 117–18 [54]). If French has not progressed satisfactorily, it is because of the ignorance of Frenchmen in past centuries (I, iii, 66 [23]) and because of the unwillingness of Frenchmen of today to desert Latin and Greek in favor of their own language. If this latter unwillingness is now overcome, if modern writers work for the development of their own language, the French language "se poura egaler aux mesmes Grecz & Romains" (I, iii, 73 [28]). This is the general end proposed for the work.

The goal of improvement implies the existence of certain standards for a language, standards not yet met by the French language—at least, not in full. For French has already made some steps in the right direction; on the one hand, it is capable of producing adequate translations—"nostre Langue Francoyse n'est si pauvre, qu'elle ne puysse rendre fidelement ce qu'elle emprunte des autres"; on the other hand, it is sufficiently advanced to permit of the writing of original works—"si infertile, qu'elle ne puysse produyre de soy quelque fruict de bonne invention" (I, iv, 76 [29]). But it still lacks certain qualities and possesses certain defects; the lists of words referring to qualities and defects are revelatory of the criteria which Du Bellay had in mind for the excellence of language. I give them below as they appear in the text:

Qualities	*Defects*
copieuse (pp. 66, 78, 81, 104, 143) [22, 30, 31, 46, 72]	nue (pp. 67, 110) [23, 49]
riche (pp. 66, 73, 104) [22, 27, 46]	pauvre (pp. 66, 76) [23, 29]
eloquence (pp. 71, 73) [26, 27]	infertile (p. 76) [29]
nombre (pp. 71, 73) [26, 27]	scabreux (p. 78) [30]
liaison (p. 71) [26]	mal poly (p. 78) [30]
	contrainte (p. 88) [36]

Qualities	*Defects*
grace (p. 73) [27]	froide (p. 88) [36]
elegant (pp. 78, 109, 111, 142) [30, 48, 49, 79]	mauvaise grace (p. 88) [36]
fidele (pp. 78, 81) [30, 31]	sans art (p. 110) [49]
venusté (p. 111) [49]	sans ornement (p. 110) [49]
ornement (p. 118) [54]	
artifice (p. 118) [54]	
douceur (p. 118) [54]	
son (p. 118) [54]	

Most of the defects, it is clear, are the contraries of the qualities or indicate their absence. As for the qualities, they relate to various aspects of linguistic expression. Such words as "copieuse, riche, fidele" refer to vocabulary, to the number and adequacy of the words in the language, and Du Bellay will be concerned constantly with problems of vocabulary. Others, such as "douceur, son" (note the contrary "scabreux"), refer to the sounds of these same words. Still others, such as "nombre, liaison, grace," refer to the rhythms of the language; Du Bellay, throughout, will be concerned with matters of harmony and rhythm. The remaining terms, "eloquence, elegant, venusté, ornement, artifice," seem to refer to the over-all effect of the language, its capacity for figures of speech, for prosodic effects, and for decoration of all kinds. Languages which lack these qualities are "infirmes & debiles en leurs espéces"; those which possess them are "saines & robustes, & plus aptes à porter le faiz des conceptions humaines" (I, i, 41 [12]).

With these criteria in mind, Frenchmen should devote themselves to the development of their language. Three groups are specifically charged with the task, the translators, the orators, and the poets. But, as we have already seen, the role of the translator is secondary. Chapter V of Book I is entitled "Que les Traductions ne sont suffisantes pour donner perfection à la Langue Francoyse"; the principal reason alleged is that elocution, the main "partie de bien dire," is essentially untranslatable:

> je ne croyray jamais qu'on puisse bien apprendre tout cela des traducteurs, pour ce qu'il est impossible de le rendre avecques la mesme grace dont l'autheur en a usé: d'autant que chacune Langue a je ne scay quoy propre seulement à elle, dont si vous efforcez exprimer le naif en une autre Langue, observant la loy de traduyre, qui est n'espacier point hors des limites de l'aucteur, vostre diction sera contrainte, froide, & de mauvaise grace (I, v, 87–88 [36]).

At best, translators can instruct those who are ignorant of Latin and Greek about the many subjects treated in those languages; they can assimilate into French the concepts and the terms of philosophy and the sciences, either by translation or by paraphrase; they can add to the wealth of "invention" of writers in French. Contrariwise, they must especially avoid the translation of the poets; because of their special nature, poems are the least susceptible of translation of all works, and they must not be profaned (I, vi, 93–97 [39–42]). The orator shares with the poet the major task of improving the French language. To all intents and purposes, his approach and methods will be the same as those of the poet; Du Bellay will concentrate upon the latter, supplementing Dolet's work on the former. I shall indicate the special functioning of the poet later, in connection with the discussion of poetry.

Both poet and orator will use as their chief device for perfecting the language the method of imitation. In so doing, they should be guided by the example of the Romans, who developed Latin through the imitation of Greek:

> Si les Romains ... n'ont vaqué à ce labeur de traduction, par quelz moyens donques ont ilz peu ainsi enrichir leur Langue, voyre jusques à l'egaller quasi à la Grecque? Immitant les meilleurs aucteurs Grecz, se transformant en eux, les devorant, & apres les avoir bien digerez, les convertissant en sang & nouriture, se proposant, chacun selon son naturel & l'argument qu'il vouloit elire, le meilleur aucteur, dont ilz observoint diligemment toutes les plus rares & exquises vertuz, & icelles comme grephes, ainsi que j'ay dict devant, entoint & apliquoint à leur Langue. Cela faisant (dy-je) les Romains ont baty tous ces beaux ecriz, que nous louons & admirons si fort: egalant ores quelqu'un d'iceux, ores le preferant aux Grecz (I, vii, 98–99 [42–43]).

This process of imitation is described in various passages. It is likened to the grafting of branches onto a plant (I, iii, 70 [25]), to the transformation of oneself into one's model (I, viii, 104 [46]). No specific instructions for imitation are given in Book I, where Du Bellay is discussing general problems of language; such instructions are reserved for Book II, where he outlines the program for the poet.

In general, then, the French man of letters, and especially the poet, will devote himself to an ardent campaign to improve his language. He will do so in order to make it an adequate instrument for the production of a great literature, which will in turn add to the glory of France. If he can do so, it is because France in every other respect has reached the cultural level of the ancients, and because nature is still sufficiently bountiful to supply Frenchmen with the same capacities that enabled the Greeks and the Romans to achieve linguistic excellence. Language is a necessary preliminary step to literature, since the most important ingredient of the latter, elocution, consists in the proper handling of language on the levels of meaning and of sound. The principal device for the improvement of the French language will be the imitation of Greek and Latin writings.

Two special kinds of writing, poetry and oratory, provide the models which the French writer is to imitate. Du Bellay tends to emphasize the similarities rather than the dissimilarities of the two types. He classifies them together under a common heading, "ceux qui font profession de bien dire, comme les poëtes & les orateurs" (I, x, 124 [58]). He calls the poet and the orator "les deux piliers qui soutiennent l'edifice de chacune Langue" (II, i, 167–69 [87]). He accepts the assumption that "les vertuz de l'un sont pour la plus grand' part communes à l'autre" (I, xii, 161 [85]). The proper pronunciation of verse bears the same relationship to poetry as does the "pronunciation & geste approprié à la matiere" to oratory (II, x, 296 [167]). If he thinks of the two types as so closely allied, it is probably because, once again, he is thinking primarily of diction and of linguistic matters rather than of the total form or the total effect of either kind of work. If he does not contrast them specifically, it is because he sets aside all formal treatment of oratory in accordance with his announced plan. What he does say about oratory is incidental to other discussions, and comes largely indirectly from his mention of the works of orators.

We have already seen the passages in which Du Bellay distinguishes the five parts of Ciceronian rhetoric and assigns places of relative importance to each. We might note that if we apply to these five parts a distinction which exists elsewhere in the work, that of nature *vs.* art, three of the parts, disposition, memory, and pronunciation, come under nature (Du Bellay eliminates them from the discussion for this reason), and the remaining two, invention and elocution, under art. It is of interest further to note that disposition includes "les evenementz du tens, la circunstance des lieux, la condition des personnes & la diversité des occasions" (I, v, 83 [33]), that is, the elements of decorum which apparently belong as much at this time to the art of rhetoric as they will later, in French criticism, belong to the art of poetry—especially tragedy. Finally, in connection with rhetoric, an important fact emerges from a listing of rhetorical qualities and defects: these are all characteristics which were similarly listed as qualities and defects of language.

Qualities	*Defects*
elegamment (p. 84) [33]	nue (p. 87) [36]
copieusement (p. 84) [33]	manque (p. 87) [36]
copie (pp. 84, 100) [33, 43]	debile (p. 87) [36]
richesse (p. 84) [33]	
vehemence (p. 100) [43]	
douceur (p. 100) [43]	

The critic would therefore apply to a rhetorical document the same criteria that he would apply to any kind of a written document; this is not surprising, since he would be, even when judging rhetoric, a critic of language and of diction.

In Du Bellay's discussion of poetry itself, it is important to distinguish those elements of theory which are an integral part of the whole discussion and those ideas which appear here incidentally only because they are a part of the critical baggage of the century. This distinction is sometimes difficult to make. Let us take for example Du Bellay's various remarks on the nature of the poet. In Book II, Chapter III, he establishes the relationship between nature and art in the poet: "c'est chose accordée entre les plus scavans, le naturel faire plus sans la doctrine que la doctrine sans le naturel" (II, iii, 193 [103]). This is expanded somewhat later: "Qu'on ne m'allegue point aussi que les poëtes naissent, car cela s'entend de ceste ardeur & allegresse d'esprit qui naturellement excite les poëtes, & sans la quele toute doctrine leur seroit manque et inutile" (II, iii, 197 [105]). Still later, the notion of poetic furor is introduced: "cete fureur divine, qui quelquesfois agite & echaufe les espris poëtiques, & sans la quele ne fault point que nul espere faire chose qui dure" (II, xi, 300 [170]). All these are current concepts. But the precedence of nature over art is essentially inoperative in the treatise, since Du Bellay has ruled out all consideration of matters not subject to precept. Similarly, his conception of the epic poet is compounded of elements ascribed by Cicero to the perfect orator, many of which appear at no other place in Du Bellay's theory:

> toy, qui doué d'une excellente felicité de nature, instruict de tous bons Ars et Sciences, principalement naturelles & mathematiques, versé en tous genres de bons aucteurs Grecz & Latins, non ignorant des parties & offices de la vie humaine, non de trop haulte condition, ou appellé au regime publiq', non aussi abject & pauvre, non troublé d'afaires domestiques, mais en repoz & tranquilité d'esprit, acquise premierement par la magnanimité de ton couraige, puis entretenue par ta prudence et saige gouvernement (II, v, 234 [127–28]).

However, when these same distinctions are applied to poetry and poems, they become much more meaningful. For already a similar division had been made of the five parts of rhetoric. Now the two parts which come from art, invention and elocution, are regarded as especially appropriate to poetry: "à cause de ceste divinité d'invention qu'ilz ont plus que les autres, de ceste grandeur de style, magnificence de motz, gravité de sentences, audace & varieté de figures, & mil' autres lumieres de poësie: bref ceste energie, & ne scay quel esprit, qui est en leurs ecriz, que les Latins appelleroient *genius*" (I, vi, 95 [40]). Again, it is a special kind of diction which very largely distinguishes poetry from other forms—a kind which is so peculiar to the individual poet as to make poetry untranslatable. As for the "divinité d'invention," it is difficult to see how this should be interpreted, in the light of the fact that elsewhere in the text invention is equated with "l'intelligence parfaite des Sciences" (I, v, 84 [33], on the orator) and that in the description of the epic poet (cited above) the faculties of the poet attributable to invention, "tous bons ars & sciences," are such as are acquired through the poet's efforts (note the terms "instruict, versé, non ignorant").

A similar lack of integration into the system is discovered in an examination of the ends proposed for poetry. The poet will of course set as one of his ends the improvement of the French language (cf. p. 238 [128]). Another will be the pursuit of glory, "la Gloire, seule echelle par les degrez de la quele les mortelz d'un pié leger montent au Ciel & se font compaignons des Dieux" (II, v, 246 [136]), for the glory of the individual is indistinguishable from the glory of the French people. Both of these ends spring from the general philosophy of the work. But the Horatian "mesle le profitable avecques le doulz" (II, iv, 207 [111]), introduced in connection with the epigram, would seem to be no more than a random reminiscence; so also would be the end of affecting an audience in a given way: "celuy sera veritablement le poëte que je cherche en nostre Langue, qui me fera indigner, apayser, ejouyr, douloir, aymer, hayr, admirer, etonner, bref, qui tiendra la bride de mes affections, me tournant ça & la à son plaisir" (II, xi, 314 [179]). What is said about the practice of poetry in general or about the pursuit of the individual genres has very little to do with the achievement of either of these ends.

With respect to the individual genres, Du Bellay gives in a few pages (II, iv) a kind of counterpart of Sebillet's *Art poëtique françoys*, although he eliminates, in accordance with his stated intention, all prosodic matters; he gives, for most genres, a statement of the subject matter, or of the general effect, or of the kind of style, and indicates one or more models to be followed. The following table summarizes these ideas:

Genre	*Subject, Effect, Style, etc.*	*Models*
epigramme	plaisans mesle le profitable avecques le doulz	Martial
elegie	style coulant & non scabreux pitoyables fables anciennes	Ovide Tibule Properce
ode	d'un luc, bien accordé au son de la lyre Greque & Romaine rare & antique erudition matiere: louanges des Dieux & des hommes vertueux, le discours fatal des choses mondaines, la solicitude des jeunes hommes, comme l'amour, les vins libres, & toute bonne chere eloingné du vulgaire	Horace

Genre	*Subject, Effect, Style, etc.*	*Models*
	enrichy & illustré de motz propres & epithetes non oysifz, orné de graves sentences varié de toutes manieres de couleurs & ornementz poëtiques toutes manieres de vers	
epistre (?)	choses familieres & domestiques à l'immitation d'elegies sentencieuses & graves	 Ovide Horace
satyre (?)	mal dire vers heroiques taxer modestement les vices de ton tens, & pardonner aux noms des personnes vicieuses	Horace
sonnet	docte, plaisante conforme de nom à l'ode certains vers reiglez & limitez	Petrarque
ecclogue	plaisantes, rustiques marines	Thëocrit Virgile Sennazar (Marot)
hendecasyllabes	coulans et mignars	Catulle Pontan Second
comedie		
tragedie		
long poëme (= epic)	beaux vieulx romans Francoys admirable, laborieuse exacte perfection (cf. the qualifications of the epic poet, cited above)	Homere Virgile Arioste

Satire and the epistle are considered as of doubtful value for the "illustration" of the language. Certain other genres are specifically prohibited, "rondeaux, ballades, vyrelaiz, chantz royaulx, chansons" (II, iv, 202 [108]), to which are later added the coq-à-l'âne, the farce, and the morality (II, iv, 219, 230 [118, 126]). Among the ones recommended above, there is great disparity as to the kind and extent of criteria set up and as to the relative desirability. But there is no doubt with respect to the preferred genre; it is the epic, to which Du Bellay devotes all of Book II, Chapter V. The epic is proposed as the surest means of attaining the highest glory; it requires of the poet the highest qualifications. The reasons are not stated directly, but from the argument in general it would seem that this high place of the epic results from two factors: the richness and variety of knowledge necessary for its "invention," the richness and variety of language possible in its "elocution." Knowledge and diction are again the cornerstones of the approach.

These same topics of knowledge and diction supply the headings under which one may group the criteria for poetry. Once again, if we remove the qualities belonging to knowledge, those remaining are almost precisely the ones established as criteria for language and for rhetoric. A listing follows:

Qualities	*Defects*
doctrine (p. 194) [104]	nue (p. 87) [36]
erudition (pp. 194, 209, 316) [104, 113, 180]	manque (p. 87) [36]
plaisant (pp. 203, 222, 225) [109, 120, 122]	debile (p. 87) [36]
coulant (pp. 207, 228) [111, 124]	scabreux (p. 207) [111]
pitoyable (p. 207) [111]	dure (p. 293) [165]
mignard (p. 228) [124]	hyulque (p. 293) [165]
majesté (p. 259) [143]	redondant (p. 293) [165]
armonieuse (p. 263) [146]	aspre (p. 296) [168]
docte (p. 265) [147]	rude (p. 296) [168]
grace (p. 284) [160]	
vehemence (p. 284) [160]	
numereux (p. 294) [166]	
comparaisons (p. 304) [172]	
descriptions (p. 304) [172]	
savoir (p. 314) [179]	

Such terms as "doctrine, erudition, docte, savoir" fall under the heading of invention, one of the two parts of *bien dire* with which Du Bellay is concerned; they are the counterpart, in poetry, of the elements of knowledge contributed to language by the translator. The qualities related to diction (and their contrary defects) again involve matters of vocabulary, of sound, of rhythm and harmony, and of over-all "eloquent" effect. The critic of poetry will apply to his special art criteria almost identical with those of the critic of rhetoric and of the critic of language in itself.

The application of such criteria shows that in Du Bellay's time French poetry, like the French language, is not nearly as good as it might be. As in the case of language, some progress has been made; but much remains still to be done:

> je repondroy' ... qu'ilz ont bien ecrit, qu'ilz ont illustré notre Langue, que la France leur est obligée: mais aussi diroy-je bien qu'on pouroit trouver en notre Langue (si quelque scavant homme y vouloit mettre la main) une forme de poësie beaucoup plus exquise (II, ii, 189 [99–100]).

The goal of a better poetry is a possible one: "j'ay tousjours estimé notre poësie Francoyse estre capable de quelque plus hault & meilleur style que celuy dont nous sommes si longuement contentez" (II, i, 172–73 [91]). If it is possible, it is again because of the constant fertility of nature and because of the generally high cultural level of the French people; linguistic and literary arguments are here indistinguishable.

Imitation is the chief method by which French poetry will be improved. The poet should choose with care the model whom he will imitate:

> regarde nostre immitateur premierement ceux qu'il voudra immiter, & ce qu'en eux il poura, & qui se doit immiter, pour ne faire comme ceux qui, voulans aparoitre semblables à quelque grand seigneur, immiteront plus tost un petit geste & facon de faire vicieuse de luy, que ses vertuz & bonnes graces. Avant toutes choses, fault qu'il ait ce jugement de cognoitre ses forces & tenter combien ses epaules peuvent porter: qu'il sonde diligemment son naturel, & se compose à l'immitation de celuy dont il se sentira approcher de plus pres. Autrement son immitation ressembleroit celle du singe (II, iii, 199–200 [106-107]).

Once the choice is made, the poet should proceed by a method which is neither translation nor a copying of superficial tricks of style, but which consists in extracting from the model "la chair, les oz, les nerfz & le sang" (II, ii, 189 [100]) and converting them into one's own work. The model must always be a Greek or Latin author, never a Frenchman, since the latter has only superficial things to contribute (II, ii, 189 [100]).

When he does give specific instructions for this imitation (Bk. II, Ch. VI), Du Bellay once more operates on the linguistic level. He urges the poet to "inventer, adopter & composer" new French words (p. 248 [137]); to borrow words from the arts, sciences and trades (p. 250 [138]); to use the French form of foreign names whenever possible (p. 255 [141]); to prefer words which are neither uncommon nor too common, except when a rare word will add color and majesty (pp. 256–59 [142–43]); to use the infinitive as a noun, the adjective as a noun, etc. (II, ix, 284 [160] ff.). In many of these processes, the criterion will be the sound of the new word; in innovation, proceed with "modestie, ... analogie & jugement de l'oreille" (p. 253 [140]); for foreign names, "je renvoye tout au jugement de ton oreille" (p. 256 [142]). There are also suggestions for the use of epithets and figures of speech (II, ix, 285 [161] ff.) and for the use of rime and other prosodic devices (II, vii and viii). The end of all these is to produce poetry of pleasant sound and rhythm:

> Regarde principalement qu'en ton vers n'y ait rien dur, hyulque [= L. *hiulcus*, disconnected] ou redundant. Que les periodes soint bien joinctz, numereux, bien remplissans l'oreille, & telz qu'ilz n'excedent point ce terme & but, que naturellement nous sentons, soit en lisant ou ecoutant (II, ix, 293–94 [165–66]).

A summary of Du Bellay's ideas on poetry will thus sound very much like a summary of his ideas on language. The poet will strive to improve French poetry as a means to improving the French language and of adding to the glory of France. Living in a country of great achievement along other lines, he should have no difficulty in doing so, given the constancy of nature. He will proceed by imitation, selecting an author and transmuting the works of that author into his own. In whatever genre he works, he will strive for the particular kind of style or effect proper to that genre. In all genres, he will seek a form having pleasant sound and appropriate vocabulary; in the highest genre, the epic, the form will be majestic and eloquent and the vocabulary rich and abundant. His wisdom as one versed in all disciplines will enable him to provide an invention capable of supporting this elegant elocution.

Poetic theory in Du Bellay is an adjunct to linguistic theory; the former would be unintelligible without a prior knowledge of the latter. For poetry, and oratory, and all of the other arts of discourse are—for purposes of this treatise—auxiliary or subsidiary arts to the broader discipline of language. If the essence of oratory is diction, and the essence of poetry is diction—if no mention is made of the structure of the argument in the one or of the nature of the form in the other—then they both are readily assimilable to any discussion of language. It becomes possible to discover a single set of qualities and defects proposed as criteria for language and poetry and oratory; it becomes impossible (except for the random introduction of a few extraneous ends) to discover any set of criteria which will be germane to one of these arts but inappropriate to the others. All three are reduced to a common treatment on the level of language.

3. Jacques Peletier du Mans

The *Art poëtique* of Jacques Peletier du Mans, 1555,[7] is distinguished from those of his predecessors by the fact that it considers poetry primarily in the context of Nature, rather than in relation to the divine character of the poet (as in Sebillet) or in relation to the problem of improving the French language (as in Du Bellay). Both of these considerations do appear, since Peletier echoes much of the current thinking about poetic matters; but they appear as subsidiary to another conception which gives direction and synthesis to that thinking. His sources are likewise eclectic, although he tends to borrow most constantly from writers on rhetoric, especially Cicero and Quintilian. The rhetorical influence is apparent in some of the special aspects of this theory.

The term "Nature" is used by Peletier with a variety of meanings. In the first place, he makes the traditional distinction between Nature and Art as contributing to the product of the poet. Nature is here defined in two ways: (1) a broad definition as "cetę́ grand' ouurierę́, qui agìt uniuęr-

[7] Ed. André Boulanger, Paris: Société d'Edition "Les Belles Lettres," 1930.

sęlėmant sus tout cė qui ęt au mondė, e sus tout cę qui tombė an la cogitacion des hommės": (2) a narrower definition as "cė qui ęt imposè an nous, sans notrė peinė et sans notrė prėmierė intancion." According to the first of these definitions there would be only nature in the poet, since art itself would be a part of this all-inclusive nature; according to the second, natural gifts would be supplemented by the "excęrcicė" which is art (I, ii, 73). Peletier pursues the argument on the basis of this latter distinction, indicating the parts of poetry attributable to nature (largely the "matière") and those attributable to art (largely the "forme"). In the second place, Nature is used to designate the creative principle in the universe, responsible for the physical world and for man and his attributes. The arts, for example, have their origin "an cetė grandeur dė Naturė: laquelė ocultėmant e insansiblėmant les à fęt antrer an l'esprit des mortęz" (I, i, 65). Nature in this sense is a kind of equivalent of God. In the third place, Nature means those physical phenomena which may serve as the subjects of poetry: "Les fez dė la Naturė sė peuuėt aussi tręter en Poësiė" (I, iii, 82). Although such facts or phenomena may be used—witness the example of Lucretius—their usefulness is restricted.

It is this third conception of nature which gives a cue to much of Peletier's theory of poetry. For it establishes a relationship between the poem and the things represented in the poem. The word "nature" itself is not used to include all these things; such words as "vie, choses, choses de la nature" have the broader significance. But it would perhaps be justifiable to extend Peletier's conception of "nature" in this third sense to include all objects, persons, and actions represented in the poem, just as he himself had interpreted Nature both "amplėmant" and "etroętėmant" in its application to the character of the poet (I, ii, 73). Such an extension will provide us with a term for all things represented, which may then be used for distinctions among these things and for distinctions among poems resulting from the distinctions among things.

In any event, the reference from the poem back to the real things represented in the poem is a constant part of Peletier's method. In one of his own works he has introduced "chosės naturęlės, Cosmografiė, Astrologiė" (I, Preface, 63). All poets introduce "toutės sortės dė pęrsonnės: Roęs, Princės, Capiteinės, Magistraz: e dė chacun depeignėt au vif les façons, gracės e oficės, pour l'imagė dė la viė" (I, i, 67). Indeed, the function of the poet is to "donner nouueaute aus chosės vielhės, autorite aus nouuęlės, beaute aus rudės, lumierė aus obscurės, foę aus douteusės, e a toutės leur naturęl e a leur naturęl toutės" (I, v, 97). Many other passages might be cited. The fact that the poet does represent things in nature imposes certain restrictions upon his activity. For he must represent things as they are. If he is speaking of material objects, he must know them first-hand—

"Alhɇ contãpler les viuɇs imagɇs des chosɇs dɇ la Naturɇ" (Conclusion, p. 221)—or through a study of the sciences which treat them (*ibid.*, pp. 216–17); thus the requirement of great erudition on the part of the poet. Pindar, giving horns to a hind, would show "ignorancɇ dɇ la naturɇ ni dɇ l'essancɇ dɇ la Bischɇ," were it not mere inadvertence (I, v, 103). If the poet is speaking of persons, he must give them proper characters. For personages in comedy, proper characters are those which correspond to the traditional conceptions of the comic types:

> an ęlɇ s'introduisɇt pęrsonnɇs populerɇs: déquelɇs faut garder la bienseancɇ, sɇlon la condicion e etat dɇ chacunɇ. C'ę̂t assauoęr, qu'il faut fęrɇ voę̂r bien ocuelerɇmant l'auaricɇ ou la prudancɇ des vielhars: les amours e ardeurs des jeunɇs anfans dɇ męson: les astucɇs e rusɇs dɇ leurs Amiɇs: la vilɇniɇ e deshonnętɇte des Maquɇreaus: la façon des Perɇs tantót seuerɇs, tantót facilɇs: l'assantacion e vilɇte des Parasitɇs: la vantɇriɇ e brauɇte d'un Soudart rɇtire dɇ la guęrrɇ: la dilig'ancɇ des Nourricɇs: l'indulg'ancɇ des Merɇs (II, vii, 186–87).

For personages in tragedy, proper characters are those which correspond to the traditional conceptions of the individual, as they had already been summarized by Horace (II, vii, 191). The actions of all personages must be in keeping with their characters—Homer is criticized for allowing the prudent, wily, and vigilant Ulysses to fall asleep in the port of the Phæacians (I, v, 101)—and with a kind of general expectation of human behavior; Vergil sins against the latter, for example, when he makes Aeneas tarry so long in the burning city of Troy (I, v, 99–100). Even on the level of diction, figures of speech must involve things commonly known in nature (I, ix, 129–130); dialogue must be appropriate to the age and station of the persons speaking (I, ix, 131); rhythms themselves should reflect the ideas to which they are adapted: "les soudeinɇs e hatiuɇs, par moz briéz e legers: e les pɇsantɇs ou dɇ traualh, par moz lons e tardiz" (I, ix, 133). It would almost seem, from this preliminary survey of the relationship of poems to nature, that the principal canon for appropriateness of parts or elements of a poem is their appropriateness to the "nature" represented in the poem, not to any structural or internal requirements of the poem. This is indeed true, but in a special way.

The nature represented in a given poem is not undifferentiated. Peletier makes two kinds of distinctions among the objects of nature, and these distinctions affect later divisions in his thought; they are distinctions of quality and of quantity. For some objects in nature are "higher" than others, some "lower"; and a given poem may include a "greater" or a "lesser" segment of nature. With respect to quality, the higher things will be the more serious ones: "la dinite e le dɇuoęr des Ecriz Poëtiques: c'ę̂t quand iz sont dɇ chosɇs serieusɇs adrecèz aus amis" (I, ii, 79); the lower things will be the less serious ones, like those "futile" stories and anecdotes which Ariosto introduces into his work: "sont cęlɇs qui nɇ peuuɇt donner splandeur aus Ecriz, e qu'il faut expręssemant delęsser" (I, v, 104). Among the highest things would be such subjects as war (II, viii, 194), among the lowest, the buffooneries of a Plautus (II, vii, 188). With respect to quantity, some poems will include all of nature within their scope; thus the epic is "une formɇ e imagɇ d'Vniuęrs: d'autant qu'il n'ę̂t matierɇ, tant soę̂t ęlɇ arduɇ, precieusɇ, ou excęlantɇ an la naturɇ des chosɇs: qui nɇ s'i puissɇ aporter, e qui n'i puissɇ antrer" (II, viii, 194). Other poems will include a very restricted segment of nature; thus because of the brevity of the epigram "Il n'ę̂t pas rɇquis ... qu'il compregnɇ beaucoup" (II, iii, 161). It is easy to see how, from such a distinction of qualities and quantities of the natural objects represented in poems, Peletier will proceed to the creation of a hierarchy of genres based upon these distinctions.

But before such a hierarchy is established, Peletier proceeds to a similar set of distinctions with respect to the audiences of various kinds of poems. Again, they are distinctions of quality and of quantity. For just as poems represent higher or lower things in nature, and more or less of nature, so they are addressed to audiences which are higher or lower in character and greater or less in number. This is another kind of "nature" affecting the composition of the poem. On the side of quality, some works will be written for the "plus nętɇs e plus grauɇs oreilhɇs" (I, Preface, 63), for "les doctɇs" (I, x, 141), for "les Princɇs e Signeurs dɇ notrɇ tans" (I, iii, 82), for the "grans Signeurs" (II, vi, 181). Others will be written for the "moins sauans" (I, x, 141), for the "Peuplɇ" (I, iii, 85), for the "commun" (II, ix, 212). On the side of quantity, the distinction is really between poetic and non-poetic writings; for the former are addressed to a universal, eternal audience, while the latter are meant for a specific, contemporary audience. The poet "parlɇ a unɇ etęrnite," the orator "parlɇ aus hommɇs presans" (I, iii, 84). But even some poetic genres are written for a more restricted audience than others; comedy "sɇ doę̂t acommoder aus condicions des tans e des hommɇs presans" (II, vii, 188), and satire exists largely for contemporaries, although it may have a historical interest for those of later generations (II, vi, 184).

This double distinction of quality and quantity applied on the one hand to nature and on the other hand to the audience provides the framework for practically all further subdivisions of Peletier's ideas. It makes possible, notably, the differentiation between poetry and other forms of writing, the hierarchy of genres, and the hierarchy of styles appropriate to the various genres.

Poetry is distinguished from oratory in keeping with these distinctions. Whereas poetry has an extremely broad scope of subjects in nature, that of oratory is much more restricted. Poetry is like painting in this respect:

> lɇ Peintrɇ peùt librɇmant fantęsier sus son ouuragɇ an ordonnancɇ, an habiz, an qualitez dɇ pęrsonnɇs: an païsagɇs, arbrɇs, fleurs e autrɇs ambęlicɇmans: Comme aussi lɇ Poëtɇ an disposicion, discours, digressions, e tant dɇ sortɇs d'ornɇmans. ... commɇ lɇ Tableau ę̇t susceptiblɇ dɇ toutɇs sortɇs dɇ protręz, einsi lɇ Poę̇mɇ dɇ tous Sugęz (I, iii, 80).

The poet may "s'ebatrɇ an tous g'anrɇs d'argumans"; he may make the Gods speak, introduce "l'Amour, les Ieus festiz, les Anfęrs, les Astrɇs, les regiõs, les chans, les prez, les fonteinɇs e telɇs beautez d'Ecriz" (*ibid.*, p. 83). But all these subjects are denied to the orator, who is "astreint aus chosɇs particulierɇs"; "sɇ tiendra dɇdans les causɇs dɇ ses clians: mouura les afęz, deduira ses ręsons, refutɇra cęlɇs dɇ son auęrserɇ" (*ibid.*, pp. 83–84). This difference arises from the difference between their audiences:

> Car lui [le Poëtɇ] qui parlɇ a unɇ etęrnite, doę̇t seulɇmant toucher lɇ neu, lɇ sɇgręt et lɇ fons d'un argumant, e parler plus resolumant, lęssant les mɇnuɇs naraccions. L'Orateur, qui parlɇ aus hommɇs presans, e lɇ plus souuant au peuplɇ, fę̇t assez s'il à unɇ accion, e unɇ façon cõuɇnablɇ a pouuoę̇r gagner ses g'ans seulɇmant pour unɇ heurɇ (I, iii, 84).

Among the poetic genres, the highest in the hierarchy will be the one which at the same time treats the best and the most varied nature and is written for the highest and the most universal audience. This is the "euurɇ heroïquɇ" or epic, whose subject is war, "lɇ plus dinɇ e lɇ plus grauɇ dɇ toutɇ la Poësiɇ: a ręson quɇ les hautɇs pęrsonnɇs i antrɇt, commɇ Roęs e Princɇs: léquez seuz ont puissancɇ dɇ fęrɇ la guęrrɇ. E par cɇ qu'iz sont suiuìz e accompagnèz dɇ toutɇs sortɇs dɇ g'ans: lɇ Poëtɇ à ocasion dɇ parler dɇ toutɇs sortɇs d'argumans" (I, iii, 83). If the *Aeneid* contains all manner of subjects, all possible styles, all sorts of precepts, it is because it attempts to reach all audiences, "satifęrɇ a tant de sortɇs dɇ Lecteurs a tant d'apetiz e a tant dɇ jugɇmans" (II, viii, 208). The ode is second to the epic in its capacity for varied subject matter: "L'Odɇ ę̇t lɇ g'anrɇ d'ecrirɇ lɇ plus spacieus por s'ebatrɇ, qui soę̇t au dɇssous dɇ l'euurɇ Heroïquɇ, an cas dɇ toutɇ libęrte Poëtiquɇ: commɇ Fablɇs, Figurɇs, e autrɇs naïuɇtez" (II, v, 179). But its matter is not as exalted as that of the epic, "Car il i à diferancɇ dɇ dirɇ les louangɇs des grans, e dɇ chanter leurs gestɇs" (II, v, 178). No special audience is indicated for the ode, although we may assume that it would be similar to that of the epic, since for Peletier the dignity and universality of the audience is always commensurate with the loftiness and variety of the nature represented. Tragedy, again, is on a par with the epic as far as elevation is concerned: "La Tragediɇ ę̇t sublimɇ, capablɇ dɇ grandɇs matierɇs tant principalɇs quɇ depandantɇs: an sommɇ, nɇ diferant rien dɇ l'Euurɇ Heroïquɇ, quant aus pęrsonnɇs" (II, vii, 190). But comedy, meant for a popular audience, will treat a definitely less dignified segment of nature: "la Comediɇ ę̀t expręssemant introduitɇ, pour complerɇ au Peuplɇ (non pourtant sans artificɇ e jugɇmant) e ... ęlɇ sɇ doę̀t acommoder aus condicions des tans e des hommɇs presans" (II, vii, 188). Its actors are "pęrsonnɇs populerɇs: déquelɇs faut garder la bienseancɇ, sɇlon la condicion e etat dɇ chacunɇ" (*ibid.*, p. 186); elsewhere (p. 189) they are characterized as "dɇ bassɇ condicion." Similar distinctions are made for the epistle, which is of lower or higher material depending upon the persons addressed, and in which even the verse form is adapted to such differences: "Si on ecrìt aus grans Signeurs, a causɇ quɇ cɇ doęuɇt ę̀trɇ propos plus importans, on usɇra dɇ vęrs Decassilabɇs. Aus autrɇs pęrsonnɇs, sɇlon leur dinite e sɇlon lɇ meritɇ dɇ l'afęrɇ, on chãgɇra dɇ mɇsurɇ" (II, vi, 181).

Each genre is thus controlled, as it were, by two considerations, of "nature" or subject matter and of audience. What is more, these two are approximately equivalent: kings and lords in the audience will be pleased by the epic or the tragedy or the ode representing kinds and lords; the "people" will be appealed to by comedy which selects from nature similarly "popular" persons. The genres treated are the epigram, sonnet, ode, epistle, elegy, satire, comedy, tragedy, and epic, in that order—an order which seems to depend upon the length of the poem involved rather than a progressive gradation from "low" to "high" subjects; witness the positions of the ode and of comedy. Since each genre is so controlled, it becomes improper to introduce elements which are out of keeping with the nature or the audience of the particular genre. Lucan, for example, shows himself a bad poet when he introduces into the epic persons of insufficiently high station: "fęsant parler un Nautonnier ou quelquɇ hommɇ ignoblɇ (quelɇs pęrsonnɇs ancorɇs nɇ doęuɇt quasi point ę̀trɇ introduitɇs an un Euurɇ Heroïquɇ) d'aussi grand respęt, commɇ un Cesar ou un Pompeɇ" (I, v, 104); and in Ariosto the humorous episodes previously mentioned are "indinɇs du Poę̀mɇ Heroïquɇ" (*ibid.*). In general, it is the highest genres which are to be practiced by the French poet. Throughout, examples are taken from the epic, and the two principal models are Homer and Vergil. Such subjects as agriculture, popular among the ancients, are no longer desirable, since they are not "capablɇ dɇ grand faueur anuęrs les Princɇs e Signeurs dɇ notrɇ tans" (I, iii, 82). Any form which uses the language of the people is inferior to a form which uses a more choice expression, and the latter alone is to be cultivated:

> notrɇ Poësiɇ Frãçoęsɇ n'ę̀t point ancorɇs an sa grandeur: d'autant qu'ęlɇ ę̀t jusquɇ ici trop voęsinɇ du langagɇ vulguerɇ: voęrɇ e sommɇs ancorɇs si sugę̀z au jugɇmãt du Peuplɇ, quɇ la louãgɇ du Poę̀mɇ samblɇ de-

> pandrɇ dɇ la procheinɇte du parler vulguerɇ: chosɇ qui arguɇ unɇ anfancɇ e impęrfeccion dɇ notre Art. Pourcɇ, jɇ conseilhɇre a noz Poëtɇs de dɇuɇnir un peu plus hardiz, e moins populerɇs: toutɇfoęs auęc jugɇmant...Cɇ qui sɇ fɇra par l'antrɇprisɇ dɇ l'Euurɇ Heroïquɇ, e non point plus tót (I, iii, 85–86).

As is indicated by this last passage, there is a hierarchy of literary styles corresponding to the hierarchy of genres, and these styles are doubly determined by nature and audience. Poetry itself is distinguished from oratory by the language it uses, a language characterized by highly metaphorical expression: "Les moz aussi doęuɇt ętrɇ diferans au Poëtɇ e a l'Orateur. Commɇ par examplɇ, an Latin, l'Orateur nɇ dira pas *altum* pour la mer: ni la poupɇ pour toutɇ la nauirɇ. E autrɇs samblablɇs moz figurez" (I, iii, 85). Similarly historians, in contrast with poets, "contɇt leur fęt nuɇmant e par moz dɇ primitiuɇ sinificacion" (I, ix, 128). Prose in general is inferior to verse with respect to its capacities for ornamentation: "il i à téz discours quɇ la prosɇ nɇ rɇcɇuroęt pas dɇ si bonnɇ gracɇ, commɇ fɇra lɇ vęrs: Commɇ quand on à anuiɇ dɇ parler alegoriquɇmant e souz ficcion: e qu'on à fantęsiɇ dɇ s'ebatrɇ par comparęsons, raconter songɇs, e autrɇs guęyɇtez" (II, vi, 181). Among the poetic genres, comedy speaks "facilɇmant, e ... populerɇmant" (II, vii, 190); poems on nature, such as that of Lucretius, are attempted only rarely because of "l'áprɇte des tęrmɇs e la contreintɇ dɇ la matierɇ, qui ęt sans ornɇmans e figurɇs" (I, iii, 82); Vergil has written works "dɇ pɇtit stilɇ" (presumably the *Georgics* and the *Bucolics*) in addition to his epic (I, Preface, 64). Against these are placed the works in a high style: the epic of Homer, where we see "unɇ infinite d'ornɇmans, dɇ sutilitez, d'exquisicions industrieusɇs" (I, ii, 74); the sonnet, which compared to the epigram "à plus dɇ majeste: e ęt capablɇ dɇ discours grauɇ, męs qui soęt brief" (II, iv, 166); the ode, "capablɇ dɇ diuęrs argumans e dɇ diuęrs stilɇ" (II, v, 177), especially as it is practiced by Horace, who displays "unɇ magnifiçancɇ d'ęr, santancɇs, figurɇs, eureusɇ copiɇ dɇ nons e dɇ moz: e quasi unɇ manierɇ dɇ fleuuɇ an elocucion" (II, v, 180); tragedy, to which are applied such epithets as "grauɇ dɇ stilɇ, hautein, santancieux, filosofiquɇ, magnifiquɇ" (II, vii, 192).

Apparently, from these brief passages, the differentiating element between a low and a high style is ornamentation. Those genres which treat the greatest segment of nature will be capable of the most ornate style, and this is considered to be a virtue. Although there are warnings against excessive or inappropriate ornateness (cf. I, ix, 126 ff.), Peletier everywhere prefers the "copious" and "florid" styles to the "brief" and "dry" among the four oratorical styles which he distinguishes (II, viii, 207). From the chapter on the "Ornɇmans de Poësiɇ" (I, ix) it is evident that ornamentation is achieved primarily through the use of the traditional rhetorical figures; the proper employment of these is a matter of such complexity and diversity that it cannot be taught, and must rather be referred to the native gifts of the poet and to what he can learn from the study of other poets (I, ix, 137). The highest and most complex style will be achieved in part through the use of the longest verse line, the Alexandrine (II, ii, 155), and in part through the cultivation of rich rime (II, i, 149). Moreover, in Peletier's conception of the epic the beginning *in medias res* is in itself a kind of ornament and aid to complexity; to begin simply at the beginning of the action and follow through chronologically to the end would be beneath the dignity of the genre (II, viii, 196–97).

All in all, this establishment of distinctions of quality and quantity in the nature represented in poems and in the audiences for which poems are written is productive of the major classifications of the work. There is no evidence, I believe, to show that either of the two elements, nature or the audience, is the predominant one; Peletier does not develop a purely rhetorical system by subordinating all considerations to the character of the audience, nor does he develop a purely "representative" system in which all criteria would derive from nature. Instead, the poem occupies a middle position between nature and the audience, and is influenced by both. As for the distinctions within nature and the audience, they are of an aristocratic character, since they concern primarily persons and rank persons in a gradation from the lower classes represented in comedy, through the lords and kings represented in tragedy, to the heroes, demigods, and gods represented in the epic. For each step in the gradation, there is an appropriate genre with its proper magnitude, long or short, its proper line length, from the shortest to the longest, its proper degree of ornamentation, its proper level of general complexity. Such matters as these figure much more prominently in the discussion of the genres than they had in the work of Sebillet, and the prosodic questions to which Sebillet had devoted so much attention are almost completely lacking here. Peletier breaks more completely with the tradition of the "second rhetorics" and approaches more satisfactorily the proper realm of the "poetic arts."

Not all the major ideas of the work, however, are to be accounted for by these distinctions of nature and audience. Certain others are present because they are in the current tradition, others are introduced as ornaments. The notion of the pleasure which accompanies all doing, and which makes it impossible to desist from writing poetry once one has begun (I, Preface), would seem to belong to the latter category. To the former probably belong the various ends suggested, at various places, for the poetic art. The double end of utility and pleasure is mentioned in passing in connection with the subject of agriculture, which "n'ęt point pour donner recreacion grandę, ni mę̂mɇ utilite" (I, iii, 82; cf. I, ii, 79). But singly these two Horatian ends frequently appear. A poem must give pleasure to its audience; such adjectives as "delectablɇ, agreablɇ" and such nouns as "contentement, plaisir" are used fairly regularly (cf. I, ix, 127; II, i, 149–50; II, iii, 162), usually as referring to the delight which the ear derives from rhythm and rime. Some poems will also have the utility of moral precept or of the castigation of vices. Satire does the latter, but Peletier doubts whether it ever has the desired effect (II, vi, 184). The chorus in tragedy should "parler santancieusɇmant, creindrɇ les Dieus, rɇprandrɇ les vicɇs, mɇnacer les mechans, ammonę̂ter a la vęrtu" (II, vii, 190–91). Vergil scatters through his epic various "preceptɇs dɇ la viɇ" (II, viii, 203). An end which is perhaps related to this kind of utility is the offering to the reader of an image of life; again, the *Aeneid* is the example: "le Poëtɇ, pour montrer les chosɇs du mondɇ, ou plus tót les fęz humeins, ę̂trɇ altęrnatiz auęc auęrsite e felecite: à rampli tout son Poę̂mɇ dɇ joęɇ e dɇ tristęcɇ, successiuɇs l'unɇ a l'autrɇ"; and again "Voęla commant d'unɇ Ideɇ dɇ sagęcɇ e dɇ vęrtu conçuɇ par lɇ grand esprit Poëtiquɇ, sɇ formɇ lɇ grand e parfęt imagɇ dɇ la viɇ" (II, viii, 197, 206). But such notions of a utilitarian end are occasional in the work; they do not account for the major distinctions of the treatise, whose tone is certainly not moralistic.

Another consideration which enters only imperfectly into the general framework of the treatise is that of the models. Peletier recommends imitation of ancient and Italian authors and proposes specific models for each genre: Martial for the epigram, Petrarch for the sonnet, Horace and Pindar for the ode, Horace for the epistle, Tibullus and Propertius for the elegy, Marot for satire, Terence for comedy, Sophocles and Euripides for tragedy, Homer and Vergil for the epic. The greatest model of all is of course Vergil. The models are the real masters; the work of the writer of precepts is merely to point out what is to be sought in the models: "Les preceptɇs d'un Art, nɇ sont quɇ manierɇs dɇ Memoęrɇs, qui eueilhɇt lɇ Lecteur pour aler pratiquer parmi lɇ mondɇ des Auteurs: e rɇconnoę̂tre an l'imagɇ vif, la sutilite des tręz qu'on lui à balhèz par auęrticɇmant" (I, ii, 76). For such subtle problems as ornamentation, Peletier admits the inefficacy of instruction: "Nous ranuoyɇrons donq tousjours a la lecturɇ des Poëtɇs" (I, ix, 137). The poet is not to limit himself to imitation, nor is he to follow any one model slavishly. He should have the greatest models in mind, compare others with them: "les ę̂t commɇ incorporèz an sa memoęrɇ pour son principal fons, e commɇ pour son ordinerɇ patron: afin quɇ quand cɇ viendra a lirɇ les autrɇs Poëtɇs , il soę̂t preparè a an pouuoęr conuęrtir la lecturɇ an cetɇ felicite prɇmierɇ imbuɇ" (I, v, 96). When he comes to write himself, he will have in his mind a store of examples of how the best poets have solved the main problems of poetry, especially those of disposition and elocution, and he will be able to follow these examples in his own work. It is to be noted that the models do not take the place in Peletier, as they do in some theorists, of nature itself. He insists that the poet be an observer of nature and of things, and that he use imitation for the best representation of nature and of things. It would perhaps not be a misstatement of the theory to say that the poet will go to nature itself for "invention," that he will be aided by imitation in "disposition" and "elocution."

Even these somewhat miscellaneous ideas, these commonplaces of Renaissance critical parlance, are not without some relationship to Peletier's general theory. That theory is on the whole less heterogeneous than it would seem to be on first consideration; most of the materials from a wide variety of sources, poetic and rhetorical, are fairly well integrated into a single point of view. That point of view is distinct from the one of any other major critic of the century, and may serve as an example of the critical approach which made poetry doubly responsible to a hierarchy in nature on the one hand and a hierarchy in the audience on the other.

4. Pierre Delaudun

Coming as late in the century as 1597, Pierre Delaudun's *Art poëtique françois*[8] represents a stage in French thought about the poetic art that is at once more complete and less systematic than that reflected in earlier documents. It is more complete in the sense that Delaudun treats more numerous literary genres than did his predecessors, and that he gives a more complete poetics of such genres as comedy and tragedy. It is less systematic in the sense that the various elements adopted from earlier theorists are less successfully welded into an independent system with its own dominating idea and its own hierarchy of concepts. Delaudun, rather than borrowing from a variety of classical authors (as had Sebillet, for example), compounds his treatise out of the writings of earlier theorists in French—Sebillet, Du Bellay, Peletier, Ronsard—and recent humanists writing in Latin—Scaliger and Viperanus. But in many cases this compounding is hardly more than a transcription, with no attempt to adjust the individual fragment to others adopted from other sources. The result is a kind of anthology of ideas, arranged in an order that is not in itself clear and is frequently expressed in a confused and verbose diction.

It is this anthological character of the work which makes it interesting to the student of critical ideas in the sixteenth century, since in it he may find a kind of summation of the notions current towards the end of the century. In those places where Delaudun does express an original or personal idea, he gives a glimpse of some of the newer considerations affecting thought about poetry. In the following analysis of his *Art poëtique françois,* I shall

[8] Ed. J. Dedieu, Toulouse: Facultés libres, 1909.

attempt to group the ideas according to five major distinctions: (1) the character and qualities of the poet as they affect the poem, and criteria to be derived from them; (2) the nature of the poetic art as distinguished from other literary arts; (3) the poem in relation to nature, and criteria derived from this relation; (4) the poem in relation to the audience, and criteria derived from this relation; (5) the poem as an independent form, and resulting criteria. Furthermore, I shall attempt to discover whether any one of these distinctions provides a first principle for his science of poetry, in the light of which the others would become more meaningful.

Before this analysis is attempted, however, I should point out for the sake of completeness that two other types of ideas are recurrent in the work. First, Delaudun repeats the current Renaissance ideas about the history and excellence of poetry—its origins and invention, its religious uses, its cultivation by kings and emperors, the first exponents of the various genres and the etymologies of the names of those genres. Second, he echoes Du Bellay's and Ronsard's theories of poetry as a means of "illustrating" the French language, and he determines the excellence of specific genres by their capacity for contributing to that "illustration."

(1) *The character and qualities of the poet.* The poet is a poet by virtue of a divine gift: "les poëtes sont sacrez, et ont quelque chose de divin en eux" (I, i, 74); he is born a poet, and without this natural disposition nothing else will avail (I, i, 78). Even Aristotle, great as he was, did not possess the necessary gift, and could only aid poets in their work (I, i, 74). In all statements about the achieving of perfection in poetry, this natural qualification is included (cf. IV, i, 130; IV, ii, 133). But when we examine what specific qualities of the poem spring from this natural gift, we find very few indeed. There is an implied connection between divine inspiration in the poet and invention in the poem (I, ii, 75) and a specific statement that "l'invention est un dessein provenant de l'imagination de l'entendement" (I, ii, 76). Good riming is a product of this gift: "Si le poëte est naturel, il ne manquera de rime non plus que d'eau un torrent" (I, v, 79). Finally, the invention and use of words depends upon "la felicité d'un bon esprit" (IV, iii, 133). But that is all, and it seems like very little in comparison with the whole mass of qualities which go to make up the perfect poem.

To this gift the poet must add art or artifice. Art consists in two types of activity, the following of such precepts as those which Delaudun provides and the imitation of the models, ancient or modern. Delaudun's task in the treatise is to "donner quelques preceptes de ceste sacree vacation à un esprit bien né" (I, iv, 78). The precepts which he gives relate largely to the forms of the various genres—number and kinds of verses, rime schemes, special subject matters and kinds of style (cf. II, "Au Lecteur," 94 and III, x, 128). This notion of precepts is complemented by that of rules; the limitation of tragedy to five acts is a rule (V, vi, 166). There seems to be no difference, however, between a precept and a rule, unless it be that a rule must invariably be observed. As for imitation, Delaudun uses the word in the traditional sixteenth-century meaning: the selection of some model, excellent in the genre which the poet wishes to practice, and the copying of the best features of that model. He himself, in the writing of his *bergerie*, has proceeded by "l'imitation d'un docte, et gentil esprit" (III, viii, 125). It is for purposes of this imitation that the poet must know Greek and Latin, so that he may read in the original the ancient poets who provide the best models for most genres (IV, i, 169). The relationship of this imitation to the poet's natural talents is not clear. On the one hand, from such a passage as the following, it would almost seem as if the poet could dispense with talent:

> Homere en son Iliade, Virgile en son Éneide et Bartas en sa Sepmaine, la lecture desquels servira beaucoup, et y regardant de pres, considerant la façon de dire, cela enflammera tellement le lecteur, qu'il le fera devenir poëte, ne fust-il qu'un rocher (IV, ix, 145).

On the other hand, imitation in itself is insufficient to produce the perfect poem, and it must be supplemented by the poet's "esprit": "il ne les faut pas aussi tant imiter qu'apres il ne soit besoin d'adjouster quelque chose de son esprit au surplus" (IV, i, 129). Moreover, the poet must possess a certain quality of discernment (the source of which is not stated) which will enable him to know what is to be imitated in a given model, what to be avoided (IV, i, 130).

Finally, the poet must have a general fund of erudition to assist him in his work. Just as the models he imitates are "tous les poëtes qui ont escript en une mer profonde de science" (IV, i, 130), so he must have at his call:

> la cognoissance de la Logique, Physique et Metaphysique, Medicine, Loix, Geometrie, Cosmographie, Astrologie, sans quoy on ne peut parvenir à la perfection, ou au moins s'il n'en a la cognoissance parfaicte, qu'il en sçache les adresses pour traicter des lieux et les aller veoir lorsqu'il en aura besoin (IV, vii, 141).

We may now determine what qualities of the poem spring from the art (as distinguished from the nature) of the poet. First, all prosodic aspects of the work are artistic—although Delaudun seems to speak of them with some disdain: "en vain un homme s'adonne à la poësie, si premierement il n'y a le naturel, et ... seulement il luy doit suffire de sçavoir comme se font les vers, et de juger à part soy ceux qui sont ou bien ou mal faicts" (I, iv, 78). Next, as we have already seen, the special conventions and rules relating to the individual genres are a matter of precept, hence artificial. Imitation is the source of a variety of qualities; different poets will be imitated for different virtues, "Homere, pour la comparaison, Virgile, pour la belle invention, Horace, pour la facondité des sentences et paroles choisies" (I, iii, 77; there is a discrepancy between this statement and the earlier one relating invention to natural talent). The matter of comparisons is very important, since they are characterized as the very soul of poetry (*ibid.*). His erudition will also enable the poet to make "quelques vives comparaisons" (IV, vii, 141). This summation of the contribution of art to the poem hardly seems more impressive than did the estimate of the part of nature; but when we analyze the poem itself and the divers features which are deemed important in its structure, we shall find that many more of these fall under the category of art than of nature.

With respect to the poet, one further point merits investigation: What end or ends does he propose for his literary work? The answer is simple; the poet seeks honor, glory, immortality. Works which are not written in French "ne franchiront jamais le pas de la mort" (IV, iv, 135); "ce n'est pas assez de s'estre immortalizé pour mil ans, ains ... il faut tendre et aspirer à une eternité" (IV, vii, 142); Delaudun will aid the poet to "parvenir au comble de tout honneur" (IV, ix, 145). True, poetry has also brought profit to poets in the form of "richesses et faveurs," but the honor is greater still and is the end especially to be sought (I, i, 74).

(2) *The nature of the poetic art.* The one characteristic which for Delaudun distinguishes poetry from other forms of the literary art is the use of "number" or measured diction. The one attempt at a definition of poetry contains this condition in a secondary way: "ce n'estoit que theologie sacrée allegorique ... dont les plus subtils esprits faisoient leur mesure en certain nombre de pieds et syllabes" (I, i, 72); but in later statements, as we shall see, it becomes the primary condition. For French poetry, rime is almost equally indispensable. In a paragraph on unrimed verse, Delaudun dismisses it summarily: "ne sont que lignes en prose, et ne valent pas le parler, si ce n'est comme prose" (II, xv, 109). Is all rimed verse then to be called poetry? The theorist answers in the negative, but his distinction is neither very complete nor very intelligible. In the chapter on rime (I, v) he sees the difference in the "worthiness to be read":

> un rimeur c'est un qui agence quelques mots en une ligne, comme des buchettes en un fagot, mettant deux ou trois lettres à la fin fraternisant à la precedente ou suivante ligne qui sert de rioterie; lorsque c'est quelque chose de mesme estoffe c'est rime, mais quand c'est quelque chose digne d'estre leüe, ce n'est plus rime, jaçoit qu'elle y soit mise, c'est poëme, et l'autheur est appellé poëte (p. 79).

Perhaps this is explained by later statements. With respect to the panegyric he says: "Il faut que tout soit bien disposé et grave: car autrement ce ne seroit que prose rimée" (III, vi, 123). Comparisons must be used appropriately, "car autrement le poëte feroit des vers qui ne sonneroient non plus qu'une piece de pain, et seroit plustost prose rimassée que d'avoir forme de vers" (IV, v, 138). In the discussion of the epic, proper "ornament" becomes the differentiating factor:

> Tous ceux qui escrivent en carmes ne sont pas Poëtes, quoyqu'il leur semble que s'ils ont observé les regles des vers ils sont parfaicts; mais tant s'en faut, car ils ne meritent que le nom de rimeurs; si, quoyque leurs carmes soient doctes, ils ne sont ornez comme cy-dessus j'ay dict (IV, ix, 148).

It would seem, then, that the distinction between poetry and rimed verse lies partly in subject matter or content, partly in order and gravity of tone, partly in ornament; the significance of all these terms will be somewhat clearer when we study the poem considered *qua* poem.

Poetry differs from rhetoric in the use of measured diction: "le poëte en son poëme garde toutes les parties d'oraison, comme l'orateur, excepté que l'un est plus contrainct de nombre que l'autre" (I, ii, 75–76). A later passage identifies the "parties d'oraison" as "exorde, narration, confirmation et conclusion" (III, vi, 123), i.e. the traditional divisions of a speech which are apparently common to a poem also. The figures are also common to both: "Faut user de ... toutes les figures de rhetorique, desquelles on se pourra servir sans ressembler ne sentir rien de son proseur" (IV, v, 538–39). In all this, there is no sharp differentiation between the two, except for the use of verse. Poetry differs from history in two ways, the natural order of history as opposed to the beginning *in medias res* or at the end in poetry, the truthful quality of history as opposed to the right of the poet to "lie" (IV, ix, 146, 147).

(3) *The poem in relation to nature.* Delaudun does not conceive of poetry as an imitation of nature in the Aristotelean sense, nor does he speak specifically of a poem as a "representation" of natural objects. But in many places in his work he discusses the kinds of things of which poetry treats and how they should be treated in it, and he derives certain criteria for poetry from these discussions. The kinds of things represented in poems are varied. In one passage at least they seem to be Platonic ideas:

> l'invention est un dessein provenant de l'imagination de l'entendement, ou bien c'est une conception des Idées, et formes de toutes choses celestes et terrestres, lesquelles enfin l'on met en effect (I, ii, 76).

More usually they are natural objects, "les forets, montagnes, rivieres, vallees, nuict, jour, soir, matin, vents et autre choses" (I, iii, 77); "le naturel des choses, comme des arbres, fontaines, jardins" (IV, ix, 148); "le battement des pieds des chevaux, la piste, les coups, le son des trompettes, le bruict des tambours" (*ibid.*, p. 149). From the contexts of these passages it is evident that such objects are introduced as decorations. The poems in which they appear concern themselves more essentially with people, their actions and their passions. Thus one of the ways of defining genres is by indicating the types of persons whom they represent and the types of actions involving these persons: the eclogue, "bergers, et gens rustiques qui discourent le plus souvent de leurs calamitez, de leurs ayses" (II, ix, 104); comedy, "vieillards, bonnes femmes, chambrieres, boulangers, tisserans, compagnons, capitaines, muguets de cour et autres personnes" (V, i, 152); tragedy, "des hommes illustres et de grand renommée" (V, iv, 156; cf. p. 158); and so on. In other cases, the type of event is the basis of the distinction; the complaint has as its subject "toute perte, mort, batterie ou autre misere" (II, xiv, 108). Or the material may be characterized merely as joyful or sorrowful; the octosyllabic ballade "n'est que pour risée," whereas the decasyllabic "est pour choses graves" (II, v, 101); the subject of the farce is "gay et de risée" (II, ix, 105). Supernatural objects—gods, furies, ghosts—are sometimes represented in given genres and under special circumstances (V, iv, 157–58).

All such subjects and persons are not of equal worth or importance. For Delaudun reflects the tradition of his predecessors who established a hierarchy of subjects and from it derived a hierarchy of genres. The basic criterion is a kind of nobility—nobility of station which places kings and heroes at the top of the social scale and commoners at the bottom, nobility of action, decoration, objects described and language used to describe them. This way of evaluating subject matters and genres is already familiar from earlier analyses, and Delaudun adds nothing new to the tradition.

The way in which these divers objects are to be represented in poetry will also vary from genre to genre, but throughout the treatise one criterion is emphasized: things must be portrayed "naturally." Such objects as trees, mountains, etc., are to be described "proprement," and since no other canon of propriety is here suggested, we must assume that the description is to be "proper" to the nature of the things themselves (I, iii, 77). This interpretation would agree with such a statement as the following: "exprimer les choses selon leur naturel, sçavoir, parlant de l'amour, que ce soit mignonement, parlant de la guerre, que ce soit furieusement" (IV, v, 138). When persons are depicted, it must be according to the conventions of the type: "Il faut surtout observer estroictement le decore des personnes, et que chacun parle selon sa dignité" (II, ix, 105). If objects are not represented as prescribed, a monstrosity will result. Delaudun insists upon this point, and although he draws no distinction between what is natural and what is monstrous, the various pertinent passages indicate that excessive variety, improper order, and unrestrained fancy produce the monstrous: "il faut garder de ne se former point de ces imaginations frenetiques ou comme disent les Philosophes, especes intelligibles, de peur de n'enfanter quelque monstre" (I, ii, 76); "Il faut garder de s'extravaguer en voulant enrichir son poëme de varietez comme un frenetique. Car voulant trop varier l'on pourroit plustost faire un monstre" (IV, ix, 148). A proper order and disposition of things in the poem seems to be an antidote against such monstrosity: "si les choses qui doibvent estre dictes ou mises premierement estoient dernieres, et les dernieres premieres, ce seroit plustost un monstre, ou confusion ... qu'autre chose" (I, iii, 76).

Actions and plots bear a slightly different relationship to nature. One difference between the historian and the poet, as we have seen, is that the poet may tell "lies," that is, he is not a mere recorder of historical or actual truth. The lies he tells are the fictions or invented actions included in his poems. But even these are affected by considerations of what can and cannot happen in nature. The terms used in this connection might be arranged as follows:

1. Historian:	Truth		
2. Good Poet:	Fiction	Like Truth	Possible
3. Bad Poet:	Falsity	Unlike Truth	Impossible

For example in the epic, "quoyque ce ne soit rien que fiction ... si est-il que cela pouvoit estre: car il ne faut jamais fonder son œuvre sur un impossible" (IV, ix, 145); in the epic again, but applicable to the poet in general: "il est permis au poëte de mentir, pourveu que ce qu'il controuve puisse estre ou avoir esté" (IV, ix, 147); and again, "Le bon poëte pour faire bien son œuvre se sert plus du possible que de la verité" (IV, ix, 148). A special case is made of tragedy, for in tragedy the poet uses the truth, not fiction: "L'argument ne doit point estre feinct, mais vray" (V, iv, 156); for this reason supernatural characters are excluded from the genre:

> si on y introduisoit un dieu ou deesse, qui sont choses fausses, l'argument aussi seroit faux, et par consequent ne representeroit pas les faicts des hommes illustres selon la verité (V, iv, 157).

This limitation of poetry to true or truthlike actions on the one hand makes it impossible to show certain actions on the stage, since the audience would recognize them as feigned and not true (V, iv, 160); on the other hand, it makes undesirable the observance of the unity of time, since such observance would lead to "des grandes absurditez pour estre contraincts introduire des choses impossibles et incredibles" (V, ix, 166). In a word, the distinction between reality and poetry is lost, and the conditions of the one are imposed on the other.

These many relationships of poetry to nature provide the poet and the critic with a number of criteria—all of them natural rather than poetic. Poems will be good in so far as they depict natural objects as they are. Poems will be good when the decorum of persons is observed carefully (for additional passages, see IV, i, 130; IV, v, 138; IV, ix, 148; V, vi, 163). Poems will be good when the actions represented are recognized as true (in tragedy) or truthlike (in the other genres).

(4) *The poem in relation to the audience.* Two specific audiences are distinguished by Delaudun, the audience of simple, uneducated people, and the audience of learned connoisseurs. It is for the former that verse was first invented: "les plus subtils esprits faisoient leur mesure en certain nombre de pieds et syllabes, pour donner plus facilement à entendre leurs conceptions aux plus grossiers" (I, i, 72). This audience still exists; even today "la tragedie n'est faicte que pour contenter le peuple" (V, iv, 159). We know certain things about its characteristics. It is lazy, and will not apply great effort to its reading: "On ne trouve plus de ceux qui autrefois se sont pleus et ont faict presse à qui entendroit une chose obscure ... , mais un chacun veut sçavoir et apprendre à peu de frais" (IV, vi, 140). It is apt to be distracted if, for example, choruses do not appear between the acts of a tragedy (V, vii, 163). It may even be ignorant of the mythology, the history, or the philosophy which the poet might introduce into his work (IV, vi, 139). The other audience, that of the "doctes," is mentioned only in passing; it is by definition learned, will know about such things as the four oratorical styles and their proper mixture. But for general purposes of the work it is not distinguished from the other group of readers (IV, ix, 150).

Certain features will have to appear in a poem if an audience of this type is to be pleased. Fables (to be taken in the sense of mythology) and comparisons will have to abound (I, i, 72). The invention will have to be such that it will be "easily understood and well accepted by everybody" (I, ii , 76). Above all, the poem will have to be clear; clarity is the first ornament of poetry (IV, v, 137). Contrariwise, obscurity is the first vice, for "il vaudroit mieux ne parler point, que de parler sans estre entendu" (IV, vi, 139). Even if the material of the poem is sometimes difficult, the words used to express it must be easily intelligible (IV, vi, 139–40). Finally, words of a certain character only may be used; they must not be harsh in sound or gross in meaning, but rather sweet and proper (I, iii, 77). These features, of course, amount to so many criteria which are derived from the audience: ornamentation through fables and comparisons, clarity, good invention and disposition, the right kind of words.

Further desiderata of the poem result from the nature of its end with respect to this audience. This end is manifold. It is at least in part ethical; the subject of the coq-à-l'âne is "la reprehension des vices des hommes"

(II, x, 105), the *bergerie* often contains "un sens moral" (III, viii, 124), in comedy "on reprend la vie des hommes" (V, i, 151) and "l'on touche le vice de chacun" (V, i, 153). The epic mingles joy and sorrow "pour monstrer les faicts humains et qu'en ce monde il n'y a rien de stable " (IV, ix, 147). No specific statement is made to the effect that the reader is bettered by these works. In part, though, the end is to give certain kinds of delight to the audience. The plot of an epic must be such that it will "delight the reader and even move him to pity" (IV, ix, 150). It must be so handled that it will arouse in the reader a kind of suspense. He will not know how the plot is to terminate, and when the story becomes interesting the thread of the narrative will be broken "pour tenir le lecteur beant et desireux de sçavoir l'evenement de ce que paravant il a leu" (IV, ix, 147). In tragedy, also, the parts must be so ordered as to "tenir tousjours les spectateurs beants" (V, iv, 158). The end of admiration, achieved through a proper admixture of the true and the false, the old and the new, is probably related to this end of the pleasure of the audience (IV, ix, 146).

(5) *The poem as a work of art.* From the preceding discussions of the poem in relationship to various external factors, it is evident that Delaudun's theory does not admit of any consideration of the poem as an independent art form. The poet, nature, the audience—all determine or affect various characteristics of the poem and impose criteria upon it. Yet there are in the treatise a large number of statements about poetry which do not spring from any of the external factors mentioned and which can be related to them only by a dialectic which is not provided by the work itself. These statements concern certain ends which seem not to be determined by external causes, certain means for achieving these ends, the poetic genres, and prosodic matters.

First, the ends. They are such things as excellence—"si on veut faire quelque chose d'excellent" (I, ii, 76); "lustre" (I, iii, 76); grace (II, x, 106; III, vi, 123; V, ix, 166); beauty—"quelque belle invention" (I, ii, 76), "un beau subject" (I, iii, 76); elegance (*ibid.*); order—"la disposition et autres belles parties du poëme" (I, v, 79), "la bonne disposition que l'autheur y faict, rapportant les choses vieilles aux nouvelles et vrayes, de sorte que l'on ne puisse cognoistre par où l'œuvre ... a esté cousue" (IV, ix, 145–46). These are vague, general terms, and we are given neither definitions nor specifications with respect to them. If we were to look for definitions for them, we should probably find them in classical rhetorical documents. Another such end, that of richness or embellishment, is similarly derived from the rhetoricians; but it is more completely discussed than the others, and probably was considered as more important by Delaudun. A poem must be "ornamented" by such things as mythological tales, told briefly or alluded to in passing (IV, v, 137), by descriptions of all kinds of objects (*ibid.*), by comparisons and all the other rhetorical figures of speech (*ibid.*), by visions, descriptions of paintings, prophecies (IV, ix, 147), by onomatopoeic effects (IV, ix, 149). Of these, as we have already seen, comparisons are seemingly the most important: "la comparaison est l'ame de la poësie françoise" (I, iii, 76–77; cf. IV, v, 139 and IV, ix, 149). All these things are to be introduced abundantly in such "ornate" genres as the ode and the epic, and less frequently in other genres. In this way an over-all effect of richness will be achieved, and the achievement of this end is desirable in itself.

Second, the means for achieving these ends. Presumably, the observance of the precepts and rules provided for the various genres will lead to the construction of poems within those genres which will have the desired effect; otherwise there would be no reason for providing them. There are, in addition, certain general canons of procedure which will insure the beauty, elegance, etc., of the poem. The most important of these is the canon of appropriateness, which is invoked on various occasions. Even harsh words may be admitted when the subject permits: "Il ne faut jamais chercher les mots rudes ou epithetes, si ce n'est en leur propre subject" (I, iii, 77). The number of personages in a tragedy will be appropriate to the subject. Delaudun takes direct issue with other theorists on this point: "il y faut mettre autant de personnages que l'histoire le requiert" (V, iv, 159). Similarly, more than three persons may appear in a given scene, contrary to the rule of Horace: "il en faut autant, qu'il est besoing" (V, vi, 163). Persons of low social rank may also appear in tragedy: "rarement hommes de bas estat, si l'argument necessairement ne le requiert" (V, iv, 158). The same requirement of appropriateness applies to ornamentation:

> je luy monstre de quoy il doit orner sa poësie, soit petit poëme ou grand, selon que la capacité d'iceluy le peut permettre: car...la chose reçeuë se comporte selon la recevante. Donc, il faut que cela soit à l'esprit du poëte, d'accomoder ses ornemens selon le suject (IV, v, 136–37).

On comparisons, Delaudun cites the opinion of Ronsard that "n'en faut pas user si souvent que bien à-propos" (IV, v, 138). There is a proper length for tragedy—"Il ne faut pas non plus que la tragedie soit ne trop longue ne trop courte, mais y tenir une mediocrité" (V, iv, 160)—and a proper plot for each epic—"l'histoire ou fable appartenant à l'essence de l'œuvre" (IV, ix, 148), whatever that "essence" may be. It is important to note that in all this insistence upon appropriateness, there is no indication as to how appropriateness is determined by the poet or tested by the critic; the recommendation remains a very general one and only the most subjective judgments are possible.

Further canons require consistency ("garder de ne se contredire point, et qu'en son œuvre, il n'y aye point de repugnances," IV, vi, 140) and a proper joining of the parts of the work. The latter is merely a repetition of the Horatian admonishment:

> Et faire qu'en la fin les parties de l'œuvre soient si bien liées et collées les unes aux autres, que la fin se rapporte au commencement, et que dextrement à la fin de l'œuvre on puisse entendre tout l'argument par ordre (IV, ix, 147).

They demand the use of paraphrase instead of direct statement, the separation of the diction from that of common speech, and the inclusion of numerous "poincts et œillets de philosophie" (*ibid.*, pp. 147–148). These general practices, while they apply equally to all genres, apply more especially to the more complicated and noble genres such as the epic and the tragedy.

Third, the poetic genres. In most of what he has to say about the various poetic genres, Delaudun departs but little from the tradition of his predecessors. He does add treatment of a number of types—the demi-sonnet, epitaph, Pindaric ode, *cartel* or *mascarade*, hymn, *stances*, panegyric, epithalamium, acrostic, and anagram—and gives more complete analysis of such types as the *bergerie*, the ode, the epic, tragedy and comedy. To these he applies the same kinds of inquiry as his predecessors had used; he makes a few remarks about the subject matter, discusses at greater length the type of verse and the rime scheme, records the current conventions and something of the history pertaining to the genre, suggests a model. What is of greater interest, however, is the fact that there is a breaking down, in Delaudun's treatise, of some of the rigorous distinctions between genres which his predecessors had sought to maintain. This abandonment of distinctions pertains both to subject matter and to the conventions of verse form. For example, the sonnet no longer has a fixed subject matter: "La matiere du Sonnet debvroit estre grande, mais pour le jourd'huy on s'en sert en toutes choses" (II, ii, 95). It is distinguishable from the madrigal only in its restriction to fourteen lines. The elegy and the epistle are the same form (II, viii, 103). The matter of the lay and virelay is "telle qu'il plaist au poëte" (II, xv, 108). The complaint is indistinguishable from the elegy, the epistle, or the epitaph, and may even be assimilated to the dialogue, "En quoy l'on peut veoir que c'est un poëme qui gist à la disposition du poëte" (II, xiv, 108). The phrase "à la disposition du poëte," which occurs several times in the work, is symptomatic of the unwillingness to lay down inviolable precepts. The same applies to the conventions of verse form. The epitaph, for one, has no fixed form: "la façon est autant diverse comme il y a diversité de poëmes, car l'on les accommode tous à l'epitaphe" (II, xii, 107); so for the ode: "chacune Ode a presque sa façon, et ... cela gist au vouloir du poëte" (III, i, 116); so for the acrostic (III, ix, 127), the anagram (III, x, 128). But this tendency does not extend to all genres, and many of the precepts of Sebillet and Peletier are repeated; even in a genre which Delaudun treates for the first time, the *stances*, there is a complete set of recommendations both for subject matter and for verse form (III, v, 120–22).

If the sharp line between genres is lost in this fashion, all poems will tend to become similar and to have more characteristics in common than those which differentiate them. Such a complete collapse of distinctions, however, is far from being accomplished by Delaudun.

Finally, prosodic matters. Delaudun's stand on matters of versification is entirely conventional. With Du Bellay and Sebillet, he asserts that the ear (rather than the eye) is the judge in such processes as riming (I, xii, 92). With Ronsard he insists upon the alternation of masculine and feminine rimes (I, vi, 80). He follows the general tradition in establishing a hierarchy of verses , and in adapting them to a similar hierarchy of genres. In a "noble genre" such as the panegyric the Alexandrine must be used, "car autrement le vers ne correspondroit pas à la matiere" (III, vi, 123). Decasyllables are employed in the elegy "et autres poëmes de peu d'importance" (I, vii, 82). Only in the lessening of rigidity with respect to verse forms, already noted, does he display any originality.

If now we reconsider the statements made with respect to the various topics distinguished in the above analysis, we shall be in a position to characterize the structure and the argument of the treatise as a whole. If it be asked "What are the ends of poetry?" several answers are discovered. Certain ends are proposed as those sought by the poet; others are indicated with respect to the audience, and they are not the same; still others emerge for the poem itself. Of these various ends variously stated, it cannot be said that any one is the most important or that others are intermediate or contributory to it. Each set of ends is of equal importance with the others, and Delaudun merely shifts from one to the other as his point of view changes. The same is true for criteria. In judging a poem according to the standards set up in this *Art poëtique*, we should be led to different conclusions on it depending upon whether we regarded it in relationship to nature, or to certain conventions and traditions of poetic composition, or to the demands of a rather vaguely defined audience. Again there would be no way of saying that any one criterion was the essential one, that others could be disregarded or discounted. If we were to write a poem according to the precepts here included, we should similarly find no dominating guide to its composition. Instead we should be obliged to include certain features in certain ways because of the requirements of the audience, other features in other ways because of the demands of a certain kind of adherence to nature, a whole mass of features in various specific ways because of the current traditions as expressed in the precepts and the rules. We should not find for our assistance any suggestions for unifying the poem, for establishing an ordering or subordination of component parts; all features from all sources are of equal value.

A poem for Delaudun would thus be a composite of miscellaneous parts, ordered to no central element, pursuing no single, all-informing end, judgable by no main criterion. In that respect it would resemble his own treatise on poetry, which is a composite of miscellaneous ideas, ordered to no central principle, having no structure of ideas or recognizable argument, supplying no single criterion. It remains rather a collection than a system of ideas. The only unifying factor in this collection is a preference—vague and imperfectly expressed—for the complicated, the ornate, and the elegant in poetry.

5. Jean Vauquelin de la Fresnaye

Although Vauquelin's *Art poëtique françois* was not published until 1605,[9] its composition goes back to a much earlier period. In his edition (pp. xxxv–xxxvi), Georges Pellissier indicates that the project was undertaken by Vauquelin as early as 1574, but that in 1589 the work had not yet been completed. The greater part of the verse treatise was probably finished, therefore, before the publication of Delaudun's study in 1597; in any case, Vauquelin's *art poëtique* may be considered as roughly contemporary with Delaudun's and as representing the same period in French thinking about the poetic art. It is like Delaudun's, again, in its assemblage of a large number of current notions about poetry and in its failure to combine those notions into a systematic treatise.

Much of the difficulty in reading Vauquelin arises from his method of writing. Essentially, the work is a paraphrase and expansion of Horace's *Ars poetica*. The entire *Ars poetica* passes over into the *Art poëtique françois*, much diluted to be sure, but with few exceptions in the exact order of verses of the original. Now Horace's epistle is one in which the order is not immediately clear to the reader and can be distinguished only after considerable analysis. It is doubtful that that order was apparent to Vauquelin himself. Add to this the fact that Vauquelin at times misreads Horace or applies his text to poetic problems in a way not justified by the original readings, and you have as the skeleton upon which the *Art poëtique françois* is hung a structure which is in itself extremely weak and disjointed. The translation or paraphrase of the *Ars poetica* is supplemented or interrupted by a wide variety of materials: introductions and finales for each canto (sometimes

[9] Ed. Georges Pellissier, Paris: Garnier Frères, 1885.

borrowed from Vida), a few excerpts from Aristotle's *Poetics*, long passages on the history of poetry and of the various genres, and on French poetry and poets, personal reminiscences, considerations on language, miscellaneous ideas borrowed from earlier theorists of French poetry. The result of this method of composition is that even the tenuous divisions of the *Ars poetica* are destroyed, and it becomes impossible to follow the line of development. Roughly, certain broad fields of operation are distinguishable for each canto: in the first, the nature of poetry, some general precepts for the writing of poetry, and the lyrical genres; in the second, the epic, tragedy, and satire, and their special treatment in French; in the third, comedy, general precepts for drama, the remainder of the genres, the character and work of the poet. But this does not prevent the repetition of the same materials in two or three cantos, nor does it guarantee that all the ideas relevant to a given point will be found at the place where that point is being treated.

Even with this kind of internal organization, it would be possible for a poetic treatise to present an integrated system of ideas. Unfortunately, that does not seem to be the case for Vauquelin's *Art poëtique françois*. I shall be obliged, therefore, in this case, as in the case of Delaudun, to present a summary rather than an analysis of the ideas; the summary will be according to the same categories and the same arrangement as those used for Delaudun.

(1) *The character and qualities of the poet.* Most of what Vauquelin has to say about the nature and the activities of the poet comes from Horace; much of it has to do with the problem of Nature and Art and their interrelationship. He does take over, from Aristotle's *Poetics*, the notion that different poets practiced different genres in accordance with their characters (I, 119 ff.), and that the imitative process in the poetic art is a natural one (I, 189); but these are accretions to the general distinction, not parts of it. In general, the poet is born a poet (I, 116), he is visited by the poetic fury (I, 97), his genius is celestial rather than terrestrial (I, 733). But Nature alone is not enough. It must be supplemented by Art, which is a product of practice and an aid to Nature:

> Mais l'vsage fist l'Art; l'Art par apprentissage (I, 147)
> Renouuelle, embellit, regle et maintient l'vsage:
> Et ce bel Art nous sert d'escalier pour monter
> A Dieu, quand du nectar nous desirons gouster.

Art is not only the poetic art; it is any and all of the arts and sciences which may serve poetry (I, 169). In so far as it is equivalent to judgment, it enables the poet to avoid faults (I, 277 ff.) and serves as a check on his "fureur" (I, 942). But art itself is subject to "le bon iugement" and "la discretion" (I, 1131 ff.), and its relation to the muses (or nature) is determined by these additional faculties.

In these remarks on art and nature in the poet, no allusion is made to the separate or distinctive qualities of the poem derived from each, nor are any criteria for the poem obtained from the fact that it is the product of a natural gift on the one hand and an artistic process on the other. We know merely that these two faculties are involved, and that they are of approximately equal importance for the poet (III, 905 ff.). We are hence less well equipped to judge of a poem in the light of its origins than we should be, for example, after a reading of Delaudun.

At least a part of the poet's art is related to the process of imitation in which he engages. And although "imitation" is at times used in the Aristotelean sense of an imitation of nature, in most passages Vauquelin uses it in the customary Renaissance meaning of an imitation of models. The distinction between imitation and simple translation is made (I, 951) and the general procedure for following models is suggested, if only in the vaguest terms (III, 527; cf. II, 887); as each genre is taken up, Vauquelin names the poet to be used as a model for that genre.

The remainder of the material on the poet is even more commonplace than that already outlined. The poet must select a task to which his capacities are fitted (I, 298), he must have knowledge and inspiration (III, 403, 444), he must cultivate good friends and severe critics (III, 787), he must work hard (III, 917). Mediocrity in poetry is intolerable (III, 694), but occasional faults are pardoned in the light of great qualities (III, 617). For his end, the poet seeks renown (II, 895; III, 616). These notions are directly out of Horace, and little is gained by their reiteration.

(2) *The nature of the poetic art.* Vauquelin's treatise is not one in which distinctions are carefully made and followed; the very way that he uses verse would militate against that. Hence there is no attempt to distinguish poetry from the other arts of discourse. Its own special characteristic is the use of verse, and the "art de poësie" is frequently synonymous with the "art des vers" (cf. I, 2 with I, 5, e.g.). Thus far the conception of poetry does not differ from that of Delaudun, for example, or from that of most Renaissance theorists. But Vauquelin does enrich the theory by certain additions, largely from Aristotle. First, the notion of music or harmony is added:

> Le Nombre et la Musique en leur douce Harmonie, (I, 151)
> Sont quasi comme l'ame en la sainte manie
> De tout genre de vers, de qui faut emprunter
> Le sucre et la douceur pour les faire gouster.

This is not peculiar to Vauquelin, but it does seem to be more specifically stated than elsewhere. Second, he includes "contrefaisance" or imitation as an essential element of poetry:

> C'est vn Art d'imiter, Vn Art de contrefaire (I, 187)
> Que toute Poësie, ainsi que de pourtraire,
> Et l'imitation est naturelle en nous.

The idea is repeated on various occasions in the work, for example in connection with the treatment of character:

> Le docte imitateur, qui voudra contrefaire (III, 499)
> De cette vie au vray le parfait exemplaire
> ...
> que Nature il sçache imiter tellement
> Que la Nature au vray ne soit point autrement.

In the latter connection, the question arises as to whether the inclusion of imitation in the definition does any more than establish a relationship between the poem and nature; imitation is not defined nor are its processes described. Moreover, we shall see that the models function in this work, as elsewhere, as the "originals" which the poet follows. Third, and on Aristotle's authority, Vauquelin permits the poet to write in prose:

> En Prose tu pourras poëtiser aussi: (II, 261)
> Le grand Stagiritain te le permet ainsi.

He thereby comes into direct opposition, on the one hand, with such a theorist as Delaudun, and on the other hand he introduces a kind of contradiction within his own work, since almost everywhere else poetry is synonymous with verse. By such additions as these, however, there does appear to be some enlarging of the conception of poetry.

(3) *The poem in relation to nature.* We have already seen that poetry is an imitation or "contrefaisance" of nature, that the nature of the poet is supplemented by his art—in a word, that the term "nature" is used in various contexts and with various meanings. In so far as it means that which is imitated or represented in the poem, it refers essentially to "life" and to the characters of men. A few general principles of imitation are stated. That which is ugly in nature, for example, may become beautiful in art through the process of imitation:

> nous plaist en peinture vne chose hideuse, (I, 191)
> Qui seroit à la voir en essence facheuse.

This is adapted from Aristotle; from a misreading of the opening lines of Horace comes another principle: that things disparate in nature may, when combined in art, form a pleasurable whole (I, 217 ff.). The concept which determines the relationship of the imitation to the object in nature is that of "vraisemblance" or verisimilitude. What is represented in the poem need not be true; it may be a fiction or "menterie," but it must have the appearance of truth (I, 911–12). In the epic, some readers will be interested

> aux fictions, aux contes delectables (I, 463)
> Qui semblent plus au vray qu'ils ne sont veritables.

As a matter of fact, a strict adherence to historical or actual truth is held undesirable (cf. I, 911–12), and fictional elements are essential:

> Ainsi dedans les vers le faux entrelassé, (II, 273)
> Auec le vray-semblant d'vn conte du passé,
> Nous emeut, nous chatouille et nous poind dauantage,
> Que l'estude qu'on met à polir son ouurage,
> Sans faire vne meslange, vne variété,
> Qui ne suit, mensongere, en rien la verité.

Nature itself is thought to have certain characteristics. One of these is a kind of consistency or predictability of behavior of persons in given situations: a man in a tragic situation will always speak appropriately to that situation. This characteristic must be reflected in the poem, and hence a tragedy would use one kind of verse, a comedy another:

> Chacune chose doit en sa naïfue grace (I, 811)
> Retenir proprement sa naturelle place.

For this relationship Vauquelin uses the word "conuenant," which later becomes a part of the canon of classical French criticism—beggars would not use pompous language "Comme mal conuenant aux banis souffretteux" (I, 826; cf. I, 873). Persons also speak and act in accordance with their characters as old men or young men, rich men or poor men, masters or slaves—all the elements which went into the Roman theory of decorum:

> Tu dois de chacun âge aux mœurs bien regarder, (II, 329)
> La bienseance en tout soigneusement garder—

and for this relationship Vauquelin uses another term of classical criticism, "bienseance." These terms and the discussions to which they apply relate exclusively to conceptions of character, and it should be noted that nature as conceived of in this work is essentially human nature.

One special aspect of subject matter treated by Vauquelin is the exploitation of Christian materials in poetry. Use of these materials imposes new rules on poetry, such as the exclusion of mention of the pagan gods (I, 901–904). Vauquelin urges the development of such subjects, and in Book III lists a number of modern poets who have practiced them and suggests some possible themes (ll. 844–904).

(4) *The poem in relation to the audience.* Practically everything that Vauquelin has to say about the audience-poem relationship is related to the *utile dulci* principle of his Horatian original. The only notable exception is the statement, derived from Aristotle, that poetry pleases essentially because imitation is pleasurable to men. The statement itself is not clear-cut, but takes such forms as the following:

> Car tant de grace auient par cette vray-semblance, (I, 203)
> Que surtout agreable est la contrefaisance.

Contrariwise, the statements to the effect that poetry is at once useful and pleasurable to the men who read it are numerous and unambiguous. The utility is a moral or ethical one, since men's characters are formed and their actions directed by the reading of poetry; for example:

> Des raisons, des discours, pour y former leurs mœurs (I, 466)
>
> conduit les humains à leur bien-heureté (I, 469)
>
> des beaus vers la ioyeuse alegresse (I, 743)
> Nous conduit aux vertus d'vne plaisante addresse.

The pleasure, as we have seen, is one which springs from the natural delight in imitation, in rhythm and harmony; it is indicated by such phrases as "quelque chose ... de gentil" (I, 750); "rendra beaucoup plus contentees, "Et les amusera" (III, 512–13); "Pour donner du plaisir et du contentement" (III, 766).

Again building upon the suggestions found in Horace, Vauquelin proceeds to a differentiation of audiences and to a specification of the kinds of pleasure and utility proper to each. Among the poet's functions is to teach virtue to the youth (II, 620). He may use low jests for an audience of commoners, but not for people who are "riches, grands, sages" (II, 805–9). Old men will be attracted by "utilité," grave men by grave things, but young men will be adverse to anything severe (III, 604–8). To amuse a king one must use "paroles de soye" and treat some thing which will please him (I, 1140). Once again, however, the distinction is not made integral to the rest of the work; there is no attempt, for example, to relate given genres to given types of audiences and to make their qualities relevant to those audiences, as was the case with Peletier.

(5) *The poem as a work of art.* Even when considered by itself and outside the context of the audience, of nature, of the other arts, poetry is still, for Vauquelin, subject to a great body of tradition. This is the complex of accepted rules embodied in the theories of Aristotle, Horace, Vida, and Minturno, and referred to in the phrase "sentier tracé":

> Car nos sçauans maieurs nous ont desia tracé (I, 61)
> Vn sentier qui de nous ne doit estre laissé.

This means that an individual poem, in any genre, will be developed not according to any internal structural principle, but according to the mass of conventions and historical precedents for poems in that genre. In his own treatise, Vauquelin devotes a great deal of space to the retailing of such conventions and precedents, although less of this space proportionately is given to matters of riming and prosody than was the case in most earlier treatises. Otherwise the materials included are the usual ones: some remarks on appropriate subject matters for the genre, some criteria and some indications with respect to the general tone or effect, and the model or models to be followed. The poem is thus caught between the dicta of the theorists on the one hand and the example of the models on the other, and there remains little room for experiment or for an individual conception of the work.

When he speaks in terms of poetry as a whole rather than in terms of a specific genre, Vauquelin restricts his remarks to variations on a surprisingly small number of ideas. First, and no matter what the genre, a poem must have a given tone or quality which must be consistently maintained throughout. This means that a mixture of verses from different genres would not be tolerated (I, 807; II, 751 ff.), that the laws of decorum must be strictly applied to all persons (I, 888), that there must be no intermixture of the high and the low poetic styles (I, 267). This idea gives rise to a second, that everything which enters into the poem must be judged by the canon of appropriateness; both the order of things and their fitness are involved here:

> La grace et la beauté de cet ordre sera, (I, 301)
> Si ie ne me deçoy, quand bien on dressera
> Ce qui dire se doit, et non se dire à l'heure.

Good invention, disposition, and elocution are thus included (I, 307). Third, in so far as the poem has an end contained within itself, that end is its perfection. This means that not only every part must be perfect, but that the whole must be perfect (cf. I, 289 ff.); that verse, whose difficulty lends an added virtue to poetry (I, 83), must be polished to the point of perfection (cf. III, 365 ff.); that language must be sweet, beautiful (I, 829; I, 460).

Thus in his recommendations for the poem itself Vauquelin does not go beyond the vague Horatian prescripts—beauty, perfection, order, appropriateness. The problem of how any one of these is to be achieved is treated only in the most general terms.

If now it be asked what line of development or evolution is discernible in the poetic arts from Sebillet in 1548 to Vauquelin in 1605, some such statement as the following might be hazarded : With Sebillet, the problem is still that of the first half of the century, the problem of prosody and of the traditions of the current genres; but this is affected by certain broader conceptions of poetry derived from the Platonists. With Du Bellay, the importance of language and of writing in the vernacular comes to the fore, and poetic considerations are assimilated to linguistic considerations. Peletier, while echoing both of these earlier concerns, propounds a theory of poetry which closely reflects an aristocratic theory of society; this theory he develops in what is probably the most self-consistent of the five documents analyzed here. Delaudun, using French rather than ancient sources, produces a compendium of the critical ideas of his time, and this is again done by Vauquelin; but Vauquelin leans more heavily on classical theorists, especially Horace, and his product shows somewhat less eclecticism. Neither of the last two succeeds in developing a theory of the poetic art.

Aside from these statements on the individual authors, some generalizations such as these might be in order: The tendency through the century is away from prosody and towards poetic; away from the traditional French genres and towards the genres of Greece and Rome and Italy; away from the grammarians and Horace as sources and towards Plato and Aristotle (although the grammarians and Horace remain the dominant influences throughout the century); away from a kind of imitation which is classical in subject matter and towards the use of French and Christian subject matters within the classical molds.

To these five texts and to the generalizations which they suggest, the prefaces which follow will add detail and variation, contradiction and confirmation, and will serve in this way to complete and enrich the picture of French literary criticism in the Renaissance.

BIBLIOGRAPHICAL REFERENCES

British Museum, *Short-title Catalogue of Books printed in France and of French Books printed in other countries from 1470 to 1600 now in the British Museum*, London, 1924.

Brunet, Jacques-Charles, *Manuel du Libraire et de l'amateur de livres*, Paris: F. Didot Frères, Fils, et Cie, 1860–1880. Fifth edition, 8 vols. including 2 vols. of *Supplément*.

Du Verdier, Antoine, *Les Bibliothèques françoises de La Croix du Maine et de Du Verdier*, ed. Rigoley de Juvigny, Paris: Saillant et Nyon; Lambert, 1772–1773, 6 vols.

Graesse, Jean George Théodore, *Trésor le Livres rares et précieux*, Dresden: Kuntze, 1859–1869, 7 vols. including 1 vol. of *Supplément* (photographic reprint, Berlin: Altmann, 1922).

La Croix du Maine, François Grudé, sieur de. See Du Verdier.

Le Petit, Jules, *Bibliographie des principales éditions originales d'écrivains français du XVe au XVIIIe siècle*, Paris: Jeanne et Brulon, 1927.

Murray, C. Fairfax, *Catalogue of a Collection of Early French Books in the Library of C. Fairfax Murray*, Compiled by Hugh Wm. Davies, London: Privately printed, 1910, 2 vols.

Praet, J. B. B. van, *Catalogue des livres imprimés sur vélin de la Bibliothéque du roi*, Paris: De Bure Frères, 1822–28, 6 vols.

Ricci, Seymour de, *Catalogue of a Unique Collection of Early Editions of Ronsard*, London: Maggs Bros., 1927.

Rothschild, James de, *Catalogue des livres composant la bibliothèque de feu M. le baron James de Rothschild*, [by Emile Picot], Paris: Morgand, 1884–1920, 5 vols.

Tchemerzine, Avenir, *Bibliographie d'éditions originales et rares d'auteurs français des XVe, XVIe, XVIIe et XVIIIe siècles*, Paris: Plée, 1927–1933, 10 vols.

SYMPHORIEN CHAMPIER

DEDICATION TO HIS *Bayard*

1525

TEXT:

Les gestes ensemble la vie du preulx Cheualier Bayard: auec sa genealogie: comparaisons aulx anciens preulx cheualiers: gentilx: Ysraelitiques: et chrestiens. Ensemble oraisons: lamentations: Epitaphes du dit cheualier Bayard. Contenant plusieurs victoyres des roys de France. Charles. viij. Loys. xii. et Francoys premier de ce nom. Ont vent lesditz liures a Lyon en rue merciere a lenseigne sainct Jehan baptiste en la maison de Gilbert de villiers. [Colophon dated "M.CCCCC.xxv. le. xxiiij. de Nouembre." B.N., Paris.]
[Cf. Brunet, I, 1773–74.]

COLLATED:

(1558) La vie & les gestes du preux cheualier Bayard. Contenant plusieurs victoires par luy faictes du Resgne des roys de France Charles huytiesme Loys douziesme. Et de Francoys premier de ce nom. Tant es Italie, Naples, et Picardie que aultres pays et regions. On les vend a Lyon au pres de nostre dame de Confort chez Oliuier Arnoullet. [Colophon dated "le .viij. De apuril mil. ccccc.lviij." Newberry Library.]
[Cf. Brunet, I, 1774; Baudrier, *Bibliographie lyonnaise*, X, 89–90.]

Symphorien Champier had married the cousin of Bayard, Marguerite du Terrail de Bernin, and through her came to know the hero of Marignano. His work on Bayard (which should be distinguished from the biography by the "loyal serviteur") appeared almost immediately after the death of the knight, and was an essay in contemporary history. Champier's other writings, in French and in Latin, are on such diverse matters as medicine, physics, philosophy, and history (cf. Du Verdier, ed. Rigoley de Juvigny, III, 478–79, and La Croix du Maine, II, 417 ff.).

[vj *v*] A MONSIEUR MERLIN DE SAINCT GELAYS, AULMOSNIER DE MONSEIGNEUR LE DAULPHIN, SYMPHORIEM CHAMPIER SALUT

Le tesmonaige du temps passé, la lumiere de verité, le messagier des antiquités,[1] la vie de memoyre que maintenant on appelle histoyre, les anciens ont[2] preferés[3] devant tous aultres genrres d'escripture. Et on dit estre utile et très necessayre aulx hommes pource que elle nous demonstre comme debvons vivre, ce que debvons ensuyvre et pareillement fouyr, et comme noz operations par bons moyens se doibvent diriger en vertu.

1. iniquitez *1558* 2. on *1525* 3. *sic; for* preferée?

Tout ce nous monstrent histoires apertement et par exemples; car tout demeureroyt en tenebres si la lumiere des histoyres n'estoit et ne[4] demonstroyt les[5] choses passées. Et comme dient les anciens, il n'est pas plus de honneur aulx victorieulx que aulx scripteurs[6] et historyens des[7] victoyres, et n'est pas moyns à louer Homere descripvant les gestes Troyennes que[8] Hector ou Achilles qui d'icelles ont esté la gloyre. Si histoyre n'eust esté trouvé, les hommes ne parleroyent que des choses[9] de leurs temps seulement.

A toy doncques, chier amy Merlyn, ay voulu ceste histoyre envoyer pource que elle est d'ung preulx entre tous les aultres qui ont esté au pays de monseigneur le Daulphin, au service duquel tu es ordinayrement et des plus familiers. Et d'aultant que monseigneur le Daulphin est filz du premier filz de l'esglise Aisné,[a] n'est de merveilles si en son pays du[10] Daulphiné est né ung des plus chevaleureulx qui aye esté de son temps. Car ainsi que le daulphin est le plus noble poyson, et beau, bening, et de doulce nature, qui soyt en la mer, ainsy monseigneur [vij] le Daulphin est entre tous jeunes princes très noble, beau, bening, et de nature courtoyse. Et veu qu'il est ainsy, d'aultant que son pere a voulu prendre l'ordre de chevalerie par les mains du feu noble Bayard,[b] à plus forte raison vouldra mon dit seigneur prandre recreation aulx gestes et histoyres du preulx Bayard, lequel a prins naisance au pays dont[11] il est souverain seigneur et duquel il porte le tiltre.

Et tu sces assés[12] comme les gestes en[13] ceste histoyre contenues peuvent donner exemples à tous jeusnes chevaliers qui veulent armes pourter. Lucius Luculus, lequel escript en Grec les batailles de Marsus,[14] par la seulle congnoisance des histoyres d'ung historien devint très saige, prudent et hardy capitaine sur les aultres de son temps.[c] La congnoisance des histoyres non seulement deleicte l'entendement de l'homme, mais aussy est utile à tous humains pour[15] la congnoisance des choses passées, par laquelle plusieurs foys les jeunes sont reputés plus saiges que aulcuns anciens, et[16] ce est par la seulle lecture des histoyres.

Si en ceste histoyre je recite aulcunes infortunes que les Françoys ont eues de nostre temps, pour ce n'en doibs estre reprins. Car ung vray historien doibt escripre aussi tost les infortunes et adversités comme les

4. se *1558* 5. les *omitted 1558* 6. escriptures *1558* 7. et *1558*
8. de *1558* 9. des choses *omitted 1558* 10. de *1558* 11. don *1525*
12. assés *omitted 1558* 13. de *1558* 14. Marcus *1558* 15. par *1558*
16. et *omitted 1558*

a. Rigoley de Juvigny, in his edition of La Croix du Maine, II, 418, points out that Champier "publia un Catalogue des Abbés d'Aisnay."

b. Francis I received knighthood from Bayard on the field of Marignano, 1515.

c. Cicero, *Academica*, II.i.2.

prosperités. Et n'est pas moins à louer Titus Livius Romain de ce qu'il a escript comme Romme fust prinse et brulée par ceulx de Gaule, dicte maintenant France, que quant il descript le triumphe de Paulus Emilius, lequel il eust des Macedoniens, ou quant il descript les victoyres de Scipion Aphricain.[d] La nature des historiens est d'escripre prosperités et adversités ensemble. Xenophon, très grand philosophe, quant il descript[17] la destruction de Athenes et la famine d'icelle cité, triste et doulent et avec larmes descript; mais non obstant, pource que il estimoyt estre utile [vij *v*] à la posterité, ne delaissat à ce fayre.[e]

Doncques, mon amy Merlin, je[18] te prie, vueille[19] excuser les faultes de ce petit livre (si aulcunes en y a), et si ne sont escriptes en vraye rethoricque Françoyse comme les *Epistres* de Ovide translatées[20] de Latin en nostre langue Gallicaine par feu ton oncle evesque de Angolesme.[f] Je te ay bien voulu ceste epistre envoyer pour te donner à congnoistre que à celle foys que tu fustz en ma mayson à Lyon avec plusieurs aultres docteurs et litterés, entre tous aultres me pleust ton eloquence et adorné langaige. Vueilles doncques recongnoistre l'amour de moy envers toy, et faictz que elle soyt reciproque, et soye juge de noz labeurs. Et atant[21] prie celluy que la terre par sa providence colloquast au centre du monde, qu'il luy plaise donner vie longue à monseigneur le Daulphin Françoys, duquel es serviteur ordinayre, et à messeigneurs ses freres, et à toy ensemble vie en[22] longueur Nestorienne et Davidtique en meurs et devotion.

17. escript *1558* 18. je *omitted 1558* 19. vueilles *1558*
20. translateur *1525*; translatees *1558* 21. autant *1558* 22. et *1558*

d. References to Livy, *Ab Urbe Condita*, V.xl.4 ff., XLV.vii, and Bks. XXIX–XXX, respectively.

e. Xenophon, *Hellenica*, II.ii.21 ff.

f. The translation of the *Epistles* of Ovid by Octavien de Saint-Gelais was printed in Paris by Vérard about 1500; cf. Tchemerzine, X, 136.

ANONYMOUS

PREFACE TO THE *Roman de la Rose*

1526

TEXT:

Cy est le Romant de la roze
Ou tout lart damour est enclose
Histoires et auctoritez
Et maintz beaulx propos vsitez
Qui a este nouuellement
Corrige suffisantement
Et cotte bien a lauantaige
Com on voit en chascune page.

On les vend a Paris en la grand salle du Palais au premier pillier en la boutique de Galliot du pre Libraire iure de Luniuersite. Auec priuilege, [Not dated; the *privilège* is dated "le ieudy dixneufiesme iour dapvril Mil cinq cens vingtsix apres pasques." B.N., Paris.]

[Cf. Brunet, III, 1174; Tchemerzine, VII, 244; Fairfax Murray, I, 426, No. 328; Bourdillon, *Early Editions of the Roman de la Rose*, pp. 32, 57–58. Some copies of the edition were sold by Jean Petit and bear his name.]

COLLATED:

(1529) Le Rommant de la Rose nouuellement Reueu et corrige oultre les precedentes Impressions. On le vend a Paris par Galliot du pre Libraire iure ayant sa bouticque au premier pillier de la grant salle du Pallays, 1529. [Colophon dated "Au moys de Mars, mil cinq centz. xxix. auant pasques" (=1530 n.s.). Library of Congress, Pierpont Morgan Library.]

[Cf. Brunet, III, 1174; Tchemerzine, VII, 245; Cat. Rothschild, No. 437; Fairfax Murray, I, 427–28, No. 329; Bourdillon, pp. 58–60.]

(1531) Cy est le Rommant de la Roze...[verse title as for 1526 ed.] On les vend a Paris en la rue sainct Jaques en la bouticque de Jean petit Libraire iure de luniuersite a lenseigne de la fleur de Lys dor. Mil. v.C. xxxi. [Newberry Library.]

[Cf. Brunet, III, 1175; Tchemerzine, VII, 246; Fairfax Murray, I, 428, No. 330; Bourdillon, pp. 60–62. Some copies of the edition were sold by Galiot du Pré and bear his name.]

(1538) Le rommant de la Rose nouuellement reueu et corrige oultre les precedentes Impressions. On les vend a Paris au clou Brennio a lenseigne de la corne de Serf pour Guillaume le Bret. [Colophon dated "Lan mil cinq cens. xxxviii." Newberry Library.]

[This edition, dated either 1537 or 1538, was sold by ten different printers. The copy at the Pierpont Morgan Library bears the name of "Arnoul et Charles les angeliers freres." Cf. Brunet, III, 1175; Tchemerzine, VII, 247–48; Bourdillon, pp. 62–64.]

Until 1912, this version of the text of *Le Roman de la Rose* was referred to as "Clément Marot's Recension," and the preface as well as the text itself were ascribed to the poet. But in that year Philipp August Becker, in an article on "Clément Marot und der Rosenroman," *Germanisch-Romanische Monatsschrift*, IV (1912), 684–87, presented excellent arguments against the attribution. He pointed out that the attribution had first been made by Estienne Pasquier on very unsure grounds, traced its history, and outlined arguments of an internal and an external character against it. Becker's case against ascribing the recension to Marot has been accepted by Henry Guy (*Histoire de la poésie française au XVIe siècle*. Vol. II, "Clément Marot et son école," Paris: Champion, 1926, p. 95); it has been rejected by K. Sneyders de Vogel (*Neophilologus*, XVII [1932], 269–71), whose arguments are not all equally convincing. Guy mentioned only two editions of the text, which was the only one printed in the sixteenth century after 1526; actually, there were four separate editions, all of which have been collated for the present text. The preface was reprinted by Guiffrey in his edition of the works of Marot (Vol. II, Paris: Claye, 1875, pp. 143–52).

For my suggested attribution of the preface and the modernization to Guillaume Michel de Tours see "Guillaume Michel, dit de Tours, The Editor of the 1526 *Roman de la Rose*," *Bibliothèque d'Humanisme et Renaissance*, XI (1949), 72–85.

[ii] PREAMBULE DU LIVRE[1]

S'il est ainsi que les choses dignes de memoire pour leur proffit et utilité soient à demeurer perpetuellement sans estre du tout assopies par trop longue saison et labilité de temps caduc et transitoire, l'esguillon et stimulement de juste raison et non simulée causé m'a, semont et enhorté, comme tuteresse de tout bien et honneur, à reintegrer et en son entier remettre le livre qui par long temps devant ceste moderne saison tant a esté de tous gens d'esprit estimé, que bien la daigne chascun veoir et tenir au plus hault anglet de sa librairie pour les bonnes sentences, propos, et ditz naturelz et moraulx qui dedans sont mis et inserez. C'est le plaisant livre du *Rommant de la Rose*, lequel fut poetiquement composé par deux nobles aucteurs dignes[2] de l'estimation de tout bon sens et louable sçavoir, maistre Jehan de Meung et maistre Guillaume de Loris. Cestuy livre present a esté auparavant par la faulte comme je croy des imprimeurs assez mal correct, ou par advanture de ceulx qui ont baillé le double pour l'imprimer, car l'ung et l'autre peult estre cause de son incorrection. Pour laquelle chose restituer en meilleur estat et plus expediente forme pour

1. Exposition moralle du romant de la rose *1529, 1538* 2. digne *1529, 1538*

l'intelligence des lecteurs et auditeurs, nonobstant la foyblesse du mien pueril[3] entendement et indignité de rural engin, j'ay[4] bien voulu relire ce present livre dès le commencement jusques à la fin, à laquelle chose faire fort laborieuse me suis employé et l'ay corrigé au moins mal que j'ay peu, y adjoustant les quottations des plus principaulx notables et auctoritez venans à propos; sans le mien voluntaire consentement comme devez entendre, mais comme j'ay dict, à l'instigation, priere et requeste de honnorable personne Galiot du Pré, libraire marchant juré en l'université de Paris, qui nouvellement l'a faict imprimer après avoir veu [ii *v*] sa correction, tant du mauvais et trop ancien langaige sentant son inveteré commencement et origine de parler, que de l'imparfaicte quantité des mettres, tous quasi corrompuz.[5]

Et pourautant qu'on[6] pourroit dire, comme jà plusieurs ont dict, que ce livre, parlant en vain de l'estat d'amours, peult estre cause de tourner les entendemens à[7] mal et les applicquer à choses dissolues, à cause de la persuasible matiere de fol amour dedans tout au long contenue, pour cause que fol appetit sensuel ou sensualité, nourrisse de tout mal et marastre de vertu, est moteur d'icelluy propos (tout honneur sauvé et premis), je respons que l'intention de l'aucteur n'est point simplement et de soy-mesmes mal fondée ne mauvaise. Car bien peult estre que ledit aucteur ne gettoit pas seullement son penser et fantasie sus le sens litteral, ains plustost attiroit son esprit au sens allegoric et moral, comme l'ung disant et entendant l'autre. Je ne veulx pas ce que je dis affermer, mais il me semble qu'il peult ainsi avoir faict. Et si celluy aucteur n'a ainsi son sens reiglé et n'est entré soubz la moralle couverture, penetrant jusques à la moelle[8] du nouveau sens misticque, toutesfois l'on le peult morallement exposer et en diverses sortes.

Je dis doncques premierement que par la rose qui tant est appettée de l'amant est entendu l'estat de sapience, bien et justement à la rose conforme pour les valeurs, doulceurs, et odeurs qui en elle sont, laquelle moult est à avoir difficile pour les empeschemens entreposez, ausquelz arrester ne me veulx pour le present. Et en ceste maniere d'exposer sera la rose figurée par la rose papalle,[a] qui est de trois choses composée, c'est assavoir d'or, de musq, et de basme. Car vraye sapience doit estre d'or, signifiant l'honneur et reverence que nous devons à Dieu le createur; de musq, à cause de la fidelité et justice que devons avoir à nostre prochain; et de basme quant à nous-mesmes, entant que nous devons tenir noz ames cheres et precieuses comme le basme pur et cher sur toutes les choses du monde.

3. petit *1529, 1538* 4. j' *omitted 1529, 1538* 5. mais...corrompuz *omitted 1538*
6. on *1526*; qu'on *1529 ff.* 7. en *1538* 8. moralle *1538*

a. Guiffrey, ed. Marot, II, 148, n. 1, refers to the *Rituum ecclesiasticorum*, I, sect. vii.

Secondement, on peult entendre par la rose l'estat de grace qui semblablement est à avoir difficile; non pas de la part de celluy qui la donne, car c'est Dieu le tout puissant, mais de la partie du pecheur qui tousjours est empesché et eslongné du collateur d'icelle grace.[9] Ceste maniere de rose spirituelle, tant bien spirant et refragant, pouons aux roses figurer par la vertu desquelles retourna en sa premiere forme le grant Apulée, selon qu'il est[10] escript au livre de l'*Asne doré*,[b] quant il eut trouvé le chappelet de fleurs de rosier pendant au sistre de Ceres, deesse des bledz. Car tout ainsi que ledit Apulée, qui avoit esté transmué en asne, retrouva sa premiere figure d'homme sensé et raisonnable, pareillement le pecheur humain, faict et converty en beste brute par irraisonnable similitude, reprent son estat premier d'innocence par la grace de Dieu qui luy est conferée lorsqu'il trouve le chappelet ou couronne de roses, c'est assavoir l'estat de penitence, pendu au doulx sistre de Ceres, c'est à[11] la doulceur de la misericorde divine.

Tiercement, nous pouons entendre par la rose la glorieuse vierge Marie, pour ses bontez, doulceurs, et perfections de grace, desquelles je me tais pour le present. Et sachez que ceste virginalle rose n'est aux hereticques facile d'avoir, et n'y eust-il seullement que Malle Bouche[c] qui les empesche d'approcher de sa bonté; car ilz ont mal d'elle parlé, voulant maculer et denigrer son honneur maternel[12] en disant qu'il ne la fault saluer et appeller mere de pitié et misericorde. C'est la blanche rose que nous trouverons en Hierico plantée, comme dit le saige: "quasi plantatio rose in Hierico."[d]

Quartement, nous pouons par la rose comprendre le souverain bien infiny et la gloire d'eter[iii]nelle beatitude, laquelle comme vrays amateurs de sa doulceur et amenité perpetuelle pourrons obtenir en evitant les vices qui nous empeschent et ayant secours des vertus qui nous introduiront au verger d'infinie lyesse, jusques au rosier de tout bien et gloire qui est la beatificque vision de l'essence de Dieu. Ce rosier peult estre figuré nompas aux roses de Pestum en Ytallie, qui florissent deux fois en[13] l'an,[e] car c'est peu souvent, mais à la rose que presenta au saige roy Salomon la noble royne de Sabba Ethiopienne, comme nous lisons[14] au livre de ses probleumes et des questions qu'elle luy demanda pour resprouver sa sapience; dont tant fut esmerveillée que son sens defailloit en elle, selon qu'il est escript au

9. grace *omitted 1529, 1538* 10. que l'ont *1538* 11. à *omitted 1529, 1538*
12. son naturel honneur *1529, 1538* 13. en *omitted 1529, 1538*
14. et apper *added 1529, 1538*

b. The *editio princeps* of Apuleius appeared in Rome in 1469; others followed in 1500, 1501, 1504, 1512, etc. The first translation into French, by Guillaume Michel de Tours, was printed in Paris: Galiot du Pré, 1518; cf. Brunet, I, 363–64.

c. Male Bouche is a character in the *Roman de la Rose*.

d. Ecclesiasticus 24:18.

e. Cf. Vergil, *Georgics* IV, 119: "biferique rosaria Paesti."

Livre des Roys.[f] Elle print deux roses, desquelles l'une venoit de l'arbre naturellement et l'autre procedoit par simulation, car elle l'avoit faicte sophisticquement et par art bien ressemblant à la rose naturelle, tant estoit subtillement ouvrée. "Voyla, dit-elle, deux roses devant vostre pacificque majesté presentes, dont l'une vrayement est naturelle mais l'autre non. Pourtant dictes-moy, sire, qui est la naturelle rose; monstrez-la-moy avec le doy." Salomon, ce voyant, fit apporter aulcunes mouches à miel, pensant et considerant par la science qu'il avoit de toutes choses naturelles que lesdictes mouches, selon leur proprieté, yroient incontinent à la rose naturelle, nompas à la sophisticquée; car telz oyseletz celestes, plaisans et mellificques, desirent et appetent les doulces fleurs sur toutes choses. Par quoy il monstra à la royne la vraye rose, la decernant de l'autre qui estoit faicte de senteurs contrefaisans nature.[g] Celle rose naturelle peult donc signifier le bien infini et vraye gloire celeste qui point n'est sophisticque ne decepvable comme la gloire du monde present, qui nous deçoit entant que nous cuidons qu'elle soit vraye, mais non est.

Doncques qui ainsi vouldroit interpreter le *Rommant de la Rose*, je dis qu'il y trouveroit grant bien, proffit et utilité cachez soubz l'escorce du texte, qui pas n'est à despriser; car il y a double gaing, recreation d'esprit et plaisir delectable quant au sens litteral et utilité quant à l'intelligence moralle. Fables sont faictes et inventées pour les exposer au sens misticque, par quoy on ne les doit contemner. Si le grant aigle duquel parla Ezechiel quant il dist, "Aquila grandis magnarum allarum plena plumis et varietate

f. I Kings 10:5, "non habebat ultra spiritum."

g. I have been unable to discover the author's source for this legend, which was apparently a written source, since he refers to the "livre de ses probleumes, etc." The story is recorded, for example, by the Rev. S. Baring-Gould, *Legends of Old Testament Characters, from the Talmud and Other Sources*, London and New York: Macmillan, 1871, II, 197–98, but the references there given do not refer to this particular episode. Guiffrey, ed. Marot, II, 151, n. 1, asserts that the legend "vient en droite ligne du Talmud, où il est mentionné dans le Guemara"; see Isaac Disraeli in his *Curiosities of Literature* (London, 1865), I, 202–203. Against this opinion, Professor Louis Ginzberg of the Jewish Theological Seminary of America assures me that the story is definitely not found in Jewish sources but that it is a typical Arabic story.

If no literary source before 1526 can be indicated, there is at least evidence of the existence of the tradition before that time in a pictorial representation dated 1506. K. Müllenhoff, *Zeitschrift für deutsches Altertum*, XXIII (1879), 47–49, in a note entitled "Gerätinschriften," described a tapestry of that date depicting the scene as we find it in this preface. In a later article on "Die Rätsel der Königin von Saba," *Gesammelte Abhandlungen von Wilhelm Hertz* (Stuttgart and Berlin, 1905), pp. 413–55, Wilhelm Hertz discussed a second tapestry of 1566 and pointed out the relationship to two separate literary treatments by Calderon. Hertz concluded, p. 451, that "Die Quelle, welcher Calderon dieses Rätsel entnommen hat, ist völlig unbekannt."

venit ad Libanum et tulit medullam cedri,"[h] je dis que si celluy aigle[15] qui tant avoit estandu son volatif plumaige se fust seullement arresté sus l'escorce du cedre quant il volla au mont du Liban, point n'eust trouvé la mouelle de l'arbre, mais s'en fust en vain retourné et eust perdu son vol. Semblablement, si nous ne creusions plus avant que l'escorce du sens litteral, nous n'aurions que le plaisir des fables et histoires sans obtenir le singulier proffit de la mouelle neupmaticque, c'est assavoir venant par l'inspiration du sainct esprit quant à l'intelligence moralle.

Qui ne penseroit sinon au sens litteral, encor y a-il grant proffit pour les doctrines et diverses sciences dedans contenues. Car neantmoins que le principal soit ung train d'amours, toutesfois il est tout confit de bons[16] incidens qui dedans sont comprins et alleguez, causans maintes bonnes disciplines. Les philosophes naturelz et moraulx y peuent apprendre, les theologiens, les astrologues, les geometriens, les archimistres, faiseurs de mirouers, paintres,[17] et autres gens naiz soubz la constellation et influence des bons astres ayans leur aspect sur les ingenieux et autres qui desirent sçavoir toutes manieres d'ars et sciences.

Cy fine le prologue.[18]

15. je dis que si celluy aigle *omitted 1529, 1538* 16. bous *1526*
17. paintes *1529, 1538* 18. Fin par tout *1529, 1538*

h. Ezekiel 17:3: "Aquila grandis magnarum alarum, longo membrorum ductu, plena plumis, & varietate, venit ad Libanum, & tulit medullam cedri."

CLÉMENT MAROT

PREFACE TO THE *Oeuvres de Françoys Villon*

1533

TEXT:

Les Oevvres de Françoys Villon de Paris, reueues & remises en leur entier par Clement Marot valet de chambre du Roy. Distique du dict Marot: Peu de Villons en bon sauoir, Trop de Villons pour deceuoir. On les vend a Paris en la grant salle du Palais, en la bouticque de Galiot du Pre. [Not dated; *privilège* and *achevé d'imprimer* both dated September, 1533. B.N., Paris.]

[Cf. Brunet, V, 1248 and *Supplément*, II, 898; Tchemerzine, X, 476; Cat. Rothschild, No. 453.]

COLLATED:

(1537) Les Oevvres de Francoys Villon de Paris, reueues & remises en leur entier par Clement Marot varlet de chambre du Roy. Distique du dict Marot [as above]. M.D.XXXVII. On les vend a Lyon chez Francoys Iuste deuant nostre Dame de Confort. [Pierpont Morgan Library.]

[Cf. Brunet, V, 1249; Tchemerzine, X, 478.]

(1540) Les oeuures de Francoys Villon de Paris, reveves et remises en leur entier par Clement Marot valet de chambre du Roy. Distique du dict Marot [as above]. On les vent a Paris en la grand salle du Palais en la boutique de Iehan Andry deuant la Chapelle de Messieurs. [Not dated; the date "1540" is only approximate. Pierpont Morgan Library.]

[Cf. Brunet, V, 1249 and *Supplément*, II, 899; Tchemerzine, X, 478. Other editions of ca. 1535, ca. 1540, and 1542, listed by Brunet, Tchemerzine, and the British Museum, have not been collated.]

Clément Marot's restoration or *rifacimento* of the text of Villon is a well-known phase of his literary activity. He may have modified the text at the instance of the enterprising printer, Galiot du Pré, who in 1532 had brought out a very poor edition of the same poet. Marot's version became the standard one for readers of the sixteenth century, and was issued by various printers and publishers between 1533 and 1542, date of the last edition of Villon in that century. The text and the preface are discussed briefly by Henri Guy in his *Clément Marot et son école* (Paris: Champion, 1926, pp. 94–95); the text is reprinted in Guiffrey's edition of Marot, II, 261–70.

[Aiij] CLEMENT MAROT DE CAHORS, VALET DE CHAMBRE DU ROY, AUX LECTEURS S.

Entre tous les bons livres imprimez de la langue Françoise, ne s'en veoit ung si incorrect ne si lourdement corrompu que celluy de Villon; et m'esbahy (veu que c'est le meilleur poete Parisien qui[1] se trouve) comment les imprimeurs de Paris et les enfans de la ville n'en ont eu plus grant soing. Je ne suys (certes) en rien son voysin; mais pour l'amour de son gentil entendement et en recompense de ce que je puys avoir aprins de luy en lisant ses œuvres, j'ay faict à icelles ce que je vouldroys estre faict aux myennes si elles estoient tombées en semblable inconvenient. Tant y ay trouvé de broillerie en l'ordre des coupletz et des vers, en mesure, en langaige, en la ryme et en la raison, que je ne sçay duquel [A iij *v*] je doy plus avoir pitié, ou de l'œuvre ainsi oultrement[2] gastée, ou de l'ignorance de ceulx qui l'imprimerent. Et pour vous en faire preuve, me suys advisé (lecteurs) de vous mettre icy ung des coupletz incorrectz du mal imprimé Villon, qui vous sera exemple et tesmoing d'ung grant nombre d'autres autant broillez et gastez que luy, lequel est tel:[a]

> Or est vray qu'apres plainctz & pleurs
> Et angoisseux gemissemens
> Apres tristesses & douleurs
> Labeurs & griefz cheminemens
> Trauaille mes lubres sentemens
> Aguysez ronds, comme vne pelote
> Monstrent plus que les comments
> En sens moral de Aristote.

Qui est celluy qui vouldroit nyer le sens n'en estre grandement corrompu? Ainsi pour vray l'ay-je trouvé aux vieilles impressions, et encorez pis aux nouvelles. Or voyez maintenant comment il a esté rabillé, et en jugez gratieusement:

> Or est vray qu'apres plainctz & pleurs [A iiii]
> Et angoisseux gemissemens
> Apres tristesses & douleurs

---

1. bien qui *1537* 2. oultrageusement *1540*

a. The quotation may be from the edition published by Galiot du Pré the year before, 1532, fol. a. iiii:

> Or est vray quapres plains & pleurs
> Et angoysseux gemissemens,
> Apres tristesses & douleurs,
> Labeurs & griefz cheminemens,
> Trauaille mes lubres sentemens,
> Aguisez, rondz comme vne pelotte,
> Monstrent plus que le communs
> En sens moral de Aristote.

Cf. also the edition of 1489 (facsimile, 1924), fols. a iii *v*-a iiii. For a modern critical text of the passage, see the Longnon-Foulet ed. of Villon's *Œuvres*, Paris: Champion, 1923, "Testament," ll. 89–96.

Labeurs & griefz cheminemens
Trauail mes lubres sentemens
Aguysa (ronds comme pelote)
Me monstrant plus que les comments
Sur le sens moral d'aristote.

Voyla comment il me semble que l'autheur l'entendoit, et vous suffise ce petit amendement pour vous rendre advertiz de ce que puys avoir amendé en mille autres passaiges, dont les aucuns me ont esté aysez et les autres très difficiles. Toutesfoys, partie avecques les vieulx imprimez, partie avecques l'ayde des bons vieillards qui en savent par cueur, et partie par deviner avecques jugement naturel, a esté reduict nostre Villon en meilleure et plus entiere forme qu'on ne l'a veu de noz aages, et ce sans avoir touché à l'antiquité de son parler, à sa façon de rimer, à ses meslées et longues parentheses, à la quantité de ses sillabes, ne à ses couppes tant feminines que masculines; esquelles choses il n'a suffisament observé les vrayes reigles[3] [A iiij *v*] de Françoise poesie. Et ne suys d'advis que en cela les jeunes poetes l'ensuyvent, mais bien qu'ilz cueillent ses sentences comme belles fleurs, qu'ilz contemplent l'esprit qu'il avoit, que de luy apreignent à proprement descrire, et qu'ilz contrefacent sa veine, mesmement celle dont il use en ses ballades, qui est vrayement belle et heroique. Et ne fay doubte qu'il n'eust emporté le chapeau de laurier devant tous les poetes de son temps s'il eust esté nourry en la court des roys et des princes, là où les jugemens se amendent et les langaiges se pollissent. Quant à l'industrie des lays qu'il feit en ses testamens, pour suffisamment la cognoistre et entendre il fauldroit avoir esté de son temps à Paris, et avoir congneu les lieux, les choses, et les hommes dont il parle; la memoire desquelz tant plus se passera, tant moins se congnoistra icelle industrie de sez lays dictz. Pour ceste cause qui vouldra faire une œuvre de longue durée ne preigne son soubgect sur telles choses basses et particulieres. Le reste des œuvres de nostre Villon (hors cela) est [A v] de tel artifice, tant plain de bonne doctrine, et tellement painct de mille belles couleurs, que le temps, qui tout efface, jusques icy ne l'a sceu effacer. Et moins encor l'effacera ores et d'icy en avant, que les bonnes escriptures Françoises sont et seront myeulx congneues et recueillies que jamais.

Et pource (comme j'ay dit) que je n'ay touché à son antique façon de parler, je vous ay exposé sur la marge avecques les annotacions ce qui m'a semblé le plus dur à entendre, laissant le reste à voz promptes intelligences, comme *ly Roys* pour *le Roy*, *homs* pour *homme*, *compaing* pour *compaignon*; aussi force pluriers pour singuliers et plusieurs autres incongruitez dont estoit plain le langaige mal lymé d'icelluy temps.

3. riegles *1533*

Après, quant il s'est trouvé faulte de vers entiers, j'ay prins peine de les refaire au plus près (selon mon possible) de l'intencion de l'autheur; et les trouverez expressement mar[A v *v*]quez de ceste marque, *; affin que ceulx qui les sauront en la sorte que Villon les fist, effacent les nouveaulx pour faire place aux vieulx.

Oultre plus, les termes et les vers qui estoient interposez, trouverez reduictz en leurs places; les lignes trop courtes, alongées; les trop longues, acoursies; les motz obmys, remys; les adjoustez, ostez; et les tiltres myeulx attiltrez.

Finablement, j'ay changé l'ordre du livre, et m'a semblé plus raisonnable de le faire commencer par le *Petit Testament,* d'autant qu'il fut faict cinq ans avant l'autre.

Touchant le jargon, je le laisse à corriger et exposer aux successeurs de Villon en l'art de la pinse et du croq.

Et si quelq'un d'aventure veult dire que tout ne soit racoustré ainsi qu'il appartient, je luy respons dès maintenant que s'il estoit [A vi] autant navré en sa personne comme j'ay trouvé Villon blessé en ses œuvres, il n'y a si expert chirurgien qui le sceust penser sans apparence de cicatrice; et me suffira que le labeur qu'en ce j'ay employé soit agreable au Roy mon souverain, qui est cause et motif de ceste emprise et de l'execution d'icelle, pour l'avoir veu voulentiers escouter et par très bon jugement estimer plusieurs passages des œuvres qui s'ensuyvent.

CLÉMENT MAROT

PREFACE TO OVID'S *Metamorphoses*

1534

TEXT:

(1536) L'Adolescence Clementine, avltrement Les Oeuures de Clement Marot, de Cahors en Quercy, Valet de chambre du Roy, faictes en son adolescence, auec aultres œuures par luy composees depuis sa dicte adolescence. Reueues & corrigees selon sa derniere recongnoissance oultre toutes autres impressions contrefaictes, ausquelles a son grant deshonneur ont esté adioustees aulcunes œuures scandaleuses mal composees & incorrectes, desquelles craignant yceluy non seullement le blasme de chose si mal faicte, aussy le grant dommaige qui luy pourroit venir a cause desdictes œuures scandaleuses, a desauoue les dictes œuures ainsi quon voirra par le contenu du liure. Oles vent a Paris a Lhostel Dalebret deuant Sainct Hylaire. M.D.XXXVI. [B.N., Paris.]

[The Ovid has a separate t.p. which reads: Le Premier Livre de la Metamorphose Dovide, translate de Latin en Francoys par Clement Marot de Cahors en Quercy, Valet de chambre du Roy. Item Certaines œuures quil feit en prison, non encores Imprimeez. On les vent a Paris deuant sainct Hilaire a Lhostel Dalebret par Anthoine Bonnemere. M.D.XXXVI.]

[The first edition of the Ovid was published in 1534; cf. Cat. Rothschild, No. 601; Brunet, III, 1448 and *Supplément*, I, 956–57; Tchemerzine, VIII, 2. There were also editions of 1535, on which cf. Brunet, III, 1448–50; Tchemerzine, VIII, 5. On the 1536 Bonnemère ed., cf. Brunet, III, 1450; Tchemerzine, VIII, 9.]

COLLATED:

(1539) Les Oeuures de Clement Marot Valet de Chambre du Roy. Desquelles le contenu sensuit...Le premier liure de la Metamorphose d'Ouide...On les uend a Lyon chez Francoys Iuste. [Colophon dated M.D.XXXIX. Pierpont Morgan Library.]

[Cf. Brunet, III, 1453; Tchemerzine, VIII, 21. This edition was also issued by Jean Barbou.]

(1540) Les oeuures de Clement Marot Valet de Chambre du Roy, Desquelles le contenu sensuyt...Le premier Liure de la Metamorphose de Ouide...Imprime a Paris par Iehan Bignon imprimeur demourant en la Rue Iudas. [Undated, but the t.p. to the *Suite de l'Adolescence* is dated 1540. Newberry Library.]

[Cf. Brunet, III, 1453; Tchemerzine, VIII, 25.]

(1544) Les Oevvres de Clement Marot, de Cahors,Vallet de chambre dv Roy. Plus amples, & en meilleur ordre que parauant. A Lyon, à l'enseigne du Rocher. 1545. [Library of Congress.]

[This is identical with the 1544 ed. except for the t.p.; cf. Le Petit, pp. 35–36; Cat. Rothschild, No. 609; Baudrier, *Bibliographie lyonnaise*, 2e série, 1896, pp. 36–37; Brunet, III, 1454–55; Tchemerzine, VIII, 30.]

(1549) Les Oevvres de Clement Marot, de Cahors, Vallet de Chambre dv Roy. A Lyon, par Iean de Tovrnes. M.D.XLIX. [Library of Congress.]

[Cf. Brunet, III, 1456; Tchemerzine, VIII, 35. The same sources list numerous other editions which were not collated.]

Although Marot's translation of Book I of Ovid's *Metamorphoses* was first published in 1534, the translation itself was made at a much earlier date. Henry Guy (*Clément Marot et son école*, p. 149) states that part of it at least was read by Marot to Francis I in August or September, 1526, and that a copy was presented to Duke Antoine de Lorraine in March of 1531 (p. 183). As for the prefatory dedication to Francis I, it was probably written especially for the publication. From 1534 on, the Ovid was a standard part of Marot's works and went through a great many editions during his lifetime and after his death. The preface appears in Guiffrey's edition, II, 299–302.

[aA. i. *v*] PROLOGUE AU TRÈS ILLUSTRE ET TRÈS CHRESTIEN ROY DES FRANÇOYS, PREMIER DE CE NOM, CLEMENT MAROT DE CAHORS EN QUERCY TRÈS HUMBLE SALUT ET DEUE OBEISSANCE[1]

Longtemps avant que vostre liberalité[2] royalle m'eust faict successeur de l'estat de mon pere,[a] le mien plus affectionné et non petit desir avoit tousjours esté, Sire, de pouoir faire œuvre en mon labeur poetique qui tant vous agreast que par là je peusse devenir, au fort, le moindre de voz domestiques. Et pour ce faire mys en avant, come pour mon roy, le[3] tout ce que je peu, et tant importunay les muses qu'elles enfin offrirent à ma plume inventions nouvelles et antiques, luy donnant le choys ou de tourner en nostre langue aucune chose de la Latine, ou d'escrire œuvre nouvelle par cy devant non jamais veue. Lors je consideray que à prince de hault esprit haultes choses affierent,[4] et tant ne me fiay en mes propres inventions que pour vous trop basses ne les sentisse. Parquoy, les laissant reposer, gettay l'oeil sur les livres Latins, dont la gravité des sentences et le plaisir de la lecture, si peu que je y comprins, m'ont espris mes espritz, mené ma main, et amusé ma muse. Que dy-je amusée?[5] Mais incitée[6] à renouveller, pour vous en faire offre, l'une des plus Latines antiquitez et des plus antiques Latinitez; entre lesquelles celle[7] de la [aA. ij.] *Metamorphose* d'Ovide me sembla la plus belle, tant pour la[8] grande doulceur du stille que pour le

1. Marot av Roy, tovchant la Metamorphose *1544, 1549* 2. liberaltite *1536*
3. le *omitted 1539 ff.* 4. luy affierent *1544, 1549* 5. amuser *1540*
6. inciter *1540* 7. cella *1536*; celle *1539 ff.* 8. sa *1540*

a. Marot's father died in 1526. Succession to his father's functions was granted Marot by Francis I in the same year, but through an oversight he did not officially obtain the title until 1527–28. Cf. H. Guy, *Clément Marot et son école*, pp. 149 ff.

grand nombre des propos tumbans de l'ung en[9] l'autre par lyaisons si artificielles qu'il semble que tout ne soit[10] q'ung. Et toutesfois,[11] aiséement et peut estre point ne se trouva[12] livre qui tant de diversitez de choses racompte. Parquoy, Sire, si la nature en la diversité se resjouyst, là ne se devra-elle melencolier. Pour ces raisons et autres maintes deliberay mettre la main à la besongne, et de tout mon pouoir suyvre et contrefaire la veine du noble poete Ovide, pour mieulx faire entendre et sçavoir à ceulx qui n'ont la langue Latine de quelle sorte il escrivoit et quelle difference peult[13] estre entre les anciens et les modernes. Oultre plus, tel list en maint passage les noms d'Apollo, Daphne, Pyramus et Thisbée, qui a l'hystoire aussi loing de l'esperit que les noms près de la bouche; ce que[14] pas ainsi n'iroit si en facile vulgaire estoit mise ceste belle *Metamorphose*, laquelle aux poetes vulgaires et aux paintres seroit très profitable, et aussi decoration grande en nostre langue, veu mesmement[15] que l'arrogance Grecque l'a bien voulu mettre en la sienne.[b]

Or est ainsi que *metamorphose* est une diction Grecque vulgairement signifiant "transformation." Et a voulu Ovide ainsi intituler son livre, contenant quinze volumes, pource qu'en icelluy il transforme les ungz en arbres, les autres en pierres, les autres en bestes, et les autres en autres formes. Et pour ceste mesme cause je me suys pensé trop[16] entreprendre de vouloir transmuer celluy qui les autres transmue. Et après j'ay contre-[aA. ij. *v*]pensé que double louenge peult venir de transmuer ung transmueur, comme d'assaillir ung assailleur, de tromper ung trompeur, et mocquer ung mocqueur. Mais pour rendre l'œuvre presentable à si grande majesté, fauldroit premierement que vostre plus que humaine puissance transmuast la muse de Marot en celle de Maro. Toutesfois, telle qu'elle est, soubz la confiance de vostre acoustumé bon recueil, elle a (par maniere d'essay) traduict et parachevé de ces[17] quinze livres le premier, dont au chasteau d'Amboise vous en pleut ouyr quelque commencement.[c] Si l'eschantillon vous plaist, par temps aurez la piece entiere; car la plume du petit ouvrier ne desire voler sinon là où le vent de vostre royalle bouche la vouldra poulser.[18] Et à tant me tairay; Ovide veult parler.

9. a *1540* 10. feit *1540* 11. touteffois *1536* 12. trouvera *1539 ff.* 13. pour *1536*; peult *1539 ff.* 14. qui *1544, 1549* 15. mesmẽt *1536* 16. trop *omitted 1540* 17. ses *1539, 1540* 18. par commandement *added 1540 only*

b. Guiffrey regards this as an "allusion à la traduction grecque du moine Maximus Planudes, un érudit de la décadence, qui vivait à Constantinople au XIVe siècle" (ed. of Marot, II, 301, n. 2).

c. Marot read a part of his translation to Francis I in August or September, 1526; cf. H. Guy, *op. cit.*, p. 149.

LAZARE DE BAÏF

PREFACE AND PROLOGUE TO SOPHOCLES' *Electra*

1537

TEXT:

[For the Preface:]
Tragedie de Sophocles intitvlee Electra, contenant la vengence de l'inhvmaine & trespiteuse mort d'Agamemnon Roy de Mycenes la grand, faicte par sa femme Clytemnestra, & son adultere Egistus. Ladicte Tragedie traduicte du grec dudit Sophocles en rythme Francoyse, ligne pour ligne, & vers pour vers: en faueur & commodite des amateurs de lune & lautre langue. Imprimee a Paris pour Estienne Roffet demourant sur le pont Sainct Michel a lenseigne de la Rose. 1537. Auec Priuilege. [B.N., Paris.]

[For the Prologue:]
MS Marciana Français XXIV (No. 235), fol. 1.

COLLATED:

[For the Preface:]
MS Marciana Français XXIV (No. 235), fol. 44 verso.
[Cf. Brunet, V, 452–53 and *Supplément*, II, 670; Tchemerzine, I, 344; also listed by British Museum.]

Baïf's translation of Sophocles' *Electra*, published in 1537, was preceded by a short "Diffinition de Tragedie." The manuscript of the same work at the Biblioteca di San Marco in Venice contained a slightly shorter version of this "Diffinition" after the translation, and was prefaced by a "Prologue" in the form of a dedicatory epistle. René Sturel, in his "Essai sur les traductions du théâtre grec en français avant 1550" (*Revue d'histoire littéraire de la France*, XX [1913], 273–80), maintained that this manuscript was anterior to the printed version and thought that it may have been written before 1530. I give the text of the "Diffinition" from the 1537 edition and of the Prologue from the Venice manuscript. Details on Baïf's life may be found in Lucien Pinvert's *Lazare de Baïf (1496?–1550)*, (Paris: Fontemoing, 1900).

[Aij] DIFFINITION DE TRAGEDIE[1]

Tragedie est une moralité composée des grandes calamitez, meurtres et adversitez survenues aux nobles et excellentz personnaiges, comme Ajas, qui se occist pour avoir esté frustré des armes d'Achilles; Oedipus, qui se creva les yeulx après qu'il luy fut declairé comme il avoit eu des enfans de sa propre mere après avoir tué son pere; et plusieurs aultres semblables.[2]

1. Que cest que Tragedie. *Venice MS* 2. Et tout plain daultres. *MS*

Tant que Sophocles en a escript six vingtz, entre lesquelles est ceste presente, intitulée *Electra* pource qu'elle y est introduicte et y parle tant bien et virilement que ung chascun s'en peult donner merveille.[3] Euripides aussi et plusieurs aultres ont composé pareilles tragedies.[4] Et la grace d'icelles[5] a anciennement si bien regné que les roys et princes se mesloyent d'en composer, mesmement Dionysius Roy de Sicile[a] et Herodes[6] Roy des Perses,[b] et assez d'aultres.[7]

[1] PROLOGUE

Sire, pour vous donner aulcunement la congnoissance des inventions des Grecz et de leur grande et inestimable prudence à bien coucher icelles et mettre par escript, j'ay entrepris de vous translater une tragedie de Sophocles; laquelle est intitulée *Electra* pource qu'elle est en ce introduicte et y parle tant bien et virilement que ung chascun s'en peult donner merveille. Mais, Sire, en lisant ceste presente tragedie en Françoys, ayez s'il vous plaist souvenance de ce que Themistocles dist au roy des Perses,[c] lequel vouloit parler à luy des affaires de la guerre par truchement et interprete. Auquel fist response (luy monstrant l'envers d'une tapisserie) que telle estoit l'interpretation d'un langaige comme l'envers d'un tapiz. Parquoy luy supplia qu'il luy pleust donner ung an de terme pour apprendre la langue Persienne. Semblablement vous, Sire, ayez estime que par la mienne translation je n'ay pouoir de vous monstrer aultre chose que l'envers de la triumphante et excellente tapisserie de Sophocles, laquelle en son endroit est tant bien ornée de fleurs d'antique et aultres figures et couleurs que je ne puys penser que depuys mille ans ait esté homme en ce monde qui en peust faire une semblable; telle est l'art de laquelle il a usé pour esmouvoir les affections et passions des hommes.

3. entre lesquelles...merveille, *omitted MS. (The passage is found in what was probably its original form in the first sentence of the "Prologue," printed below)*

4. Et Euripides beaucoup. Et plusieurs aultres. *MS* 5. icelle *MS*

6. *(In the Venice MS, a blank space was originally left at this point and no name for the king appeared. The space was later filled, by another hand, with the name "Artawasdes" and the word "Armeniens" was written in the space above the original "Perses.")*

7. infiniz aultres. *MS*

a. Suidas (s.v. Διονύσιος) tells of the literary compositions of Dionysius; also Aelian, *Varia Historia*, XIII. xviii. Lilio Gregorio Giraldi, *Historiae poetarum* (Basel, 1545), notes that "Dionysius etiam notissimus ille Siciliae tyrannus in tabulis & ipse inter poëtas locum habuit: nam Tragoedias & Comoedias, ut alia mittam, condidit" (Dialogue VII, p. 818).

b. I have found no source for this statement. If the reading of the Venice MS represents Baïf's original, he may have been referring to Plutarch, *Crassus*, XXXIII.2, ὁ δ' Ἀρταουάσδης καὶ τραγῳδίας ἐποίει.

c. The story is told by Plutarch, *Themistocles*, XXIX.

Et nonobstant que ce ne soit ma [1 *v*] profession de composer en ryme, ce neantmoins pour donner quelque grace à l'œuvre et aussi en suyvant mon aucteur, j'ay observé les nombres de ses mettres autant qui m'a esté possible et y ay adjousté rythme telle quelle. A laquelle il vous plaira n'avoir grand egard, mais seullement à la disposition de l'aucteur et merveilleuse œconomie. Car de moy je ne suys que son simple truchement fidele pour certain autant qui m'a esté possible, mais non suffisamment exercité en l'un et l'aultre langaige pour me debvoir paragonner à luy. Ce neantmoins, Sire, si je m'apperçoy que mon labeur vous soit agreable, j'auray pour le temps advenir plus grande promptitude à faire pour vous quelque meilleure chose, aydant le createur, lequel par sa saincte grace vous vueille donner très bonne et longue vie.

ESTIENNE DOLET

La Maniere de Bien Traduire d'Une Langue en Aultre

1540

TEXT:

La Maniere De Bien Tradvire D'vne Langve En Avltre. D'aduantage. De la punctuation de la langue Francoyse. Plus. Des accents d'ycelle. Le tout faict par Estienne Dolet natif d'Orleans. [Undated; printed by Dolet in Lyon, 1540. B.N., Paris.]
[Cf. Brunet, II, 795–96.]

After various works written in Latin, Dolet undertook the publication of a long treatise in French, bearing the general title of *L'Orateur Françoys.* The preface of the volume described above, addressed "au peuple Françoys," contains a prospectus listing the parts of the work as "La grammaire, l'orthographe, les accents, la punctuation, la pronunciation, l'origine d'aulcunes dictions, la maniere de bien traduire d'une langue en aultre, l'art oratoire, l'art poëtique." The *Manière,* the *Accents,* and the *Pronunciation* were included in the 1540 volume, but no more was ever published, although Dolet had promised completion in two or three years (cf. p. 80 below). Dolet was burned at the stake in 1546, and in 1549 Du Bellay regretfully referred to the rest of the work as still unpublished (*Deffence,* ed. Chamard, p. 86). There has been a modern reprint of the 1540 volume (Paris: Techener, 1830) as one of a series of reprints of Dolet's works. On Dolet, see Ph. Aug. Becker, *Aus Frankreichs Frührenaissance* (Munich, 1927), pp. 85–118, and Marc Chassaigne, *Etienne Dolet* (Paris: Michel, 1930).

[a 2] ESTIENNE DOLET À MONSEIGNEUR DE LANGEI[a] HUMBLE SALUT ET RECONGNOISSANCE DE SA LIBERALITÉ ENVERS LUY

Je n'ignore pas (seigneur par gloire immortel) que plusieurs ne s'ebaissent grandement de veoir sortir de moy ce present oeuvre, attendu que par le passé j'ay faict et fais encores maintenant profession totalle de la langue Latine. Mais à cecy je donne deux raisons; l'une, que mon affection est telle envers l'honneur de mon païs que je veulx trouver tout moyen de l'illustrer, et ne le puis myeulx faire que de celebrer sa langue comme ont faict Grecs et Rommains la leur. L'aultre raison est que non sans exemple de plusieurs je m'addonne à ceste exercitation.[1] Quant aux antiques, tant Grecs que Latins, ilz n'ont prins aultre instrument de leur eloquence que la langue maternelle. De la Grece seront pour tesmoings Demo[a 2 *v*]sthene, Aristote,

1. Autheurs antiques illustrateurs de leur langue. *Margin 1540*

a. Guillaume du Bellay, seigneur de Langey.

[Platon, Isocrate][2] Thucydide, Herodote, Homere, et des Latins je produis Ciceron, Cæsar, Salluste, Virgille, Ovide; lesquelz n'ont delaissé leur langue pour estre renommés en une aultre. Et ont mesprisé toute aultre, sinon qu'aulcuns des Latins ont apprins la Grecque affin de sçavoir les arts et disciplines traictées par les autheurs d'ycelle. Quant aux[3] modernes,[4] semblable chose que moy a faict Leonard Aretin, Sannazare, Petracque, Bembe (ceulx-là Italiens), et en France Budée, Fabri, Boville, et maistre Jacques Sylvius.[b] Doncques non sans l'exemple de plusieurs excellents personnages j'entreprends ce labeur; lequel (seigneur plein de bon jugement) tu recepvras non comme parfaict en la demonstration de nostre langue, mais seulement comme ung commencement d'ycelle. Car je sçay que quand on voulut reduire la langue Grecque et Latine en art, cela ne fut absolu par ung homme mais par plusieurs; ce qui se faira pareillement en la langue Françoyse, et peu à peu par le moyen et travail des gens doctes elle pourra estre reduicte en telle parfection que les langues dessusdictes. A ceste cause (seigneur tout humain) je te requiers de prendre ce mien labeur en gré, et s'il ne reforme totallement no[a 3]stre langue, pour le moyns pense que c'est commencement qui pourra parvenir à fin telle que les estrangiers ne nous appelleront plus barbares. Te soubvienne aussi en cest endroict qu'il est bien difficille qu'une chose soit inventée et parfaicte tout à ung coup. Parquoy tu te doibs contenter de mon invention et en attendre ou par moy ou par aultres la parfection avec le temps; joinct aussi qu'en choses grandes et difficilles le vouloir doibt estre assés.

Je laisse ce propos et te veulx dire ce qui m'a esmeu de te dedier ce livre.[5] Certes l'opinion et estime grande que j'ay de ton sçavoir, eloquence, et jugement en tout esmerveillable, m'a induict à ce faire aultant ou plus que l'humanité et liberalité de laquelle tu uses de jour en jour de plus en plus en mon endroict; et ce sans aulcun mien merite. Car de te faire aulcun

2. *Lacking 1540, torn page; supplied from 1830 reprint* 3. aut *1540*

4. Aulcuns Autheurs modernes illustrateurs de leur langue, tant en Italien, qu'en Francoys. *Margin 1540*

5. Le comble des uertus de Monsieur de Langei. *Margin 1540*

b. Guillaume Budé, the celebrated humanist; Pierre Fabri, author of the *Grand et vray art de pleine rhétorique* (1521); Charles de Bouvelles (probably), author of the first treatise on geometry in French, *Geometrie en francoys*, Paris: H. Estienne, 1511 (the name is diversely given as Bouvelle, Bovelle, Bouvelles, and in Latin, Bovilles, Bovillus; see Brunet, I, 1188 and Graesse, I, 514); and Jacques Dubois (*dit* Sylvius), author of an *In linguam gallicam isagoge*, Paris: R. Estienne, 1531. I have no trace of any works by Dubois in French, unless he actually did write the lost *Grammaire françoise* which has been attributed to him but whose actual existence is questioned (cf. Brunet, V, 610). Dubois later (1546) translated Ficino's commentary on the *Symposium* into French, Poitiers: Marnef; cf. R. V. Merrill, *The Platonism of Joachim du Bellay*, Chicago, 1925, p. 15 and note.

service meritant telle amour que me la portes et monstres par effect, cela est hors totallement de mon pouvoir. Toutesfoys pour suppliment du pouvoir la vouluntė te doibt satisfaire, laquelle est telle que sans exception d'aulcun humain je te revere comme ung demi-dieu habitant en ces lieux terrestres et estincellant de tous costés par une lumiere de vertus à toy seul octroiées par l'Omnipotent—Omnipotent envers toy prodigue de ses graces si jamais il en [a 3 *v*] eslargist à aulcune sienne creature. Et qui est celuy qui puisse à mon dict contredire[6] s'il a congnoissance de tes faicts? Nul ne doubte de la bonté de ta nature. Chascun se sent de ta munificence. Toutes nations estranges ne preferent aulcun à toy, touchant l'art militaire et conduicte de guerre. Quant à la politique et gouvernement equitable d'ung païs, le Piedmont en donnera tesmoignage, en laquelle province tu es à present gouverneur soubs l'autorité du Roy, qui t'a esleu à ceste charge comme personne idoine à touts faicts de grand conseil et prudence. Croy (seigneur le premier des humains) que je suis l'homme le moins admirant les hommes sans raison et cause vehemente. Mais tes vertus et parfections infinies m'ont ravy jusques à là que sur touts je t'adore; et ceste affection la posterité n'ignorera si mes oeuvres meritent immortalité de nom. Icy feray fin de mon epistre, te priant derechef avoir ce mien livre pour aggreable.

De Lyon ce dernier jour de may, mil cinq cents quarante.

[a 4] ESTIENNE DOLET AU PEUPLE FRANÇOYS HUMBLE SALUT ET ACCROYSSEMENT D'HONNEUR ET PUISSANCE

Depuis six ans (ô peuple Françoys), desrobbant quelcques heures de mon estude principalle (qui est en la lecture de la langue Latine et Grecque), te voulant aussi illustrer par touts moyens, j'ay composé en nostre langage ung oeuvre intitulé l'*Orateur Françoys*,[7] duquel oeuvre les traictés sont telz:

La grammaire.
L'orthographe.
Les accents.
La punctuation.
La pronunciation.
L'origine d'aulcunes dictions.
La maniere de bien traduire d'une langue en aultre.
L'art oratoire.
L'art poëtique. [a 4 *v*]

Mais pource que ledict oeuvre est de grande importance, et qu'il y eschet ung grand labeur, sçavoir, et extreme jugement, j'en differeray la publica-

6. coutredire *1540* 7. l'Orateur Francoys. *Margin 1540*

tion (pour ne le precipiter) jusques à deux ou troys ans. Ce pendant tu t'ayderas des instructions qui sont en ce present livre; lequel si je congnois t'estre aggreable, je seray plus enclin à te bien polir et parfaire le demeurant de mon entreprinse. Combien que j'en attends plustost contentement de la posterité que du siecle present; car le cours des choses humaines est tel que la vertu du vivant est tousjours enviée et deprimée par detracteurs,[8] qui se pensent advantager en reputation s'ilz mesprisent les labeurs d'aultruy. Mais l'homme de sçavoir et de bon jugement ne doibt regarder à telz resveurs et plustost s'en mocquer du tout. Ainsi faisant, je poursuivray mon effort et attendray legitime los de la posterité, non d'aulcuns vivants par trop pleins d'ingratitude et maulvais vouloir.

Contente-toy pour ceste heure (ô peuple Françoys) de ce petit oeuvre, et prends pour pleige l'affection que je porte à ma renommée que dedans quelcque temps je te rendray parfaict l'oeuvre dessusdict. Et si aulcuns se delectent en tel labeur, cela n'est que bon. Que pleust à Dieu que pour ung il y en eust mille, [b] car par telz efforts le plus parfaict sera congneu et en demeurera la gloire au bien entendant la langue Latine et Françoyse. Pour le moins de mon costé je tascheray de faire mon debvoir en si noble et louable passetemps. Vray est que si j'estois envieux du bien d'aultruy je me deporteroys de ce mien labeur, pource que j'ay congneu telle ingratitude[9] entre les hommes de mon temps que ceulx qui ont le plus proffité sur mes oeuvres sont les premiers qui taschent de deprimer mon renom. Mais pour leur meschante nature je ne laisseray de produire par oeuvres le don de grace que le Creatur m'a faict tant en la congnoissance de la langue Latine que de ma maternelle Françoyse. Et ce tout à l'honneur et gloire de luy (luy seul autheur de tout bien) et à l'utilité de la chose publicque, laquelle je prefere aux maldicts de touts mes envieux et detracteurs, qui à la fin se trouveront trompés en moy. Car leur meschant langage ne me sert que d'ung esguillon à la vertu, tout au rebours de ce qu'ilz vouldroient de moy proceder. Mais je sçay comme il fault tromper telles bestes chaussées, et en telle prudence consumeray le demeurant de ma vie, taschant tousjours de perpetuer mon nom par oeuvres recommendables à la posterité et aage futur; lequel se trouvant [b *v*] vuide d'envie en mon endroict et muni de bon vouloir ne se monstrera ingrat, mais par une equité et raison louera ce qui est de louer. Ceste esperance m'a tousjours esmeu à escrire et donné cueur de prendre les labeurs que j'ay jusques icy prins en la vacation literaire. Car au jugement des vivants il y a bien peu d'equité et racueil pour les doctes. Adieu, peuple le plus triumphant du monde, soit en vertu, soit en puissance.

A Lyon, ce dernier jour de may, l'an de grace mil cinq cents quarante.

8. La uertu du uiuant est tousiours enuiée. *Margin 1540*
9. L'ingratitude d'aulcuns personnages de ce temps. *Margin 1540*

[b 2] LA MANIERE DE BIEN TRADUIRE D'UNE LANGUE EN AULTRE
Autheur Estienne Dolet natif d'Orleans

La maniere de bien traduire d'une langue en aultre requiert principallement cinq choses. En premier lieu,[10] il fault que le traducteur entende parfaictement le sens et matiere de l'autheur qu'il traduict; car par ceste intelligence il ne sera jamais obscur en sa traduction, et si l'autheur lequel il traduict est aulcunement scabreux, il le pourra rendre facile et du tout intelligible. Et de ce je te vois bailler exemple familierement. Dedans le premier livre des *Questions Tusculanes* de Ciceron il y a ung tel passage Latin:[11] "Animum autem animam etiam fere nostri declarant nominari; nam et *agere animam* et *efflare* dicimus et *ani*[b 2 *v*]*mosos*, et *bene animatos*: et *ex animi sententia*. Ipse autem animus ab anima dictus est."[c] Traduisant cest oeuvre de Ciceron, j'ay parlé comme il s'ensuict: "Quant à la difference (dy-je) de ces dictions *animus* et *anima*, il ne s'i fault poinct arrester. Car les façons de parler Latines qui sont deduictes de ces deux mots nous donnent à entendre qu'ilz signifient presque une mesme chose. Et est certain que *animus* est dict de *anima* et que *anima* est l'organe de *animus*, comme si tu voulois dire la vertu et instruments vitaulx estre origine de l'esprit, et iceluy esprit estre ung effect de ladicte vertu vitale." Dy-moy, toy qui entends Latin, estoit-il possible de bien traduire ce passage sans une grande intelligence du sens de Ciceron? Or saiche doncques qu'il est besoing et necessaire à tout traducteur d'entendre parfaictement le sens de l'autheur qu'il tourne d'une langue en aultre. Et sans cela, il ne peut traduire seurement et fidellement.

La seconde chose[12] qui est requise en traduction, c'est que le traducteur ait parfaicte congnoissance de la langue de l'autheur qu'il traduict, et soit pareillement excellent en la langue en laquelle il se mect à traduire. Par ainsi il ne violera et n'amoindrira la majesté de l'une et l'aultre langue. Cuydes-tu que si ung homme n'est parfaict en la langue Latine et Françoyse il puisse bien traduire en Françoys quelcque oraison de Ciceron?[13] Entends que chascune langue a ses proprietés, translations en diction, locu[b 3]tions, subtilités et vehemences à elle particulieres; lesquelles, si le traducteur ignore, il faict tort à l'autheur qu'il traduict et aussi à la langue en laquelle il le tourne. Car il ne represente et n'exprime la dignité et richesse de ces deux langues desquelles il prend le manîment.

Le tiers poinct[14] est qu'en traduisant il ne se fault pas asservir jusques à là

10. La premiere reigle pour bien traduire. *Margin 1540*
11. Lieu de Ciceron interpreté. *Margin 1540*
12. La seconde reigle. *Margin 1540*
13. Chascune langue a ses proprietés. *Margin 1540*
14. La tierce reigle. *Margin 1540*

c. Cicero, *Tusculan Disputations*, I.ix.19. Dolet's translation appeared in 1543.

que l'on rende mot pour mot. Et si aulcun le faict, cela luy procede de pauvreté et deffault d'esprit. Car s'il a les qualités dessusdictes (lesquelles il est besoing estre en ung bon traducteur), sans avoir esgard à l'ordre des mots il s'arrestera aux sentences et faira en sorte que l'intention de l'autheur sera exprimée, gardant curieusement la proprieté de l'une et l'aultre langue. Et par ainsi, c'est superstition trop grande (diray-je besterie ou ignorance?) de commencer sa traduction au commencement de la clausule. Mais si, l'ordre des mots perverti, tu exprimes l'intention de celuy que tu traduis, aulcun ne t'en peult reprendre.[15] Je ne veulx taire icy la follie d'aulcuns traducteurs lesquelz, au lieu de liberté, se submettent à servitude. C'est assçavoir qu'ilz sont si sots qu'ilz s'efforcent de rendre ligne pour ligne ou vers pour vers, par laquelle erreur ilz depravent souvent le sens de l'autheur qu'ilz traduisent et n'expriment la grace et parfection de l'une et l'aultre langue. Tu te garderas diligemment de ce vice, qui ne demonstre aultre chose que l'ignorance du traducteur. [b 3 *v*]

La quatriesme reigle[16] que je veulx bailler en cest endroict est plus à observer en langues non reduictes en art qu'en aultres; j'appelle langues non reduictes encores en art certain et repceu, comme est la Françoyse, l'Italienne, l'Hespaignole, celle d'Allemaigne, d'Angleterre, et aultres vulgaires. S'il advient doncques que tu traduises quelcque livre Latin en ycelles, mesmement en la Françoyse, il te fault garder d'usurper mots trop approchants du Latin[17] et peu usités par le passé; mais contente-toy du commun sans innover aulcunes dictions follement et par curiosité reprehensible. Ce que si aulcuns font, ne les ensuy en cela; car leur arrogance ne vault rien et n'est tolerable entre les gens sçavants. Pour cela n'entends pas que je dye que le traducteur s'abstienne totallement de mots qui sont hors de l'usage commun; car on sçait bien que la langue Grecque ou Latine est trop plus riche en dictions que la Françoyse,[18] qui nous contrainct souvent d'user de mots peu frequentés. Mais cela se doibt faire à l'extreme necessité. Je sçay bien en oultre qu'aulcuns pourroient dire que la pluspart des dictions de la langue Françoyse est derivée de la Latine, et que si noz predecesseurs ont heu l'authorité de les mettre en usage les modernes et posterieurs en peuvent aultant faire. Tout cela se peult debattre entre babillarts; mais le meilleur est de suivre le commun langage. En mon *Orateur Françoys*, je traicteray ce poinct plus amplement et avec plus grand' demonstration. [b 4]

Venons maintenant à la cinquiesme reigle[19] que doibt observer ung bon

15. C'est follie de vouloir rendre ligne pour ligne, ou vers pour vers. *Margin 1540* 16. La quarte reigle. *Margin 1540*

17. Il se fault garder d'usurper mots trop approchants du Latin. *Margin 1540*

18. La langue Grecque, ou Latine est plus riche en dictions, que la Francoyse. *Margin 1540* 19. La cinquiesme reigle. *Margin 1540*

traducteur; laquelle est de si grand' vertu que sans elle toute composition est lourde et mal plaisante. Mais qu'est-ce qu'elle contient? Rien aultre chose que l'observation des nombres oratoires,[20] c'est assçavoir une liaison et assemblement des dictions avec telle doulceur que non seulement l'ame s'en contente, mais aussi les oreilles en sont toutes ravies, et ne se faschent jamais d'une telle harmonie de langage. D'yceulx nombres oratoires je parle plus copieusement en mon *Orateur*; parquoy n'en feray icy plus long discours. Et derechef advertiray le traducteur d'y prendre garde; car sans l'observation des nombres on ne peult estre esmerveillable en quelcque composition que ce soit, et sans yceulx les sentences ne peuvent estre graves et avoir leur poix requis et legitime. Car pense-tu que ce soict assés d'avoir la diction propre et elegante sans une bonne copulation des mots? Je t'advise que c'est aultant que d'ung monceau de diverses pierres precieuses mal ordonnées, lesquelles ne peuvent avoir leur lustre à cause d'une collocation impertinente. Ou c'est aultant que de divers instruments musicaulx mal conduicts par les joueurs ignorantz de l'art et peu congnoissantz les tons et mesures de la musique. En somme, c'est peu de la splendeur des mots, si l'ordre et collocation d'yceulx n'est telle qu'il appartient. En cela sur touts fut jadis estimé Isocrate, orateur Grec, et pareillement Demosthene. [b 4 *v*] Entre les Latins, Marc Tulle Ciceron a[21] esté grand observateur des nombres. Mais ne pense pas que cela se doibve plus observer par les orateurs que par les historiographes. Et qu'ainsi soit, tu ne trouveras Cæsar et Salluste moins nombreux que Ciceron. Conclusion quant à ce propos: sans grande observation des nombres ung autheur n'est rien, et avec yceulx il ne peult faillir à avoir bruict en eloquence si pareillement il est propre en diction, et grave en sentences, et en arguments subtil. Qui sont les poincts d'ung orateur parfaict et vrayment comblé de toute gloire d'eloquence.

20. Nombres oratoires. *Margin 1540* 21. à *1540*.

NICOLAS DE HERBERAY DES ESSARTS

PROLOGUE TO *Amadis de Gaule*

1540

TEXT:

Le Premier Liure de Amadis de Gaule, qui traicte de maintes adventvres D'armes & D'amours, qu'eurent plusieurs Cheualiers & Dames, tant du royaulme de la grand Bretaigne, que d'aultres pays. Traduict nouuellement D'espagnol en Francoys par le Seigneur des Essars, Nicolas de Herberay. Acuerdo Oluido. Auec priuilege du Roy. 1540. Nouuellement imprimé à Paris par Denys Ianot libraire & imprimeur, demourant en la rue neufue nostre dame, à L'enseigne Sainct Iehan Baptiste, contre Sainte Geneuiefue des Ardens. [New York Public Library.]

[Cf. Brunet, I, 214–15; Vaganay, *Amadis en français*, Florence: Olschki, 1906, pp. 3–6, for the text of the prologue as it appears in the 1544 ed.]

COLLATED:

(1548) Le Premier Liure de Amadis de Gaule, traitant de maintes avantvres d'Armes & d'Amours, qu'eurent plusieurs Cheualiers & Dames, tant du royaume de la grand' Bretaigne, que d'autres païs: Traduit nouuellement d'Espagnol en Françoys, par le Seigneur des Essars Nicolas de Herberay. Acuerdo Oluido. Auecq' priuilege du Roy. A Paris, Par Estienne Groulleau, demourant en la rue neuue nostre Dame, à l'enseigne saint Ian Baptiste. 1548. [Newberry Library.]

[Cf. Brunet, I, 215. The 1548 ed. cited by Vaganay, *op. cit.*, p. 14, is apparently a different edition.]

(1550) Le Premier Livre d'Amadis de Gavle, mis en Francoys par le Seigneur des Essars Nicolas de Herberay, Commissaire ordinaire de l'artillerie du Roy, & Lieutenant en icelle es païs & gouvernement de Picardie de monsieur de Brissac, Cheualier de l'ordre, grand Maistre & Capitaine general d'icelle artillerie. Acverdo Olvido. Auecq' Priuilege du Roy. A Paris. Pour Vincent Sertenas Libraire, tenant sa boutique au Palays en la galerie par ou l'on va à la Chancellerie, & au mont saint Hylaire à l'hostel d'Albret. 1550. [University of Chicago Libraries.]

[Cf. Brunet, I, 215.]

With the spread of printing in the sixteenth century, many of the prose romances which had delighted readers in the Middle Ages were published in popular editions. To them were added many new romances imported from other countries. Herberay des Essarts's version of the Amadis story soon became one of the most current of these, and it was regarded by many contemporaries as one of the finest French works of the century. The bibliography of the work has been treated by Hugues Vaganay in his *Amadis en français, Livres I–XII*: Essai de Bibliographie et d'Iconographie,

Florence: Olschki, 1906 (Extrait de *La Bibliofilía*, 1903–1905), which reprints the translator's prologue (pp. 4–6). The prologue is also found in Vaganay's edition of *Le Premier Livre d'Amadis de Gaule*, Paris: Hachette, 1918 ("Société des textes français modernes"), I, xi–xiii.

[ã iii] PROLOGUE DU TRANSLATEUR DU LIVRE D'AMADIS D'ESPAGNOL EN FRANÇOYS[1]

A TRÈS HAULT ET TRÈS ILLUSTRE PRINCE CHARLES DUC D'ORLEANS ET D'ANGOULESME, SECOND FILZ DU ROY, NICOLAS DE HERBERAY SEIGNEUR DES ESSARS TRÈS HUMBLE SALUT

Depuis deux ou trois ans en ça que Mars s'est eslongné d'entre les princes Chrestiens, contrainct laisser enrouiller ses armes et instrumens belliqueux à l'occasion de la treufve qui est de present entre le très Chrestien et magnanime Roy vostre pere et Charles cinqiesme Empereur,[a] estant par ce moyen reduict de l'impetueuse vie des armes au[2] bien du repos et loisir, me suis mis (pour eviter la trop pernitieuse oysiveté) à lire plusieurs sortes de livres, tant vulgaires qu'estranges; entre lesquelz m'estant tombé ès mains celluy d'*Amadis de Gaule* en langue Castillane,[b] lequel maintes fois plusieurs gentilzhommes d'Espaigne m'avoient loué et estimé sur tous les romans, et le trouvant tel qu'ilz me l'avoient asseuré, tant pour la diversité des plaisantes matieres dont il traicte que de representation[3] subtilement descripte qu'il fait des personnes suyvant les armes ou amours, ay prins plaisir à le communiquer par translation (soubz vostre auctorité) à ceulx qui n'entendront le langaige Espagnol, pour faire revivre la renommée d'Amadis (laquelle par l'injure et antiquité du temps estoit estaincte en ceste nostre France) et aussi pource qu'il est tout certain qu'il fut premier mis en nostre langue Françoyse, estant Amadis Gaulois et non Espaignol. Et qu'ainsi soit, j'en ay trouvé encores quelque reste d'un vieil livre escript à la main en langaige Picard,[c] sur lequel j'estime que les Espaignolz ont fait leur traduction, non pas du tout suyvant le vray original comme l'on pourra veoir par cestuy; car ilz en ont obmis en d'aulcuns[4] endroictz et augmenté aux aultres; parquoy suppliant à leur obmission elle se trouvera en ce livre, dans lequel je n'ay voulu coucher la plus part de leur dicte augmentation,

1. *Omitted 1550* 2. ou *1540*; au *1548, 1550* 3. de la reputation *1550*
4. aucuns *1550*

a. Pope Paul III effected a truce between Francis I and Charles V on June 18, 1538; although it was to last for ten years, the peace was broken by Francis after only four years.

b. The first edition of the *Amadis* in Spanish appeared ca. 1496, and there were eleven additional editions before 1540. Cf. G. S. Williams, *The Amadis Question*, New York and Paris: 1909 (Extrait de la *Revue hispanique*, XXI), pp. 155 ff.

c. This Picard version has never been discovered; cf. Brunet, I, 215.

qu'ilz nomment en leur langaige *consiliaria* (qui vault autant à dire au nostre comme "advis" ou "conseil"), semblans[5] telz sermons mal propres à la matiere dont parle l'histoire; laquelle j'ay expressement mise en lumiere, non pour esperance d'en rapporter louenge (estant l'œuvre de trop peu de merite) mais seulement pour tesmoigner à tout le monde combien je vouldrois pouoir pour vous faire très humble service, mesmement pour vous donner quelquefois de quoy recréer[6] vostre gentil esprit lorsqu'il sera ennuyé de lire choses plus haultes et ardues.

Toutesfois, je n'eusse esté jamais si temeraire [ã iii *v*] ny ne me fusse jusques là oublié de le presenter devant vostre excellence, n'estoit qu'à l'imitation[7] de vostre très illustre progeniteur vous estes estimé le prince qui plus humainement et gratieusement reçoit aussitost les moindres presens des petitz que les bien grans des majeurs, conformant vostre grandeur et magnanimité à la volunté de ceulx qui vous desirent faire service. Et combien que ce qui s'offre en ceste traduction d'*Amadis* ne soit tiré de nul auteur fameux pour luy donner couleur de verité, si trouvera-on en elle tant de rencontres chevaleureuses et plaisantes, avec infiniz propos d'amours si delectables à ceulx qui ayment ou sont dignes d'aymer, que toute personne de bon jugement se doit persuader (voyre quasi contraindre) à lire son histoire pour le passetemps et plaisir qu'il pourra recevoir en la bien voyant. A ceste cause, monseigneur, je m'ose asseurer que si elle treuve grace devant voz yeulx ou soit quelque peu favorisée de vous, que non seulement elle sera estimée beaucoup, mais acquerra le premier lieu entre toutes les aultres histoires semblables; qui est en partie la cause pour laquelle j'ay entreprins la traduire, et aussi pour faire cognoistre à chascun mon intention qui tend à exalter la Gaule en laquelle passe de present un siecle bien heureux, par la grace que Dieu nous donne de nous[8] avoir fait naistre en voz[9] jours, durant lesquelz nous esperons tant de vous que de vous veoir quelquefois aussi grand par dessus les princes estranges que vous estes aymé et honoré des vostres.

Doncques, monseigneur, je vous supplie très humblement recevoir ce premier livre d'*Amadis* et le fruict de mon labeur avec telle facilité et bon visaige que vous avez accoustumé recevoir les presens de chascun; entre lesquelz nul ne vous est offert plus grand que les cœurs et bonnes voluntez des gentilzhommes, qui vous sont du tout acquis tant pour le bon recueil que vous leur[10] faites que pour la bonne grace que vous avez, accompaignée de voz aultres perfections et vertuz. Et si vous appercevez en quelque endroict que je ne me soye assubjecty à le rendre de mot à mot, je vous supplie croyre que je l'ay fait tant pource qu'il m'a semblé beaucoup de choses

5. me semblant *1550* 6. recreér *1540*
7. a'imitation *1540*; a l'imitation *1548*, *1550* 8. vous *1550*
9. noz *1550* 10. leurs *1540*, *1548*; leur *1550*

estre mal seantes aux personnes introduictes, eu regard ès[11] meurs et façons du jourd'huy, qu'aussi pour[12] l'advis d'aulcuns mes amys qui ont trouvé bon me delivrer de la commune superstition des translateurs, mesmement que ce n'est matiere où soit requise si scrupuleuse observance; ce que, pourtant, si je cognois vous avoir despleu en ce premier livre, je mettray peine aux aultres de faire mieulx pour vous obeyr et faire toute ma vie très humble service.

11. aux *1548, 1550* 12. pous *1540*; par *1550*

CHARLES ESTIENNE

PREFACE TO TERENCE'S *Andria*

1542

TEXT:

Premiere Comedie de Terence, intitvlee l'Andrie, Nouuellement traduicte de Latin en François, en faueur des bons espritz, studieux des antiques recreations. 1542. Auec priuilege. On les vend à Paris, en la rue neufue nostre Dame, à l'enseigne du Faulcheur, deuant saincte Geneuiefue des ardens, par Andry roffet. [Privilège dated "le xii. iour de Feburier Mil.v c. xli." Printer's device of Pierre Roffet at end. British Museum.]

[Cf. Brunet, III, 454–55.]

The "Epistre du translateur au lecteur" which Charles Estienne used as a preface to his translation of Terence's *Andria* was to have a long career as a preface to other works. But its original form was also its most complete and its most interesting form; subsequent versions were much shorter and considerably changed. For information on the second and later redactions, the reader is referred to the introductory note on Charles Estienne's "Preface to *Les Abusez*," pp. 135–38 below. On Estienne, see Erich Lau, *Charles Estienne* (*Biographie und Bibliographie*), Wertheim a. M.: Bechstein, 1930; Lau suggests Donatus, Horace, and Vitruvius as the sources of the epistle.

[ã ii] EPISTRE DU TRANSLATEUR AU LECTEUR, EN LAQUELLE EST DECLAIRÉE LA MANIERE QUE LES ANCIENS ONT OBSERVÉE EN LEURS COMEDIES

Pourautant que plusieurs me semblent beaucoup travaillez à entendre la raison et maniere des comedies anciennes, asçavoir comment elles se faisoient, et le lieu où elles se jouoient, et par quel moyen on en usoit; à ceste cause je vous ay bien en bref icy voulu declairer ce que j'en ay peu comprendre par les bons autheurs, et aussi par les vestiges qui restent au-[a ii *v*]jourdhuy des choses antiques, tant au pays d'Italie comme en Provence et aultres lieux de la noble France. Et l'ay faict principalement affin que l'on prenne desormais quelque goust à l'autheur qui entre les anciens a esté tousjours estimé le bien eloquent et très excellent compositeur de comedies. Faulte duquel entendre, et la maniere qu'il avoit à bien disposer et ordonner le sens et la matiere dont il escripvoit, nostre vulgaire du jourdhuy est tumbé en telle ignorance et cecité, que ce qu'il faict pour le present en telles matieres ne sent riens moins que sa comedie.

Parquoy m'est aussi venu en fantaisie de traduyre et mettre en nostre langue vulgaire la premiere des comedies dudit Terence, seulement en prose, pour plus facilement monstrer le stile, la maniere [ã iii] de proceder, et le bon esprit qu'avoit le comique en la façon d'icelles. Je ne l'ay point mise en rithme pour deux causes: l'une, pourautant que la liberté d'ung traducteur, tel que les Græcz appelloient *paraphraste* (c'est-à-dire, qui rend le sens, la phrase, et l'esprit d'une matiere, sans contrainte du langaige), facilement se pert soubz la subjection du vers; l'aultre à cause que vous avez en ce royaulme grandement des bons rithmeurs, lesquelz facilement après ceste premiere traduction la pourront mettre en meilleure rithme que je ne sçauroye faire. Il me suffit d'avoir rendu le principal sens, et vous enseigner par le present escript, premierement, dont vindrent les comedies et les differences d'icelles; puis, comment elles se jouoient et en quelz lieux se proposoient pu[ã iii *v*]bliquement, tant à Romme que aultre part; ensemble la façon et les aornementz des theatres et scenes faictes pour les jeux comiques; puis les vestementz des joueurs avec leur maniere et pronunciation. Toutes lesquelles choses pendant que je m'efforceray vous declairer, il vous plaise me donner ung bien peu de vostre bonne faveur et attention, et m'excuser si possible aulcun des plus sçavans me desdit en quelque passaige. Car pour tout certain, la chose est ung peu difficile, et qui pour la pluspart gist en conjecture; parquoy ne se peult aulcunesfois faire qu'il n'y ayt quelque vacilation de jugement. Je commenceray donc par la difference des comedies, pour vous donner à entendre que c'estoit que les anciens apelloient la fable, tragedie, satyre, comedie vieille [ã iiii] et nouvelle; et ce pour mieulx parvenir au surplus de mon intention.

Qu'estoit ce que les anciens appelloient fable, tragedie, satyre, comedie vieille, et comedie nouvelle

Fable estoit ung nom commun et general tant à la tragedie que à la comedie et satyre, mesmement encores à toute poesye·ainsi qu'il plaist à d'aulcuns. Car la fable n'est aultre chose sinon une deduction de matiere faicte et inventée, bien et proprement disposée, soubz le sens de laquelle gist une reprehention de vice ou remonstrance de vertu.

La tragedie estoit une maniere de fable sumptueuse qui se jouoit par personnaiges et se recitoit publiquement aux theatres, par laquelle les anciens reprenoient non seulement les faultes qui[1] [ã iiii *v*] se commettoient ès choses privées et civiles, mais encores ès choses haultaines et ardues, jusques à toucher et taxer les princes. Aux anciennes tragedies, les joueurs (devant que l'usaige des masques feust trouvé) se souloient brouiller le visaige de marc d'huille, que les Græcz appeloient τρύγας, dont est venu le nom de tragedie. En icelle se menoient grands bruytz et en estoit l'argument grave et haultain, le commencement doulx et paisible avec joyeuseté,

1. qui qui *1542*

la fin funeste et douloureuse. L'argument se prenoit le plus souvent de quelque histoire, comme d'Hercules furieux (lequel personnaige joua Neron aultresfois, luy estant empereur)[a] et de Thyestes, qui sont deux noms de tragedies du senateur Senecque qui feust aussi maistre dudit empereur.

Les empereurs [ã v] qui feurent depuis Domitian et ses successeurs se fascherent de ceste tragedie;[b] au moyen dequoy l'on n'en joua plus à Romme, et demeura seulement pour les jeux sceniques une sorte de comedie que les posterieurs ont appellé la comedie vieille. En laquelle ne se descripvoient que comme par maniere de foy hystorique les choses qui avoient esté commises par les citoyens et bourgeois de la ville, avec la declaration le plus souvent de leurs noms propres; car les anciens poetes comiques n'avoient point de coustume de faindre du tout leurs argumentz, mais descripvoient assez appertement les choses qui avoient esté faictes en nommans ceulx mesmes qui les commettoient, qui fut une maniere de faire pour quelque temps assez proffitable pour la cité. Car par ce [ã v *v*] moyen chascun mettoit peine à ne faire chose parquoy il peust estre joué aux comedies. Mais depuis que les poetes trop licentieux commencerent à injurier pour leur plaisir plusieurs gens de bien, fut faict une ordonnance par Domitian qu'ilz se teussent du tout,[c] et qu'il reservoit la correction de telles faultes à soy, feussent des hommes ou des femmes; tellement qu'il abolit par edict tous libelles et vers diffamatoires avec le nom des autheurs. Mesmement toutes personnes d'authorité, et notamment du senat, feussent princes ou aultres, tenoit pour infames s'ilz s'addonnoient à jeux sceniques et gesticulatoires; de sorte qu'il priva ung questeur de son office pour s'en estre meslé.[d]

De mesmes la vieille comedie fut aussi la satyre, qui estoit une sorte de fable et maniere de taxer les [ã vi] meurs des citoyens, en forme obscure et agreste, sans nommer personne aulcunement; et en la scene de ladicte satyre n'estoient introduys que faunes et dieux petulantz, lascives, et sauvaiges, que l'on appelloit aussi satyres. En icelle ne se declairoit riens que par enigmes et circumlocutions, principalement touchant les haultes et ardues matieres. Ceste maniere de fable fut prejudiciable à beaucoup de poetes, à cause du souspeçon qu'ilz bailloient aux riches bourgeois de Romme, par ce que chascun d'eulx se doubtoit estre celuy de qui l'on parloit; au moyen dequoy se teurent les satyriques et n'oserent plus jouer.

a. Cf. Suetonius, *De Vita Caesarum,* Nero, XXI, 3: "Inter cetera cantavit Canacen parturientem, Oresten matricidam, Oedipodem excaecatum, Herculem insanum."

b. Unidentified.

c. Unidentified; cf. note d.

d. Cf. Suetonius, Domitian, VIII,3: "scripta famosa vulgoque edita, quibus primores viri ac feminae notabantur, abolevit non sine auctorum ignominia; quaestorium virum, quod gesticulandi saltandique studio teneretur, movit senatu."

Ceste maniere estoit plus Græcque que Latine, car les Latins composoient plus leurs satyres par poemes et libelles que aultrement.

Toutes ces fables mises hors [ã vi *v*] d'usaige, vint en bruict et estimation la comedie qu'ilz ont appellée nouvelle pour ceste cause; car elle ne laissoit pas auparavant de se jouer, mesmement ne touchoit qu'en general toutes persones par manieres d'esbat, et ne parloit que d'amours, et n'introduysoit que personnaiges de basse condition. En icelle y avoit motz pour rire, sentences joyeuses, argument bien disposé et conduyt, reformations de mœurs corrumpues et lascives. Parquoy l'eloquent Ciceron, voulant definir la comedie, dit que c'est ung poeme ou une fable remonstrant la maniere et imitation de vivre, mirouer de bonnes mœurs, ymaige de verité.[e] En ceste comedie nouvelle se trouvoit quant à l'argument tout lé contraire de la tragedie; c'est assçavoir fascherie au commencement et [ã vii] joye à la fin.

Le nom des comedies nouvelles, desquelles ont esté compositeurs Latins Plaute et Terence entre les aultres, se prenoit aulcunesfois du nom d'ung personnaige principal de la comedie, comme Phormion; aulcunesfois d'ung lieu, comme *Andrie* de l'isle d'Andros; aulcunesfois d'ung faict, comme d'ung chastré, qui est le nom de la seconde comedie de Terence; et aulcunesfois d'ung accident, commes les freres, qui est aultre nom de comedie dudit facteur.

En quelz lieux, premierement, se jouoyent les tragedies et comedies

Les premieres tragedies et comedies anciennes se jouerent aux villaiges, près de la ville, sur ung [ã vii *v*] verd pré, et proposoit l'on pris aux facteurs ou compositeurs d'icelles affin d'exciter tousjours de mieulx en mieulx les bons espritz des poetes. L'on faisoit aussi present aux joueurs et leur donnoit-on quelque chevreau ou aultre beste, affin de plus voluntiers mettre peine à moderer leur voix et donner recreation au peuple. Depuis l'on trouva moyen de jouer aux carrefours de ville, qu'ilz appelloient *compita*, et les jeux qui là se proposoient aux spectateurs s'appelloient *ludi compitalitii*; telz que fit aulcunesfois Auguste, donnant plusieurs scenes par toutes les rues, et hystrions de toutes langues.[f] Et le moyen de proposer lesdictes comedies ou tragedies par lesditz carrefours estoit de faire les eschauffaulx qu'ilz appelloient scenes, posez et assis sus [ã viii] des chariotz qu'ilz nommoient *plaustres*, et se transportoient au moyen des roues facilement deça et dela, parquoy les appelloient *scenes ductiles*.

e. Cited by Donatus, *Commentum Terenti* (ed. Wessner, Leipzig: Teubner, 1902, I, 22): "comoediam esse Cicero ait imitationem uitae, speculum consuetudinis, imaginem ueritatis." Cf. note f. to Grévin's "Prefaces in the *Théâtre*," p. 186 below.

f. Cf. Suetonius, Divus Augustus, XLIII,1: "Fecitque nonnumquam etiam vicatim ac pluribus scaenis per omnium linguarum histriones..."

Tant sont venues en recommendation du peuple à traict de temps les comedies et tragedies que l'on leur a[2] faict cet honneur de les reduire au nombre des jeux publiques lesquelz estoient instituez d'ancienneté, ou à l'honneur des dieux, ou pour donner recreation au peuple. Et se jouoient aux cirques, theatres, et amphitheatres faictz et edifiez ou par la chose publique ou par quelque empereur ou gros citoyen, pour la commodité et appropriation des spectateurs; se faisoient aussi aux communs despens de la ville, avec pris proposé aux fraiz de la chose publique. Et y avoit gens deputez et offices communes de la ville, lesquelz [ã viii *v*] n'avoient aultre charge ou vacation que de soliciter et entendre tant ausditz jeux sceniques comme aussi aux aultres jeux publiques dediez à leurs dieux, selon leur religion. Et s'appelloient iceulx officiers *aediles curules*.

Des jeux sceniques en general et des acteurs et joueurs d'iceulx

Or est-il ainsi que les theatres ne servoient qu'aux jeux sceniques principalement, de la partie desquelz appellée scene se nommoient aussi sceniques, entre lesquelz estoit comprinse la tragedie, satyre, et comedie, recit de poemes, vers lyriques, et choses semblables; et y avoit personnaiges propres à jouer lesdictes tragedies, comedies, et satyres, les[ẽ]quelz personnaiges s'appelloient hystrions, mimes, et pantomimes; toutesfois que les hystrions estoient proprement ceulx qui recitoient les comedies, et les mimes, ceulx qui contrefaisoient les gestes. Parquoy est dit de Neron qu'il produit une foys en la scene plusieurs femmes desguisées pour jouer comme les mimes.[g] Iceulx estoient les plus excellentz de tous les joueurs, et aux tragedies et comedies avoient l'industrie de contrefaire toutes personnes avec masques et vestementz propres aux personnaiges qu'ilz contrefaisoient; de sorte qu'il est memoire de Neron empereur susdit qu'il fit faire masques au propre pour jouer des demys dieux et déesses aux tragedies, lesquelz masques estoient faictz à la semblance de son visaige et de la dame qu'il aymoit [ẽ *v*] le mieulx.[h] Ledit Neron encores recita au theatre, sur la scene, aulcuns vers qu'il avoit composez, avec si grand joye d'ung chascun que à cause de tel recit le senat luy ordonna estre faicte supplication publique en son nom; et fut une partie desditz vers escripte en lettre d'or et dediée à Jupiter

2. à *1542*

g. Possibly Suetonius, Nero, XI, 2: "Ludis, quos pro aeternitate imperii susceptos appellari 'maximos' voluit, ex utroque ordine et sexu plerique ludicras partes sustinuerunt."

h. Cf. Suetonius, Nero, XXI, 3: "Tragoedias quoque cantavit personatus heroum deorumque, item heroidum ac dearum, personis effectis ad similitudinem oris sui et feminae, prout quamque diligeret."

du Capitole.[i] Il est aussi memoire qu'il chanta des tragedies luy estant emmasqué, comme l'*Hercules furieux* que composa son maistre Senecque, et *Orestes meurdrier de sa mere*, *Oedipus aveugle*, et aultres semblables;[j] pendant qu'il chantoit lesquelles choses n'estoit loysible au peuple soy partir du theatre, feust pour aulcun empeschement necessaire ou aultrement, en sorte que (recite Suetone) plusieurs femmes grosses enfanterent au theatre pendant qu'il chantoit, et beaucoup de personnaiges, ennuyez de l'escouter et de le louer, [ẽ ii] se faisoient porter dehors, faignantz d'estre esvanouiz.[k] Ledit Neron observoit si bien les loix des joueurs et histrions sceniques que jamais ne crachoit en jouant ou chantant, et torchoit la sueur de son fronc avec le bras sans aultre mouschoir. Une fois entre les aultres le baston qu'il tenoit pour geste luy cheut de la main, dont fut si fasché, craignant d'avoir perdu le pris et que le monde ou les juges l'eussent apperceu (car il y avoit combat à qui chanteroit le mieulx), que si ce n'eust esté l'hypocrite (qui estoit celuy qui monstroit aux joueurs la maniere de faire les gestes) qui le conforma, il doubtoit d'estre sifflé du peuple et chassé hors de la scene.[l] Plusieurs foys rapportoit pris de la scene selon qu'il avoit bien joué; lesquelz pris, tant de couronnes que d'aultres [ẽ ii *v*] choses, il faisoit pendre près de son lict, à sa chambre secrette, et au lieu où il beuvoit et mengeoit privéement; fit aussi frapper de la monnoye en laquelle il estoit pourtraict tenant ung septre en sa main et en habit de joueur scenique.[m]

En telz jeux y avoit debat entre les joueurs bien souvent, tellement que ceulx d'entre eulx qui se nommoient pantomimi (c'estoient ceulx qui avoient la grace de contrefaire toutes personnes et toutes voix) souvent se battoient sur la scene, au combat desquelz se trouva Neron une foys. Et comme leur capitaine, estant au hault du proscene, jettoit force pierres et pieces des sieges sur le peuple pour son plaisir, de sorte qu'il bleça le

i. *Ibid.*, X, 2: "recitavit et carmina, non modo domi sed in theatro, tanta universorum laetitia, ut ob recitationem supplicatio decreta sit eaque pars carminum aureis litteris Iovi Capitolino dicata."

j. *Ibid.*, XXI, 3; see note a. above.

k. *Ibid.*, XXIII, 2: "Cantante eo ne necessaria quidem causa excedere theatro licitum est. Itaque et enixae quaedam in spectaculis dicuntur et multi taedio audiendi laudandique clausis oppidorum portis aut furtim desiluisse de muro aut morte simulata funere elati."

l. *Ibid.*, XXIV, 1: "In certando vero ita legi oboediebat, ut numquam exscreare ausus sudorem quoque frontis brachio detergeret; atque etiam in tragico quodam actu, cum elapsum baculum cito resumpsisset, pavidus et metuens ne ob delictum certamine summoveretur, non aliter confirmatus est quam adiurante hypocrita non animadversum id inter exsultationes succlamationesque populi."

m. *Ibid.*, XXV, 3: "Sacras coronas in cubiculis circum lectos posuit, item statuas suas citharoedico habitu, qua nota etiam nummum percussit."

preteur par la teste, luy-mesmes après fit ordonnance que lesditz pantomi-[ẽ iii]mi debattroient à qui mieulx gaigneroit;[n] que Domitian osta du tout, et fit defences que les hystrions ne pantomimes se trouvassent plus sur la scene, mais jouassent en privé.[o]

Lesditz pantomimi, en jouant et recitant, chantoient et dansoyent; parquoy y avoit premierement quelque musicien qui faisoit les mesures du chant et de la danse devant que la comedie fust jouée, et y avoit menestriers qui conduysoient ledit chant au son de la fleuste.[3] Et croy qu'ung pantomimus seul jouoit une grande part d'une tragedie ou comedie, en changeant souvent de masque, d'habit, et de voix, ainsi que font aujourdhuy en Italie ceulx que l'on appelle bufons. Car il est dit en la vie de Caligula qu'ung pantomime nommé Marcus Nestor saulta la trage[ẽ iii *v*]die, laquelle aultresfois avoit saultée ung aultre nommé Neoptolemus, aussi pantomime Græc, aux jeux ausquelz Philippe roy des Macedoniens fut tué.[p] Je pense que le saulter ou dancer d'une tragedie ou cantique estoit comme aujourdhuy l'on dit la danse d'une chanson; car Ciceron dit que à la premiere voix ou premier son que l'on oyoit des haultz boys, le peuple jugeoit bien quelle comedie on devoit jouer.[q] Davantaige il est dit que Caligula une fois se leva de son lict et fit appeller trois ou quatre senateurs, avec lesquelz monta sur le pulpite de la scene et feit sonner ung cantique à force d'instrumentz et bruit de sieges; puis après qu'ilz eurent dansé se retira.[r] Le tragicien pronunçoit en forme de chant, et l'histrion faisoit le geste et la maniere (dit quelqu'ung); ce [ẽ iiii] qui se conforme par ce qu'il est dit à la vie du mesmes Caligula, que quand il estoit aux jeux sceniques

3. ffeuste *1542*

n. *Ibid.*, XXVI, 2: "Interdiu quoque clam gestatoria sella delatus in theatrum seditionibus pantomimorum e parte proscaeni superiore signifer simul ac spectator aderat; et cum ad manus ventum esset lapidibusque et subselliorum fragminibus decerneretur, multa et ipse iecit in populum atque etiam praetoris caput consauciavit."

o. Cf. Suetonius, Domitian, VII, 1: "interdixit histrionibus scaenam, intra domum quidem exercendi artem iure concesso."

p. Cf. Suetonius, Gaius Caligula, LVII, 4: "pantomimus Mnester tragoediam saltavit, quam olim Neoptolemus tragoedus ludis, quibus rex Macedonum Philippus occisus est, egerat..."

q. Possibly a reference to Cicero, *Lucullus* (ed. O. Plasberg, Leipzig: Teubner, 1922), par. 20: "quam multa quae nos fugiunt in cantu exaudiunt in eo genere exercitati, qui primo inflatu tibicinis Antiopam esse aiunt aut Andromacham, cum id nos ne suspicemur quidem."

r. Cf. Suetonius, Gaius Caligula, LIV, 2: "quondam tres consulares secunda vigilia in Palatium accitos multaque et extrema metuentis super pulpitum conlocavit, deinde repente magno tibiarum et scabellorum crepitu cum palla tunicaque talari prosiluit ac desaltato cantico abiit."

il ne se pouoit tenir qu'il ne chantast quant et le tragicien, à mesmes qu'il pronunçoit, et que publiquement il ne contrefist le geste de l'histrion comme louant ou vituperant iceluy.[s]

Ces histrions et pantomimes avoyent grande liberté, à cause de ce qu'ilz se veoyent estre bien recueilliz auparavant que Domitian les chassast; et pour ceste cause engendroient noyse et debatz tant par le peuple comme sur la scene. Ilz gaignoient gros pris et leur faisoit-on gros presentz. Vaspasian donna à ung tragicien quatre centz sesterces, et aultres deux centz à deux menestriers; à d'aultres communéement quarante sesterces, oultre les couronnes d'or et aultres presentz.[t] [ẽ iiii *v*] Telle liberté avoit auparavant esté restrainte par Auguste; tellement qu'il fit donner du fouet par trois theatres à ung nommé Estienne togataire, pource qu'il avoit produit en la scene une dame ayant les cheveulx roignez et en habit de garson. Ung aultre pantomime nommé Hyla, pource qu'il se fit celer du preteur des jeux qui l'aloit querir, fut aussi puny par ledit Auguste. Ung aultre nommé Pylades, pource qu'il avoit monstré au doigt ung des spectateurs qui le siffloit, fut banny de toute l'Ytalie.[u]

Il y avoit d'aultres joueurs qui se nommoient *ludii*; mais ceulx-là recitoient motz pour rire et se trouvoient principalement aux bancquetz des seigneurs par passetemps. Aultres s'appelloient *aretalogi*, lesquelz disoient aussi motz joyeulx, mais graves et de [ẽ v] bonne portée, sans mocquerie. Iceulx appelloit souvent Auguste à ses repas pour recreation. Aultres s'appelloient fabulateurs, que nous pouons nommer faiseurs de comptes ou compteurs de fables; lesquelz aussi Auguste faisoit appeller toutesfois qu'il avoit perdu le sommeil du matin et qu'il vouloit prendre repos sus jour, ou bien au soir à son coucher; et au recit de ceulx-là, ou de quelque ung qui luy lisoit quelque hystoire ou fable, s'endormoit facilement.[v]

s. *Ibid.*, LIV, 1: "ne publicis quidem spectaculis temperaret quo minus et tragoedo pronuntianti concineret et gestum histrionis quasi laudans vel corrigens palam effingeret."

t. Cf. Suetonius, Divus Vespasianus, XIX, 1: "Apella tragoedo quadringenta, Terpno Diodoroque citharoedis ducena, nonnullis centena, quibus minimum, quadragena sestertia super plurimas coronas aureas dedit."

u. Cf. Suetonius, Divus Augustus, XLV, 4: "Nam histrionum licentiam adeo compescuit, ut Stephanionem togatarium, cui in puerilem habitum circumtonsam matronam ministrasse compererat, per trina theatra virgis caesum relegaverit, Hylan pantomimum querente praetore in atrio domus suae nemine excluso flagellis verberarit et Pyladen urbe atque Italia summoverit, quod spectatorem, a quo exsibilabatur, demonstrasset digito conspicuumque fecisset."

v. *Ibid.*, LXXIV: "et aut acroamata et histriones aut etiam triviales ex circo ludios interponebat ac frequentius aretalogos." Also LXXVIII, 2: "Si interruptum somnum reciperare, ut evenit, non posset, lectoribus aut fabulatoribus arcessitis resumebat producebatque ultra primam saepe lucem."

Les aornementz et vestementz des joueurs sceniques

Les histrions et joueurs (comme j'ay dit) estoient masquez, et pouoient soubz leurs[4] masques parler et reciter ou chanter sans fasche[ẽ v *v*]rie. Les vieillards estoyent vestuz de blanc, pource que l'on tenoit que ce feust la premiere et plus antique couleur. Les jeunes filz estoient vestus de diverses couleurs et de livrée. Les serviteurs estoient legierement et mincement accoustrez, pour demonstrer la pauvreté ancienne ou bien affin qu'ilz jouassent plus habilement. Les flateurs estoient vestus d'ung manteau, lequel ilz renversoient sus l'espaule et portoient en escharpe. Ung chevalier estoit vestu d'ung manteau ou cappe d'escarlate. Une jeune fille estoit abillée selon la mode du pays dont la comedie disoit qu'elle feust, c'est assçavoir ou de Græce ou d'aultre part. Le macquereau ou ruffian estoit vestu d'ung manteau de diverses couleurs et flory à l'entour, que les anciens appelloyent *amiculum flori*[ẽ vi]*dum*; tenoit aussi pour aornement en sa main une verge que les Græcz appelloient *arescos*. Les dames de joye avoient des sayes jaulnes et bien longues; si c'estoit en jeux funeraux, les dames portoyent sayes noyres. Et s'il estoit question de changer d'abit durant la comedie, selon les affections, à ung aymant joyeulx on donnoit ung abit blanc, à ung fasché ung abit changeant ou bien brun, à ung riche ung abit rouge, à ung pauvre ung abit pers et violet.

Les joueurs tragiques estoient plus sumptueusement accoustrez, à cause que l'argument estoit plus grave et haultain et ne parloit que de princes, dieux, et déesses. Les joueurs sceniques portoyent une maniere de souliers haultz qu'ilz appelloyent *socci*, telz que peuvent [ẽ vi *v*] estre des bottes; les joueurs de tragedies portoient des petitz brodequins bien faictz et sumptueulx qu'ilz appelloient[5] *cothurni*, et en ces deux choses principalement estoient cogneuz lesditz joueurs.

Si la comedie estoit Latine, et d'argument Latin, les joueurs portoient ung manteau de chevalier Romain qu'ilz appelloient *paludamentum*, duquel nom estoit appellée la comedie *paludata*. Ou bien selon l'argument portoient des vestementz longs, comme ceulx des senateurs, qu'ilz appelloient *toga*, et s'appelloit *togata* pour ceste cause; et ainsi des aultres. Et si l'argument estoit Græc ilz usoient d'ung manteau à la Græcque que l'on nommoit *pallium*, parquoy estoit aussi la comedie nommée *palliata*.

Que signifient les actes et les [ẽ vii] *scenes en la comedie*

Toutes comedies antiques estoient divisées en cinq ou six actes, et le plus communéement en cinq. Chascun desditz actes contenoit sens parfaict (dont en est descendu le nom), parquoy à la fin d'iceulx, pour recreer les

4. leur *1542* 5. ap-/apelloient *1542*

assistans, se faisoient plusieurs esbatementz sur la scene, par maniere d'intervalle et pour relascher les espritz des auditeurs; puis rentroient aux aultres actes et ainsi poursuyvoient leur comedie. Quand deux personnaiges ou trois avoyent devisé et tenu propos ensemble, et que l'ung se retiroit ou qu'il en venoit ung aultre en nouveau propos, ilz appelloient cela une scene, c'est-à-dire commutation ou variation de propos; de sorte que chascun acte, selon la variation [ẽ vii *v*] des personnaiges et deviz qu'ilz tenoient, estoit aussi divisé en cinq ou six scenes pour le moins. Et par ce moyen jamais ne demeuroit l'eschauffault vuyde, et n'y avoit personnaige sur le pulpite qui n'y feust necessaire, ou pour parler ou pour escouter les aultres à quelque intention; qui est une des choses où plus nous faillons, et que plus je trouve inepte en noz jeux et fainctes comedies. Somme, l'acte comprent sens parfaict, la scene, propos parfaict. L'ung fut inventé pour ne detenir trop longuement les auditeurs en une mesme chose et pour recréer les espritz par intervalles; l'aultre pour excuser (ce qui est de faulte en noz jeux) quand ung personnaige fainct d'aller parler à l'aultre ou qu'il se retire en quelque part pour ses affaires, qui n'est jà mestier de repre[ẽ viii]senter au peuple; puis à l'aultre scene ensuyvant retourne exprimer ce qu'il a faict autant que si le peuple l'avoit veu en presence.

Description du theatre et de la façon d'iceluy

Le bastiment (feust de boys ou de pierre) sur lequel les spectateurs des jeux sceniques estoyent commodéement assiz s'appelloit theatre, et estoit faict à demy rond avec troys ordres de galeries au hault pour retirer les auditeurs en temps de pluye; au bas desquelles y avoit ung eschauffault en pente, pour le moins hault eslevé de quinze grands degrez selon le long d'iceluy estenduz, sur lesquelz estoit le peu[ẽ viii *v*]ple assis chascun pour sa dignité, asçavoir aux degrez plus près de la scene et au lieu où les plus anciens souloient faire leur orchestra (qui estoit lieu dedié aux saulteurs et danceurs) estoient assiz les senateurs, pour plus facilement veoir les gestes et mouvementz des piedz des joueurs. Ung peu plus hault estoient assiz les aultres officiers du senat, et ainsi jusques au reste des degrez, chascun selon sa qualité comme plus amplement descriprons cy après. Entre chasque trois degrez y en avoit ung plus large deux fois que les aultres, et s'appelloit ceste largeur la *precinction*, dans laquelle y avoit petites huysseries par lesquelles des degrez de dessoubz on entroit sus le theatre, puis discouroit-on partout chascun à son lieu. Encores y avoit selon la longitude entre chasque cinq [õ] degrez une espace large à menuz degrez, pour se transporter de la *precinction* à tel grand degré que l'on vouloit; et telle espace, depuis la *precinction* jusques ausditz petitz degrez, faisoit une separation que l'on nommoit *cuneus*. Par le moyen de ces *precinctions* les serviteurs, sans fascherie du peuple, pouoient facilement venir cercher leurs maistres estantz aux jeux et parler à eulx sans riens destourber ne fascher, qui estoit fort grande commodité. Et pourautant que la pente estoit grande et non pas trop droicte, affin que l'eaue de la pluye ne feust retenue (ou aussi pour les urines, à ung besoing), y avoit certains petitz canaulx[6] engravez dans les degrez des *precinctions* et allées traverses, par lesquelz l'eau s'escouloit sans nuire à personne; ce que très bien descript Seba[ỏ *v*]stian Serlio en ses protraictz d'architecture antique.[w]

Description de la scene

Au devant du theatre estoit eslevé ung eschauffault de la haulteur de cinq piedz ou environ et de la longueur du dernier et inferieur degré du theatre; et s'appelloit cest eschauffault le pulpite, lequel aulcunesfois estoit de bois (combien que la scene fust de pierre) et se pouoit oster quand on vouloit. Depuis cest eschauffault, à la haulteur de deux petitz degrez, estoient situées plusieurs columnes soubstenantes comme quelque forme d'edifice, percé de force de fenestraiges, avec paramentz fort honnestes de paintures diverses et aultres cas; peu au derriere desquelles [ỏ ii] columnes, comme dans une galerie, se veoyent certaines portes et entrées de diverses maisons, desquelles sailloient les joueurs et ausquelles se retiroient selon ce qu'il appartenoit, et d'icelles sortantz venoient jouer sur l'eschauffault. Et estoient ces portes fermées et ne s'ouvroient sinon quand ung joueur entroit leans, puis soubdain se refermoient. Vers le meilleu de la scene y avoit une grande porte ouverte, faicte en forme d'entrée de ville, en laquelle entroient les joueurs quand ilz signifioient vouloir aller ou à la ville ou au marché ou aux champs, ou ailleurs que à leur logis, et de laquelle porte aussi retournoient ou de la ville ou de quelque aultre lieu. Par les fenestres susdictes, au-dessus des columnes, l'on veoit quelquesfois les personnaiges parler, [ỏ ii *v*] comme quand l'on bucquoit à la porte de quelqu'ung et celuy qui est leans respondoit par la fenestre. Aulcunesfois on veoit des jongleurs, buffons, gesticulateurs, et aultres telz se mettre par intervalles ausdictes fenestres et dire motz à plaisir ou bien chanter et faire diverses gestes. Au-dessus de l'estaige sus ung perron estoient les musiciens, qui par les intervalles des actes delectoient le peuple, comme dict est. Des deux costez de ladicte scene, depuis l'alignement droit des columnes, poursuyvoit en avant vers le theatre et sailloit l'edifice de ladicte scene, comme recontrant aux deux courbes et extremitez du theatre; toutesfois en carré, non pas en rond, mais bien à l'equipolent d'iceluy. Et ceste addition

6. cauaulx *1542*

w. Cf. Serlio, *Tutte le opere d'architettura*, Venice, 1600, p. 79*r*, in his description of the Coliseum, Bk. III: "ne' quai gradi ci sono alcuni canaletti da alto a basso per scolare le acque, & anco per le orine..."

desditz deux costez s'appelloit le *proscene,* lequel estoit [õ iii] faict du mesme artifice et architecture que la galerie frontale. De columne en columne (hors mises celles qui estoient près de la grande porte, nommée *regia,* et aussi celles qui estoient au droict des maisonnettes, desquelles sailloient les joueurs), y avoit à la haulteur de trois piedz ou environ ung appuy de massonnerie faict à cleres veues, pour y mettre quelques personnes privées, ou feussent seigneurs estrangiers ou aultres princes ausquelz on faisoit cest honneur de regarder la scene. Et continuoit cesditz appuys jusques aux deux costez et proscenes (en comprenant toutesfois iceulx) et s'appelloit cela *podium;* auquel lieu Neron le plus souvent se souloit mettre pour regarder les jeux, aulcunesfoys en secret que l'on ne le veoit point, aulcunes[õ iii *v*]fois appuyé sur ledit *podium* pour estre plus à son ayse, comme plus amplement declairerons cy après.[x]

Les aornementz des theatres

Aux theatres, les anciens Græcz applicquoient des vaisseaulx de fonte bien resonantz, posez dans des pertuys propres tant aux paroitz d'en hault comme aux intervalles des degrez, dans lesquelz vaisseaulx la voix des joueurs se formoit si bien qu'elle en estoit plus intelligible et gracieuse. Les Romains n'ont guieres usé de cela, au moins que j'en aye leu. L'on espandoit (dit Pline)[y] de la fleur de saffran bastard par le theatre, plustost pour aornement et plaisir des yeux que pour bonne odeur. [õ iiii]

Au-dessus dudit theatre et cirque ou amphitheatre estoient des voylles estandues pour garder les spectateurs de l'ardeur du soleil, et estoient ycelles voylles estandues sus des cordes attachées à des grandes solives debout, enclavées dans l'edifice à la maniere que demonstre l'architecteur Sebastian Serlio au protraict de l'amphitheatre de Rome et à celuy de Pole.[z] Neron fit paindre d'azur les voylles du theatre et au-dessus semer d'estoilles[7] d'or, pour beaulté comme d'ung ciel.[aa] Caligula, à la grand ardeur du soleil, fit pour son plaisir abaisser et oster lesditz voylles, affin de nuyre au peuple, et defendoit que nul feust si hardy de partir du lieu.[bb]

7. *for* des estoilles?

x. Cf. Suetonius, Nero, XII, 2: "Nam perraro praesidere, ceterum accubans, parvis primum foraminibus, deinde toto podio adaperto spectare consueverat."

y. Cf. Pliny, *Natural History,* XXI. 6 (17), "tritum ad theatra replenda..."; ed. Mayhoff, Leipzig: Teubner, 1892, III, 391.

z. The amphitheater of Rome is described in Bk. III, pp. 78*v*–81*r* (edition of Venice, 1600); that of Pola, Bk. III, pp. 85*r*–86*v*. I have found no specific reference to these beams; Estienne may be referring only to the drawings.

aa. Unidentified.

bb. Cf. Suetonius, Gaius Caligula, XXVI, 5: "Gladiatorio munere reductis interdum flagrantissimo sole velis emitti quemquam vetabat..."

L'on faisoit au bas dudit theatre ung lieu, qu'ilz appelloient *tribunal*, [õ iiii *v*] pour les preteurs et curateurs du jeu, aussi pour les juges. En l'orchestre l'on tappissoit les sieges et y mettoit-on des aornementz pour les senateurs et pour le prince, s'il luy plaisoit estre en ce lieu.

Les aornementz de la scene

La scene estoit bien paincte et parée, et y mettoit-on des statues entre les columnes. S'il n'y avoit point de pulpite en ladicte scene, on y en mettoit ung de bois. Semblablement au costé droit on y mettoit l'ymaige de Bacchus et à l'aultre l'ymaige du[8] dieu en l'honneur de qui les jeux se faisoient. [õ v]

Si la scene estoit pour jouer satyre, on l'accoustroit d'arbres, de cavernes, de montaigne et choses agrestes faictes en ouvraige de jardinerie bien jolyement et mygnonnement.

La scene comique: les edifices desquelz sailloient les joueurs estoient faictz en villaige à petites maisonnettes, ou bien bastimentz communs avec fenestraiges à la mode commune. Car selon l'argument on faisoit l'aornement de la scene. Et aux costez desdictes maisons y avoit des yssues faictes comme petites rues ou allées vuydes sans huysserie, comme ruelles; à l'une desquelles alloient les joueurs quand ilz se vouloient retirer au marché. De l'aultre ilz retournoient quand ilz venoient de la ville ou d'aultre lieu que de leur logis. [õ v *v*] Au meilleu y avoit ung grand portail divisé en deux, pour aornement et à plaisir.

Si la scene estoit pour une tragedie, l'on faisoit plus grand appareil et accoustrement qu'à la comique ou satyrique. Et y avoit columnes sumptueuses, richement accoustrées et aornées, avec maisons faictes en forme de chasteaulx et villes, force medales, statues et accoustrementz royaulx. La porte du meilleu, qu'ilz nommoient *regia*, estoit comme ung arc triumphal, de laquelle sortoient gens à cheval et grande compaignie de personnes. Aux costez dudict arc estoient les lieux ditz *hospitalia*, assçavoir les maisons. Aux coings, vers les lieux de la scene qui demeuroient pour aornement, estoy[õ vi]ent deux machines comme tours triangulaires, dans lesquelles se faisoyent les fainctes, comme quand il failloit quelque pluye, ou tonnoirre, ou quelque advenement des dieux, et telles choses. Cesdictes tours se changeoient, muoient, et tournoient face à mesmes que les scenes se changeoient et varioient.

Comme estoit assis le peuple au theatre ou amphitheatre, selon ses degrez

Pour eviter confusion (comme j'ay dit), il fut ordonné par arrest du senat que chascun auroit son lieu pour se asseoir au theatre, amphitheatre, ou lieu publicque de spectacle, et personnaiges creez [õ vi *v*] et decernez

8. de *1542*

pour garder que nul s'assist à la place d'ung aultre. Et quand ung senateur ou chevalier viendroit, fut conduict par aulcuns (ainsi que font les bedeaux aux actes publiques en l'université de Paris) jusque en son lieu.

Le premier ordre en l'orchestre, et près d'icelle, estoit pour le prince et les senateurs; toutesfois que le prince se mettoit où il luy[9] plaisoit. Car Auguste regardoit aulcunesfoys des cenacles de ses amys quand c'estoit au cirque; et Neron se mettoit le plus souvent au perron et appuy de la scene entre les columnes (comme dict est), appellé *podium*, et estoit courbé ou à son seand sur ung lict bas, regardant par certains treilliz qui estoient au-devant de luy.[cc] Car il prenoit plaisir luy-mesmes (comme [õ vii] dict est) à jouer aulcunesfois, et quand il luy venoit en fantaisie ouvroit tout le perron et se laissoit veoir. Doncques le premier ordre des degrez fut institué pour les senateurs et l'empereur, dont est dit en la vie de Tiberius Cesar que l'on mist des libelles diffamatoires au premier degré de l'orchestre affin qu'il les apperceust plus facilement quand il reviendroit s'asseoir en ce degré.[dd] Et fut en ce temps deffendu que nul des ambassadeurs d'estrange pays s'y vint asseoir, toutesfoys que Claude Cesar laissa les ambassadeurs d'Alemaigne s'y asseoir. Mais ce fut pource que quand ilz arriverent au theatre, le bedeau par ignorance les avoit mis entre le peuple et aux sieges populaires; mais voyans que les ambassadeurs des Partiens et Armeni-[õ vii *v*]ens estoient assis entre les senateurs, ilz descendirent de leur place et s'y asseirent comme les aultres, disantz qu'ilz n'estoient de riens moindres n'inferieurs aux aultres; ce que permist facilement ledict Cesar pour leur simplicité et bonne foy.[ee]

Les chevaliers Romains avoient ung coing à part eulx au theatre, par ordonnance; et appelloient le coing une partie des degrez dudict theatre ou amphitheatre, divisée par allée de costé et d'aultre comme dict est cy-dessus. Vray est que Caligula, fasché et pour semer noyse pour son plaisir entre le commun et les gentilzhommes ou chevaliers, bailla et distribua les dismes plustost qu'il n'estoit de raison, et par ce moyen sema discord entre le peuple et l'ordre de chevalerie; à cause dequoy le peuple jusque aux [õ viii] infimes[10] se asseoit aux degrez des chevaliers.[ff] Mais cela fut contre l'ordonnance du senat.

9. il il luy *1542* 10. infinies *1542*; *cf. note ff.*

cc. *Ibid.*, Divus Augustus, XLV, 1: "Ipse circenses ex amicorum fere libertorumque cenaculis spectabat..." On Nero, see note x. above.

dd. *Ibid.*, Tiberius, LXVI, 1: "vel per libellos in orchestra positos ingerente."

ee. *Ibid.*, Divus Claudius, XXV, 4: "Germanorum legatis in orchestra sedere permisit, simplicitate eorum et fiducia commotus, quod in popularia deducti, cum animadvertissent Parthos et Armenios sedentis in senatu, ad eadem loca sponte transierant, nihilo deteriorem virtutem aut condicionem suam praedicantes."

ff. *Ibid.*, Caligula, XXVI, 4: "Scaenicis ludis, inter plebem et equitem causam discordiarum ferens, decimas maturius dabat, ut equestria ab infimo quoque occuparentur."

Le commun peuple avoit aussi ung coing à part. Les hommes du peuple qui estoient mariez avoient ung ordre à part. Les pretextes (c'est-à-dire les jeunes gens qui commençoient avoir dignité au senat) avoient leur coing semblablement separé, auprès duquel estoit le coing des pedagogues et maistres d'escoles. Et estoit l'ordonnance que nul portant le dueil s'assist au meilleu des degrez. Les degrez et coingz pour les femmes estoient au hault du theatre; ausquelles n'estoit permis de regarder les gladiateurs. Les vierges vestables seules avoyent ung lieu à part au theatre separé des aultres, et estoient auprès du tribunal [õ viii *v*] du preteur; ausquelles n'estoit licite veoir les athletes ou combatz et joustes, jaçoit que Neron puis après leur eust permis.[gg]

Ces choses premises et entendues (lecteur), me semble maintenant bien facile l'intelligence, non seulement de la comedie qui s'ensuyt, mais encores des aultres que (Dieu aydant) avons espoir vous traduire par bon loysir.

gg. Ibid., Nero, XII, 4: "Ad athletarum spectaculum invitavit et virgines Vestales, quia Olympiae quoque Cereris sacerdotibus spectare conceditur."

GUILLAUME BOUCHETEL

DEDICATION TO EURIPIDES' *Hecuba*

1544

TEXT:

(1550) La Tragedie d'Evripide, nommee Hecvba: Traduicte de Grec en rhythme Francoise, dediee au Roy. A Paris. De l'imprimerie de Rob. Estienne, Imprimeur du Roy. M.D.L. Avec privilege dv Roy. [B.N., Paris.]

[First edition, Paris: Robert Estienne, 1544; cf. Cat. Rothschild, No. 1060, and Vol. V, "Additions et Corrections," p. 192, where the attribution to Bouchetel (cf. below) is accepted. On the 1550 ed., see Tchemerzine, I, 343; also listed by British Museum. The copy at the B.N. has the words "par Lazare de Baif" written in ink on the t.p.]

Within a few years of its appearance in 1544 and its reprinting in 1550, this anonymous translation of Euripides' *Hecuba* was attributed to two different authors. In 1551, in his *Epistre à Mellin de Saint-Gelais sur l'immortalité des poëtes françois*, François Habert attributed a translation of Euripides, presumably this one, to Guillaume Bouchetel:

> Melpomene le los ne voulut faire
> De *Bouchetel*, le Royal Secretaire,
> Qui fait si bien Euripide tonner
> En vers François, qu'on doit s'en estonner...[1]

In 1555, in his *Art poëtique*, Jacques Peletier du Mans spoke of "l'Hecubé d'Euripidé, par Lazaré Débaïf."[2] This double attribution persisted through the centuries. For Bouchetel there was the support, in 1585, of the famous bibliographer Du Verdier, who said that "Guillaume Bouchetel Secretaire de Finances du Roy François Premier a traduit de Grec en rime Françoise la Tragedie d'Euripide nommée Hecuba: impr. à Paris 8. par Robert Estienne 1550." This attribution was noted and accepted, in the eighteenth century, by Michael Maittaire in the *Annales Typographici*.[3] For Lazare de Baïf, on the other hand, there was the support of Du Verdier's rival, La Croix du Maine, in 1584:[4]

> Lazare de Baif a traduit de Grec en Vers François l'Electra de Sophocle, impr. à Paris 1537. par Estienne Roffet, & l'Hecuba d'Euripide, impr. à Paris 1550. par Robert Estienne. Il n'a voulu mettre son nom à pas une de ces deux traductions, sinon qu'il se voit dans l'Electra,

[1] Reprinted by Niceron, *Mémoires*, XXXIII, 195.

[2] Ed. Boulanger, Paris, 1930, p. 192.

[3] Vol. III (Hagae-Comitum, 1725), pp. 372 and 593.

[4] Quoted by Maittaire, *op. cit.*, III, 372.

> compris dans les lettres capitales d'un dizain; & dans l'Hecuba, par sa devise Latine seulement, qui est *Rerum vices*.

Later, in 1790, it was again accepted by R. Duclos in his *Dictionnaire bibliographique*, which lists "La Tragédie d'EURIPIDE, nommée *Hécuba*; trad. du grec en rhytme françoise par Lazare de Bayf. Paris, Robert Estienne, 1544 ou 1550. in-8."[5]

Indeed, during the eighteenth century a whole group of scholars attributed translations to both Baïf and Bouchetel—probably because they copied one from the other. The earliest of these texts that I have examined, Maupoint's *Biblioteque des Theatres* of 1733, contains the following entries:

> "*Hecuba*. 1537. Par Lazare de Baïf.
> *Vne autre*. Par Bouchetel en 1550."

It will be noted that the date of Baïf's translation of Sophocles' *Electra* is wrongly assigned to his supposed translation of the *Hecuba*.[6] The same erroneous attribution of a *Hecuba* of 1537 to Baïf and the correct designation of Bouchetel for the 1550 edition occur in other works, e.g. Léris's *Dictionnaire portatif des théatres* of 1754 and Clément's *Anecdotes dramatiques* of 1775.[7]

In modern times, Baïf has most generally been thought to be the author; thus Lucien Pinvert treats the publication of this work in his life of Baïf[8] and as late as 1922 he repeats the attribution in his edition of Jacques Grévin's works.[9]

But already in 1910 René Sturel had clearly demonstrated that Bouchetel was the author.[10] Sturel pointed out the weakness of La Croix du Maine's argument based on the device *Rerum vices* and of Pinvert's argument based on an interpretation of the dedicatory epistle. He produced evidence to show that both the biographical facts contained in the epistle

[5] Paris: Cailleau et Fils, 1790, I, 420.

[6] Paris: Prault, 1733, p. 158.

[7] Antoine de Léris, *Dictionnaire portatif des théatres*, Paris: Jombert, 1754, pp. 171, 398; Jean Marie Bernard Clément, *Anecdotes dramatiques*, Paris: Veuve Duchesne, 1775, I, 420 and III, 62.

[8] Paris: Fontemoing, 1900, pp. 83, 87, 103.

[9] Paris: Garnier, 1922, p. 1 of the "Notes," where he attributes the 1544 edition to Baïf and the 1550 edition to Bouchetel!

[10] "A Propos d'un manuscrit du Musée Condé," *Mélanges offerts à M. Emile Chatelain*, Paris: Champion, 1910, pp. 575–83; cf. Sturel, "Essai sur les traductions du théâtre grec en français avant 1550," *Revue d'histoire littéraire de la France*, XX (1913), 280–96.

and the character of the translation itself made it likely that Bouchetel was the author. This attribution has since been generally accepted.[11]

[A. ij.] AU ROY MON SOUVERAIN SEIGNEUR

Gorgias Leontin, homme de grand nom entre les anciens qui ont esté celebrez par leurs lettres et sçavoir, disoit que la tragedie est une tromperie et deception, par laquelle celuy qui trompe est plus juste que celuy qui ne trompe pas, et celuy qui est trompé plus sage que celuy qui n'est point trompé: chose qui semble contre raison, et toutesfois est veritable. Car la tragedie nous trompe et deçoit en ce que bien souvent elle traicte argumens fabuleux si sagement controuvez que nous cuidons qu'ils soyent veritables. Or celuy qui trompe ung autre, et par ceste tromperie luy monstre et enseigne ce qui[1] luy est proffitable ou nuysible, bon ou mauvais, honneste ou deshonneste, est sans doubte plus juste que celuy qui n'ha pouvoir ou vouloir de ce faire.[a] Car il n'y a point d'acte plus vertueux ne tant convenable à l'homme que de bien merir et proffiter à la communaulté des autres. D'autre part, celuy à qui par la fiction de la tragedie demeure la congnoissance de vice et de vertu et de bien et de mal est beaucoup plus sage et advisé en tous ses affaires que celuy qui, pour n'avoir esté si heureusement trompé, n'ha ceste cognoissance. Et comme l'on voit, la coustume des poetes, premiers aucteurs et inventeurs de la philosophie, a tousjours esté de couvrir et cacher soubs le voile des fables la verité des choses qu'ils vouloyent enseigner, ou bien mesler le plaisir qu'on ha de leur ingenieuse fiction avec bons et proffitables documens. Et pour ce dit Horace que le poete apprend aux hommes à honnestement parler, instruit l'en[A. ij. *v*]tendement de bons enseignemens, reprend les vices, et loue

[11] Cf. Félix Gaiffe in his edition of Sebillet's *Art poëtique*, Paris: Droz, 1932, p. ix, n. (2), where Gaiffe also points out that the translation was at one time, by Colletet, attributed to Sebillet.

1. qu'il *1550*

a. The first sentence of the passage is quoted by Plutarch, "How the Young Man Should Study Poetry," in *Moralia*, I, 79: "... and Gorgias called tragedy a deception wherein he who deceives is more honest than he who does not, and he who is deceived is wiser than he who is not deceived." But Bouchetel probably took the whole passage from Erasmus, *Apophthegmata*, Bk. VIII, which supplies the interpretation: "Dicebat [Gorgias] tragœdiam esse deceptionem, qua qui alterum decepisset, iustior esset eo qui non decepisset: & qui deceptus esset, sapientior foret eo qui non esset deceptus. Fallit enim tragœdia tractans argumenta conficta, sed adeo scite, ut uera credantur. Iustior autem ille uidetur qui fallendo prodest: & sapientior est qui per fictas fabulas discit, quid sit turpe, quid sit honestum. Refert Plutarchus de poëtis audiendis" (ed. Basel, 1539, pp. 782–83).

la vertu.[b] Et oultre plus nous donne congnoissance de l'advenir par exemples du passé, et en adversité et affliction console nostre esprit troublé.

Mais entre tous, il semble que les tragicques, ainsi qu'ils surpassent tous autres escripts en haulteur de style, grandeur d'argumens, et gravité de sentences, aussi ont-ils plus amené de proffit aux hommes, d'autant qu'ils ont prins à instruire et enseigner les plus grans et ceulx-là que fortune a plus haultement eslevez, comme princes et roys; dont ils ont amené grand proffit à la posterité, laissant mesmement par escript monumens de si grande utilité comme l'instruction d'ung bon prince, laquelle se peult tirer des tragedies. Car à ces fins ont-elles esté premierement inventées, pour remonstrer aux roys et grans seigneurs l'incertitude et lubrique instabilité des choses temporelles, afin qu'ils n'ayent confiance qu'en la seule vertu. Ce qu'ils peuvent veoir et entendre par les grans inconveniens, miseres et calamitez qui autresfois sont advenues à ceulx qui ont esté en fortune semblable. Car ce sont les propres argumens des tragedies, comme monstra Euripide, lequel estant en Macedoine le roy Archelaus pria d'escrire une tragedie de luy; et le poete luy refusa, priant aux dieux que jamais chose ne luy advint qui peust estre bon argument d'escrire une tragedie.[c] Pource que ce ne sont que pleurs, captivitez, ruines et desolations de grans princes, et quelquefois des plus vertueux. Ce qui sert aux successeurs, afin qu'en prosperité ils ne s'eslevent par trop et provoquent malheur en abusant de leur fortune; et aussi en adversité n'ayent le cueur abaissé ne failly, à l'exemple de plusieurs vertueux princes qui [A. iij.] jamais pour quelque envie que fortune ait porté à leur gloire, et pour quelque affliction qu'ils ayent soustenue, n'ont aucunement flechy; laissant preuve à la posterité que la vertu peult bien estre affligée mais non vaincue—comme, Syre, on le peult veritablement et sans flaterie dire de vous.

Or est-il, Syre, que quelques jours passez, me retrouvant en ma petite maison, mes enfans, tant pour me faire apparoir du labeur de leur estude que pour me donner plaisir et recreation, m'apportoyent chascun jour la lecture qui leur estoit faicte par leur precepteur de la tragedie d'Euripide denommée *Hecuba*, me la rendant de mot à mot de Grec en Latin. Laquelle pour la sublimité du style et gravité des sentences que je y trouvay, il me prinst envie, Syre, de la mettre en vostre langue Françoise, seulement pour

b. Horace, *Epistles*, II.i.126 ff.

c. Related by Diomedes, *Artis grammaticae*, Bk. III (ed. Keil, *Grammatici Latini*, Vol. I, Leipzig: Teubner, 1857, p. 488); "ideoque Euripides petente Archelao rege ut de se tragoediam scriberet abnuit ac precatus est ne accideret Archelao aliquid tragoediae proprium, ostendens nihil aliud esse tragoediam quam miseriarum conprehensionem." Diomedes was printed many times in the 15th and 16th centuries, notably (with Donatus) by Badius, Paris, 1527. The anecdote about Archelaus was included in various collections during the century and was repeated in numerous literary discussions.

occuper ce peu de temps de repos à quelque honneste exercice. Et depuis vous voyant, Syre, travaillé de maladie, pour vous donner quelque recreation je prins la hardiesse de vous lire le commencement que j'en avoye tourné; que benignement vous ouistes et me commandastes l'achever. Ce que j'ay faict, non tant pour l'asseurance que j'ay eue de le sçavoir bien faire, congnoissant ma foible puissance, que pour le desir de vous obeir. Car trop plus m'a aidé l'efficace de vostre commandement que ne m'a empesché la congnoissance de mon infirmité au parachevement de la traduction de ceste tragedie. Laquelle, Syre, très humblement je vous presente, en esperance que de vostre accoustumée bonté et benignité prendrez en gré le service de celuy qui n'a en cest œuvre pretendu autre louange ny loyer fors seulement de vous donner contentement et plaisir.

JACQUES PELETIER DU MANS

PREFACES TO HORACE'S *Ars Poetica*

1545

TEXT:

L'Art poetiqve d'Horace, traduit en Vers Francois par Iacques Peletier du Mans, recongnu par l'auteur depuis la premiere impression. Moins & meilleur. Imprimé a Paris par Michel de Vascosan, au mois d'Aoust. Auec priuilege de la Court. M.D.XLV. [B.N., Paris.]
[Cf. Graesse, III, 368; Tchemerzine, IX, 146.]

In 1932, when André Boulanger published his edition of Peletier's *Art poëtique*, he knew only the 1545 edition of the same author's Horace; an edition of 1544, referred to by La Croix du Maine, had never been discovered. But many years earlier Graesse had listed the first edition of 1541, and in 1933 Tchemerzine published a description and a title page of that edition, "Paris en la rue des Carmes a l'enseigne de l'homme Sauluage" (Tchemerzine, IX, 146). No location is given for this volume, which is listed as "Très rare." It is apparently this edition to which Peletier refers on the title page of the second edition, 1545. Tchemerzine gives no indication as to whether the two prefaces to the Horace, printed below, were included in the 1541 edition, except the negative evidence contained in the fact that he mentions the dedication to Perot in the 1545 edition and does not mention it in connection with the 1541 edition. The Horace was again printed in 1584 with corrections by Luc de la Porte. On Peletier's life and works, see the Boulanger edition of the *Art poëtique* (Paris: Les Belles Lettres, 1932, pp. 7–35), which also prints the dedication to Perot (pp. 227–30), as does the Abbé Clément Jugé in his *Jacques Peletier du Mans* (Paris: Lemerre, 1907, pp. 423–27); see also Ph. Aug. Becker, *Aus Frankreichs Frührenaissance* (Munich, 1927), pp. 177–206.

[A ij] AU LECTEUR

Lecteur, tu trouveras en ce livret l'orthographe Françoise aucunement diverse de celle qui est vulgairement prattiquée. A cette cause t'a eté premis ce petit avertissement, pour en passant te declairer les principalles raisons de l'auteur. L'une est que tout ainsi que la parolle est significative de la pensée, semblablement l'orthographe de la parolle, à laquelle elle doit obeir fidelement; de sorte que ecrire autrement qu'on ne prononce est comme si on parloit autrement qu'on ne pense. L'autre raison, qui depend de la premiere, est pour eviter superfluité, laquelle sans ce qu'en toutes choses est reprenable tient nostre langue Françoise en subgetion, si bien qu'elle la garde de passer aux nations etranges, qui pour le grand entassement de lettres ne la peuent prononcer ni apprendre s'ilz ne sont sur les lieux. La tierce raison est pour commencer à regler et mettre au net notre langage, et faire à tout pouoir que prononciation pareille n'ait orthographe diverse; qui est le plus expeditif moien qui puisse aquerir honneur et majesté à une langue, comme on voit de la Greque et de la Latine, desquelles l'orthographe est la prononciation mesme sinon qu'elle est mue. Il est bien vrai que telle en[A ij *v*]treprise ne se peut pas achever ni resoudre si à coup; et mesmes n'a semblé bon à l'auteur d'observer sa fantaisie de point en point et à la rigueur, bien congnoissant que trop soudaines mutations ne s'acceptent pas volontiers, mais a eté content d'ouvrir le chemin par le plus facile et commun endroit en attendant que le temps, qui addoussit et consomme toutes choses, donne peu à peu à congnoitre combien doit valoir raison artificielle contre abus irregulier.

Atant te suffira, ami lecteur, n'etant ici le lieu de deduire toutes les raisons à ce appartenantes; joint que jà ont eté pour la plus grand part decouvertes par autres bien entenduz, ainsi que tu puis voir à ce qu'ilz en ont publié.[a] Cependant tu prendras en gré ce qu'on fait pour le mieux et en faveur de notre langue Françoise.

[A iij] A TRÈS VERTUEUX ET NOBLE HOMME CRETOFLE PEROT,[b] ECUIER SENESCHAL DU MAINE, JACQUES PELETIER SALUT

Si de bien près on veut considerer le stile des ecrivains du temps present, seigneur de renom, on voirra clairement qu'ilz n'approchent pas de celle copieuse vehemence et gracieuse proprieté qu'on voit luire ès auteurs anciens. Et toutesfois on ne sauroit raisonnablement dire que ce fut faute de grand esprit; car si nous voulons mettre en conte les personnages qui ont nagueres flori et florissent encores de present, nous trouverons que notre secle est en cetui egard de bien peu redevable à l'ancienneté. Mais la principalle raison et plus apparente, à mon jugement, qui nous ote le merite de vrai honneur est le mepris et contennement de notre langue native, laquelle nous laissons arriere pour entretenir la langue Greque et la langue Latine, consumans tout notre temps en l'exercice d'icelles. Au moyen de quoi nous en voions plusieurs, autrement très ingenieux et doctes, lesquelz pour telle inusitation et nonchaloir commettent erreurs lours et insupportables, non pas en parler quotidien seulement mais aussi

a. Several works on the reform of French spelling had already appeared, e.g. Geoffroy Tory, *Champfleury*, 1526; Anonymous, *Briefue doctrine pour deuement escripre selon la propriete du langaige francoys*, 1533; Meigret, *Traitè touchant le commun vsage de l'escriture Françoise*, 1542. On the whole question, see Brunot, *Histoire de la Langue française*, Vol. II (Paris: Colin, 1906), pp. 93 ff.

b. Unidentified.

en composition Françoise; si bien qu'ilz semblent prendre [A iij *v*] plaisir exprès à oublier leur propre et principal langage.

Je seroie à bon droit estimé impudent calomniateur et pour vrai depourveu de sens commun si je vouloie deprimer ces deux tant celebres et honnorables langues Latine et Greque, ausquelles sans controverse (et singulierement à la Greque) nous devons toute la congnoissance des disciplines et la meilleure part des choses memorables du temps passé. Et tant suis loing de telle intention que je soutiens estre impossible proprement parler ni correctement ecrire notre langue sans aquisition de toutes deux; ou bien, affin que ne soie trop rigoreux estimateur des choses, de la Latine pour le moins. Car sans ce que la plus grand partie de notre phrase et de noz termes vulgaires est tirée des langues susdictes, encores quant à l'invention et disposition, lesquelles vertuz ne s'aquierent que par long usage et continuation de lire, c'est chose toute receue et certaine qu'homme ne sauroit rien ecrire qui lui peut demeurer à honneur et venir en commendation vers la posterité sans l'aide et appui des livres Grecz et Latins. Mais je veux bien dire qu'à une langue peregrine il ne faut faire si grand honneur que de la requeillir et priser pour regetter et contenner la sienne domestique. J'ai pour mes garens les anciens Rommains, lesquelz bien qu'ilz eussent en sin[A iiij]guliere recommendation la langue Greque, toutesfois après i avoir emploié un etude certain se retiroint à leur enseigne et s'appliquoint à illustrer et enrichir leur demaine hereditaire, redigeans les preceptes philosophiques non en autre langage que le leur propre, et demeurans contens d'entendre la langue aquisitive. Et tellement exploiterent en leur entreprise que Ciceron, prince d'eloquence Rommaine, se vente que la philosophie qu'ilz avoint empruntée des Grecz est plus ornément et copieusement ecritte en Latin qu'en Grec.[c] Et lui de sa part s'i gouverna si bien qu'à peine sauroit-on juger lequel des deux a donné plus de lumiere et dignité, ou le Latin à la philosophie ou la philosophie au Latin. A semblable Jule Cesar, qui fut monarque du monde, n'avoit moindre solicitude et affection d'amplifier l'usance de sa langue que de dilater les fins de l'empire Rommain.[d]

J'ai mesmement pour mes auteurs Petrarque et Bocace, deux hommes jadis de grande erudition et savoir, lesquelz ont voulu faire temoignage de leur doctrine en ecrivant en leur Touscan. Autant en est des souverains poetes Dante, Sannazar, aussi Italiens; lesquelz, bien qu'ilz fussent parfondement appris en langue Latine, ont eu neantmoins ce jugement qu'il vaut mieux exceller en une fonction, pourveu que de soi-mesme soit hon-

c. Cicero, *De Finibus* I.ii–iii and III.ii.5.

d. This is apparently a general reference to Caesar's writings in Latin, although it may refer more specifically to the lost *De Analogia*.

neste et [A iiij *v*] digne d'homme liberal, qu'en l'abandonnant estre seulement mediocre en un autre, bien que plus estimable. Il est bien vrai que ces auteurs-là ont aussi voulu ecrire en Latin pour la majesté et excellence d'icelui; ce qui ne leur doit moienner petite louange. Car comme c'est une preeminence incomparable d'avoir esprit naturel plus qu'un autre, ainsi doit-on reputer l'homme mal né et ingrat à soi-mesme lequel, se congnoissant capable de plusieurs louables professions, ne s'applique seulement qu'à une.

Mais quant à ceux qui totalement se vouent et adonnent à une langue peregrine (j'entens peregrine pour le respect de la domestique), il me semble qu'il ne leur est possible d'atteindre à celle naïve perfection des anciens non plus qu'à l'art d'exprimer Nature, quelque ressemblance qu'il i pretende. Partant ne puis non grandement louer plusieurs nobles espriz de notre temps, lesquelz se sont etudiez à faire valoir notre langue Françoise, laquelle n'a pas long temps commença à s'anoblir par le moien des *Illustrations de Gaule et Singularitez de Troie*, composées par Jan le Maire de Belges,[e] excellent historiographe François et digne d'estre leu plus que nul qui ait ecrit ci davant. Et maintenant elle prend un très beau et riche accroissement souz notre très Chretien roi François, lequel par sa liberalité roialle en faveur des [A v] muses s'efforce de faire renaitre celui secle très heureux auquel, souz Auguste et Mecenas à Romme, florissoint Virgile, Horace, Ovide, Tibulle, et autres poetes Latins; tellement qu'à voir la fleur où ell' est de present, il faut croire pour tout seur que si on procede tousjours si bien, nous la voirrons de brief en bonne maturité, de sorte qu'elle suppeditera la langue Italienne et Espagnole, d'autant que les François en religion et bonnes meurs surpassent les autres nations.

Et souverainement cela se pourra parfaire et mettre à chef moiennant notre poesie Françoise, à laquelle plusieurs ont de cetui temps si courageusement aspiré qu'il leur eut eté facile d'i parvenir ne fut la persuasion qu'ilz ont eue d'i estre desja parvenuz. Or n'i a-il meilleur moien d'i atteindre que de congnoitre les vices d'icelle pour les eviter et les vertuz pour les observer, combien qu'à peu près on se puisse contenter de l'un d'iceux; pource que congnu l'un de deux contraires, facilement se congnoit l'autre. Sur quoi se semble estre fondé notre present auteur Horace; car veritablement il n'a pas tant compris les vertuz et proprietez d'icelle comme les vices et abus, lesquelz il a entierement declairez en cetui livre trop plus precieux que grand. Et si on le veut bien gouter et prattiquer, chacun ne sera si hatif de mettre ses ecriz en lumiere sans [A v *v*] meure attente et prevoiance.

Donques souz espoir d'impetrer quelque faveur et aucunement meriter envers ceux qui sont studieux de notre poesie, j'ai translaté cetui livre

e. First edition, 1510.

intitulé l'*Art poetique*, et l'ai voulu approprier à icelle notre poesie Françoise entant qu'ai peu sauver l'integrité du sens. Il est vrai qu'on i trouvera quelques passages qui ne servent pas beaucoup à notre vulgaire, comme quant il parle du pié iambe, du chore des tragedies, et de quelques autres specialitez. Mais j'ai mieux aimé servir au bien publiq en communicant plusieurs belles traditions, sans lesquelles n'est aucunement possible d'ouvrer en poesie, que non pas qu'elles demeurassent cachées pour la sugetion de deux ou trois endroiz, combien qu'ilz ne soint du tout inutiles. Car si le lecteur est de bon jugement, il en pourra bien faire son profit en notre François mesme.

Ce mien labeur, de pieça entrepris et quelque temps intermis, a eté par moi nagueres repris et achevé. Et sur le point de le mettre en evidence, votre humanité singuliere, noble seigneur, et le plaisir que vous prenez ès choses qui concernent l'anoblissement et decoration de l'esprit, selon le loisir que vous ottroient les negoces civilz et urgens exercices de votre juridiction, m'ont donné l'avis, confermé le propos, et augmenté le courage de le vous addresser et [A vi] dedier. Puis le vrai point qui m'asseure qu'il sera de vous favorablement receu est que l'invention provient d'un auteur lequel par sus tous a ecrit exactement et excellé en brieveté sentencieuse, comme votre parfaict jugement pourra congnoitre.

HUGUES SALEL

DEDICATORY EPISTLE TO HOMER'S *Iliad*

1545

TEXT:

Les Dix Premiers Livres de l'Iliade d'Homere, Prince des poetes: Traduictz en vers Francois, par M. Hugues Salel, de la chambre du Roy, & Abbé de S. Cheron. Avec privilege dv Roy. On les vent à Paris, au Palais en la Gallerie, pres la Chancellerie, en la boutique de Vincent Sertenas. 1545. [Pierpont Morgan Library.]

[Cf. Brunet, III, 289, and Fairfax Murray, I, 261–62, No. 260.]

Although the first two books of Salel's translation of the *Iliad* appeared in Lyon in 1542, the "Epistre de Dame Poésie" did not appear until the publication of the first ten books in 1545. Subsequently it preceded all the many editions of the work which, through the century, was frequently revised and augmented; the "Epistre" itself was unchanged, and the edition of Paris: Gautier, 1574, shows no significant differences from the first edition. Salel's contemporaries admired his work wholeheartedly, and his name frequently appears in lists of the great littérateurs of the century. The history of the editions is given by Brunet (*loc. cit.*) and by Bergounioux in his *Un Précurseur de la Pléiade: Hugues Salel de Cazals-en-Quercy* (*1504–1553*) (Paris et Toulouse: Editions Occitania, 1929, pp. 122–25). Bergounioux also prints the prefatory epistle (pp. 279–93). Philipp August Becker, in an article on "Hugues Salel (1503–1553)," *Zeitschrift für französische Sprache und Litteratur*, LV (1932), 475–512, indicates Salel's use of Quintilian and the anonymous *Vita Homeri* as sources.

[a iij] EPISTRE DE DAME POESIE AU TRÈS CHRESTIEN ROY FRANÇOIS, PREMIER DE CE NOM, SUR LA TRADUCTION D'HOMERE, PAR SALEL

Veu le grand faix que sur tes bras soubstiens,
Roy très puissant, le plus grand des Chrestiens,
Tant pour la guerre, à bon droict commencée,
Contre celuy qui t'a la foy faulsée,[a]
Que pour le soing où ton esprit s'applique
A gouverner ce beau peuple Gallique
Qui s'esjouyst et tient à bien bon heur
D'avoir de Dieu tel roy, tel gouverneur;
Si j'entreprens te faire la lecture
De quelque basse et legere escripture,

a. In 1545, Francis I was at war with Henry VIII of England, who had been allied with Charles V.

Je doubte fort de faillir grandement,
Bien cognoissant que ton entendement,
Tousjours repeu de celeste viande,
Ne peult gouster chose qui ne soit grande.
Mais quand je voy après que je suis celle
En qui reluist souvent quelque estincelle
De ta faveur (me donnant privaulté
De conferer avec ta royaulté),
Je me resoulz, saichant que qui s'avance
Trop hardyment n'entend pas ta puissance,
Mais qui trop crainct et n'est devant toy seur
Ignore aussi ta clemence et doulceur. [a iij *v*]
J'ay alaicté et nourry, comme mere,
Plusieurs enfans, entre lesquelz Homere
Fut le premier, par qui dame Nature
Feist aux humains liberale ouverture
De ses secretz; et si très bien l'apprit
Qu'on n'a sceu veoir depuis pareil esprit
Representer les mysteres du monde
Le mieulx au vif. Car la chose profonde,
Il la traictoit haultement, et la basse
Très proprement et non sans grande grace.[b]
Si qu'on peult dire en voyant son ouvraige
Qu'il est, luy seul, de Nature l'imaige;
Dont j'ay acquis partout louange telle
Que j'en demeure à jamais immortelle,
Et tous mes filz jusqu'au ciel extollez.
C'est l'Ocean[c] d'où sont ainsi coulez
Les clairs ruysseaulx, pour l'esprit arrouser
De bon sçavoir et puys le disposer
A la vertu, le rendant susceptible
Du bien parfaict, hault et incorruptible.
De la liqueur de ceste claire source
Grecs et Latins, courans à plaine course,
Ont beu grans traictz, d'où sont après yssues
Opinions diversement receues,
Chascun pensant la sienne plus nayfve,
Venant du fonds de ceste source vive.

b. Cf. Quintilian, *Institutes*, X.i.46: "Hunc nemo in magnis rebus sublimitate, in parvis proprietate superaverit."

c. Cf. Quintilian, *Institutes*, *loc. cit.*: "Hic enim, quemadmodum ex Oceano dicit ipse omnium amnium fontiumque cursus initium capere, omnibus eloquentiae partibus exemplum et ortum dedit."

Celuy qui preuve et monstre evidemment
L'ame immortelle a prins ung fondement
En cest autheur.[d] L'autre qui admoneste
Suyvre vertu et tout office honeste
A son recours, comme par ung miracle,
A ses beaulx vers, qui luy servent d'oracle.[e] [a iiij]
Aristippus, de son sens transporté,
Lequel pensoit la seule volupté
Estre le bien où chascun debvoit tendre
Comme au vray but, s'est efforcé d'y prendre
Pied sur les motz couchez en ung passaige,
L'interpretant trop à son advantaige.[f]
Celuy qui donne[g] à la grand' providence
Du Souverain la superintendence
De l'univers, et croit la chose née
Estre subgecte à une destinée,

d. This allusion and the others following to philosophical doctrines seem to have been directly derived by Salel from an anonymous life of Homer which was at the time ascribed to Plutarch. The so-called "Vita Homeri" appeared with editions of Homer from the earliest; e.g., the Bibliothèque nationale lists the edition of Florence, 1488, as containing the "πλουτάρχομ εἰς τὸν βίον τοῦ 'Ομήρου." The Aldine editions of 1504 and 1517 also reprinted the *Vita*, as did many others. Later, scholars contested the attribution to Plutarch and even divided the work into separate treatises, one a life of Homer, the other a study of his poetry. Thus Ernesti, in the last volume (V) of Samuel Clark's edition of the *Homeri Operum* (Leipzig, 1764), prints the second part under the title "De Homeri Poesi incerti auctoris," with the remark: "Hic incipit manifeste nova Disputatio de Homero et eius Carminibus, eaque alius auctoris. Quam omnes veteres editores Homeri cum priori coniungunt sub Plutarchi nomine" (p. 151). I quote this edition with the Latin translation there given. For vss. 49 ff. cf. *De Homeri Poesi*, p. 204: "Inter placita sane Pythagorae et Platonis celeberrimum est, quod sentiunt animam immortalem esse: cui et alas Plato, vt ferunt, attribuit. Quis ergo istud pronunciavit? Homerus, qui inter alia et haec dicit: *Ast anima ex membris volitat Plutonis in aedes.*"

e. *De Homeri Poesi*, pp. 214–15: "Caeterum multis a philosophis de bonorum finibus et felicitate dictis, de hoc inter illos per omnia convenit, quod animae virtus bonorum sit maximum. At Stoici virtutem per sese ad felicitatem sufficere putant, ansa nimirum ex Homericis illis sumpta, in quibus sapientissimum et prudentissimum virum, gloriae causa laboris patientem, ac voluptatis contemnentem finxit."

f. *De Homeri Poesi*, pp. 225–26: "His Epicurus adductus, summum bonum in voluptate posuit. Ad haec, ille ipse Vlysses nonnunquam preciosa et tenera veste induebatur, nonnunquam vero pannis et pera et nunc apud Calypso ocium agebat, nunc ab Iro et Melanthio contumeliis afficiebatur. Hac vitae imagine assumpta, Aristippus non solum cum paupertate et laboribus valde conflictatus est, sed etiam voluptatibus affatim studuit."

g. *De Homeri Poesi*, p. 201: "Caeterum ad Dei mentem providentia et fatum pertinet, de quibus philosophi multa verba fecerunt. Horum autem omnium Homerus occasionem suppeditavit."

Ordre certain qui ne se peult confondre,
Y trouve assez de raisons pour respondre
A ces resveurs qui, contre verité,
Assignent tout à la temerité
Et à ne sçay quel rencontre de corps
S'entrejoignants par discordants accords.
Il n'est passaige en la philosophie,
Tant soit divers, qui ne se fortiffie
Par quelque dict ou sentence notable
De ce poëte. Et qu'il soit veritable,
Thalés le saige, entre les sept Gregeoys
Tant renommé, y lisant quelque foys
Que l'ocean donnoit estre et naissance
A tous les corps, sans autre cognoissance
Soubdainement il discourt et se fonde
Que terre, ciel, et la machine ronde
Jadis par l'eau fut produicte et forgée
Et de sa main humide ainsy rengée.[h]
Xenophanés qui s'efforce d'enquerre
Le vray principe, et dict l'eau et la terre
Estre premiers;[i] puis d'autre opinion
Empedoclés, affermant l'union [a iiij *v*]
Et le debat avoir faict toute chose;[j]
Ung chascun d'eulx sa sentence dispose
Selon qu'il l'a dans Homere trouvée,
Et la maintient veritable et prouvée.
Les mouvementz, les maisons, les distances[k]
Des corps des cieulx, leurs aspectz, leurs puissances,

h. *De Homeri Poesi*, p. 189: "Exordiamur itaque a totius vniversi principio, ac generatione, quam Thales Milesius ad aquae substantiam refert, et videamus num Homerus primus hoc invenerit, dicens: *Oceanus, qui cuncta creat, gignitque creata.*"

i. *De Homeri Poesi*, p. 189: "Post illum [Thales] vero Xenophanes Colophonius, aquam et terram inter prima initia constituens, eam occasionem ab Homericis illis sumpsisse videtur: *Sed vos et tellus omnes fiatis et vnda.*"

j. *De Homeri Poesi*, p. 192: "Empedocles cuncta ad hunc modum constare inquit: *Est vbi conveniunt in amore bene, est vbi rursus Singula discordant, litem, pugnamque capessunt*: Vbi elementorum concordiam et vnitatem, amicitiam: discordiam autem, contentionem appellat. Ante hunc autem Homerus concordiam et discordiam in iis obscure ostendit... "

k. The general idea of a catalogue of Homer's scientific knowledge comes from the *De Homeri Poesi*. On the heavenly bodies and their movements, see pp. 194–99; on arithmetic, p. 220; on politics, pp. 242–43; on military art (Salel, vss. 169 ff.), pp. 246–49. The section on military art is especially close to the *De Homeri Poesi* in details and in expression.

Tonnerre, esclair, gresle, vent, pluyes, nues,
Par ses beaux vers sont clairement cognues.
Il monstre aussy qu'il a eu le sçavoir
D'arithmetique. Encor y peult-on veoir
Beaucoup de l'art, enseignant la mesure.
Quand Phidias feit la belle figure
De Juppiter, des Grecs tant estimée,
Il se venta l'avoir ainsy formée
De quatre vers du poëte gentil
Qui luy servoient de pourtraict et d'outil.[l]
Oultre cecy, tout l'estat politique,
L'agriculture et soing oeconomique
Tant necessaire à ceste vie humaine,
Le vray mespris de toute chose vaine
Et l'honneur deu par les hommes aux dieux,
Y est descript et se presente aux yeulx
De tout lisant comme vive paincture.
O noble esprit, O gente creature,
Bien heureux est qui tes oeuvres contemple
Et qui s'en sert de miroir et d'exemple.
Merveille n'est doncques si tant de villes
Du païs Grec et des prochaines ysles
Ont essayé à trouver le moyen
De le nommer leur natif citoyen;
Comme feroient plusieurs grandes princesses,
Qui cognoissans les vertuz, les richesses [a v]
D'ung puissant prince et très hault roy de France,
Desireroyent avoir son accoinctance,
Mettant chascune en avant sa valeur
Pour à l'amour donner quelque couleur.
Et de là vint qu'ung très grand personnaige,
Voulant monstrer clairement son lignaige
Et le païs, dit que son origine
Estoit du ciel, et sa mere divine
Calliopé, principale des muses;[m]
Car en voyant tant de graces infuses
En ung subgect, il pensoit impossible
Qu'engendré feust de quelque corps passible.

l. Valerius Maximus, *Memorabilium*, III. vii. Ext. 4 (ed. Teubner).

m. The *Vita Homeri* attributed to Plutarch quotes the epigram of Antipater (the "très grand personnaige"?) which assigns this parentage to Homer; cf. ed. Ernesti, p. 148.

Et toutesfois ceste perfection
Oncques ne fut d'aucune ambition
Sollicitée, onc l'esguillon de gloire
Ne le picqua, pour laisser la memoire
De son seul nom, et moins de sa patrie;
Tout au rebours d'une grande partie
D'autres autheurs qui (mettans en lumiere
Quelques escriptz) en la page premiere
Couchent leurs noms pour acquerir louange,
Qui bien souvent en deshonneur se change.
La peur que j'ay qu'on me tienne suspecte,
Roy très puissant, parlant de ce poëte,
Me contraindra de passer en silence
Tout le meilleur de sa grande excellence.
Je m'abstiendray pour l'heure à declairer
Comme les dieux l'ont voulu decorer
De prophetie, en ce qu'il a predit
L'autorité, le regne, et le credit
Que les Troiens, après leurs grans dangers,
Auroyent ung jour ès païs estrangers. [a v *v*]
Je me tairay des contrées diverses
Qu'il voyagea, des perilz, des traverses
Qu'il luy convint plusieurs fois soubstenir
Pour le desir ardant de parvenir
A la notice et science certaine
De toute chose, et divine et humaine;
Comme l'esprit d'Achilles l'agita
Divinement et les yeulx luy osta,
En luy rendant après l'ame pourveue
De trop plus claire et plus subtile veue;
Ne plus ne moins que l'on compte du sage
Tiresias, qui veit le nud corsaige
De la deesse[1] et prophete en devint;[n]
Et si j'osois le dire, ainsy qu'advint
Au bon sainct Pol, que Jesu Christ ravit
Et aveugla avant qu'il s'en servit,
Luy faisant veoir au ciel choses en somme
Qu'il n'est permis de dire à langue d'homme.[o]

1. Pallas *Margin 1545*

n. The version of the Tiresias legend which comes closest to that represented by Salel is the one recorded by Callimachus, *Hymns*, V, 75 ff.

o. Acts 13, 11: "Et nunc ecce manus Domini super te, et eris caecus, non videns solem usque ad tempus."

Je diray bien, et ne m'en sçaurois taire,
Que le plus beau de tout l'art militaire
Est tellement en son ouvraige espars
Que l'on le peult cueillir de toutes pars.
Et sembleroit, veu ceste affection,
Qu'en escripvant il eust intention
Monstrer en quoy l'heur ou malheur consiste
D'ung assaillant ou de cil qui resiste.
Car on y voit deux puissantes armées
Souventesfois à combatre animées,
Et les deux chefz enhorter les souldards
A se renger dessoubz leurs estendards,
Leur proposant pour la belle victoire
Honneur, prouffict, et immortelle gloire. [a vj]
L'on y apprent à villes assieger,
Et ses souldards camper et diriger
Commodement; et pour n'estre forcez,
Se remparer de paliz et fossez,
Mettant tousjours en place plus patente,
Droit au mylieu, la grand royale tente,
Consequemment les plus adroitz et fors
Sur les deux coings, pour servir de renforts.
Là peult-on veoir la prudence requise
A bien fournir quelque haulte entreprise;
Comme il convient que le chef se conseille
Aux plus experts, et leur preste l'oreille;
Comme il luy fault avec iceulx traicter,
Puis estre prompt quand à l'executer,
Mesmes en chose adventureuse et grande
Où bien souvent la fortune commande
Et où peu vault subtile invention
Si mise n'est à execution;
Qu'il fault punir mutins, sedicieux,
Et mesdisans, puis louer jusqu'aux cieulx
Et guerdonner les plus forts et puissans
Qui par effect sont très obeïssans.
Quand aux souldards, chascun y peult apprendre
Maint tour subtil pour l'ennemy surprendre;
Et mesmement qu'on ne doit s'esbaÿr
D'ung seul malheur, mais tousjours obeÿr.
Et s'il advient qu'ilz se trouvent vaincqueurs,
Estre advisez de ne mettre leurs cueurs

Tant au butin qu'ilz ne voyent sur l'heure
Si la campaigne et le camp leur demeure.
  Encor y est la façon de combatre
Seul, corps à corps, et le moyen d'abbatre [a vj *v*]
Aucunesfois la noyse commencée.
Course, saillie, escarmousche dressée,
Embusche aux champs, guet prins, faulses alarmes,
Tout y est clair. Brief, c'est ung miroir d'armes.
  Dont à bon droict le preux roy Alexandre,
Qui desiroit sa renommée espandre
Trop plus avant que ses grandes conquestes
Ne s'estendoyent, entre tous les poëtes
Il souhaictoit ung seul Homere avoir,
Bien cognoissant le prince de sçavoir
Qu'il n'y a mort ne long temps qui consume
Ce que faict vivre une bien docte plume.
  Face qui veult en marbre ou fer graver
Sa pourtraicture, et la face eslever
Sur pyramide ou bien haulte colomne;
A tout cela le temps quelque fin donne.
Mais les beaulx vers d'ung clair esprit tissuz,
Maulgré le temps, obtiennent le dessus;
Immortelz sont et les mortz font revivre,
Car plume vole où metal ne peult suyvre.
  Ce jeune roy, voyant donc que Nature
Ne monstroit plus si digne creature,
Il proposa en lieu du personnaige
Avoir au moins près de soy son ouvraige,
Usant tousjours du poete royal
(Tel le nommoit) comme d'ung serf loyal.
  Onc ne revint d'assault ou d'escarmouche,
Tant feust-il las, qu'avant se mettre en couche
Il n'en apprint quelque vers singulier;
Puis s'en servoit comme d'vng orilier.
Et bien souvent disoit que cest autheur
Luy tenoit lieu de guyde et conducteur, [b]
Et qu'il devoit plus à sa poësie
Qu'à ses souldards la conqueste d'Asie.
Disoit encor que sur lucz et violes
On pouvoit bien chanter choses frivoles,

Mais il faloit ses beaulx vers heroïques
Chanter au son des trompetes belliques.[p]
  Pareil vouloir eut le roy Ptolomée,
J'entens celuy duquel la renommée
Florist encor, pour la solicitude
Qu'il eut tousjours envers les gens d'estude,
Faisant recueil de tant de librairie.
Car il punit l'audace et baverie
Du mesdisant et superbe Zoïle
Qui tant osa que d'aguyser son stile
Encontre Homere; et pour son faulx libelle,
Après tourmentz luy donna mort cruele.[q]
  Croire convient aussy que les Romains
Reveremment l'ont tenu en leurs mains.
Car Scipion, le vainqueur de Carthage,
Prisant ung jour l'heur et grand advantage
D'Achilles Grec, chanté dedans ses vers,
Cria tout hault (ayant les yeulx ouvers
Tournez au ciel): "Or pleust à Dieu que Rome
Fust maintenant ornée d'ung tel homme;
Certainement les marciaulx espritz
Et leurs beaulx faictz seroient en plus grand pris."[r]
  Mais de quoy sert, prince très redoubté,
Dire cecy devant ta majesté?
De quoy te sert, si je te ramentoy
Tout ce dessus? Qui le sçait mieulx que toy?

p. Cf. Erasmus, *Apophthegmata* (ed. Basel, 1539), Bk. VIII, p. 835: "Alexander Macedo præter modum delectatus est Homero, adeo ut illum ad uerbum edidicerit, ac dormiens etiam ceruicali suppositum haberet. Eum aliâs summum virtutis præconem, interdum poëtam βασιλικὸν appellare consueuit: cuius carmina censebat ad non citharam ut aliorum, sed ad tubam potius esse canenda ..." Alexander's admiration for Homer is recorded by various ancient writers, notably Plutarch (*Alexander* XV) and Cicero (*Pro Archia* X).

q. Cf. Torrentinus, *Elucidarius Carminum et Historiarum* ... (Daventry: R. Paffroet, 1505): "Zoilus quidam malignus poeta scripsit contra libros Homeri ... Que scripta cum recitasset ptholomeo regi rex indignatus nullum ei verbum fecit. Cumque Zoilus inopia pressus regem rogaret ut sibi daret aliquid quo viveret. ait rex Homerus multos pascit quare tu qui illo doctior es saltem teipsum pasce. Tandem Zoilus paricidii damnatus iussu regis cruci affixus est." The story appeared in various works of antiquity and in numerous modern collections; cf. Vitruvius, *De Architectura*, VII. Preface. 8, for the most detailed version; also Robert Estienne, *Dictionarium propriorum nominum ... in libris prophanis ...*, Paris: R. Estienne, 1542, p. 556, and Polydorus Vergilius, *Proverbiorum et Adagiorum*, Paris: Lefevre, 1511, fol. ix *v*.

r. Source not identified.

Qui est l'esprit ayant plus en reserve
De bon sçavoir? Veulx-je enseigner Minerve? [b *v*]
Certes, nenny. Une aultre chose, Sire,
M'a mis en main la plume pour t'escrire;
Voyant par toy les arts croistre et flourir,
Qui ont cuydé auparavant perir,
Et que desja deux deesses courtoises,
Litterature et les Armes Françoises,
Par ton moyen tele amour ont ensemble
Qu'impossible est que l'on les desassemble;
Tant reluysans que leur claire splendeur
Faict du beau lis cognoistre la grandeur;
J'estois marrye, et non pas sans raison,
Qu'en si heureuse et dorée saison
Ta France fust d'ung Homere privée.
  Si de son nom la gloire est arrivée
(Comme l'on dict) aux plus loingtains barbares,
Indois, Persans, Boristhenois, Tartares,
Et si les mers et desers n'ont peu faire
Qu'eulx esloignez du present hemysphere,
Privez encor de veoir le Pol Arctique,
N'ayent entendu cest oeuvre poëtique,
Saichans au vray la perte et les regretz
Des bons Troiens, et la joye des Grecs;
  Il m'a semblé que ta France prisée,
Tant de Pallas et Mars favorisée,
Devoit avoir pour sa perfection
De cest autheur propre traduction.
  Et pour ce faire, O prince très puissant,
J'ay destiné ung tien obeïssant
Humble subgect, Salel, que tu reçois
Et mectz au renc des poëtes François;[s]
Auquel desja ta royale faveur
A faict gouster du fruict de son labeur.[t] [b ij]
Par iceluy, qui n'a aultre desir
Qu'à faire chose où tu prennes plaisir,
Tu pourras veoir en brief l'oeuvre avancée
De l'*Iliade* et puis de l'*Odyssée*;
Non vers pour vers, car persone vivante,

s. Salel had earlier published *Les OEuvres de Hugues Salel*, Paris: Estienne Roffet, [1539], and a *Dialogue* ... , [Lyon, 1538?].

t. Salel had already received from Francis I the gift of the Abbey of St. Chéron.

Tant elle soit docte et bien escrivante,
Ne sçauroit faire entrer les epithetes
Du tout en rythme. Il souffist des poëtes
La volunté estre bien entendue
Et la sentence avec grace rendue.
  Les anciens disoient estre impossible
Tirer des mains d'Herculés invincible
La grand massue; encore plus d'oster
L'horrible fouldre au grand dieu Juppiter;
Et pour le tiers, à Homere ravir
Ung vers entier, pour après s'en servir.[u]
  Or si Salel s'efforce de le rendre
En ton vulgaire, en est-il à reprendre?
Je croy que non. Ains fault que l'on le prise,
Sinon du faict, au moins de l'entreprise;
Veu mesmement que par là l'on peult veoir
Que ceste langue est duisante au sçavoir,
Et qu'il n'est rien trop dur au translateur
Ayant ung Roy à maistre et protecteur.
  Ce neantmoins, combien que ta sentence,
Roy très Chrestien, luy serve de defence,
Comme venant du très sain jugement
De ton divin et noble entendement,
Et que celuy du conseil duquel uses,
Ton Castellan,[v] le bien aimé des muses,
Luy favorise et à tous ses semblables
Quand il cognoist qu'ilz te sont agreables, [b ij *v*]
On trouvera une grand compaignie
D'aultres espritz promptz à la calumnie,
Qui retiendroyent dedans leur bouche fole
Ung charbon vif plustost qu'une parole
Injurieuse; et en lisant ces vers,
Soubdainement donneront à travers
En les blasmant. Puis (ressemblans la mousche)
S'envoleront, laissans la dure touche
Et l'esguillon de leur langue mauvaise.
  A tous ceulx-là, Sire, mais qu'il te plaise,

u. Two of these feats regarded as difficult by the ancients are reported by Donatus, *Vita Vergilii*, ed. I. Brummer (Leipzig: Teubner, 1912): "Verum intellecturos facilius esse Herculi clavam quam Homero versum subripere." I have found no source for the third.

v. Pierre Du Chastel (1480–1552), Bishop of Tulle.

Je respondray, non pour seul excuser
Ce traduisant ne pour eulx accuser,
Mais soubstenant la publique querele
Des translateurs, nourriz de ma mammelle.
  En premier lieu, c'est ung inique faict
Vituperer le labeur lequel faict
Que plusieurs artz, qui n'estoient en lumiere,
Sont jà renduz en leur clarté premiere;
Et le sçavoir, aultresfois tant couvert,
Est maintenant à chascun descouvert.
  Secondement, puisque c'est une peine
Qui grand travail et peu d'honeur ameine
(Car quoy que face ung parfaict traducteur,
Tousjours l'honeur retourne à l'inventeur),
Devroit-on pas leur vouloir accepter
En bonne part, sans point les molester,
Considerant qu'ilz n'ont entente aucune
Fors d'augmenter l'utilité commune?
  Je vouldrois bien que ces beaulx repreneurs
Fussent ung jour si bons entrepreneurs,
Que l'on veist d'eulx et leur veine gentile
Quelque argument plus honeste et utile. [b iij]
Certainement en lieu d'estre censeurs
Il leur fauldroit patrons et defenseurs.
Car on verroit, de leurs traictz, la pluspart
Prise d'ailleurs; et qui mettroit à part
Le larrecin (laissant leur muse franche),
On trouveroit la charte toute blanche.
  Et quant à ceulx qui font petite estime
De translater ou faire vers en rhythme,
S'il leur plaisoit ung petit esprouver
Cest exercice, ilz pourroyent lors trouver
Leurs bons cerveaulx si confuz du desordre
Qu'on les[2] verroit souvent les ongles mordre;
Recognoissans qu'il y a difference
Entre penser et mectre en apparence.
  J'ameneroys encor quelque raison
Pour cest effect; mais que vault l'oraison,
Tant elle soit docte et bien terminée,
Ayant affaire à cervele obstinée?
  Ung seul confort que je prens en cecy

2. le *1545*

(Roy très puissant) amoindrist mon soucy;
C'est qu'il ne fault defence preparer
Où l'on se peult d'ung grand roy remparer,
D'ung roy François qui en vertu royale
Tous aultres roys ou surpasse ou esgale;
Le nom duquel fera mourir l'envie,
Donnant à l'oeuvre une durable vie.
  A toy s'adresse, à toy seul est vouée;
Il suffira que de toy soit louée;
A tout le moins que tes clairvoyans yeulx
Passent dessus: je ne requiers pas myeulx.
Atant faict fin ton humble chambriere,
Faisant à Dieu très devote priere [b iij *v*]
Qu'en longue vie et saine te maintiene,
Et les fleurons de la fleur très Chrestiene.

FIN DE L'EPISTRE

JEAN MAUGIN

PREFACE TO *Palmerin d'Olive*

1546

TEXT:

Le Premier Livre de Palmerin d'Oliue, filz du Roy Florendos de Macedone et de la belle Griane, fille de Remicivs emperevr de Constantinople. Histoire plaisante & de singuliere recreacion, traduite iadis par vn auteur incertain de Castillan en Françoys, lourd & inusité, sans art, ou disposicion quelconque. Maintenant reueuë, & mise en son entier selon nostre vulgaire, par Iean Maugin natif d'Angiers. Soing & Secret. Auecq' Priuilege du Roy. A Paris. 1546. De l'Imprimerie de Ieanne de Marnef, Pour Iean Longis libraire, tenant sa boutique au Palays en la galerie par ou l'on va à la Chancelerie. [Columbia University Library.]

[Cf. Brunet, IV, 330; Graesse, V, 113.]

COLLATED:

(1553) L'Histoire de Palmerin d'Oliue, filz du roy Florendos de Macedone, et de la belle Griane, fille de Remicivs emperevr de Constantinople: discours plaisant & de singuliere recreation, traduit iadis par vn Auteur incertain de Castillan en Françoys, mis en lumiere & en son entier, selon nostre vulgaire, par Ian Maugin, dit le petit Angeuin. Reueu & emendé par le mesme Auteur. Probé & Tacité. Auec priuilege du Roy. A Paris. Par Estienne Groulleau, libraire demourant en la rue Neuue nostre Dame, à l'enseigne saint Iean Baptiste, pres Sainte Geneuieue des Ardans. 1553. [Newberry Library.]

[Cf. Brunet, IV, 330–31.]

Palmerin d'Olive was another of the romances of chivalry which, in the sixteenth century, were extensively read in translations and prosifications. Jean Maugin, who translated and adapted it, mentions an "auteur incertain" as his source; this predecessor is assumed by Brunet to be "Jean de Voyer, vicomte de Paulmy, seigneur d'Argenson, à qui La Croix du Maine attribue une traduction de Palmerin d'Olive" (IV, 331). Maugin himself also wrote versions of the *Tristan de Léonnois* story (1554) and of the *Orgueilleuse d'Amours*, and translated such ancient works as Apuleius and such Italians as Machiavelli (cf. Du Verdier, ed. Rigoley de Juvigny, II, 466–67). The *Palmerin d'Olive* was apparently very popular in the second half of the century, as witnessed by later editions in 1553, 1572, 1573, 1576, 1593, and 1619.

[ã ij] AUX NOBLES, VERTUEUX ET ILLUSTRES FRANÇOYS,[1] JEAN MAUGIN DIT LE PETIT ANGEVIN BAISE LES MAINS DE LEUR SEIGNEURIE

Les anciens Romains (manifiques[2] seigneurs) pour mieux atirer leurs citoyens à l'amour de vertu et avoir en horreur le vice, non seulement escrivirent loix, fisrent publier editz, créerent censeurs, entretindrent gents

1. Aux Gentilzhommes nobles et vertueux Françoys *1553* 2. tres illustres *1553*

letrez du tresor publicq' pour rediger par escrit les actes heroïques et vertueux[3] faitz de leurs majeurs, ains à grands fraiz eurent à leurs gaiges gladiateurs, poëtes, basteleurs, musiciens, et menestriers de diverses sortes; les uns, à fin de leur mettre devant les yeux le commun vivre des hommes, pour l'ensuyvre ou fuyr; les autres, pour leur recreacion seulement.[4] De ce font assez foy les ordonnances de leurs roys, decretz de consulz, les[5] loix des douze tables, les[5] saintes constitucions imperiales, nombre infiny de vrayes et bien belles histoires, et les satyres et comedies que nous avons d'eulx encores pour le jourd'huy. Les Françoys (precellants entre tous peuples à faire leur proffit des meurs de leurs voysins) les ont ensuyviz en cecy; ont mis en livres les vies de leurs ancestres, gouverneurs, ducz, roys,[6] princes, et jusques aux modernes, traduit fables, et inventé romants qui ne sont autre chose que comedies prosaïques; et en abolissant le paganisme Romain ont defendu les convives publiques, monopoles, libelles diffamatoires et[7] tous jeux lubriques et deshonnestes comme estoient ceulx de Saturne, Bachus et Flora. Mesmement ont eu en abhominacion les spectacles cruelz et inhumains des meurdres des gladiateurs et occisions d'hommes par elephants, lyons, ours, tigres, et autres bestes sanguinaires.

Or si quelqu'un des monarques et dominateurs qui ont par cy devant regné en Gaule a monstré un bon zele et affection à son peuple, touchant les artz et sçavoir, certainement nostre Roy très Chrestien à present regnant a excellé et triumphé sur tous. Qu'ainsi soit,[8] voyant à l'avenement de sa monarchie les letres estre presque estaintes et peries en la France, a mandé ses sujetz, quis[9] Latins et Græcz,[a] pour mettre en lumiere l'Hebreu, Græc, et elegant Latin, qui jà cinq ou six siecles avoient demouré en tenebres. Non content de ce, a remis en leur pristine forme les artz liberaux et mathematiques, si bien que ses lecteurs publiques le rendront immortel et feront fleurir à jamais, maugré envie et ses ennemys. Davantage les sciences de prospective, pourtraiture, painture, orfevrie, et architecture, dont il n'estoit plus nouvelles deça les montz, les a rendues si communes et faciles que les Italiens et Alemans nous viennent maintenant voir pour en aprendre. Et en ce a et aura la seule vile de Paris autant de bruit que l'antique Rome.

Oultre plus, considerant que la langue Françoyse demouroit abjecte et desprisée mesmes des siens, a alaité en sa court et incité par ses biensfaitz

3. haux *1553* 4. seulement *omitted 1553* 5. les *omitted 1553*
6. roys, ducz *1553* 7. et *omitted 1553* 8. ne soit *1546*; soit *1553*
9. *so 1546, 1553*

a. "Latins et Græcz" here apparently means "knowing, who knew, Latin and Greek." Cf. the *privilège* to the 1538 ed. of Justinus, *Oeuvres*, translated by Guillaume Michel de Tours, Paris: Les Angeliers, fol. [a *v*]: "il a faict translater de latin en francoys / Iustin hystorien fort recreatif / et auquel plusieurs gentilz hommes (non latins) pourront prendre grande recreation ... "

un grand nombre d'espritz poëtiques à escrire si proprement, soit de leur invencion ou traduction, que leur renomée a penetré jusques au-dessus des nues. Entre lesquelz Salel a eu tant de grace au translat du poëte Græc[b] que non moins est à priser que l'auteur. Semblablement a esmeu plusieurs gents de bien à travailler en prose, le plus à estimer desquelz est le seigneur des Essars,[c] si le lecteur ne veult desdaigner la douceur de sa phrase, proprieté de ses[10] termes, liaison de ses[10] propoz, et richesse[11] de sentences telle que plusieurs lisants ceste nouveauté de bien parler desperent de l'ensuyvre, tant s'en fault qu'ilz le[12] puissent esgaler.[13] Ce que venu à ma cognoissance, neantmoins que de mon vouloir et d'autruy j'eusse souvent esté importuné mettre devant voz yeux quelque romant en nostre vulgaire, j'avois[14] tousjours differé, craignant (au lieu de vous complaire) vous esmouvoir à fascherie et mespriser ma peine. Et n'eust esté qu'au contraire de ce je me persuadois qu'œuvre, tant petite soit-elle, moyennant qu'elle procede d'un bon cueur pour proffiter à la posterité, peult aucunement delecter[15] les lecteurs, je n'eusse jamais paind caracthere. Estant doncq' meu de ceste per-[ã ij *v*]suasion et asseuré que toutes choses nouvelles peuvent quelque temps recréer, je me mis à revoir une vieille minute prinse de l'auteur Espaignol du *Palmerin d'Olive*, tant pource que je la trouvay assez ample que pourautant qu'elle estoit pleine d'arguments amoureux et contes de regretz lamentables (matieres, au temps qui court, sur toutes autres pratiquées), toutesfois si confuz, mal ordonnez, et indisposez qu'onques la statue que descrit Horace au commencement de son *Art poëtique* ne fut composée de la sorte. Et si ce mauvais ordre avecq' mon peu d'experience me garderent assez longuement d'y toucher, l'avertissement que j'eu que le noble de Herberay (traducteur de nostre fleurissant *Amadis*) en avoit mis au net aucuns des premiers cayers, m'en cuyda descourager du tout. Et ne puis penser la cause qui l'auroit empesché d'y faire poursuyte,[16] sinon la lourderie de la vieille traduction ou la commission ordinaire[d] qu'il a du Roy.

"Quoy?" me dist lors quelqu'un mien amy, "laisseras-tu pour ce à suyvre ton entreprinse? Sçais-tu pas que Fortune, par sa premiere fille Hardiesse, a tousjours haulcé les voluntaires et abaissé les nonchalants, timides, et couardz? Non, ne te faings. Et si tu n'aproches de cest heureux langaige Essardin, on dira (pour le moins) que tu as essayé de l'ataindre.[17] Qui plus est, l'architecte qui a bien ensuivy le plant[18] et basty n'est moins à

10. ses *omitted 1553* 11. richesses *1546*; richesse *1553* 12. y *1553*
13. attaindre *1553* 14. j' *omitted 1553* 15. delecter aucunement *1553*
16. la poursuyte *1553* 17. ensuyvre *1553* 18. bien imité le desceing *1553*

b. Salel's translation of the *Iliad* was published in 1545; see pp. 117–29 above.

c. Herberay des Essarts's version of the *Amadis* was published in 1540; see pp. 85–88 above.

d. Herberay had the official title of "commissaire ordinaire de l'artillerie." Cf. the title page of the 1550 edition of the *Amadis*, p. 85 above.

estimer que celuy qui a inventé et ordonné." Persuadé doncq' de ces paroles, je[19] continuay en ma premiere volunté tant que je trouvay derechef aucun nombre de chapitres corrigez par un que je n'ay sceu cognoistre;[e] pour lesquelz lier, unir, et rendre conformes au principe, je[19] n'ay eu moindre peine qu'à une invencion, et m'a falu entierement les reffaire. Depuys j'ay[20] tant suivy ma pointe que mes amys m'ont contraint mettre le tout en impression.

Et à fin (seigneurs) que soyez avertiz de ma maniere d'escrire, je n'ay prins de l'original que la matiere principale, sans m'assujetir aux propoz du traducteur antique mal entenduz et pirement poursuyviz. Les discours des affaires ay abregez le plus succintement qu'il m'a esté possible; les guerres selon leur forme ancienne, sans canons ou harquebuzes; et les amours à la moderne, sauf les foles, pource que je les cuyde faintes et qu'il n'en soit point de semblables. Et si en passant j'ay usé de metaphores,[21] similitudes, et comparaisons, allegué fables, poësies, histoires, et inventé vers, excusez le desir que j'ay eu de monstrer qu'en cest endroit le François y est plus propre que l'Espaignol. Au reste, si prenez plaisir et tant soit peu vous contentez de ce mien labeur, suportant mon ramage Angevin (lequel impossible est qu'aucunesfois je ne sente), je me tiendray pour plus qu'assez satisfait[22] et m'induirez à poursuyvre davantage, mesmes l'*Orgueilleuse d'amours*[23] que j'ay intencion paindre de ses couleurs et en brief.[f]

19. je *omitted 1553* 20. j' *omitted 1553* 21. mataphores *1546*
22. satiffait *1546*
23. *New conclusion substituted 1553*: l'Orgueilleuse d'amours, & autres Romans tant de mon inuention, qu'estranges, & trop mieux correctz, que la premiere edition de cestuy, que i'ay amendé au moins mal que i'ay peu, pour vous satisfaire de promesse. Neantmoins le hazard m'a esté tant contraire, ne sçay si par fortune ou mon malheur ainsi le voulant: si est-ce, que si ie fuz precipité à la premiere fois, tant qu'à grand' peine pouuois lire vn cayer de copie, qu'il me faloit bailler à l'Imprimeur, à ce coup n'ay peu voir les espreuues: ains est tombée successiuemen es mains de deux correcteurs, qui n'auoient acoustumé le Françoys: ce que vous prie suporter, & penser l'Impression sans fautes estre presque impossible. Ce qui fasche & ennuye trop plus l'auteur, qu'il ne desplaist à vousmesmes. A Dieu.

e. This may be Jean de Voyer, as suggested by Brunet; cf. the prefatory note to this text.

f. In fact, the *privilège* for the *Palmerin*, dated April 17, 1545, "apres Paques," also covers "vne autre histoire traduite de langaige Picard fort ancien en ceste nostre langue, intitulée l'Orgueilleuse d'Amours"; cf. the 1546 edition, fol. [ã *v*]. I have found no trace of the publication of this edition.

CHARLES ESTIENNE

PREFACE TO *Les Abusez*

1548

TEXT:

Les Abvsez. Comedie faite à la mode des anciens Comiques, premierement composée en langue Tuscane, par les professeurs de l'Academie Senoise, & nommée Intronati, depuys traduite en Françoys par Charles Estienne, & nouuellement reueuë & corrigée. A Paris. Par Estienne Groulleau, demourant en la rue Neuue nostre Dame, à l'enseigne saint Ian Baptiste. 1548. [B.N., Paris.]

[Cf. Brunet, III, 454–55.]

For his translation of the *Comedia del Sacrificio degli Intronati da Siena*, Charles Estienne reworked the preface written for his translation of Terence's *Andria* (see above, pp. 89–103). The new preface probably appeared for the first time in the first edition of the translation from the Italian, then called *Comédie du Sacrifice*, published at Lyon in 1543; but Harold Walter Lawton, *Térence en France au XVIe siècle* (Paris: Jouve, 1926, p.488), was able to find no copy of this rare volume, and I have not been more fortunate. If it did appear there, then the present preface to *Les Abusez* should really be dated 1543 rather than 1548. The new preface was essentially a rewriting, introducing many new ideas and omitting many of the old; only a few passages represent literal transcriptions from the original version, and I omit them from the text given below. *Les Abusez* went through two later editions, in 1549 and 1556. Later still, the first seven of the original ten paragraphs of the preface were published with a collection of *Six Comédies de Térence*, Antwerp, 1566 and Paris, 1572, 1574, and 1578. On the history of these various editions of the preface, consult Harold Walter Lawton's "Charles Estienne et le théâtre," *Revue du seizième siècle*, XIV (1927), 336–47; on its influence on Jean de la Taille, see my "Charles Estienne and Jean de la Taille," *Modern Language Notes*, LXI (1946), 262–65.

[A ij] EPISTRE DU TRADUCTEUR À MONSEIGNEUR LE DAUPHIN DE FRANCE, DECLARATIVE DE LA MANIERE QUE TENOIENT LES ANCIENS TANT À LA COMPOSITION DU JEU QU'À L'APAREIL DE LEURS COMEDIES

Je ne puis assez louër, monseigneur, la coustume des anciens en leurs comedies qu'ilz apelloient nouvelles, et la façon de disposer et poursuyvre leur sens et argument en icelles pour donner recreation aux auditeurs; laquelle maniere, si jusques à nous ce jourd'huy estoit parvenue, je ne croy point que ne fussions aussi heureux en ce cas qu'ilz estoient, consideré que nostre langage, tant pour exprimer comme aussi pour aorner et decorer quelque chose, n'est de rien[1] pour le present inferieur au leur; combien que pour la pluspart du leur soit descendu. Mais à ce que maintenant j'en aperçoy, nostre rude vulgaire a fort sincopé la maniere ancienne en matiere de comedie, ou pourautant qu'elle luy sembloit de trop de fraiz, ou possible pource qu'il ne l'entendoit point [A ij *v*] bonnement. De sorte que pour nostre comedie vulgaire n'avons retenu qu'un acte simple de leur comedie nouvelle, n'ayants encor' observé la maniere de taire et suplier ce que[2] facilement sans exprimer se pourroit[3] entendre, qui est un des poinctz en quoy les anciens facteurs mettoient plus de peine; dont est avenu qu'en plusieurs de noz comedies ne se trouve sens, rithme, ne raison, seulement des paroles ridicules avecq' quelque badinage, sans autre invention ne conclusion.

Les aucuns ont bien pris et retenu le mal que les anciens commettoient en leurs satyres, comedies vieilles, et tragedies, quand souz ombre de personnes lascives taxoient les plus grands et notables. Mesmement s'ilz parloient de quelques personnes civiles, ne se gardoient de les nommer par nom et surnom, ou en bailloient telle signifiance qu'il n'y avoit celuy des auditeurs qui ne l'aperceust facilement. Et telle fois est avenu que le personnage de qui l'on parloit estoit en presence, ce qui ne se pouvoit faire sans impudence trop temeraire; au moyen de quoy l'on a veu avenir grands scandales.

Autres, imitans les tragedies, ont[4] fait moralitez et semblables choses avecq' telle grace et ornement [A iij] d'antiquité, que rien ne se peult dire semblable, sinon la couverture et le taxer des superieurs qui fut la raison pour laquelle les anciens abolirent telles folies comme pernicieuses et plustost incitatives de noyses et debatz que de plaisir et delectation; au lieu desquelles folies trouverent la comedie qu'ilz apelloient nouvelle,[5] en laquelle n'introduysoient que villageoys ou personnages de vile qualité, ne parlans d'autre cas que de mariages, amours, et semblables choses; lesquelles, à fin qu'elles fussent delectables aux auditeurs, deduysoient en telle sorte et si commodement, avecq' changements de propoz, choses inopinées, celées et puys descouvertes, laissants un propos pour entrer à l'autre, puis reprenants le premier poinct et le faisants convenir au dernier avecq' si grande dexterité et maniere, que cela rendoit un plaisir incredible aux spectateurs.

Et pour vous donner à entendre, monseigneur, l'apareil et aornement qui se faisoit en telles recreations, il vous convient sçavoir que le lieu auquel les spectateurs des comedies anciennes estoient commodement assiz s'apelloit theatre. [The description of the theater which follows repeats the one given

1. riens *1548* 2. que *for* qui? 3. pourrroit *1548* 4. on *1548*
5. uouuelle *1548*

in the "Preface to Terence's *Andria,*" pp. 98–99 above, although it omits much of the material contained in the earlier version.]

[A iiij *v*] Toutes comedies estoient divisées en cinq ou six actes, et le plus communément en cinq. Chacun acte contenoit sens parfait; parquoy à la fin d'iceux, pour recréer les assistans, se faisoient plusieurs et divers esbatements, puis rentroient[6] aux autres actes, et ainsi poursuyvoient leur comedie. Et quand deux personnes ou troys avoient devisé et tenu propos ensemble, et que l'on se retiroit ou qu'il en venoit un autre en nouveau propos, ilz apelloient celà une scene, de sorte que chacun acte selon la variation des personnages et deviz qu'ilz tenoient estoit aussi divisée en cinq ou six scenes pour le moins. Et par ce moyen jamais ne demeuroit sur l'eschauffault [A v] personnage qui n'y fust necessaire, ou pour parler ou pour escouter les autres à quelque intention; qui est une des choses en laquelle plus nous faillons et que plus je trouve inepte en noz jeux et faintes comedies.

Plusieurs autres choses y avoit à l'ornement de la scene et theatre antique, qui seroient fort longues à raconter; comme certains lieux deputez pour les princes, auxquelz ne pouvoient estre veuz du peuple; aussi paramentz divers et vestements de personnages, ornement de theatre par hault et par bas, certains pertuys où estoient posez vaisseaux de fonte penduz la gueule à mont, pour leans faire retentir la voix et la rendre plus gracieuse et intelligible aux auditeurs; semblablement aussi certains pris ordonnez aux meilleurs joueurs de la bande. Car telz jeux se faisoient communément aux despens de la ville pour la recreation du peuple, non pas pour en recevoir deniers ne autrement. Lesquelles choses, si je vouloys plus au long reciter, j'auroys peur, monseigneur, de vous donner ennuy en faisant la matiere trop longue. Car d'expliquer la forme des amphitheatres (qui furent puys inventez pour servir tant aux comedies qu'autres jeux de [A v *v*] pris comme combatz d'hommes et de bestes et autres choses semblables, à ce que après la comedie recitée le peuple soudain, en changeant de place, se retirast du costé oposite pour voir l'autre deduyt), celà me sembleroit superflu, consideré qu'il n'apartient du tout à nostre propos.

Parquoy ces premiers cas seulement atenduz, j'ay espoir que vostre noble esprit s'adonnera facilement et inclinera à vouloir prendre plaisir de la lecture de ceste comedie, laquelle à present je (le moindre de tous voz serviteurs) luy presente et dedie, comme pour luy donner esbat de quelque petite resjouyssance en y lisant parfois et par maniere d'esbat un acte seulement qui soit cause de vous donner à cognoistre la grace que les anciens eurent à bailler recreation[7] par leurs comedies. Car de ce, monseigneur,[8] je vous vueil asseurer, que ceste presente comedie, jasoit que des

6. rentroiont *1548* 7. recrecreation *1548* 8. mon Seigueur *1548*

anciens n'aye esté faite, mais de bons et modernes espritz Senoys,[a] studieux de toute antiquité et honnesteté, faisants de leur langage Tuscan une profession et academie qu'ilz nomment Intronati, toutesfois en lisant j'espere que la trouverez telle que si Terence mesmes l'eust composée en Italien, à peine mieux l'eust-il [A vi] sceu diter, inventer, ou deduyre. Du langage je m'en tais; toutesfois que pour vulgaire Italien, je pense que c'est le meilleur qui oncques fut prononcé. Et quant au reste, ne croiray jamais que touchant l'invention et deduction à l'imitacion ancienne, nul des poëtes modernes, soient Italiens ou Françoys, jusques à present en ayent faite la pareille.

J'y mettray Pietro Aretino avecq' sa *Cortesane*[b] et plusieurs autres, Pietro Ariosto avecq' sa *Lena*[c] et son *Mareschal*[d] et son *Negromant*,[e] et semblables facteurs Italiens. Et quant aux Françoys, j'y mettray Pathelin avecq' sa Guillemette et son drapier (combien que soit chose aussi bien composée pour nostre temps que l'on sçache trouver), Coquillart avecq' son plaidoyer,[f] Cretin avecq' son Thibault Chenevote,[g] et plusieurs autres de noz facteurs Françoys. Bien est vray que la pluspart des Italiens que j'ay nommez, et semblablement tous noz Françoys, se sont contraints aux rithmes de leur langue, comme aussi les anciens ont tousjours fait à leurs metres. Mais les bons personnages compositeurs de ceste comedie, voyants que les vers ostent la liberté du langage et proprieté d'aucunes phrases, ont beaucoup mieux aymé faire reciter [A vi *v*] leur comedie en belle prose (pour mieux monstrer l'efait et sens d'icelle) que de s'assubjetir à la rithme.

A ceste cause, je la vous ay bien voulu traduire en nostre vulgaire Françoys, monseigneur, au mieux que j'ay peu, en reservant les noms et proprietez Tuscanes; toutesfois que non si bien ne si proprement que le naturel Italien, mais au moins en telle sorte (quoyque rude et mal polie) que vous en pourriez prendre quelque plaisir parfois s'il vous vient en fantasie d'en lire une ou deux scenes par passetemps. En quoy faisant, accepterez le petit don de vostre moindre serviteur en jouissant paisiblement de si peu de plaisir que pourrez recouvrer de la lecture d'iceluy.

a. *Comedia del Sacrificio degli Intronati*, Venice, [1537?].

b. *La Cortigiana*, written *ca.* 1525, published 1534.

c. *La Lena*, 1535.

d. Probably a confusion on the part of Estienne with the *Marescalco* of Pietro Aretino, 1535.

e. *Il Negromante*, 1535; this comedy was later translated by Jean de la Taille.

f. Guillaume Coquillart, *Plaidoyé d'entre la Simple et la Rusée*, 1477; cf. H. G. Harvey, *The Theatre of the Basoche* (Cambridge: Harvard University Press, 1941), pp. 83–102.

g. Unidentified.

JOACHIM DU BELLAY

PREFACE TO *L'Olive*

1549

TEXT:

L'Olive et qvelqves avtres oevvres poeticqves. Le contenu de ce liure. Cinquante Sonnetz à la louange de l'Oliue. L'Anterotique de la vieille, & de la ieune Amye. Vers Lyriques. Par I. D. B. A. Caelo Mvsa Beat. Imprimé à Paris pour Arnoul l'Angelier tenant sa Bouticque au second pillier de la grand' sale du Palays. 1549. Auec priuilege. [Yale University Library.]

[Cf. Brunet, I, 750; Tchemerzine, V, 42.]

Du Bellay's preface to the first edition of the *Olive* was suppressed in the second and later editions in favor of a new preface. It has been reprinted in various modern editions, notably that of Léon Séché (*Œuvres complètes*, Paris: Revue de la Renaissance, 1903, I, 87–88) and that of Chamard (*Œuvres poétiques*, Paris: Cornély, 1908, I, 7–9).

[A ii] AU LECTEUR

Quand j'ecrivoy' ces petiz ouvraiges poëtiques, lecteur, je ne pensoy' rien moins qu'à les exposer en lumiere; et me suffisoit qu'ilz fussent aggreables à celle qui m'a donné la hardiesse de m'essayer en ce genre d'ecrire, à mon avis encore aussi peu usité entre les François comme elle est excellente sur toutes, voyre quasi une deesse entre les femmes. Or depuis, ayant fait part de ces miens ecriz à quelques amys curieux de telles choses, qui les ont aussi communiquez à beaucoup d'autres, j'ay esté adverty que quelqu'un les avoit baillez à l'imprimeur; au moyen de quoy, doutant ou qu'il voulust les publier soubz son nom (en quoy toutesfois il m'eust paravanture vengé de luy-mesmes) ou faire tort à ma renommée, les exposant soubz le mien incorrectz et pleins d'erreurs, cela craignant (dy-je) je me suis hasté d'en faire un petit recueil et tumultuairement le jecter en lumiere avecques la permission de celle qui est et sera seule mon laurier, ma muse, et mon Apolon. Je croy, lecteur, entendu ceste contrainte, que je te jure par la troupe sacrée des neuf sœurs estre veritable, que tu excuseras benignement les faultes de cest ouvraige precipité, semblable à un fruict abortif ou à ces tableaux ausquelz le peintre n'a encores donné la derniere main; protestant si je congnois que ces fragmentz te plaisent te faire bientost present de l'oeuvre entier. Ce[A ii *v*]pendant tu jugeras (comme on dit) le lyon aux ungles.

Si je ne craignois que le prologue fust plus long que la farce, je respondroy' voluntiers à ceulx qui, congnoissans Petrarque de nom seulement, diront incontinent que je l'ay desrobé, que je n'apporte rien du mien, non pour autre raison sinon qu'il a escript des sonnetz et moy aussi. Vrayment, je confesse avoir imité Petrarque, et non luy seulement mais aussi l'Arioste et d'autres modernes Italiens, pource qu'en l'argument que je traicte je n'en ay point trouvé de meilleurs. Et si les anciens Romains pour l'enrichissement de leur langue n'ont fait le semblable en l'imitation des Grecz, je suis content n'avoir point d'excuse. Non que je me vante d'y avoir bien fait mon debvoir; mais j'espere que ce mien petit essay donnera occasion de faire dadvantaige à tant de bons esprits dont la France est aujourd'huy ennoblye. Quand à ceulx qui ne vouldroient recevoir ce genre d'escripre, qu'ilz appellent obscur pource qu'il excede leur jugement, je les laisse avecq' ceulx qui après l'invention du bléd vouloient encores vivre de glan. Je ne cerche point les applaudissemens populaires. Il me suffit pour tous lecteurs avoir un S. Gelays, un Heroët, un de Ronsart, un Carles, un Sceve, un Bouju, un Salel, un Martin;[a] et si quelques autres sont encor' à mettre en ce ranc, à ceulx-là s'addressent mes petiz ouvraiges. Car s'ilz ne les approuvent, je suis certain pour le moins qu'ilz louront mon entreprinse. A Dieu.

a. Du Bellay addressed poems to most of these fellow poets in the *Vers lyriques* and in the *Recueil de poësie*; cf. ed. Chamard, III, 40, 93, 120, 130, 135.

THOMAS SEBILLET

PREFACE TO EURIPIDES' *Iphigenia*

1549

TEXT:

L'Iphigene d'Evripide poete tragiq: tovrne de Grec en Francois par l'Auteur de l'Art poëtique, dédié a Monsieur Ian Brinon, Seigneur de Villénes, & Conseilher du Roy nottre Sire en sa Court de Parlement a Paris. A Paris. Auec priuilége. On les vend en la salle du Palais, en la boutique de Gilles Corrozet. 1549. [Harvard College Library.]

[Cf. Brunet, II, 1105; the edition was reissued in 1550 with a new title page.]

Thomas Sebillet bore a curious relationship to the group of the Pléiade. As is apparent from the analysis of his *Art poétique françoys* given above (Introduction, pp. 1–11), he added to the practice of the *rhétoriqueurs* a philosophy of poetry largely derived from the classics, hence in the humanistic tradition. Yet this same *Art poétique* served as a spur to the younger group to produce a theory in opposition to Sebillet's, the theory of Du Bellay's *Deffence et Illustration de la langue françoyse.* Similarly, by translating Euripides' *Iphigenia* into French, Sebillet was contributing to the dissemination of the works of antiquity which was a part of the program of the Renaissance; yet the preface to this translation contains many open and unveiled attacks upon the theory and practice of Du Bellay. Much of Du Bellay's second preface to the *Olive* is an answer to Sebillet's attacks. Still again, Sebillet was interested in the current proposals for a reform of French orthography, and the present text shows his application of a system much more moderate than Meigret's or Peletier's in its departure from tradition. In order that the reader may be able to judge the nature of these reforms, a special case has been made of this text and all accents have been reproduced exactly as in the original; also, the "ȩ" has been retained. Otherwise, the general editorial practices applied to other texts have been followed.

On the translation of Euripides, see René Sturel's "Essai sur les traductions du théâtre grec en français avant 1550," *Revue d'histoire littéraire de la France*, XX (1913), 637–43; on the preface, Henri Chamard's *Joachim du Bellay* (Lille, 1900), pp. 146–47; on Sebillet, Félix Gaiffe's introduction to his edition of the *Art poétique françoys* (Paris, Droz, 1932).

[A iiij] AUS LECTEURS

Amys lecteurs, je vous voeil bien avisér de ma conception en quelques particularitéz que pourréz trouver éttranges et a l'aventure trop rudes avant qu'entendre ma raison, laquéle découverte lés pourra aussi beaucoup adoucir. En premiér lieu, je me suy conformé au stile de ma version tout au plus prés que j'ay peu a la gravité de l'auteur; et au demourant l'ay suivy quasi a pié levé en la forme dés vers, rendant lés trocaïques Grés en alexandrins François, lés iambiques trimétres et quelques anapéstiques en heroïques, lés autres méllés de divers genres plus petis (et usurpés par Euripide au cœur introduit en cétte tragédie) en diverses sortes aussi de moindres vers, et aucunefois tant petis et pour leur petitésse tant malaisés a vétir de leur livrée, que j'ay bien grande peur que la rudésse par endrois ne vous en déplaise. Mais vottre douceur et grandɇ humanité me récrée et donnɇ éspor que ne trouverés rien tant rudɇ et mauvais commɇ il sera, mais balançeant l'appreté dés vers contre vottre equanimité et la raison (a laquele savéz tant bien réduire toutes choses) jugeréz promtement que la difficulté de traduire augmentée par la sugétion du petit vérs, rymé le plus souvent a quatre et a sis, est assés forte pour empéchér le fluïde et gracieus cours de la fontaine Caballine.

Et a cela me suy-je quasi contreinct exprés, pour faire qu'en ce petit poëme toute sorte de ryme et tous genres de vers fussent a peu prés compris, comme connoittrés que [A iiij *v*] j'ay fait si vous y aviséz de prés. Car vous y lirés dés vers depuis deus sylabes[1] jusques a tréze et la plus grande part dés assiétes de ryme aujourduy usurpées en nottre langue Françoise, voire jusques au sonnét, lay, virelay,[2] et ryme altérée; et n'y eusse omis le rondeau s'il y fût autant bien venu a propos. Cétte mienne mignardise a l'aventure déplaira a la délicatésse de la délicatésse de quelques hardis repreneurs; mais si je say que la friandise vous en plaise, ce me sera plaisir de leur déplairɇ en vous plaisant.

J'ay davantage tant ausé que de me retirér en quelques choses de l'opinion et abus vulgaire et du grand chemin dés vaches. Ce que le Gréc a dit χόρος, le Latin *Chorus*, et savans hommes François ont qui retenu *chorus*, qui retourné *chore*, je l'ay traduit et écrit *Cœur*—traduit, pource que le Gréc et Latin, entendans par ce mot troupe d'hommes ou de femmes ou personne la representant, ne seront point mal exprimés en disant *Cœur*, qui en nottre langage François sinifie méme chose aus colléges ecclésiastiques; écrit, afin que le lisant ne dissiés "chœur" comme "chose."

J'ay aussi observé qu'un vieilhart serviteur parlant au roy Agamemnon son maittre, Ménélaɇ a son frére, Iphigénɇ a son pére, Clytemnestra au princɇ Achillés, et autres en mémɇ analogie ne dissent "toy" mais "vous," pource qu'il m'a semblé que nottre phrase Françoise, l'usurpant ainsi suyvant la dignité dés personnes, ne doit ettre regettée pour se mancipér a l'arogance Romainɇ, et luy donnér occasion tous lés jours plus grande de nous reprochér sés richésses. Quant a l'ortographe, je ne m'amuseray icy a

1. sybabes *1549* 2. virerelay *1549*

m'en excuser; car j'ay en autre endroit[a] dit lés raisons pour lesquelles je m'assuget[A v]ty avec le grand César Auguste[b] a exprimer par l'écriture le naïf de ma prononciation. Et s'il vous prend par fortunɇ envie de me reprochér qu'en cest endroit j'entrepren avéques d'autres (gens nonobstant ce de bon ésprit) forcer l'usage commun au grand contennement de la vénérablɇ antiquité, je vous suppliɇ humblement, lecteurs, éstimér que j'admirɇ et révére nos majeurs et lés suy pas a pas partout ou raison lés a conduis. Mais pensés aussi que sans elle je ne m'arretteray au plaisir d'un pratticien qui, écrivant, prend plus prés gardɇ a emplir son bout de papier qu'a raison qu'il seût rendre—ny autre pour luy—pourquoy il écrit ainsi. Si au réste je n'ay traduit vers pour vers, ç'a étté pource que je ne l'ay peu et que je croy qu'il ne se peut faire, et l'eussent entrepris ceus qui fondent l'immortalité de leur nom sur moindre chose que cela. Si j'ay dit icy "Ménélaüs, Tyndarus, " etc., là "Ménélae, Tyndare," etc., la sugétion de la couppɇ et quelquefois de la ryme m'y a contreint; mais aussi m'aidant du mot Latin a mon besoin, je ne suy tant loin de raison que je ne le facɇ a l'éxemple de Virgilɇ et autres classiques poëtes Latins, lesquelz souvent diënt "Pallada, Thesea," etc. semblables, là ou le pié du vers les contreint et ne veut recevoir "Palladem, Theseum," et semblables purs Latins. Je ne daigneroie réppondre a celuy qui voudroit dire qu'il ne m'est permis de faire tout ce que Virgilɇ a fait; car c'est la raison de ceus qui n'hont autre pilliér plus seur pour souttenir leur calumnie.

Finablement, si je n'ay tant purement, doucement, naïvement, elegamment, richement, et mignonnement tourné l'*Iphigéne* d'Euripide que Marot a fait le *Léandre* du poéte Musée,[c] [A v *v*] aussy ne suy-je, ne pense-je éttre Marot. Si la langue Françoise n'est illustrée par la version dés poëmes, on ne s'en doit attachér a moy qui n'en suy illustrateur ne gagé ne renommé. Si je fay moins pour moy en traduisant anciëns auteurs qu'en cérchant inventions nouvelles, je ne suy toutefois tant a reprendre que celuy qui se vante d'avoir trouvé ce qu'il ha mot a mot traduit dés autres.

Si cétte version n'est suffisante pour immortalisér mon nom, aussi ne l'y vœil-je méttrɇ en tittre. Si je ne suy leu et loüé dés poétes de la premiére douzaine, aussi n'ay-je pas écrit a cétte intention. Car j'écry aus muses et a moy; et si quéqu'un par fortune prend plaisir a més passetems, je ne suy pas tant ennuyeus de son aise que je luy vœilhe défendre la communication de més ébbas pour lés resérvér a une afféctée demye-douzaine dés estimés princes de nottre langue et par ce moyen cércher leur applaudissement.

a. *Art poëtique* (1548), I, ix; ed. Gaiffe, pp. 97–98.

b. Cf. Suetonius, *Divus Augustus*, LXXXVIII (Loeb, I, 257): "videtur eorum potius sequi opinionem, qui perinde scribendum ac loquamur existiment."

c. *Museus ancien Poete Grec, des amours de Leander & Hero, traduict en Rithme francoise, par Clement marot de Cahors en quercy, valet de Chambre du Roy.* Paris: Jehan André, 1541.

Et c'est la cause pourquoy aisément je vous communique la présente traduction, n'en affectant ne louenge d'industrie n'immortalité de nom, mais simplement satisfaisant a la requêtte que m'en ont faitte aucuns més amys, suyvant la bonne volunté qu'il[3] leur plaît me departir. Pour laquelle entretenir et poursuyvre vottre bonne grace, vous pouvéz croire, lecteurs, que je ne craindray me méttre en plus grand hazard d'éttre abbayé dés chiéns gardans lés boutiques en tous lés déttrois et endrois ou je penseray passant vous donnér quelque plaisir.

Fin.

3. ilz *1549*

PIERRE DE RONSARD

PREFACE TO HIS *Odes*

1550

TEXT:

Les Qvatre Premiers liures des Odes de Pierre de Ronsard, Vandomois. Ensemble son Bocage. [Greek distich of Jean Dorat.] A Paris. Chez Guillaume Cauellart libraire iuré de l'uniuersité de Paris, demeurant deuant le College de Cambrai, a la poulle grasse. M.D.L. Avec previlege dv Roi. [Pierpont Morgan Library.]

[Cf. Brunet, IV, 1378; Tchemerzine, IX, 416; Le Petit, p. 84; Cat. Rothschild, No. 671; De Ricci, No. 4, p. 23.]

Ronsard's preface to his *Odes* was printed only once during his lifetime, with the first edition of 1550; the next appearance was with the edition of Lyon, 1592. Essentially, it was a controversial document, belonging to the same group as the *Deffence* and Du Bellay's second preface to *L'Olive;* as such, its timeliness decreased as the controversy was won. But its immediate effect, in 1550, was to inflame further the opposition party; the *Quintil Horatian* was in part an attack upon this preface. The place of the preface in the controversy has been discussed by Laumonier (*Ronsard poète lyrique,* Paris: Hachette, 1932, pp. xxiii–xxx), who also reprints it in his edition of Ronsard's *Œuvres complètes* (Paris: Hachette, 1924, I, 43–50). Some of my notes are from that edition.

[A ij] AU LECTEUR

Si les hommes tant des siecles passés que du nostre ont merité quelque louange pour avoir piqué diligentement après les traces de ceus qui, courant par la carriere de leurs inventions, ont de bien loin franchi la borne, combien davantage doit-on vanter le coureur qui, galopant librement par les campaignes Attiques et Romaines, osa tracer un sentier inconnu pour aller à l'immortalité? Non que je soi, lecteur, si gourmand de gloire ou tant tormenté d'ambitieuse presumption que je te vueille forcer de me bailler ce que le tens, peut estre, me donnera (tant s'en faut, que c'est la moindre affection que j'aie de me voir pour si peu de frivoles jeunesses estimé). Mais quand tu m'appelleras le premier auteur lirique François et celui qui a guidé les autres au chemin de si honneste labeur, lors tu me rendras ce que tu me dois, et je m'efforcerai te faire apprendre qu'en vain je ne l'aurai receu. Bien que la jeunesse soit tousjours elongnée de toute studieuse occupation pour les plaisirs voluntaires qui la maistrisent, si est-ce que dès mon enfance j'ai tousjours estimé l'estude des bonnes lettres l'heureuse felicité de la vie, et sans laquelle on doit desesperer ne pouvoir jamais attaindre au comble du [A ij *v*] parfait contentement.

Donques desirant par elle m'approprier quelque louange encores non connue ni atrapée par mes devanciers, et ne voiant en nos poëtes François chose qui fust suffisante d'imiter, j'allai voir les étrangers et me rendi familier d'Horace, contrefaisant sa naive douceur, dès le méme tens que Clement Marot (seulle lumiere en ses ans de la vulgaire poësie) se travailloit à la poursuite de son *Psautier;* et osai le premier des nostres enrichir ma langue de ce nom "ode," comme l'on peut veoir par le titre d'une imprimée sous mon nom dedans le livre de Jaques Peletier du Mans, l'un des plus excelens poëtes de nostre âge; affin que nul ne s'atribue ce que la verité commande estre à moi. Il est certain que telle ode est imparfaite, pour n'estre mesurée ne propre à la lire ainsi que l'ode le requiert; comme sont encores douze ou treze que j'ai mises en mon *Bocage* sous autre nom que d'odes pour cette méme raison, servans de temoignage par ce vice à leur antiquité. Depuis aiant fait quelques-uns de mes amis participans de telles nouvelles inventions, approuvants mon entreprise se sont diligentés faire apparoistre combien nostre France est hardie et pleine de tout vertueus labeur, laquelle chose m'est aggreable pour veoir par mon moien les vieus liriques si heureusement resuscités.

Tu ju[A iij]geras incontinant, lecteur, que je suis un vanteur et glouton de louange. Mais si tu veus entendre le vrai, je m'assure tant de ton accoustumée honnesteté que non seulement tu me favoriseras, mais aussi quand tu liras quelques trais de mes vers qui se pourroient trouver dans les oeuvres d'autrui, inconsiderément tu ne me diras imitateur de leurs écris. Car l'imitation des nostres m'est tant odieuse (d'autant que la langue est encores en son enfance) que pour cette raison je me suis éloingné d'eus, prenant stile apart, sens apart, euvre apart, ne desirant avoir rien de commun avecq' une si monstrueuse erreur.

Donques m'acheminant par un sentier inconnu, et monstrant le moien de suivre Pindare et Horace, je puis bien dire (et certes sans vanterie) ce que lui-méme modestement témoigne de lui:

> Libera per vacuum posui vestigia princeps,
> Non aliena meo pressi pede.[a]

Je fu maintesfois avecques prieres admonesté de mes amis faire imprimer ce mien petit labeur et maintesfois j'ai refusé, apreuvant la sentence de mon sententieus auteur: "nonumque prematur in annum";[b] et mémement solicité par Joachim du Bellai, duquel le jugement, l'etude pareille, la longue frequentation, et l'ardant desir de reveiller la poësie Fran[A iij *v*]çoise avant nous foible et languissante (je excepte tousjours Heroet, Sceve, et Saint

a. Horace, *Epistles*, I.xix.21–22.
b. Horace, *Ars poetica*, l. 388.

Gelais) nous a rendus presque semblables d'esprit, d'inventions, et de labeur.

Je ne te dirai point à present que signifie strophe, antistrophe, epode (laquelle est tousjours differente du strophe et antistrophe de nombre ou de rime), ne quelle estoit la lire, ses coudes ou ses cornes; aussi peu si Mercure la façonna de l'escaille d'une tortue ou Polypheme des cornes d'un cerf, atachant les cordes aus[1] cornes du cerf, le creus de la teste servant de concavité resonante; en quel honneur estoient jadis les poëtes liriques, comme ils[2] accordoient les guerres emeues entre les rois et quelle somme d'argent ils[2] prenoient pour louer les hommes. Je tairai comme Pindare faisoit chanter les hinnes écris à la louange des vainqueurs Olympiens, Pithiens, Nemeans, Isthmiens. Je reserve tout ce discours à un meilleur loisir. Si je voi que telles choses meritent quelque breve exposition, ce ne me sera labeur de te les faire entendre, mais plaisir, t'assurant que je m'estimerai fortuné aiant fait diligence qui te soit agreable.

Je ne fai point de doute que ma poësie tant varie ne semble facheuse aus oreilles de nos rimeurs, et principalement des courtizans qui n'admirent qu'un petit sonnet petrarquizé ou quelque mignardise d'amour qui continue tousjours en [A iiij] son propos. Pour le moins, je m'assure qu'ils ne me sçauroient accuser sans condamner premierement Pindare, auteur de telle copieuse diversité, et oultre que c'est la sauce à laquelle on doit gouster l'ode. Je suis de cette opinion que nulle poësie se doit louer pour acomplie si elle ne ressemble la nature, laquelle ne fut estimée belle des anciens que pour estre inconstante et variable en ses perfections.

Il ne faut aussi que le volage lecteur me blâme de trop me louer, car s'il n'a autre argument pour médire que ce point-là, ou mon orthographe, tant s'en faut que je prenne égard à tel ignorant que ce me sera plaisir de l'ouir japper et caqueter, aiant pour ma deffence l'exemple de tous les poëtes Grecs et Latins. Et pour parler rondement, ces petis lecteurs poëtastres qui ont les yeus si agus à noter les frivoles fautes d'autrui, le blâmant pour un "A" mal écrit, pour une rime non riche ou un point superflu, et bref pour quelque legere faute survenue en l'impression, montrent evidemment leur peu de jugement de s'attacher à ce qui n'est rien, laissant couler les beaus mots sans les louer ou admirer. Pour telle vermine de gens ignorantement envieuse ce petit labeur n'est publié, mais pour les gentils espris ardans de la vertu et dedaignans mordre comme les mâtins la pierre qu'ils ne peuvent digerer.

Certes je m'assure [A iiij *v*] que tels debonnaires lecteurs ne me blâmeront, moi, de me louer quelquefois modestement, ni aussi de trop hautement celebrer les honneurs des hommes favorisés par mes vers. Car outre que ma boutique n'est chargée d'autres drogues que de louanges et d'honneurs,

1. au *1550* 2. il *1550*

c'est le vrai but d'un poëte liriq de celebrer jusques à l'extremité celui qu'il entreprend de louer. Et s'il ne connoist en lui chose qui soit dinne de grande recommandation, il doit entrer dans sa race et là chercher quelqu'un de ses aieus, jadis braves et vaillans; ou l'honnorer par le titre de son païs, ou de quelque heureuse fortune survenue soit à lui soit aux siens, ou par autres vagabondes digressions; industrieusement brouillant ores ceci, ores cela, et par l'un louant l'autre tellement que tous deus se sentent d'une méme louange.

Telles inventions encores te ferai-je veoir dans mes autres livres, où tu pourras (si les muses me favorisent comme j'espere) contempler de plus près les saintes conceptions de Pindare et ses admirables inconstances que le tens nous avoit si longuement celées. Et ferai encores revenir (si je puis) l'usage de la lire, aujourdui resuscitée en Italie, laquelle lire seule doit et peut animer les vers et leur donner le juste poix de leur gravité; n'affectant pour ce livre ici aucun titre de reputation, lequel ne t'est laché que pour al-[A v]ler découvrir ton jugement affin de t'envoier après un meilleur combatant—au moins si tu ne te faches dequoi je me travaille faire entendre aus étrangers que nostre langue (ainsi que nous les surpassons en prouesses, en foi, et religion) de bien loin devanceroit la leur si ces fameus sciamaches d'aujourdhui vouloient prendre les armes pour la defendre et victorieusement la pousser dans les païs étrangers. Mais que doit-on esperer d'eus? lesquels étants parvenus plus par opinion, peut estre, que par raison ne font trouver bon aus princes sinon ce qu'il[3] leur plaist; et ne pouvants souffrir que la clarté brusle leur ignorance, en medisant des labeurs d'autrui deçoivent le naturel jugement des hommes abusés par leurs mines. Tel fut jadis Bacchylide à l'entour d'Hieron roi de Sicile, tant notté par les vers de Pindare;[c] et tel encores fut le sçavant envieus Challimaq, impatient d'endurer qu'un autre flattast les oreilles de son roi Ptolémée, medisant de ceus qui táchoient comme lui de gouter les mannes de la roialle grandeur.[d] Bien que telles gens foisonnent en honneurs, et qu'ordinerement on les bonnette pour avoir quelque titre de faveur, si mourront-ils sans renom et reputation; et les doctes folies de poëtes survivront les innombrables siecles à venir, criants la gloire des princes consacrés par eus à l'immortalité.

3. qu'ils *1550*

c. Pindar dedicated various of the Pythian odes to Hiero. References to Bacchylides are found in the scholia to the Pythians; cf. Jebb, *Bacchylides: The Poems and Fragments* (Cambridge, 1905), p. 13. Various sixteenth-century editions of Pindar included the scholia, and the tradition is reflected by Lilio Gregorio Giraldi, *Historiae poetarum* (Basel, 1545): "Scribunt Pindari interpretes in Pythijs, Bacchylidis poëmata apud Hieronem Pindaricis esse praelata" (Dialogue IX, p. 1013).

d. The source of this tradition is in Suidas. Robert Estienne, *Dictionarium propriorum nominum* (Paris, 1542), ascribes to Callimachus an "in adversarium poema acerbissimum," and gives Suidas as his source of information.

THÉODORE DE BÈZE

PREFACE TO HIS *Sacrifice d'Abraham*

1550

TEXT:

(1576) Theod. Bezæ poemata. Psalmi Davidici XXX. Sylvæ. Elegiæ. Epigrammata, cùm alia varii argumenti, tum Epitaphia, & quæ peculiari nomine Iconas inscripsit. Omnia, in hac tertia editione, partim recognita, partim locupletata. [The printer was Henri Estienne; the dedication of the volume is dated Geneva, 1576. Newberry Library.]

[Cf. Brunet, I, 842–43, on this and the earlier editions; also Graesse, I, 359. The first edition was of 1550, probably Geneva; others followed in 1553, 1561, 1580, etc. The first edition of the *Poemata* was in 1548, and the second edition of 1569 did not contain the tragedy. Cf. also the edition of Geneva: Cherbuliez, 1856, for a listing of editions. None of these have been collated.]

Théodore de Bèze became a convert to Protestantism in 1548 and took refuge in Geneva in October of that year. He went to Lausanne in 1549, and it was there that he wrote his tragedy of the *Sacrifice d'Abraham*. According to one of his biographers, Henry Martyn Baird (*Theodore Beza*, New York: Putnam's, 1899, p. 49), the play was first performed there by students "in one of the halls of the former 'officiality' ... So favourable was its reception by the public, that it was repeatedly brought on the boards." Gustave Lanson ("Etudes sur les origines de la tragédie classique en France," *Revue d'histoire littéraire de la France*, X [1903], 185), believed that the tragedy was produced in Lausanne in 1549 or 1550, and that it thus preceded the *Cléopâtre* of Jodelle. Bèze himself referred to the performances, but without giving any date, in a letter to Johannes Jacomot prefatory to the latter's Latin translation of the *Abraham* in the *Poemata varia* of 1597:

> Istud qualecunque ante annos circiter quadraginta quinque fuisse Lausannae, vbi tunc Graecas literas profitebar, nulla sanè cura, sed leuiter, vt ludicrum quiddam perscriptum quod ab illius Gymnasij iuuenibus de more spectandum repraesentaretur, nec fortassis istud scriptionis genus quibusuis probatum iri. Respondit ille sic tamen istud & tum placuisse, & multis postea probatum, vt & in publicum prodierit, & multis Galliae locis magno cum applausu exhibitum ... (pp. 285–86).

The *Abraham* was translated into English by Arthur Golding in 1575 (published 1577). Its preface, dated 1550, went through many editions with the tragedy; it has been reprinted in the edition of Geneva: Cherbuliez, 1856, and in Malcolm W. Wallace's edition of the Golding translation, Toronto: University of Toronto Library, 1906.

[m. vi.] THEODORE DE BEZE AUX LECTEURS, SALUT EN NOSTRE SEIGNEUR

Il y a environ deux ans que Dieu m'a fait la grace d'abandonner le pays auquel il est persecuté[a] pour le servir selon sa saincte volonté; durant lequel temps, pource qu'en mes afflictions diverses fantasies se sont presentées à mon esprit, j'ay eu mon recours à la parole du Seigneur, en laquelle j'ay trouvé deux choses qui m'ont merveilleusement consolé. L'une est une infinité de promesses sorties de la bouche de celui qui est la verité mesmes et la parole duquel est tousjours accompagnée de l'effect. L'autre est une multitude d'exemples, desquels le moindre est suffisant non seulement pour enhardir mais aussi pour rendre invincibles les plus foibles et descouragez du monde; ce que nous voyons aussi estre avenu si nous considerons par quels moyens la verité de Dieu a esté maintenue jusques ici. Mais entre tous ceux qui nous sont mis en avant pour exemple au Vieil Testament, je trouve trois personnages ausquels il me semble que le Seigneur a voulu representer ses plus grandes merveilles, assavoir Abraham, Moyse, et David, en la vie desquels si on se miroit aujourdhui on se cognoistroit mieux qu'on ne fait.

Lisant donc ces histoires sainctes avec un merveilleux plaisir et singulier profit, il m'est pris un desir de m'exercer à escrire en vers tels argumens, non seulement pour les mieux considerer et retenir mais aussi pour louer Dieu en toutes sortes à moy possibles. Car je confesse que de mon naturel j'ay tousjours pris plaisir à la [m. vi. *v*] poesie, et ne m'en puis encores repentir. Mais bien ay-je regret d'avoir employé ce peu de grace que Dieu m'a donné en cest endroit en choses desquelles la seule souvenance me fait maintenant rougir.[b] Je me suis donques adonné à telles matieres plus sainctes, esperant de continuer ci-après, mesmement en la translation des Pseaumes que j'ay maintenant en main.[c]

Que pleust à Dieu que tant de bons esprits que je cognoy en France, en lieu de s'amuser à ces malheureuses inventions ou imitations de fantasies vaines et deshonnestes (si on veut juger à la verité), regardassent plustost à magnifier la bonté de ce grand Dieu, duquel ils ont receu tant de graces, qu'à flatter leurs idoles, c'est-à-dire leurs seigneurs ou leurs dames qu'ils entretienent en leurs vices par leurs fictions et flatteries. A la verité il leur seroit mieux seant de chanter un cantique à Dieu que de petrarquiser un sonnet et faire l'amoureux transi, digne d'avoir un chaperon à sonnettes ou de contrefaire ces fureurs poetiques à l'antique, pour distiler la gloire de ce

a. Bèze, fleeing from France, arrived in Geneva on October 24, 1548; cf. Baird, *op. cit.*, p. 33, and O. Douen, *Clément Marot et le Psautier huguenot*, Paris: Imprimerie nationale, 1878, I, 548 ff.

b. Allusion to his juvenilia published in the *Poemata* of 1548.

c. His translation of the Psalms was published the following year, *Les Trente-quatre pseaumes de David* ... , Geneva: Jean Crespin, 1551. They appeared with the Psalms of Marot in 1552, Geneva: Jacques Berjon. Cf. O. Douen, *op. cit.*, I, 552 ff.

monde et immortaliser cestuy-ci ou ceste-là; choses qui font confesser au lecteur que les auteurs d'icelles n'ont pas seulement monté en leur mont de Parnasse, mais sont parvenus jusques au cercle de la lune. Les autres (du nombre desquels j'ay esté à mon très grand regret) aiguisent un epigramme tranchant à deux costez ou picquant par le bout. Les autres s'amusent à tout renverser plustost qu'à tourner. Autres, cuidans enrichir nostre langue, l'accoustrent à la Greque et à la Romaine.

Mais quoy? dira quelcun, j'attendoy' une tragedie et tu nous donnes une satyre. Je confesse que pensant à telles phrenesies je me suis moy-mesme transporté. Toutesfois je n'entens avoir mesdit des bons esprits, mais bien voudroy'-je leur avoir descouvert si à clair l'injure qu'ils font à Dieu et le tort [m. vij.] qu'ils font à eux-mesmes, qu'il leur print envie de me surmonter en la description de tels argumens dont je leur envoye l'essay; comme je say qu'il leur sera bien aise si le moindre d'eux s'y veut employer.

Or pour venir à l'argument que je traitte, il tient de la tragedie et de la comedie, et pour cela ay-je separé le prologue et divisé le tout en pauses, à la façon des actes des comedies, sans toutesfois m'y assujettir. Et pource qu'il tient plus de l'un que de l'autre, j'ay mieux aimé l'appeller tragedie. Quant à la maniere de proceder, j'ay changé quelques petites circonstances de l'histoire pour m'approprier au theatre. Au reste j'ay poursuivi le principal au plus près du texte que j'ay peu, suivant les conjectures qui m'ont semblé les plus convenables à la matiere et aux personnes. Et combien que les affections soyent des plus grandes, toutesfois je n'ay voulu user de termes ni de manieres de parler trop eslongnées du commun, encores que je sache tel avoir esté la façon des Grecs et des Latins, principalement en leurs chorus (ainsi qu'ils les nomment). Mais tant s'en faut qu'en cela je les vueille imiter, que tout au contraire je ne trouve rien plus mal seant que ces translations tant forcées et mots tirez de si long temps qu'ils ne peuvent jamais arriver à poinct; tesmoin Aristophane, qui tant de fois et à bon droit en a repris les poetes de son temps. Mesmes j'ay faict un cantique hors le chorus, et n'ay usé de strophes, antistrophes, epirrhemes, parecbases, ni autres tels mots qui ne servent que d'espouvanter les simples gens, puisque l'usage de telles choses est aboli et n'est de soy tant recommandable qu'on se doive tormenter à le remettre sus.

Quant à l'orthographie, j'ay voulu que l'imprimeur suivist la commune, quelques maigres[d] fantasies qu'on ait mis en avant depuis trois ou quatre ans en [m. vij. *v*] ça. Et conseilleroy' volontiers aux plus opiniastres de ceux qui l'ont changée (s'ils estoyent gens qui demandassent conseil à autres qu'à eux-mesmes), puisqu'ils la veulent renger selon la prononciation, c'est-à-dire puisqu'ils veulent faire qu'il y ait quasi autant de manieres d'escrire qu'il y a non seulement de contrées mais aussi de personnes en

d. Possibly a punning allusion to the theories of Meigret.

France, ils apprenent à prononcer devant que vouloir apprendre à escrire. Car pour parler et escrire à leur façon, celui n'est pas digne de bailler les reigles d'escrire nostre langue qui ne la peut parler. Ce que je ne di pour vouloir calomnier tous ceux qui ont mis en avant leurs difficultez en ceste matiere, laquelle je confesse avoir bon besoin d'estre reformée, mais pour ceux qui proposent leurs resveries comme certaines reigles que tout le monde doit ensuivre.

Au surplus, quant au profit qui se peut tirer de ceste singuliere histoire, outre ce qui en est traitté en infinis passages de l'Escriture, j'en laisseray faire à celui qui parlera en l'epilogue,[e] vous priant quiconques vous soyez recevoir ce mien petit labeur d'aussi bon cœur qu'il vous est presenté.

De Lausanne, ce premier d'octobre. M. D. L.

e. Cf. the Epilogue, pp. 227–29 of the 1576 ed.:

Or uoyez-uous de foy la grand' puissance,
Et le loyer de uraye obeissance.
Parquoy, messieurs, & mes dames aussi,
Ie uous suppli' quand sortirez d'ici,
Que de uos cœurs ne sorte la memoire
De ceste digne & ueritable histoire.
Ce ne sont point des farces mensongeres,
Ce ne soint point quelques fables legeres:
Mais c'est un faict, un faict tresueritable,
D'un serf de Dieu, de Dieu tresredoutable.
Parquoy seigneurs, dames, maistres, maistresses,
Poures, puissans, ioyeux, pleins de destresses,
Grans & petis, en ce tant bel exemple
Chacun de uous se mire & se contemple.
Tels sont pour uray les miroirs où l'on uoid
Le beau, le laid, le bossu, & le droit.
Car qui de Dieu tasche accomplir sans feinte,
Comme Abraham, la parole tressaincte,
Qui nonobstant toutes raisons contraires,
Remet en Dieu & soy & ses affaires,
Il en aura pour certain une issue
Meilleure encor' qu'il ne l'aura conceue.
....
Or toy, grand Dieu, qui nous as fait cognoistre
Les grans abus esquels nous uoyons estre
Le poure monde, helas, tant peruerti,
Fay qu'un chacun de nous soit aduerti
En son endroit, de tourner en usage
La uiue foy de ce sainct personnage.
Voila, messieurs, l'heureuse recompense,
Que Dieu uous doint pour uostre bon silence.

JOACHIM DU BELLAY

SECOND PREFACE TO *L'Olive*

1550

TEXT:

L'Olive avgmentee depvis la premiere edition. La Mvsagnoeomachie & aultres oeuures poëtiques. Auec priuilege pour IIII ans. A Paris. 1550. On les vend au Palais es boutiques de Gilles Corrozet & Arnoul L'angelier. [Princeton University Library.]
[Cf. Brunet, I, 750; Tchemerzine, V, 42.]

COLLATED:

(1554) L'Olive avgmentee depvis la premiere edition. La Mvsagnoemachie & autres œuures poëtiques. ... A Paris. 1554. On les vend au Palais es boutiques de Gilles Corrozet & Arnoul L'angelier. [Harvard College Library.]

(1569) L'Olive, et avtres oevvres poetiqves de Ioachim Dv-Bellay Gentilhomme Angeuin. A Paris, De l'Imprimerie de Federic Morel, rue S. Ian de Beauuais, au Franc Meurier. M.D.LXVIIII. Avec Privilege dv Roy. [Yale University Library.]
[Cf. Brunet, I, 750; Tchemerzine, V, 44.]

Between 1549, when the first edition of *L'Olive* and the *Deffence* were published, and 1550, Du Bellay was vigorously attacked both for his practice in the former and his theory in the latter. Among the principal documents in the attack were the *Quintil Horatian* and Sebillet's preface to his translation of Euripides' *Iphigenia*. Therefore, in 1550, Du Bellay took the second edition of *L'Olive* as the occasion for answering these attacks, and wrote the new preface as the medium for his defence. The relationship of this second preface to the two documents mentioned has been studied by Chamard in his *Joachim du Bellay* (Lille: 1900, pp. 158–63) and in his notes to the preface in the *Œuvres poétiques* (Paris: Cornély, 1908, I, 11–25). Some of my notes are borrowed from the latter edition.

[A iii] AU LECTEUR

Combien que j'aye passé l'aage de mon enfance et la meilleure part de mon adolescence assez inutilement, lecteur, si est-ce que par je ne sçay quelle naturelle inclination j'ay tousjours aimé les bonnes lettres, singulierement nostre poësie Françoise pour m'estre plus familiere, qui vivoy' entre ignorans des langues estrangeres. Depuis, la raison m'a confirmé en cete opinion, considerant que si je vouloy' gaingner quelque nom entre les Grecz et Latins, il y fauldroit employer le reste de ma vie et (peult estre) en vain; etant jà coulé de mon aage le temps le plus apte à l'etude et me trouvant chargé d'affaires domestiques dont le soing est assez suffisant pour dégouter un homme beaucoup plus studieux que moy. Au moyen de quoy, n'ayant où passer le temps et ne voulant du tout le perdre, je me suis volontiers appliqué à nostre poësie, excité et de mon propre naturel et par l'exemple de plusieurs gentiz espritz François, mesmes de ma profession, qui ne dedaignent point manier et[1] l'epée et la plume, contre la faulse persuasion de ceux qui pensent tel exercice de[2] lettres deroger à l'estat de noblesse.

Certainement, lecteur, je ne pouroy' et ne voudroy' nier que si j'eusse ecrit en Grec ou en Latin ce ne m'eust esté un moyen plus expedié[3] pour aquerir quelque degré entre les doctes hommes de ce royaume. Mais il fault que je confesse ce que dict Ciceron en l'oraison *Pour Murene:* "Qui cum cytharoedi esse non possent,"[a] et ce qui s'ensuit. Considerant encores nostre langue estre bien loing de sa [A iii *v*] perfection, qui me donnoit espoir de pouvoir avecques mediocre labeur y gaingner quelque ranc sinon entre les premiers pour le moins entre les seconds, je voulu bien y faire quelque essay de ce peu d'esprit que la nature m'a donné. Voulant donques enrichir nostre vulgaire d'une nouvelle ou plustost ancienne renouvelée poësie, je m'adonnay à l'immitation des anciens Latins et des poëtes Italiens, dont j'ay entendu ce que m'en a peu apprendre la communication familiere de mes amis. Ce fut pourquoy à la persuasion de Jaques Peletier je choisi le sonnet et l'ode, deux poëmes de ce temps-là (c'est depuis quatre ans) encores peu usitez entre les nostres; étant le sonnet d'Italien devenu François, comme je croy, par Mellin de Sainct Gelais, et l'ode, quand à son vray et naturel stile, representée en nostre langue par Pierre de Ronsard. Ce que je vien de dire, je l'ay dict encores en quelque autre lieu,[b] s'il m'en souvient; et te l'ay bien voulu ramentevoir, lecteur, afin que tu ne penses que je me vueille attribuer les inventions d'autruy.

Or, afin que je retourne à mon premier propos, voulant satisfaire à l'instante requeste de mes plus familiers amis, je m'osay bien avanturer de mettre en lumiere mes petites poësies, après toutesfois les avoir communiquées à ceux que je pensoy' bien estre clervoyans en telles choses; singulierement à Pierre de Ronsard qui m'y donna plus grande hardiesse que tous les autres, pour la bonne opinion que j'ay tousjours eue de son vif esprit, exacte sçavoir, et solide jugement en nostre poësie Françoise. Je n'ay pas icy entrepris de respondre à ceux qui me voudroient blasmer d'avoir pre-

1. et *omitted 1554* 2. des *1569* 3. expedient *1569*

a. Cicero, *Pro Murena,* XIII, 29: "qui citharoedi fieri non potuerint ... ": "As they say of Greek musicians, those who cannot qualify to sing to the lyre, sing to the flute."

b. In the ode *Contre les envieux poëtes*, addressed to Ronsard in 1550; cf. ed. Chamard, *Œuvres poëtiques*, IV, 46.

cipité l'edition de mes œuvres, et comme on dict avoir trop tost mis la plume au vent. Car si mes ecriz sont bons, ma jeunesse ne leur doibt oster leur louange meritée. S'ilz ne sont telz, elle doibt pour le moins leur servir d'excuse, d'aultant que si [A iiii] j'ay faict en cet endroit quelque acte de jeunesse, je n'ay faict sinon ce que je devoy'. Pour le moins, ce m'est une faulte commune avecques beaucoup d'autres meilleurs espriz que le mien. Je ne suis tel que je vueille blâmer le conseil d'Horace quand à l'edition des poëmes;[c] mais aussi ne suis-je de l'opinion de ceux qui gardent religieusement leurs ecriz comme sainctes reliques pour estre publiez après leur mort, sçachant bien que tout ainsi que les mors ne mordent point, aussi ne sentent-ilz les morsures.[d]

Cete conscientieuse difficulté, lecteur, n'estoit ce qui me retardoit le plus en la premiere edition de mes ecriz. Je craignoy' un autre inconvenient qui me sembloit avoir beaucoup plus apparente raison de future reprehension. C'est que telle nouveauté de poësie pour le commencement seroit trouvée fort etrange et rude. Au moyen de quoy, voulant prevenir cete mauvaise opinion et quasi comme applanir le chemin à ceux qui excitez par mon petit labeur voudroient enrichir nostre vulgaire de figures et locutions estrangeres, je mis en lumiere ma *Deffence et Illustration de la langue Françoise*, ne pensant toutefois au commencement faire plus grand œuvre qu'une epistre et petit advertissement au lecteur. Or ay-je depuis experimenté ce qu'auparavant j'avoy assez preveu; c'est que d'un tel œuvre je ne rapporteroy jamais favorable jugement de noz rethoriqueurs Françoys, tant pour les raisons assez nouvelles et paradoxes introduites par moy en nostre vulgaire que pour avoir (ce semble) hurté un peu trop rudement à la porte de noz ineptes rimasseurs. Ce que j'ay faict, lecteur, non pour aultre raison que pour eveiller le trop long sillence des cignes et endormir l'importun croassement des corbeaux.

Ne t'esbahis donques si je ne respons à ceulx qui m'ont apellé hardy repreneur,[e] car mon intention ne feut onques d'auctorizer mes petiz oeuvres par la reprehension de telz gallans. [A iiii *v*] Si j'ay particularizé quelques ecriz, sans toutefois toucher aux noms de leurs aucteurs,[f] la juste douleur m'y a[4] contrainct, voyant nostre langue quand à sa nayfve proprieté si copieuse et belle estre souillée de tant de barbares poësies, qui par je ne sçay quel nostre malheur plaisent communement plus aux oreilles

4. à *1550*

c. Horace, *Ars poetica*, ll. 386–89.

d. Chamard believes that this is meant for Ronsard. Cf. his edition of the *Œuvres poëtiques*, I, 14, and his "L'Invention de l'ode et le différend de Ronsard et de Du Bellay," *Revue d'histoire littéraire de la France*, VI (1899), 47–50.

e. Cf. Sebillet, *Iphigenia* preface, p. 142 above.

f. *Deffence*, II, xi; ed. Chamard, pp. 310 [175] ff.

Françoises que les ecritz d'antique et solide erudition. Les gentilz espris, mesmes ceulx qui suyvent la court (seule escolle où voluntiers on apprent à bien et proprement parler), devroient vouloir pour l'enrichissement de nostre langue et pour l'honneur des espriz François que telz poëtes barbares ou feussent fouettez à la cuysine—juste punition de ceulx qui abusent de la pacience des princes et grands seigneurs par la lecture de leurs ineptes oeuvres—ou (si on les vouloit plus doucement traicter) qu'on leur donnast argent pour se taire, suyvant l'exemple du grand Alexandre qui usa de semblable liberalité en l'endroict de Cherille, poëte ignorant.[g] Certes j'ay grand' honte quand je voy' le peu d'estime que font les Italiens de nostre poësie en comparaison de la leur; et ne le treuve beaucoup etrange quand je considere que voluntiers ceulx qui ecrivent en la langue Toscane sont tous personnaiges de grand' erudition, voire jusques aux cardinaux mesmes et aultres seigneurs de renom qui daignent bien prendre la peine d'enrichir leur vulgaire par infinité de beaux ecriz; usant en cela de la diligence et discretion familiere à ceulx qui legerement n'exposent leurs conceptions au publique jugement des hommes.

Pense donques, je te prie, lecteur, quel prix doivent avoir en l'endroict de celle tant docte et ingenieuse nation Italienne les ecriz d'ung petit magister, d'un conard, d'un badault, et aultres mignons de telle farine, dont les oreilles de nostre peuple sont si abbreuvées qu'elles ne veulent aujourd'huy recevoir aultre chose. Je suis certain que tous lecteurs de bon jugement prendront ce que je [A v] dy en bonne part, veu que je ne parle du tout sans raison. Au fort, si nos petiz rimeurs s'en trouvoint un peu fachez, je leur conseilleroy' de prendre pacience, considerant que je ne suis ung Aristarque ou Aristophane dont la grave censure doive oster leurs ecriz du rôle de noz poësies ou retarder leurs aucteurs de mieux faire à l'advenir. Aussi leur mescontentement ne me doit rompre ma deliberation, qui par veu solennel me suis obligé aux muses de ne mentir jamais (que je le puisse entendre) ni en vin ni en poësie. Toutefois je ne veux pas du tout estre juge

g. The story of Alexander and Cherilus was frequently told in the sixteenth century; cf. Erasmus, *Apophthegmata*, Bk. VIII (ed. Basel, 1539, p. 835): "Cherilus erat Alexandri poëta non satis felix, qui quum fertur ita pactus, ut pro quoque bono versu acciperet Philippeum aureum, pro malo colaphum." Also L. G. Giraldi, *Historiae poetarum* (Basel, 1545), Dialogue III, pp. 324–25, for various versions of the story, e.g. "et cum eo praeterea pepigisse, ut pro singulis bonis carminibus singulos aureos acciperet, pro malis colaphos seu alapas" (p. 325). It will be noted however that this is not a case of a poet being paid for his silence; Du Bellay probably has in mind the story of Sylla and an unknown poet as also told by Erasmus, *Apophthegmata*, Bk. VI: "Idem [Sylla] quum ipsi libellum malus poëta de populo subiecisset, quòd in eum epigramma fecisset, tantummodo uersibus alternis longiusculis, statim ex his rebus quas tum uendebat iussit ei præmium tribui, sub hac conditione, quid postea scriberet. Existimabat ille etiam mali poëtae operam aliquo dignam præmio. Simul autem & silentium redemit ab eo qui scribere nesciret" (p. 602).

si severe et incorruptible en matiere de poësie que je suyve l'heresie de celuy qui disoit: "Mitte me in lapicidinas."[h]

Quelques-uns se plaignent de quoy je blâme les traductions poëtiques en nostre langue, dont ilz ne sont (disent-ilz) illustrateurs ny gaigez ny renommez.[i] Ausi ne suis-je. Mais s'ilz n'alleguent aultre raison, je n'y feray point de response; encores moins à ce qu'ilz disent que j'ay reservé la lecture de mes ecriz à une affectée demy-douzaine des plus renommez poëtes de nostre langue.[j] Car je n'avoy' entrepris de faire un catalogue de tous les aultres, mesmes de ceulx qui ne m'etoient conneuz ny à leurs noms ny à leurs oeuvres. Ceux dont je ne cherche point les applaudissemens ont occasion de gronder. Aussi me plaisent leurs aboys, car je n'en crain' gueres les morsures. Je fonde encor' (disent-ilz) l'immortalité de mon nom sur moindre chose que leurs escritz, dont toutefois ilz ne pretendent aucune louange.[k] Ce n'est à eulx ny à moy à juger de nostre cause, qui (Dieu mercy) n'est de telle importance que la court y doibve estre longuement embesongnée. Aussi n'ay-je pas fondé mon advancement sur telles magnifiques comparaisons. Si en mes poësies je me loüe quelquesfois, ce n'est sans l'imitation des anciens; et en cela je ne pense avoir encor' esté si excessif que j'aye pour illustrer le mien offensé l'hon[A v *v*]neur de personne.

Et puis je me vante d'avoir inventé ce que j'ay mot à mot traduit des aultres.[l] A peu que je ne leur fay la responce que fist Virgile à un quiddam Zoile qui le reprenoit d'emprunter les vers d'Homere.[m] J'ay (ce me semble) ailleurs assez deffendu l'immitation.[n] C'est pourquoy je ne feray longue response à cet article. Qui vouldroit à ceste ballance examiner les escritz des anciens Romains et des modernes Italiens, leur[5] arrachant toutes ces belles plumes empruntées dont ilz volent si haultement, ilz seroint en hazard d'estre accoutrez en corneille Horacienne.[o] Si par la lecture des bons livres je me suis imprimé quelques traictz en la fantaisie, qui après, venant à exposer

5. leurs *1550*

h. Cf. Diodorus Siculus, *Bibliotheca Historica*, XV.vi.3–5. Chamard indicates that Du Bellay probably knew the story through Erasmus' *Apophthegmata* (Bk. VI). Various versions of the anecdote are collected by L. G. Giraldi, *Historiae poetarum*, Dialogue IX, pp. 1018 ff.; cf. Dialogue VII, pp. 818–19.

i. Cf. Sebillet, *Iphigenia* preface, p. 143 above.

j. Cf. Du Bellay's first preface to the *Olive*, p. 140 above, and Sebillet, *Iphigenia* preface, p. 143 above.

k. Cf. Sebillet, *Iphigenia* preface, p. 143 above.

l. *Ibid.*, p. 143 above.

m. Reported by Donatus, *Vita Vergilli*, ed. I. Brummer (Leipzig: Teubner, 1912): "Verum intellecturos facilius esse Herculi clavam quam Homero versum subripere."

n. Cf. *Deffence*, I, viii and II, iii; ed. Chamard, pp. 105–108, 193–200 [45–48, 103–7].

o. Horace, *Epistles*, I.iii.18–20: "lest, if some day perchance the flock of birds come to reclaim their plumage, the poor crow, stripped of his stolen colours, awake laughter."

mes petites conceptions selon les occasions qui m'en sont données, me coulent beaucoup plus facilement en la plume qu'ilz ne me reviennent en la memoire, doibt-on pour ceste raison les appeller pieces rapportées? Encor' diray-je bien que ceulx qui ont leu les oeuvres de Virgile, d'Ovide, d'Horace, de Petrarque, et beaucoup d'aultres que j'ay leuz quelquefois assez negligemment, trouverront qu'en mes escriptz y a beaucoup plus de naturelle invention que d'artificielle ou supersticieuse immitation.

Quelques-ungs, voyans que je finissoy' ou m'efforçoy' de finir mes sonnetz par ceste grace qu'entre les aultres langues s'est faict propre, l'epigramme François, diligence qu'on peult facilement recongnoistre aux oeuvres de Cassola Italien,[p] disent pour ceste raison que je l'ay immité, bien que de ce temps-là il ne me feust congneu seulement de nom—ou Apollon jamais ne me soit en ayde! Je ne me suis beaucoup travaillé en mes ecriz de ressembler aultre que moy-mesmes; et si en quelque endroict j'ay usurpé quelques figures et façons de parler à l'imitation des estrangers, aussi n'avoit aucun loy ou privilege de le[6] me deffendre.

Je dy encores cecy, lecteur, affin que tu ne penses que j'aye [A vi] rien emprunté des nostres si d'avanture tu venois à rencontrer quelques epithetes, quelques phrases et figures prises des anciens et appropriées à l'usaige de nostre vulgaire. Si deux peintres s'efforcent de representer au naturel quelque vyf portraict,[7] il est imposible qu'ilz ne se rencontrent en mesmes traictz et lineamens, ayans mesme exemplaire devant eulx. Combien voit-on, entre les Latins immitateurs des Grecz et entre les modernes Italiens immitateurs des Latins, de commencemens et de fins de vers, de couleurs et figures poëtiques quasi semblables? Je ne parle poinct des orateurs. Ceulx qui voudront considerer le stile des Ciceroniens ou aultres ne trouverront estrange la ressemblance qu'ont ou pourront avoir les poëmes François, si chacun s'efforce d'escrire par immitation des estrangers. Tous ars et sciences ont leurs termes naturelz. Tous mestiers ont leurs propres outilz. Toutes langues ont leurs motz et loqutions usitées; et qui n'en voudroit user, il se faudroit forger à part nouveaux artz, nouveaulx mestiers, et nouvelles langues. Ce que j'ay dict, cetuy-ci l'a dict encor' et cetuy-là. Aussi les muses n'ont restrainct et enfermé en l'esprit de deux ou trois tout ce qui se peut dire de bonne grace en nostre poësie.

S'il y a quelques faultes en mes escritz, aussi ne sont tous les aultres parfaictz. Ceulx qui avecques raison me voudront faire ce bien de me reprendre, je mettray peine d'en faire mon profit. Car je ne suis du nombre de ceulx qui ayment myeux deffendre leurs faultes que les corriger. Mais si quelques-ungs directement ou indirectement (comme on dict) me vouloient

6. le *omitted 1554* 7. protraict *1550*

p. Luigi Cassola, *Madrigali del magnifico signor cavalier Luigi Cassola, Piacentino*, Venice: Giolito, 1544, published by Giuseppe Betussi.

taxer non point avecques la raison et modestie accoutumée en toutes honnestes controversies de lettres, mais seulement avecques une petite maniere d'irrision et contournement de nez, je les adverty' qu'ilz n'attendent aulcune response de moy. Car je ne veux pas faire tant d'honneur à telles bestes masquées que je les estime [A vi *v*] seulement dignes de ma cholere. Si quelques-uns vouloient renouveler la farce de Marot et de Sagon, je ne suis pour les en empescher; mais il fault qu'ilz cherchent aultre badin pour jouer ce rôle avecques eux.

Voylà ung petit desseing, lecteur, de ce que je pouroy' bien respondre à mes calomniateurs si je vouloy' prendre la peine de leur tenir plus long propoz. Quand à ceux qui blasment en moy cet etude poëtique comme totalement inutile, s'ilz veulent combatre contre la poësie, elle a des armes pour se deffendre; s'ilz plaignent l'empeschement de ma promotion, je les remercie de leur bonne volunté. Ceux qui ayment le jeu, les banquetz et aultres menuz plaisirs, qu'ilz y passent et le jour et la nuict si bon leur semble. Quand à moy, n'ayant aultre passetems de plus grand plaisir, je donneray voluntiers quelques heures à la poësie. Et combien ce m'est un labeur peu laborieux et coutumier, si ce n'est ou faisant quelque voiage ou en lieu qui n'ait aultre plus joyeuse occupation, bien l'entendent ceux qui me hantent de familiarité. J'ayme la poësie, et me tire bien souvent la muse (comme dict quelq'un)[q] furtivement en son oeuvre. Mais je n'y suis tant affecté que facilement je ne m'en retire si la fortune me veult presenter quelque chose où avecques plus grand fruict je puisse occuper mon esprit.

Je te prie donques, amy lecteur, me faire ce bien de penser que ma petite muse telle qu'elle est n'est toutefois esclave ou mercenaire comme d'ung tas de rymeurs à gaiges; elle est serve tant seulement de mon plaisir. Je te prie encores ne trouver mauvais cet advertissement ou t'ennuyer de sa longueur, comme oultrepassant les bornes d'une epistre. En recompence de quoy je te fay' present[8] de mon *Olive* augmentée de plus de la moitié et d'une *Musagnoeomachie*, c'est-à-dire "la Guerre des Muses et de l'Ignorance." Ceux qui ne treuvent rien bon sinon ce qui sort de leur main y trouverront à mordre en beaucoup de lieux, mesme en cet endroict [A vij] où je fay mention de quelques sçavans hommes de nostre France.[r] Les uns diront que j'en ay laissé que je ne devoy' pas oublier; les aultres, que je n'ay pas gardé l'ordre, nommant quelques-ungs les derniers qui meritoient bien estre au premier ranc. Je n'ay qu'une petite response à toutes ces objections frivoles: c'est que mon intention n'estoit alors d'ecrire une hystoire mais une poësie. Et combien ce genre d'escrire est peu consciencieux en telles

8. un present *1554*

q. Ovid, *Tristia*, IV.x.19–20.

r. For the list of these learned men, see the *Œuvres poétiques*, ed. Chamard, IV, 12 ff.

choses, je m'en rapporte seulement à ceux qui l'entendent. Mais pourquoy pren-je tant de peine, lecteur, à preoccuper l'excuse de ce qui sera trouvé (peult estre) la moindre faulte de mes oeuvres? J'ay tousjours estimé la poësie comme ung somptueux banquet où chacun est le bienvenu, et n'y force l'on personne de manger d'une viande ou boire d'un vin s'il n'est à son goust, qui le sera (possible) à celuy d'un aultre.

C'est encor' la raison pourquoy j'ay si peu curieusement regardé à l'orthographie, la voyant aujourdhuy aussi diverse qu'il y a de sortes d'ecrivains. J'appreuve et loue grandement les raisons de ceux qui l'ont voulu reformer. Mais voyant que telle nouveaulté desplaist autant aux doctes comme aux indoctes, j'ayme beaucoup mieulx louer leur invention que de la suyvre, pource que je[9] ne fay pas imprimer mes oeuvres en intention qu'ilz servent de cornetz aux apothequaires ou qu'on les employe à quelque aultre plus vil mestier. Si tu treuves quelques faultes en l'impression, tu ne t'en dois prendre à moy, qui m'en suis rapporté à la foy d'autruy. Puis le labeur de la correction est tel, singulierement en un œuvre nouveau, que tous les yeux d'Argus ne fourniroient à voir les faultes qui s'i treuvent.

A Dieu, ami lecteur.

9. je *omitted 1554*

JACQUES AMYOT

DEDICATION AND PREFACE TO PLUTARCH'S *Lives*

1559

TEXT:

Les Vies des Hommes Illustres Grecs & Romains, Comparees l'vne auec l'autre par Plutarque de Chæronęe, Translatees de Grec en François. A Paris, De l'imprimerie de Michel de Vascosan. M.D.LVIIII. Auec Priuilege du Roy. [Library of Congress.]

[Cf. Brunet, *Supplément*, II, 258; Van Praet, *Catalogue des livres imprimés sur vélin de la Bibliothèque du roi*, V, 49–50; Cat. Rothschild, III, No. 2735, giving a complete description of Amyot's own copy; and my "A False First Edition of Amyot's Plutarch," *Modern Language Notes*, LXI (1946), 454–58.]

COLLATED:

(1567) Les Vies des Hommes Illvstres, Grecs et Romains, comparees l'une auec l'autre par Plutarque de Chæronee, Translatees premierement de Grec en François par maistre Iaques Amyot lors Abbé de Bellozane, & depuis en ceste troisieme edition reueuës & corrigees en infinis passages par le mesme Translateur, maintenant Abbé de sainct Corneille de Compiegne, Conseiller du Roy, & grand Aumosnier de France, à l'aide de plusieurs exemplaires uieux escripts à la main, & aussi du iugement de quelques personnages excellents en sçauoir. A Paris, Par Vascosan Imprimeur du Roy. M.D.LXVII. Avec privilege. [Princeton University Library.]

[Cf. Brunet, *Supplément*, II, 258–59; Cat. Rothschild, No. 1899. The second edition, also published by Vascosan, 1565, and listed by the British Museum, has not been collated. The three editions by Vascosan are the only authentic ones; cf. René Sturel, *Jacques Amyot traducteur des Vies parallèles de Plutarque*, Paris: Champion, 1908, pp. 94 ff. I have also collated the editions of Lausanne: Le Preux, 1574 (Harvard), Lausanne: Le Preux, 1575 (University of Pennsylvania and Princeton University Library, the latter with a 1559 title page), Paris: Jaques du Puys, 1578 (Pierpont Morgan Library), and Geneva: Jacob Stoer, 1593 (Harvard); since this collation has yielded only orthographic differences, the results are not given here. To all intents and purposes, Amyot's dedication and preface were never modified after the first edition of 1559.]

As early as 1553, when he was writing the dedication to his translation of Diodorus of Sicily (published in 1554), Amyot announced his intention to compose an essay in praise of history: "je ne veux point pour ceste heure entrer plus avant en ce discours de la louange de l'histoire, le reservant à un autre plus grand et plus excellent œuvre des *Vies* de Plutarque" (cited by Sturel, *op. cit.*, p. 89). The essay appeared in 1559 with the first edition of the *Lives* and reappeared with all subsequent editions. The work itself was extremely popular—Sturel lists fifteen separate editions in the sixteenth century alone, and others are known—and the preface must thus have been one of the most widely read critical documents of the period. Auguste de Blignières, *Essai sur Amyot et les traducteurs français au XVIe siècle* (Paris: Durand, 1851, pp. 271–74), has shown the relationship of the ideas contained in the preface to the ideas of other writers on history in the same century.

[a ij] AU TRÈS PUISSANT ET TRÈS CHRESTIEN ROY DE FRANCE, HENRY DEUXIEME DE CE NOM, JACQUES AMYOT ABBÉ DE BELLOZANE SON TRÈS HUMBLE ET TRÈS OBEÏSSANT SERVITEUR S.

Ceux qui de pere en fils sont nez ou habituez soubs une juste, legitime et hereditaire principauté comme la vostre, Sire, doyvent à mon jugement au service de leur prince la devotion que les sages anciens attribuoyent à la charité du païs où l'on a pris naissance. Car ils disoyent que le premier degré en estoit deu aux dieux, le second au païs, et le troisieme aux parens, sans faire mention de roy ne de prince pourautant que c'estoyent gens qui vivoyent soubs autre forme de gouvernement que de royaume, et qui pour inciter les hommes à defendre le public (soubs lequel la vie, l'honneur et le bien de chaque particulier sont compris) et à tascher de profiter à la communauté de ceux avec lesquels on a convenance de nativité, de langue, de loix, de mœurs et de demeurance, enseignoyent que non seulement la raison de tout droict humain, mais aussi la religion de droict divin et le devoir de conscience, obligeoyent toute personne de servir à son entier pouvoir au bien public de son païs—outre la douceur d'affection que nature imprime en noz cœurs et la conformité d'humeurs qui se[1] treuve ordinairement en noz corps avec le ciel et l'air où nous avons premierement respiré, qui semble une obligation naturelle. Mais comme ainsi soit que toutes nations, non plus que tous hommes particuliers, ne sont pas propres à estre regies d'une mesme sorte de gouvernement, pource qu'il est plus expedient à aucunes de servir que de commander, et qu'au jugement du prince des philosophes la plus parfaitte des trois especes du gouvernement de la chose publique, et la plus selon Dieu et nature, est celle de la royauté,[a] ceux qui par election ou par nativité y sont soubmis doyvent bien affectueusement esvertuer toutes leurs forces, et de corps et d'entendement, pour faire chacun en son endroit et selon sa vacation service à leur souverain; attendu que servans à un ils profitent à tous, et qu'en luy seul gist l'heur et malheur de ses subjects. De luy depend le repos ou travail, l'aise ou misere de tous ceux qui vivent soubs son empire. Luy seul represente la chose publique, veu que sa volonté est loy, sa parole arrest, et sa vie discipline exemplaire de bien ou de mal faire.

Si me semble à ce propos qu'Artabanus, l'un des capitaines du roy Xerxes,

1. ce *1559;* se *1567*

a. This is the general argument emerging from Aristotle's *Politics*; cf. IV.xi.

respondit sagement à Themistocles lorsqu'il se retira fuitif de la Grece en la court de [a ij *v*] Perse:

> Les loix et coustumes des hommes, dit-il, sont differentes, Themistocles, et y a des choses tenues pour honestes en un païs qui ne le sont pas en un autre; mais bien est-il partout honeste à un chacun de maintenir et garder celles de son païs. Car quant à vous autres Grecs, on dit que vous n'avez rien si cher ny en si grande recommandation que la liberté et l'egalité. Mais nous Persiens estimons que la plus belle et la plus saincte ordonnance que nous ayons soit celle qui nous commande d'honorer, servir, et reverer nostre roy, ne plus ne moins que l'image de Dieu vivant qui regit et gouverne tout ce monde.[b]

C'est bien un tiltre auguste et venerable que celuy-là, et le plus magnifique et le plus digne qui sçauroit estre donné à un monarque souverain, prouveu qu'il s'en vueille souvenir et qu'il ait tousjours la crainte de Dieu et la raison qui luy sonne continuellement aux oreilles. Ce qui jadis s'observoit par coustume en la court de Perse, là où l'un des gentilshommes de la chambre avoit la charge de se trouver tous les matins au reveil du roy et luy dire: "Leve-toy, Sire, pour prouveoir aux affaires dont le grand Mesoromasdes (car ainsi appeloyent-ils Dieu) veut que tu ayes le soing."[c]

Ce discours de raison naturelle, Sire, quand encore le commandement des escriptures sainctes, où l'authorité des princes est si authentiquement fondée, n'y seroit point, oblige assez tous voz subjects à desirer de vous faire service. Et de ma part, ayant cherché de vous en faire en l'institution de Messeigneurs d'Orleans et d'Angoulesme, voz très heureusement nez enfans, que Dieu benie, pour employer le temps qui me demeuroit vuide à faire encore quelque autre chose qui vous fust agreable, après avoir vacqué au devoir de l'office auquel il vous a pleu me commettre de leur enseigner les lettres, je me suis mis à reveoir ce que de long temps j'avoye traduit de Grec en François des *Vies* de Plutarque, et à continuer de traduire ce qui m'en restoit; tant que finablement, ayant conduit l'œuvre totale à chef, j'ay pris la hardiesse de la vous presenter imprimée et la faire sortir soubs la sauvegarde de vostre très illustre nom, en public ès mains de voz hommes. Non que j'eusse opinion qu'il peust issir de moy, personne si basse et si petite en toute qualité, chose qui meritast d'estre mise devant les yeux de vostre majesté; mais bien ayant certaine confiance que l'œuvre de soy est si recommandable et si excellente qu'elle pourra faire excuser le defaut

b. Quoted from Plutarch, *Themistocles*, XXVII.

c. Plutarch, *Commentarium in Principe requiri doctrinam*, tr. Erasmus, in the Vascosan, 1544 ed. of the *Ethica*, p. 252A: "Nam Persarum rex unum habebat cubicularium, cui hoc negocii mandatum erat, ut diluculo ingressus illi diceret: Surge rex, atque ea cura negocia, quæ te curare uoluit Mesoromasdes. At erudito prudentíque principi intus in animo adest, qui semper idem dictet ac iubeat." Cf. notes q, r, s below for additional borrowings from this edition.

qui s'y trouvera de ma part. Pource que je confesse avoir plus estudié à rendre fidelement ce que l'autheur a voulu dire que non pas à orner ou polir le langage, ainsi que luy-mesme a mieuls aimé escrire doctement et gravement en sa langue que non pas doucement ny facilement.

Mais en recompense il y a tant de plaisir, d'instruction et de profit en la substance du livre, qu'en quelque style qu'il soit mis, prouveu qu'il s'entende, il ne peut faillir à estre bien receu de toute personne de bon jugement; pource que c'est en somme un recueil abbregé de tout ce qui a esté de plus memorable et de plus digne faict ou dict par les plus grands rois, plus excellens capitaines et plus sages hommes des deux plus nobles, plus vertueuses et plus puissantes nations qui jamais furent au monde. Et au reste j'espere, Sire, que de vostre grace et liberalité royale, laquelle se monstre aussi bien à recevoir guayement et joyeusement les petits presens comme à donner franchement et liberalement les grands, quand la bonne volonté des offrans excuse l'impuissance de mieuls faire, vous aurez pour agreable l'humble af[a iij]fection que j'ay euë en ce faisant de recommander à la posterité la memoire de vostre glorieux regne, de servir au bien public de voz subjects, et d'enrichir nostre langue Françoise selon la foible portée de mon peu de sens et de litterature. Pource que je m'asseure que d'icy à longues années, quand les survivans trouveront tant de beaux et bons livres translatez des langues Grecque et Latine en la Françoise, durant vostre heureux regne et soubs l'inscription de vostre très illustre nom, l'on vous donnera la louange d'avoir glorieusement couronné et achevé l'œuvre que ce grand roy François, vostre feu pere, avoit heureusement fondé et commencé de faire renaistre et florir en ce noble royaume les bonnes lettres; dont nostre langue va tous les jours de plus en plus recevant tel ornement et enrichissement que ny l'Italiene, ny l'Hespagnole, ny autre qui soit aujourdhuy en usage par l'Europe ne se pourra vanter de la surmonter en nombre ny en bonté des outils de sapience qui sont les livres. Et consequemment voz subjects en recueilliront ce fruict, que sans se travailler pour apprendre les nobles anciennes langues, qui coustent beaucoup de temps et de peine à apprendre, à cause qu'elles sont mortes et qu'il les faut tirer hors des monumens des livres où elles sont ensepvelies, ils auront en leur maternelle et chez eux, par maniere de dire, ce qu'il y a de plus beau et de meilleur en la Latine et en la Grecque. A raison duquel benefice ils seront de tant plus obligez à prier Dieu, comme je fay en toute humilité et toute reverence, pour la bonne prosperité, accroissement d'honneur, et continuation de longue vie en bonne santé de vous, Sire, et de tout ce qui appartient à vostre sacrée royale majesté.

En vostre royale maison de Fonteine-belleau,[2] au mois de Febvrier, M. D. LVIIII.

2. Fonteine-bleau *1567*

[a iij *v*] AUX LECTEURS

La lecture des livres qui apportent seulement une vaine et oiseuse delectation aux lisans est à bon droict reprouvée des hommes sages et de grave jugement, et celle qui profite aussi simplement, sans faire aimer le profit qu'elle apporte et addoucir la peine que l'on prend à le recueillir par quelque allechement de plaisir, semble un peu trop austere au goust de plusieurs delicats entendemens, qui pour ce defaut ne s'y peuvent arrester longuement. Mais celle qui plaist et profite, qui delecte et instruit ensemble, a tout ce que l'on sçauroit desirer pour estre universellement aimée, receuë et estimée de toute maniere de gens, suyvant le commun dire du poëte Horace:

> Qui le plaisir à l'utilité joinct,
> En ses escripts le gagne de tout poinct.[d]

Et fait mieuls ces deux effects, l'un pour l'amour de l'autre reciproquement, en profitant plus d'autant qu'elle delecte et delectant davantage d'autant qu'elle profite.

Ceste louange à mon advis est deuë proprement, ou principalement plus qu'à nulle autre, à la lecture des histoires, comme à celle où il y a plus d'honeste plaisir conjoinct avec utilité, et qui a plus d'efficace pour ensemble plaire et profiter, resjouïr et enseigner, que nulle autre sorte d'escripture ne d'invention humaine. A raison de quoy il sembleroit aussi convenable d'advouër que les hommes sont autant ou plus obligez aux bons esprits qui ont merité le nom d'historiens par leurs sages escripts, qu'ils ne sont à nulle autre maniere de lettres; pourautant que l'histoire est une narration ordonnée des choses notables dictes, faictes ou advenues par le passé, pour en conserver la souvenance à perpetuité et en servir d'instruction à la posterité. Et tout ainsi comme la memoire est le tresor de l'entendement de l'homme, sans laquelle les actions des autres deux parties demeureroyent imperfaictes et presque inutiles, aussi se peut-il dire que l'histoire est à la verité le tresor de la vie humaine, qui preserve de la mort d'oubliance les faicts et dicts memorables des hommes et les adventures merveilleuses et cas estranges que produit la longue suite du temps. C'est pourquoy le sage Platon[3] veut qu'elle ait esté appelée histoire pource qu'elle arreste le flux de nostre memoire,[e] qui autrement auroit trop peu de durée et de tenue. Et peut-on à cela recognoistre combien nous luy sommes obligez, si nous imaginons seulement en quelle horreur de tenebres et quelle fondriere d'ignorance bestiale et pestilente nous serions abysmez si la sou-

3. ἀπὸ τοῦ ἵστασθαι τον ῥοῦν τῆς μνήμης *margin 1559*

d. *Ars poetica*, ll. 343–44.

e. The marginal notation (cf. variant 3) is possibly a paraphrase of *Cratylus*, 437: ἔπειτα ἡ "ἱστορία" αὐτό που σημαίνει ὅτι ἵστησι τὸν ῥοῦν.

venance de tout ce qui s'est faict ou qui est advenu avant que nous fussions nez estoit entierement abolie et esteincte.

Je veux donques laisser à part l'excellence et la dignité de la chose en soy, veu que non seulement elle est plus ancienne que toute autre espece d'escripture qui onques ait esté au monde, mais aussi qu'elle a eu cours entre les hommes avant que l'usage des lettres mesmes y fust. Pource que lors les vivans laissoyent à leurs successeurs la memoire des choses passées en chansons qu'ils faisoyent apprendre par cœur de main à main à leurs enfans, ainsi que l'on a peu veoir de nostre temps par l'exemple des barbares habitans ès terres neufves occidentales, qui sans conserve d'aucunes lettres avoyent la cognoissance des choses advenues bien huit cens [a iiij] ans auparavant. Je laisse semblablement à deduire que c'est la plus seure garde et le plus durable monument que les hommes puissent laisser de leurs faicts en ce monde pour consacrer leur nom à immortalité. Car il n'y a ny statues, ny trophées de marbre, ny arcs de triomphe, ny coulonnes, ny sepultures magnifiques qui puissent combattre la durée d'une histoire eloquente, accomplie des qualitez qu'elle doit avoir. Aussi peu me veux-je arrester à peser qu'elle a je ne sçay quoy de venerable en ce qu'elle fait profession de dire tousjours verité et en ce que son propre subject est de traitter de toutes les plus hautes et plus grandes choses qui se facent en ce monde, pource qu'il me semble que l'utilité grande, qui est comme dit Horace presque la mere de justice et d'equité,[f] la recommande tant qu'il n'est jà besoin de luy chercher d'ailleurs authorité ny ornement de dignité.

Car c'est une regle et instruction certaine, qui par exemples du passé nous enseigne à juger du present et à prevoir l'advenir, à fin que nous sçachions ce que nous devons suyvre ou appeter et qu'il nous faut fuir et eviter. C'est une peincture qui nous met devant les yeux, ne plus ne moins qu'en un tableau, les choses dignes de memoire qu'anciennement ont faictes les puissans peuples, les rois et princes magnanimes, les sages gouverneurs et vaillans capitaines et personnes marquées de quelque notable qualité, nous representant les mœurs des nations estrangeres, les loix et coustumes anciennes, les desseings des hommes particuliers, leurs conseils et entreprises, les moyens qu'ils ont tenus pour parvenir, et leurs deportemens quand ils sont parvenus aux plus hauts ou bien qu'ils ont esté dejettez aux plus bas degrez de la fortune; tellement qu'il ne sçauroit naistre accident en paix ny en guerre, en public ny en privé, que qui aura leu diligemment, bien entendu et fidelement retenu les histoires, n'y treuve lumiere pour s'esclarcir et conseil pour se resoudre à prendre party ou à donner advis à un autre en tout douteux et dangereux passage, pour elire le plus expedient et juger à peu près le poinct auquel devra tomber un affaire

f. Horace, *Satires*, I.iii.98.

bien emmeslé: advertissement pour soy moderer en prosperité et reconfort pour se revenir et soustenir en adversité.

Et si le fait avec plus de grace, d'efficace et de dexterité que ne font les livres de philosophie morale, d'autant que les exemples sont plus aptes à esmouvoir et enseigner que ne sont les argumens et les preuves de raisons ny leurs imperieux preceptes, à cause qu'ils sont particuliers, accompagnez de toutes leurs circonstances, là où les raisons et demonstrations sont generales et tendent plus à fin de prouver ou de donner à entendre, et les exemples à mettre en œuvre et à executer. Pource qu'ils ne monstrent pas seulement comme il faut faire, mais aussi impriment affection de le vouloir faire, tant pour une inclination naturelle que tous hommes ont à imiter que pour la beauté de la vertu, qui a telle force que partout où elle se voit elle se fait desirer et aimer. Aussi le fait-elle avec plus de pois et plus de gravité que ne font les inventions et compositions poëtiques, d'autant qu'elle ne se sert jamais que de la nue verité, et la poësie ordinairement enrichit les choses qu'elle louë par dessus le merite, à cause que son but principal est de delecter; et encore plus honestement et plus doucement que ne font les loix et ordonnances civiles, d'autant qu'il est plus honeste instruire et enseigner que non pas punir et corriger.

Et toutefois l'histoire a bien aussi sa maniere de chastier les meschans par la note d'infamie perpetuelle dont elle marque leur memoire, qui est un grand moyen de retirer des vices ceux qui autrement auroyent mauvaise et lasche volonté; comme aussi est-ce un bien vif et poignant aiguillon aux [a iiij *v*] hommes de gentil cœur et de nature genereuse, pour les inciter à entreprendre toutes hautes et grandes choses, que la louange et la gloire immortelle dont elle remunere les bienfaisans. Car les livres sont pleins d'exemples d'hommes de courage et d'entendement elevé qui, pour le desir de perpetuer la memoire de leur nom par le seur et certain tesmoignage des histoires, ont volontairement abandonné leurs vies au service de la chose publique, despendu tous leurs biens, supporté travaux infinis et d'esprit et de corps, pour defendre les oppressez, bastir edifices publiques, establir loix et gouvernemens politiques, inventer arts et sciences necessaires à l'entretenement et ornement de la vie humaine: de tous lesquels grands benefices la grace est deuë à la fidele recommandation des histoires. Car encore que la vraye vertu ne demande aucun loyer mercenaire de ses actes louables et se contente à par soy de la conscience d'avoir bien fait, si est-ce chose utile et bonne, à mon advis, d'attraire par tous moyens les hommes à bien faire; et ne doit-on point defendre aux gens de bien d'esperer honneur (qui naturellement accompagne la vertu comme l'ombre le corps) de leurs vertueux faicts. Car on voit ordinairement que c'est un signe infallible de lasche, basse et vile nature que ne sentir point les estincelles du desir d'honneur, et que ceux qui estiment chose impertinente, superflue ou malseante que d'estre loué, ne font aussi rien qui merite que l'on les louë; ains sont coustumierement personnes de cœur failly, desquelles les pensées ne s'estendent point plus avant que les vies et dont la souvenance se pert aussi quand et la veuë.

Or si le conseil des vieilles gens est grandement estimé pource qu'ayans vescu longuement il est force qu'ils ayent beaucoup veu; et si ceux qui ont longuement voyagé en païs estranges, qui se sont trouvez en beaucoup d'affaires et ont grande experience des choses de ce monde, sont reputez sages et dignes à qui l'on mette en main les resnes des grands gouvernemens; combien fait à estimer la lecture des histoires, qui en un seul jour nous peut fournir plus d'exemples que ne sçauroit faire le cours entier de la plus longue vie d'un homme? Tellement que ceux qui sont exercitez à la lire (ainsi qu'il appartient) encore qu'ils soyent jeunes deviennent, quant à l'intelligence des affaires du monde, tels que s'ils estoyent vieux et chenus, et n'ayans jamais bougé de leurs maisons sont aussi advertis, informez et instruits de tout ce qui est par le monde, que ceux qui avec travaux innumerables et dangers infinis ont abbregé leurs jours à courir toute la terre habitable; comme au contraire ceux qui sont ignorans des choses faites ou advenues avant qu'ils fussent nez, quoyqu'ils soyent suraagez, demeurent tousjours enfans, et dedans le propre païs de leur naissance sont en pareille condition que les estrangers.

Brief, il se peut veritablement dire que la lecture des histoires est une eschole de prudence, que l'homme se forme en son entendement en considerant meurement l'estat du monde qui a esté par le passé et observant diligemment par quelles loix, quelles mœurs et quelle discipline les empires, royaumes et seigneuries se sont jadis premierement establies et depuis maintenues et grandies, ou au contraire changées, diminuées et perdues. Aussi lit-on qu'Alexander Severus, très sage et vertueux empereur de Rome, toutes et quantes fois qu'il avoit à deliberer de quelque chose de consequence, tant au faict de la guerre que de gouvernement, appeloit tousjours ceux qui estoyent renommez de sçavoir bien les histoires.[g]

Je sçay bien toutefois qu'il y en a qui insisteront alencontre, en soustenant que ceste lecture des histoires ne sçauroit [a v] que bien peu ou rien du tout servir à l'acquisition de prudence, veu qu'elle gist en action et que c'est experience reelle et actuelle qui l'engendre, quand l'homme re-

g. Cf. Aelius Lampridius, *Alexander Severus* (Loeb Classics, *Scriptores Historiae Augustae*, II, 208): "et omnes litteratos et maxime eos qui historiam novant, requirens quid in talibus causis quales in disceptatione versabantur veteres imperatores . . ." Aelius Lampridius was printed, with other historians, by Robert Estienne in 1544.

marque bien et retient fermement ce qu'il a veu à l'œil et qu'il a experimenté de faict, suyvant ce que dit l'ancien poëte Afranius:[h]

> Prudence suis, Usage est le mien pere,
> Qui m'engendra en Memoire ma mere;

et ce qu'entendoit le Philosophe, qui dit que la main estoit l'instrument de sapience.[i] Au moyen de quoy (disent-ils) ceux qui parlent de matieres de gouvernement et d'affaires d'estat, mesmement de ceux de la guerre, par livres en parlent comme clercs d'armes, ainsi que dit le proverbe François, rapportant à celuy des Grecs qui appellent un "pilote par livre" celuy qui n'a pas seure et certaine cognoissance des choses dont il parle, voulans dire qu'il ne se faut pas fier à l'intelligence que l'on acquiert par la lecture ès choses qui consistent en action, et qu'il faut avoir mis la main à l'œuvre; ne plus ne moins que rien ne sert à devenir bon peintre avoir ouy souvent parler et discourir de la peinture et deviser des couleurs, qui ne prent le pinceau en main; et qu'au contraire il se trouve de bien sages hommes et de bons capitaines qui ne sçavent ne lire ny escrire, joint qu'ils alleguent davantage qu'au faict des armes toutes choses se changent d'an à autre, par maniere de dire. Au moyen de quoy les ruses et subtilitez que l'on pourroit apprendre ès livres ne serviroyent non plus que les mines esventées, ainsi que Cambyses remonstre à son fils Cyrus en Xenophon, disant que comme en la musique les chansons les plus nouvelles sont ordinairement celles qui pour une fois plaisent le plus, à cause que jamais elles n'ont esté ouyes, aussi en la guerre les ruses qui n'ont point esté practiquées sont celles qui succedent le mieuls et qui sortent le plus souvent à effect, d'autant que les ennemis s'en doutent moins.[j]

Mais aussi ne suis-je pas celuy qui voudroit soustenir que l'on peust faire un sage gouverneur d'estat politique ny un grand capitaine d'un personnage qui n'auroit jamais bougé de dessus les livres en une estude; combien que Ciceron escrive de Lucius Lucullus que quand il partit de Rome capitaine general et lieutenant du peuple Romain pour aller faire la guerre au roy Mithridates, il n'avoit experience quelconque de la guerre, mais que depuis il feit si grande diligence de lire les histoires et d'interroguer sur chaque poinct les vieux capitaines et gens de longue experience qu'il menoit avec luy, que quand il fut arrivé en Asie, où il falut mettre à bon

h. From Afranius' *Sella* (cf. Bothe, *Poetarum Latii Scenicorum Fragmenta*, V², p. 188). The passage is cited by Aulus Gellius, *Attic Nights*, XIII.viii.3. Melanchthon used the lines as an example in his *Syntax*; cf. ed. Paris: R. Estienne, 1528, p. 6 *v*.

i. The general argument of the *Nicomachean Ethics*, II.i.4 ff., although the hand is not specifically mentioned.

j. Xenophon, *Cyropaedia*, I.vi.38.

esciant la main à la besongne,[4] il se trouva un très suffisant capitaine, ainsi que le tesmoignerent ses effects; attendu que par voyes d'armes toutes contraires il desfeit les deux plus puissans, plus redoutez et plus grands princes qui fussent lors en tout l'Orient.[k] Car son entendement fut si vif, son soing si vigilant, et son courage si bon qu'il n'eut point besoing du long apprentissage ny de la grossiere discipline d'usage. Et encore que je confesse qu'il se soit trouvé des gouverneurs et capitaines qui par la seule vigueur de leur nature aidée de longue rotine d'usage ont fait de belles et grandes choses, l'on ne me sçauroit aussi nier que s'ils eussent adjouxté à ces dons de nature la cognoissance des lettres et la lecture des histoires, ils n'en eussent peu faire de beaucoup plus grandes et qu'ils n'en eussent esté de beaucoup plus perfaits.

Pource qu'à la perfection de ceste suffisance de bien gouverner en paix ou en guerre, il y a trois choses necessairement requises, comme en toute autre excellence d'art ou de science: la nature, l'art, et l'exercita[a v *v*]tion. La nature, au propos que nous traittons, fournira d'un bon sens naturel, d'un corps bien composé pour endurer tout travail, et d'une bonne volonté de ce faire valoir. L'art contribuera le jugement et la cognoissance acquise par les exemples et sages discours leus et releus ès bonnes histoires. Et l'exercitation donnera la promptitude, l'asseurance et la facilité de les mettre à execution. Car prudence, quoyqu'elle regisse l'action, est neantmoins vertu de l'entendement, qui enseigne le poinct du milieu auquel consiste toute louable action entre deux vitieuses extremitez, du peu et du trop. Et qui s'attent à l'acquerir par rotine d'usage seulement, et aime mieuls apprendre à ses despens qu'à ceux d'autruy, il pourroit estre du nombre de ceux que touche l'ancien proverbe qui dit que l'experience est la maistresse des fols, pource que la vie de l'homme est courte et l'experience difficile et perilleuse, mesmement au faict de la guerre, auquel, comme disoit Lamachus capitaine Athenien, on ne peut pas faillir deux fois,[l] pource que les fautes y sont de telle consequence qu'elles apportent le plus souvent ruïne d'estat ou perte de vie à ceux qui les font. Ainsi ne faut-il pas attendre celle prudence usagere, qui couste si cher et qui est si longue à venir que l'homme bien souvent est mort en la peine avant qu'elle soit arrivée, et qu'il luy faudroit une seconde vie pour l'employer quand elle est trop tard venue. Ains la faut haster par diligence de lire continuellement ès anciennes et modernes histoires, à fin de jouïr de l'heur que dit le poëte:

> Heureux celuy qui pour devenir sage,
> Du mal d'autruy fait son apprentissage.[m]

---

4. besongue *1559*

k. Cicero, *Academica*, II.i.2.

l. Plutarch, *Moralia*, III, 101.

m. The lines translate a line of an interpolated scene in Plautus' *Mercator*, Act IV, Scene VIII, l. 40, of the old editions: "Vetus id dictum est, Feliciter is sapit, qui

Au demeurant, quant à ceux qui vont disans que le papier endure tout, s'il y en a aucuns qui à faulses enseignes usurpent le nom d'historiens et qui par haine ou faveur offensent la majesté de l'histoire en y meslant quelque mensonge, cela n'est point la faute de l'histoire, ains des hommes partiaux qui abusent indignement de ce nom pour desguiser et couvrir leurs passions. Ce qui n'adviendra jamais si celuy qui escrit l'histoire a les parties qui luy sont necessairement requises pour meriter le nom d'historien: qu'il soit despouillé de toute affection, sans envie, sans haine ny flatterie, versé aux affaires du monde, eloquent, homme de bon jugement pour sçavoir discerner ce qui se doit dire et qui se doit laisser et ce qui nuiroit plus à declarer qu'il ne profiteroit à reprendre et à condamner. Attendu que sa fin principale doit estre de servir au public, et qu'il est comme un greffier tenant registre des arrests de la court et justice divine, les uns donnez selon le style et portée de nostre foible raison naturelle, les autres procedans de puissance infinie et de sapience incomprehensible à nous, par dessus et contre tout discours d'humain entendement, lequel ne pouvant penetrer jusques au fond des jugemens de la divinité pour en sçavoir les motifs et les fondemens, en attribue la cause à ne sçay quelle fortune, qui n'est autre chose que fiction de l'esprit de l'homme s'esblouïssant à regarder une telle splendeur et se perdant à sonder un tel abysme, comme ainsi soit que rien n'advient ny ne se fait sans la permission de celuy qui est justice mesme et verité essentielle, devant qui rien n'est ne futur ny passé et qui sçait et entend les choses casuelles necessairement. Laquelle consideration enseigne aux hommes à s'humilier soubs sa puissante main en recognoissant qu'il y a une cause premiere qui gouverne supernaturellement, d'où vient que ny la hardiesse n'est pas tousjours heureuse ny la prudence bien asseurée.

Ces utilitez si notables sont partout accompagnées de delectation singuliere, qui prin[a vi]cipalement procede de la diversité et de la nouvelleté dont nostre nature s'esjouïst et en est grandement desireuse, à cause qu'ayant une affectueuse inclination à son bien souverain, elle le va cherchant en tout ce qu'elle cuide beau ou bon en ce monde. Mais ne trouvant de quoy se contenter soubs la voulte du ciel, elle s'ennuye et se fasche bientost de ce que nagueres elle avoit ardemment appeté, et va ainsi errant en la temerité de ses appetits; dont elle ne cessera jamais de changer continuellement jusques à ce qu'estant unie à ceste fin derniere de son bien souverain, où est la perfection de toute beauté et toute bonté, ses souhaits seront à un coup assouvis. Cest appetit de varieté ne se peut mieuls recreer qu'en celle qui est le repertoire et le tesmoignage du temps, pere de toute

---

periculo alieno sapit" (ed. Paris: R. Estienne, 1530, p. 160 *r*; cf. the edition of Pareus, Hanover, 1641). The scene, attributed to Hermolaus Barbarus, does not appear in modern editions. Note that the line quoted also appears in G. Major's collection of *Sententiae Veterum Poetarum*, Paris: R. Estienne, 1551, p. 98.

nouvelleté, et messagere de l'antiquité. Car si nous sentons un plaisir singulier à escouter ceux qui retournent de quelque lointain voyage, racontans les choses qu'ils ont veuës en estrange païs, les mœurs des hommes, la nature des lieux, les façons de vivre differentes des nostres; et si nous sommes quelquefois si ravis d'aise et de joye que nous ne sentons point le cours des heures en oyant deviser un sage, disert et eloquent vieillard, en la bouche duquel sourt un flux de langage plus doux que miel quand il va recitant les adventures qu'il a euës en ses verds et jeunes ans, les travaux qu'il a endurez et les perils qu'il a passez; combien plus devons-nous sentir de ravissement, d'aise et d'esbahissement de veoir en une belle, riche et veritable peincture d'eloquence les cas humains representez au vif et les variables accidens que la vieillesse du temps a produits dès et depuis l'origine du monde: les establissemens des empires, ruïnes des monarchies, accroissemens ou aneantissemens des royaumes, et tout ce qui onques a esté de plus esmerveillable par l'univers? le tout representé si vifvement qu'en le lisant nous nous sentons affectionnez comme si les choses n'avoyent pas esté faictes par le passé, ains se faisoyent presentement; et nous en trouvons passionnez de joye, de pitié, de peur et d'esperance ne plus ne moins, presque, que si nous estions sur le faict sans estre en aucune peine ou danger, ains avec le contentement qu'apporte la recordation en seureté des maux que l'on a autrefois endurez, et avec l'aise que descrit Lucrece en ses vers:[n]

C'est un plaisir, quand la mer violente
Est par les vens battue de tourmente,
Veoir de sur terre en toute seureté
Quelque autre en mer durement tourmenté;
Non que ce soit volupté agreable
De veoir autruy en peine miserable,
Mais pourautant qu'il fait grand bien de veoir
Quels maux on n'a que l'on pourroit avoir.

Aussi voit-on que ceste lecture retient et arreste tellement les bons esprits que non seulement elle leur fait bien souvent oublier tous autres plaisirs, mais aussi leur sert d'agreable divertissement en leurs ennuis et quelquefois de medecine en leurs maladies. Comme l'on trouve escrit du roy Alphonse de Naples, prince tant renommé par les chroniques pour sa sagesse et bonté, qu'estant griefvement malade en la ville de Capoue,[5] après que ses medecins eurent employé tout ce que leur art enseigne pour

5. Capone *1559*

n. Lucretius, *De Rerum Natura*, II, 1–4. At this date, no translation of Lucretius had been published, although a manuscript translation by Guillaume des Autels was in circulation. Cf. E. Belowski, *Lukrez in der französischen Literatur der Renaissance*, Berlin: Ebering, 1934, p. 16.

luy recouvrer sa santé, voyant que rien n'y valoit, il se resolut de ne prendre plus de medecines; et pour passer son temps, se feit lire devant luy l'histoire de Quintus Curtius des faicts et ge[a vi *v*]stes d'Alexandre le Grand; à la leçon de laquelle il prit si merveilleux plaisir que la nature s'en fortifiant surmonta l'obstination de la maladie. Parquoy estant retourné en sa convalescence, il donna congé aux medecins en leur disant: "Ne me faites plus de feste de vostre Hippocrates et Gallien, puisqu'ils ne m'ont sceu guarir; et vive Quintus Curtius, qui m'a si bien sceu aider à recouvrer ma santé."[o]

Mais si la lecture et cognoissance des histoires est agreable, utile et profitable à toute autre maniere de gens, je dy qu'elle est de tout poinct necessaire aux grands princes et aux rois; non seulement pource qu'ayans de plus pesantes et plus difficiles charges, la raison voudroit aussi qu'ils eussent plus grande provision des qualitez qui seroyent requises pour bien s'en acquiter; ny aussi pource qu'estant le propre subject de l'histoire traitter de toutes hautes matieres, comme sont guerres, batailles, conquestes de villes et de païs, traittez de paix ou d'alliance, il semble qu'elle leur soit plus particulierement qu'à nuls autres affectée; mais pource qu'à prendre les choses comme elles sont, estans nez et nourris tendrement en delices pour le grand soing et la crainte que l'on a de leurs personnes, ainsi qu'il appartient à leur grandeur, ils ne travaillent pas en jeunesse tant comme il est besoing à qui veut apprendre les nobles langues anciennes et les disciplines laborieuses que comprent la philosophie. Puis quand ils ont attaint l'aage d'homme, leur devoir les appelle aux actions des grands affaires, de maniere qu'il ne leur reste autre exercice d'entendement plus propre que la lecture des histoires en leur langue, laquelle sans peine leur peut enseigner, avec douceur et facilité grande, tout ce que les penibles œuvres des philosophes touchant le gouvernement de la chose publique leur sçauroyent monstrer pour sçavoir bien regir et gouverner les peuples et païs que Dieu a soubmis à leur obeïssance. Mais le pis est qu'ils sont tousjours ou le plus du temps environnez de personnes qui ne cherchent qu'à leur complaire par toutes voyes, et s'en treuve bien peu qui leur osent dire franchement la verité de toutes choses; et au contraire, l'histoire ne leur flatte rien, ains leur met à descouvert devant les yeux les fautes et vices de ceux qui en grandeur de fortune ont esté semblables à eux. A raison de quoy Demetrius le Phalerien, personnage autant renommé pour sa sagesse de bien gouverner un estat politique que pour son eminent sçavoir, conseilloit à Ptolomeus, le premier roy d'Ægypte après le trespas d'Alexan-

o. The story is related by Antonio Beccadelli (known as Panormita) in his *De dictis et factis Alphonsi regis Aragonum libri quatuor*. Enea Silvio Piccolomini wrote a commentary on the work which appears with it in the edition of Basel, 1538, and separately in the works of Piccolomini (cf. the edition of Basel, 1571, p. 476). For a modern German translation of Beccadelli, see Hermann Hefele, *Alfonso I, Ferrante I von Neapel* (Jena: Diederichs, 1912), p. 32.

dre le Grand, qu'il leust souvent et diligemment les livres qui traittent de l'administration des royaumes: "Pource que là-dedans, disoit-il, tu trouveras plusieurs choses que tes serviteurs et familiers ne t'oseroyent dire."[p]

Il y a, davantage, que tels personnages ne peuvent pas facilement sortir hors des limites de leurs seigneuries et voyager en autres païs comme font les personnes privées, pource que la jalousie de leurs estats et le regard de leur dignité requierent qu'ils ne se treuvent jamais en lieu où autre leur puisse commander. Et bien souvent, à faute d'avoir veu à l'œil les païs et cognu les forces des peuples et princes voisins, ont[6] fait des entreprises bien mal fondées; auquel defaut l'information qu'ils en peuvent avoir par la lecture des histoires est un des plus aisez et plus commodes remedes qu'ils sçauroyent trouver.

Mais quand il n'y auroit autre occasion que ceste derniere, elle seule deust bien convier les princes à lire souvent et affectueusement les livres où sont escripts les faicts heroïques des sages et vaillans hommes, mesmement des rois qui ont esté devant eux. C'est qu'en les lisant il leur prend envie d'en faire de semblables, mesmement à ceux qui ont le cœur [a vij] haut et genereux, pource que les semences des vertus royales, qui sont nées avec eux, s'esveillent alors par emulation de ceux qui ont esté ou qui sont en degré pareil à eux; et comme en noblesse de sang et en grandeur d'estat ils ne veulent ceder à personne, encore moins le veulent-ils en gloire de faicts vertueux. De quoy l'on pourroit alleguer innumerables exemples, si la chose n'estoit de soy tant notoire que la doute en seroit trop plus desraisonnable que la preuve necessaire. Ainsi peut-on veritablement conclurre que l'histoire est la maistresse des princes, de laquelle ils peuvent apprendre sans peine, en passant leur temps et avec singulier plaisir, la meilleure partie de ce qui est requis à leur office.

Or est-il que selon la diversité de la matiere qu'elle traitte ou de l'ordre et maniere d'escrire dont elle use, on luy donne noms differens. Mais il y en a entre autres deux principales especes: l'une qui expose au long les faicts et adventures des hommes et s'appelle du nom commun d'histoire; l'autre qui declare leur nature, leurs dicts et leurs mœurs, qui proprement se nomme vie. Et combien que leurs subjects soyent fort conjoincts, si est-ce que l'une regarde plus les choses, l'autre les personnes; l'une est plus publique, l'autre plus domestique; l'une concerne plus ce qui est au dehors de l'homme, l'autre ce qui procede du dedans; l'une les evenemens et l'autre les conseils, entre lesquels il y a bien souvent grande difference, suyvant ce que Siramnes Persien respondit à ceux qui s'esbahissoyent dont venoit que ses devis estoyent si sages et ses effects si peu heureux: "C'est pourau-

6. on *1559;* ont *1567*

p. Plutarch, *Apophthegmata*, III, 189.

tant, dit-il, que les devis sont en ma pleine disposition, et les effects en celle de fortune et du roy."[q]

Mais entre tous ceux qui se meslerent onques de rediger par escript les vies des illustres hommes, la palme d'excellence, au jugement des plus clairvoyans, est meritoirement adjugée à Plutarque philosophe Grec, natif de la ville de Chæronée en la province de la Bœoce, homme noble, consommé en tout rare sçavoir, ainsi comme ses œuvres ne laissent douter à qui les a entierement leuës, et ayant toute sa vie jusques en sa vieillesse manié affaires publiques comme luy-mesme tesmoigne en plusieurs lieux, mesmement au traitté qu'il a fait, *Si l'homme viel se doit entremettre du gouvernement de la chose publique*; et qui jadis eut cest heur et honneur que d'estre precepteur de l'empereur Trajan, ainsi que l'on tient communement et qu'il est expressement porté par une missive qui se lit au devant de la traduction Latine de ses *Politiques*, laquelle (à dire la verité) m'est un petit suspecte pource que je ne l'ay point trouvée entre ses œuvres Grecques, joinct qu'elle parle comme si le livre estoit dedié à Trajan, ce qui est manifestement dedict par le commencement du livre, et pour quelques autres raisons. Encore toutefois, pource qu'elle m'a semblé sagement et gravement escripte, et estre digne de luy, je l'ay inserée en ce lieu:[r]

> Plutarque à Trajan, salut. Je sçavoye bien que la moderation de ta nature n'estoit point convoiteuse de l'empire, combien que par honesteté de vie tu te sois tousjours efforcé de le meriter, à raison dequoy tu en es de tant plus estimé digne, que plus on te treuve esloigné du vice d'ambition. C'est pourquoy maintenant je m'esjouy avec ta vertu et avec ma fortune, si tant est que tu vueilles justement administrer ce que tu as deuëment merité. Car autrement je suis asseuré que tu t'es exposé à de grands dangers, et moy aux langues des mesdisans, pourautant que Rome ne peut endurer un lasche empereur et que la commune voix du peuple a tousjours accoustumé de rejetter les fautes des disciples sur leurs maistres, comme Seneque est deschiré par les langues des mesdisans pour les pechez de son Neron; la temerité des jeunes disciples

---

q. Plutarch, *Apophthegmata*, tr. by Raphael Regius in the Vascosan, 1544 ed. of the *Ethica*, p. 80A: "Quare Siramnes Persa quibusdam admirantibus, quòd sapientibus ipsius uerbis facta non responderent: Verborum, inquit, ipse quidem sum dominus, factorum autem simul cum Rege fortuna." The passage occurs in the dedication by Plutarch to Trajan, to which Amyot later refers in this preface (see p. 176 below).

r. The original Latin letter was included by John of Salisbury in his *Polycraticus*, Bk. V, Ch. 1, where it is attributed to Plutarch; cf. Migne, *Patrologia Latina*, CXCIX, col. 539. Amyot's immediate source was probably the Vascosan, 1544 ed. of the *Ethica*, where the Latin letter appears with the following prefatory remark, similar to Amyot's own: "Epistola Plutarchi ad Traianum imperatorem in nuncupatione Politicorum: quam epistolam Germani typographi omiserunt tam in græcis quàm latinis codicibus. Nos tamen eam cum pro grauitate sententiæ tum pro nostro candore dignam duximus quam uel uniuerso operi praeponeremus" (fol. [Aij *v*]).

> de Quintilian est imputée à luy-mesme; et blasme-l'on Socra[a vij *v*]tes d'avoir esté trop doux à son pupille. Mais quant à toy, tu feras bien toutes choses prouveu que tu ne te departes point d'avec toy-mesme, et si tu te composes le premier et disposes toutes autres choses à la vertu, il n'y aura rien qui ne succede selon ton desir. Je t'ay descript les moyens qu'il faut tenir pour bien administrer une chose publique, et ay monstré combien les mœurs y ont de pouvoir. Si tu y veux obtemperer, tu as Plutarque pour directeur et guide de ta vie; sinon, je proteste par ceste missive que ce n'est point de la doctrine de Plutarque que tu vas au dommage et à la ruïne de l'empire.

Ceste epistre tesmoigne disertement qu'il a esté precepteur de Trajan, à quoy il semble que s'y rapporte aussi ce que Suïdas en escript, disant:[s]

> Plutarque, natif de la ville de Cheronée en la Bœoce, fut du temps de l'empereur Trajan et encore devant. Mais Trajan luy donna l'honneur de la dignité consulaire, et voulut que les officiers et magistrats qui seroyent en toute la province de l'Esclavonnie ne feissent chose aucune sans son authorité.

Voilà ce qu'en escript Suïdas. Et me semble bien que Trajan, si sage empereur, ne luy eust pas fait ce grand honneur s'il ne se fust senty tenu à luy de quelque obligation notable. Mais ce qui plus encore me semont à le croire, c'est que l'on voit en plusieurs faicts et dicts de Trajan la mesme droitture, bonté et justice naïfvement empreinte, dont le moule et la forme est, par maniere de dire, engravée ès œuvres morales de Plutarque, de sorte que l'on remarque notoirement que l'un a bien sceu faire ce que l'autre luy a sagement enseigné. Car Dion escript qu'entre autres honneurs que le Senat de Rome decerna à Trajan, il luy donna le tiltre d'Optimus Imperator, c'est-à-dire très bon empereur.[t] Et Eutropius met que jusques à son temps, quand un nouveau empereur venoit à estre receu au Senat, entre les cris d'heureux presage et les souhaits qu'on luy faisoit, on luy crioit: "Que puisses-tu estre plus heureux qu'Auguste et meilleur que Trajan."[u] Comment que ce soit, il est bien certain que Plutarque luy dedia le recueil de ses *Apophthegmes*.

Mais estant retiré en sa maison, après avoir longuement vescu à Rome, il se meit à escrire ceste œuvre excellente des *Vies*, qu'il appela *Parallelon* comme qui diroit l'accouplement ou assortissement, pource qu'il accouple un Grec avec un Romain, mettant leurs vies l'une devant l'autre et les

s. Suidas, *Lexicon*, ed. Ada Adler, Pt. IV (Leipzig: Teubner, 1935), p. 150, No. 1793. Again, Amyot's source was probably the Vascosan, 1544 ed. of the *Ethica*, where the Latin translation of the Suidas entry appears on the same page as the "Plutarch" letter treated in the preceding note.

t. Dio, *Roman History*, LXVIII, 18 (Loeb, VIII, 401).

u. Eutropius, *Breviarium*, ed. F. Ruehl (Leipzig: Teubner, 1919), VIII.v. Note that Du Bellay wishes Henri II a similar good fortune in Bk. II, Ch. II of the *Deffence*.

conferant ensemble selon qu'ils se sont trouvez avoir entre eux conformité de nature, de mœurs et d'adventures, en examinant ce que l'un a eu de meilleur ou de pire, de plus grand ou de plus petit que l'autre; le tout avec tant de beaux et graves discours partout, tirez des plus profonds et plus cachez secrets de la philosophie morale et naturelle, tant de sages advertissemens et de fructueuses instructions, si affectueuse recommandation de la vertu et detestation du vice, tant de belles allegations d'autres autheurs, tant de propres comparaisons, et tant de hautes inventions, que le livre se doit plustost nommer un tresor de toute rare et exquise litterature que de luy donner autre nom. Aussi dit-on que Theodorus Gaza, personnage Grec d'erudition singuliere et digne de l'anciene Grece, estant quelques fois enquis par ses familiers amis, qui le voyoyent si fort affectionné à l'estude qu'il en oublioit toute autre chose, quel autheur il choisiroit entre tous s'il estoit reduit à ce poinct de n'en pouvoir retenir qu'un tout seul, il respondit qu'il eliroit Plutarque, pource que tout compris il n'y en a pas un qui soit si profitable et si delectable ensemble à lire que luy.[v]

Celuy auquel il dedie son œuvre, Sosius Senecio, estoit un senateur Romain, ainsi que tesmoigne Dion,[w] qui escript que les trois personnages que Trajan aimoit et honoroit le plus estoyent Sosius, [a viij] Parma et Celsus, jusque à leur faire à tous trois eriger des statues. Il est vray qu'il avoit escript beaucoup d'autres vies que l'injure du temps nous a enviées, comme notamment luy-mesme fait mention de celles de Scipion l'Africain et de Metellus le Numidique;[x] et j'ay leu une petite epistre d'un sien fils, où il n'y a point de nom, transcripte d'un vieil exemplaire de la librairie de S. Marc à Venize, par laquelle il escript à un sien amy la liste de tous les livres que son pere a composez;[y] là où entre les coupples des vies il met celle de Scipion et d'Epaminondas, et au bout celles d'Augustus Cesar, de Tiberius, de Caligula, de Clodius, de Neron, de Galba, de Vitellius et d'Othon. Mais ayant fait toute diligence à moy possible de les chercher ès principales librairies de Venize et de Rome, je ne les ay peu recouvrer. Seulement en ay-je tiré plusieurs diversitez de leçons et plusieurs corrections en conferant les vieux livres escripts à la main avec ceux qui sont imprimez,

v. Cf. Migne, *Patrologia Graeca*, CLXI, cols. 981–82, where the anecdote is quoted from Xylander, *Vita Plutarchi*, ed. Paris, 1624, p. 11. The *Vita* also appeared with the 1620 ed. of Xylander's translation of Plutarch, originally published between 1561 and 1570. I have been unable to discover Amyot's immediate source for the anecdote.

w. Dio, *Roman History*, LXVIII, 16 (Loeb, VIII, 393).

x. The life of Metellus is mentioned by Plutarch, *Caius Marius*, XXIX; of Scipio Africanus, in *Pyrrhus*, VIII (Loeb, IX, 546 and 366 respectively).

y. The original Greek text of the letter is given by Bernadakis, *Moralia* (Leipzig: Teubner, 1896), VII, 473–77. For discussion, see Wyttenbach ed. of the *Moralia* (Oxford: Clarendon Press, 1795), I, xxxvii–xxxix, and Babbitt ed., Loeb Classics, I, xviii.

qui m'ont grandement servy à l'intelligence de plusieurs difficiles passages. Et plusieurs y en a aussi que j'ay restituez par conjecture, avec le jugement et l'aide de quelques-uns des plus sçavans hommes de cest aage en lettres humaines. Toutefois encore est-il demeuré quelques lieux, mais peu, esquelz, pource qu'il y a en l'original omission de quelques lignes à mon advis, j'ay mieux aimé tesmoigner la defectuosité par la marque d'une estoile que de temerairement deviner ou y rien adjouxter. Mais au reste si je me suis en quelques endroits abusé, comme il est bien aisé en autheur si obscur et ouvrage si long (mesmement à personne de si peu de suffisance comme moy), je prieray les lisans de vouloir pour ma descharge accepter l'excuse que me donne le poëte Horace quand il dit:[z]

> En œuvre longue il n'est pas de merveille
> Si quelquefois l'entendement sommeille;

attendu mesmement que tant de gens de bien et de sçavoir y ayans par cy devant mis la main pour le traduire, il ne s'en est encore treuvé pas un que moy seul qui l'ait entierement achevé en quelque langue que ce soit, au moins que j'aye sceu ne veu; et que ceux qui se sont meslez d'en traduire, mesmement en Latin, ont evidemment tesmoigné la difficulté qu'il y a, ainsi que pourront facilement cognoistre ceux qui voudront prendre la peine de conferer noz traductions.

Mais si, peut estre, l'on ne treuve le langage de ceste translation si coulant comme l'on a fait de quelques autres miennes qui de pieça sont entre les mains des hommes,[aa] je prie les lecteurs de vouloir considerer que l'office d'un propre traducteur ne gist pas seulement à rendre fidelement la sentence de son autheur, mais aussi à representer aucunement et à adombrer la forme du style et maniere de parler d'iceluy, s'il ne veut commettre l'erreur que feroit le peintre qui, ayant pris à pourtraire un homme au vif, le peindroit long là où il seroit court et gros là où il seroit gresle, encore qu'il le feist naïfvement bien ressembler de visage. Car encore puis-je bien asseurer, quelque dur ou rude que soit le langage, que ma traduction sera beaucoup plus aisée aux François que l'original Grec à ceux mesmes qui sont les plus exercitez en la langue Grecque, pour une façon d'escrire plus aigue, plus docte et pressée, que claire, polie ou aisée qui est propre à Plutarque. Au fort, si je ne m'en suis acquitté si heureusement que vous eussiez pensé et desiré, seigneurs lisans, encore ay-je esperance que vous excuserez le bon vouloir de celuy qui en y aspirant a tasché de vous profiter. Et si ce mien labeur sera si heureux que de vous contenter, à Dieu en soit la louange, qui m'a donné la grace de le parachever.

z. *Ars poetica*, l. 360.

aa. Amyot had published a translation of Heliodorus, *Histoire aethiopique*, 1547; of Diodorus Siculus, *Sept livres des histoires*, 1554. In 1559, he published his translation of Longus, *Les Amours pastorales de Daphnis et Chloé*.

CLAUDE GRUGET

DEDICATION TO MARGUERITE DE NAVARRE'S *Heptaméron*

1559

TEXT:

L'Heptameron des Novvelles de Tresillvstre et Tresexcellente Princesse Marguerite de Valois, Royne de Nauarre, Remis en son vray ordre, confus au parauant en sa premiere impression: & dedié à tresillustre & tresvertueuse Princesse, Ieanne de Foix, Royne de Nauarre, par Claude Gruget Parisien. A Paris, Par Benoist Preuost, rue Frementel, à l'enseigne de l'Estoille d'or, pres le cloz Bruneau. 1559. Auec priuilege du Roy. [Pierpont Morgan Library.]

[Cf. Brunet, III, 1415–16; Tchemerzine, VII, 391; Le Petit, p. 61; Alfred Cartier, "Notes sur deux éditions de l'Heptaméron de la Reine de Navarre, Paris, 1559 et 1560, in-4," *Bulletin du Bibliophile*, 1883, pp. 214–21, 449–51.]

COLLATED:

(1560) L'Heptameron des Novvelles de Tresillvstre et Tresexcellente Princesse Marguerite de Valois, Royne de Nauarre: Remis en son vray ordre, confus au parauant en sa premiere impression: & dedié à tresillustre & tresvertueuse Princesse Ieanne, Royne de Nauarre, par Claude Gruget Parisien. A Paris, Par Benoist Preuost, rue Frementel, à l'enseigne de l'Estoille d'or pres le clos Bruneau. 1560. Auec priuilege du Roy. [Yale University Library.]

[Cf. Brunet, III, 1416–17; Tchemerzine, VII, 392–93; Fairfax Murray, I, 471–72; Cartier, *op. cit.*, who characterizes this as the most exact of the "éditions originales," p. 219.]

(1578) L'Heptameron ov Histoires des amans fortunez des Novvelles de tresillustre & tresexcellente Princesse, Marguerite de Valois Royne de Nauarre ... A Lyon, Povr Loys Cloqvemin. 1578. [Newberry Library.]

[Cf. Brunet, III, 1417; Tchemerzine, VII, 395. The editions of 1561, 1567, and 1572 have not been collated.]

Pierre Boaistuau, *dit* Launay, was the first editor of the *Heptameron*. Nine years after Marguerite's death in 1549, he published an edition containing sixty-seven of the seventy-two stories, under the title of *Histoire des Amans fortunez*. It was issued by Sertenas and other booksellers. The edition was apparently as incorrect as it was incomplete, and in the following year, 1559, Claude Gruget (a valet de chambre of Marguerite's) undertook the publication of a more complete and more correct edition. This became the accepted text, and it was accompanied by its preface in a whole series of editions during the century. The history of the first editions is given by Pierre Jourda in his *Marguerite d'Angoulême*, Paris: Champion, 1930, II, 655–60.

[ã ij] A TRÈS ILLUSTRE ET TRÈS VERTUEUSE PRINCESSE, MA DAME JEANNE DE FOIX,[1] ROYNE DE NAVARRE, CLAUDE GRUGET, SON TRÈS HUMBLE SERVITEUR, DESIRE SALUT ET FELICITÉ

Je ne me fusse ingeré, madame, vous presenter ce livre des nouvelles de la feuë Royne vostre mere si la premiere edition[a] n'eust obmis ou celé son nom et quasi changé toute sa forme, tellement que plusieurs le mescognoissoient; cause que pour le rendre digne de son auteur, aussitost qu'il fut divulgué je recueilly de toutes parts les exemplaires que j'en peu recouvrer escrits à la main, les verifiant sur ma copie, et feis en sorte que je le reduysy au vray ordre qu'elle l'avoit dressé. Puis sous la permission du Roy et vostre consentement, il a esté mis sur la presse pour le publier tel qu'il doit estre.

En quoy me revient en memoire ce que le Comte Baltazar dict de Boccace en la preface de son *Courtisan*, que ce qu'il feit en se joüant, sçavoir est son *Decameron*, luy a porté plus d'honneur que toutes ses autres œuvres Latines ou Tuscanes qu'il estimoit les plus serieuses.[b] Aussi la Royne, vray ornement de nostre siecle (de laquelle vous ne forlignez en l'amour et cognoissance des bonnes lettres), en se joüant sur les actes de la vie humaine a laissé si belles instructions qu'il n'y a celuy qui n'y trouve matiere d'eru[ã ij *v*]dition; et si a (selon tout bon jugement) passé Boccace ès beaux discours qu'elle faict sur chacun de ses comptes. Dequoy elle merite louënge, non seulement par dessus les plus excellentes dames, mais aussi entre les plus doctes hommes. Car de trois stiles d'oraison descrits par Ciceron[c] elle a choisy le simple, semblable à celuy de Terence en Latin, qui semble à chacun fort aisé à imiter, mais à qui l'experimente, rien moins.

Vray est que tel present ne vous sera point nouveau, et ne ferez que le recognoistre par heredité maternelle. Toutesfois, je m'asseure que le recevrez bien, pour le veoir par ceste seconde impression remis en son premier estat. Car (à ce que j'ay peu entendre) la premiere vous desplaisoit; non que celuy qui y avoit mis la main ne fust homme docte, qu'il n'y ait prins peine; et si est aisé à croire qu'il ne l'a voulu desguiser ainsi sans quelque

1. de Foix *omitted 1560*

a. The first edition was published by Sertenas (also Caveiller, Robinot) in 1558; cf. Tchemerzine, VII, 359–60.

b. Aldus published the first edition of the *Cortigiano* of Baldassar Castiglione in 1528; a French translation by Jacques Colin appeared in Paris in 1537. In the first edition, the passage to which reference is apparently made appears as follows: "anchor chel Boccaccio fusse di gentil ingegno secondo quei tempi, & che in alcuna parte scriuesse con discrettione, & industria, nientedimeno assai meglio scrisse quando si lassò guidar solamente dal ingegno, & instinto suo naturale senz'altro studio, o cura di limare i scritti suoi, che quando con diligentia, & fatica si sforzò d'esser piu culto, & castigato" (fols. [* ii *v*-* iii]).

c. Cf. for example *Orator*, V, 20.

occasion. Neantmoins son travail s'est trouvé peu agreable. Je le vous presente donc, madame, non pour part que j'y[2] pretende, ains seulement comme l'ayant demasqué pour le vous rendre en son naturel. C'est à vostre royale grandeur de le[3] favoriser, puisqu'il est sorty de vostre maison illustre; aussi en a-il la marque sur le front, qui luy servira de sauf-conduict par tout le monde, et le rendra bienvenu ès bonnes compagnies. Quant à moy, recognoissant l'honneur que me ferez à recevoir de ma main ce labeur de l'avoir remis à son poinct, je me sentiray perpetuellement obligé à vous faire très humble service.

2. je *1578* 3. la *1578*

JACQUES GRÉVIN

PREFACES IN THE *Théâtre*

1561

TEXT:

Le Theatre de Iaqves Grevin de Cler-mont en Beauuaisis, A Tresillvstre et Treshavlte Princesse Madame Clavde de France, Duchesse de Lorraine. Ensemble, La Seconde Partie de l'Olimpe et de la Gelodacrye. A Paris, Pour Vincent Sertenas, demeurant en la rue neuue nostre Dame, à l'enseigne sainct-Iehan l'Euangeliste, & en sa boutique au Palais, en la gallerie par ou on va à la Chancellerie. Et, Pour Guillaume Barbé rue sainct Iehan de Beauuais, deuant le Bellerophon. M.D.LXII. Avec Privilege. [Chapin Library, Williams College.]

[The 1562 edition described above is identical with the first edition of 1561 except for the t.p. Cf. Brunet, II, 1737, and Tchemerzine, VI, 12. Also Cat. Rothschild, No. 711. Copies at the Arsenal and the British Museum.]

The four selections by Jacques Grévin reprinted here consist of the "Brief Discours pour l'intelligence de ce théâtre," which is a general introduction to all his dramatic writings; the preface "Au Lecteur," which is a special introduction to his two comedies; and the "Avant-jeux" or prologues to those two comedies, *La Trésorière* and *Les Esbahis*. These constitute most of his writings of critical interest. The dates of composition are unknown, except that *La Trésorière* was first played at the Collège de Beauvais on February 5, 1558 (= 1559 n.s.), and *Les Esbahis* at the same place on February 16, 1560 (= 1561 n.s.); it is probable that the other two prefaces were written especially for the publication of the *Théâtre* later in 1561. An additional selection which may have some critical value is the "Avis au lecteur" which appeared with a separate edition of his tragedy *César*, Paris: Nicolas Bonfons, 1578; this preface has apparently never been reprinted (cf. Brunet and Tchemerzine, *loc. cit.*).

There have been several modern editions of these prefaces. The preface to the two comedies and the "Avant-jeu" of *La Trésorière* were reprinted with that play in Auguis's *Les Poètes françois depuis le XIIe siècle jusqu'a Malherbe* (Paris: Crapelet, 1824, V, 205–206, 207–209); the "Avant-jeu" to *Les Esbahis* with that comedy in Viollet Le Duc's *Ancien Théâtre françois* (Paris: Jannet, 1855, IV, 227–29). All four were edited by Lucien Pinvert in his *Théâtre complet et poésies choisies de Jacques Grévin* (Paris: Garnier, 1922, pp. 5–10, 49–50, 51–53, and 115–17); a few of my notes have been borrowed from this last edition. Biographical details on Grévin may be found in Pinvert's "Notice sur Grévin" in this edition (pp. v-xlvi) and in his *Jacques Grévin (1538–1570)*, Paris: Fontemoing, 1899. For a study of the sources of the "Brief Discours," see my "Sources of Grévin's Ideas on Comedy and Tragedy," *Modern Philology*, XLV (1947), 46–53.

[iij] BRIEF DISCOURS POUR L'INTELLIGENCE DE CE THEATRE

Ami lecteur, j'ay bien voulu discourir sur quelques poincts, lesquels paraventure pourroyent estre causes de souspeçon si librement je ne declaroy mon intention par ce discours, pourautant que premier de nostre temps je me suis hazardé de mettre la tragedie et comedie Françoise entre tes mains; veu que comme dit Martial:[a]

> ... nimium Martia turba sapit.
> Maiores nusquam rhonchi: iuvenesque senesque
> Et pueri nasum rhinocerotis habent.

Non que je me vueille dire premier qui en a composé en nostre langue. Car je sçay bien qu'Estienne Jodelle (homme qui merite beaucoup pour la promptitude et gentillesse de son esprit) a[1] esté celuy qui les a tirées des Grecs et Latins pour les replanter en France. Mais aussi je diray ceci sans arrogance, que je suis encores à voir tragedies et comedies Françoises, excepté celles de *Medée*[b] et d'*Hecuba*[c] lesquelles [iij *v*] ont esté faictes vulgaires et prises du Grec d'Euripide.

Or pourtant que je sçay bien que plusieurs pourront cheoir sur ces compositions non accoustumées en nostre langue, il me semble estre bon de declarer mon opinion touchant l'origine des tragedies et comedies et de l'heureux ou malheureux succès d'icelles et du proffict que l'on en peult retirer. La tragedie donc (comme dit Aristote en son *Art poëtique*) est une imitation ou representation de quelque faict illustre et grand de soy-mesme,[d] comme est celuy touchant la mort de Jules Cesar. Et pour sçavoir d'où vient ce mot de tragedie, il fault entendre qu'anciennement on donnoit aux poëtes tragiques, pour recompense de leur labeur, un bouc ou bien la corne d'un bouc pleine de vin; non que le present fust de grand valeur, mais plus pour l'honneur d'avoir esté aggreable et d'avoir bien faict entre tous. De ceste opinion est Horace quand il dit:

> Carmine qui tragico vilem certavit ob hircum.[e]

---

1. à *1561*

a. Martial, *Epigrams*, I.iii.

b. This is probably a confusion on the part of Grévin. The *Medea* of Euripides had not yet been translated into French, although Buchanan's Latin translation had been published in 1544. The *Médée* of La Péruse had indeed been printed in 1555; but it was based upon the tragedy of Seneca.

c. Translated by Guillaume Bouchetel, 1544 (reprinted 1550); see pp. 105–9 above.

d. *Poetics* 1449*b*24. For the sources in detail, see *Modern Philology*, XLV (1947), 46–53.

e. *Ars poetica*, l. 220.

Et pourtant que les Grecs appellent un bouc τράγος, de là est venu τραγῳδία, que nous appelons tragedie. Je pense bien que ceux [iiij] qui ont faict les premieres tragedies n'observoyent pas si estroictement ce qu'aujourdhuy on y requiert. Mais avec le temps (ainsi qu'il est facile d'adjouster aux choses inventées) on les a si bien polies que maintenant on n'y sçauroit que desirer; je dy en celles qui sont faictes selon les preceptes qu'en ont donné Aristote et Horace.

Quant est du bon accueil qu'ha eu la tragedie, je diray seulement que les escripts des poëtes Grecs nous en peuvent faire foy, entre lesquels est Æschyle, Sophocle et Euripide, que nous osons à bon droict nommer la fontaine de laquelle tous les bons poëtes tragiques ont beu, et le tresor auquel ils ont pris les richesses pour embellir leurs[2] poëmes; ainsi qu'entre les Latins nous avons Seneque.

Mais revenons à nostre tragedie de *Jules Cesar*, laquelle nous avons mise en avant en nostre langue, non que je l'aye empruntée comme quelques-uns se sont faict accroire, estimants que je l'eusse prise du Latin de Marc Anthoine de Muret; car là où elles seront confrontées, on trouvera la verité. Je ne veux pourtant nier que s'il se trouve quelque traict digne d'estre [iiij *v*] loué, qu'il ne soit de Muret, lequel a esté mon precepteur quelque temps ès lettres humaines, et auquel je donne le meilleur comme l'ayant appris de luy.

En ceste tragedie on trouvera paraventure estrange que, sans estre advoué d'aucun autheur ancien, j'ay faict la troupe interlocutoire de gensdarmes des vieilles bandes de Cesar, et non de quelques chantres ou autres ainsi qu'on a accoustumé. Mais où l'on aura entendu ma raison, possible ne leur sera-il de si difficile digestion comme il a esté à quelques-uns. J'ay eu en ceci esgard que je ne parloy pas aux Grecs ny aux Romains mais aux François, lesquels ne se plaisent pas beaucoup en ces chantres mal exercitez, ainsi que j'ay souventesfois observé aux autres endroicts où l'on en a mis en jeu. Davantage, puisqu'il est ainsi que la tragedie n'est autre chose qu'une representation de verité ou de ce qui en ha apparence, il me semble que cependant que là où les troubles (tels que l'on les descrit) sont advenues ès republiques, le simple peuple n'avoit pas grande occasion de chanter, et que par consequent que l'on ne doit faire chanter non [v] plus en les representant qu'en la verité mesme. Autrement à bon droict nous serions repris, ainsi qu'un mauvais peintre auquel on auroit donné charge de faire un pourtraict et qui auroit adjousté quelques traicts qui ne se recognoistroyent au visage qui luy auroit esté presenté. Que si l'on m'allegue ceci avoir esté observé de toute antiquité par les Grecs et Latins, je respon qu'il nous est permis d'oser quelque chose, principalement où il n'y a occasion et où la grace du poëme n'est offensée. Je sçay bien qu'on me repliquera que les anciens l'ont faict pour resjouir le

2. leur *1561*

peuple fasché, possible, des cruautez representées; à quoy je respondray que diverses nations requierent diverses manieres de faire, et qu'entre les François il y a d'autres moyens de ce faire sans interrompre le discours d'une histoire. De ceci je te laisseray le jugement, t'advertissant que je n'ay voulu (à la maniere de ceux lesquels prenants peine de s'enfler, crevent tout en coup) rechercher un tas de gros mots propres pour espouanter les petits enfans; ains plustost je me suis contenté, ensuyvant les tragiques Grecs, de ma langue, sans en emprunter une e[v *v*]strangere pour exprimer ma conception.

Or je reviens à la comedie, qui est un discours fabuleux, mais approchant de verité, contenant en soy diverses manieres de vivre entre les citadins de moyen estat, et par lequel on peult apprendre ce qui est utile pour la vie et au contraire cognoistre ce que l'on doit fuir, enseignez par le bonheur ou malheur d'autruy. C'est pourquoy Ciceron l'appelle imitation de vie, mirouer des coustumes, et image de verité.[f] Il y a eu anciennement deux sortes de comedies. L'une est appelée la vieille, laquelle comprenoit plusieurs choses fabuleuses, injures et moqueries, jusques à taxer les hommes par leurs[3] noms; ainsi que nous pouons voir en Aristophane en la comedie des *Nues*, là où il se moque apertement de Socrate. L'autre comedie est appelée la nouvelle, laquelle est faicte à l'imitation des mœurs et commune maniere de vivre des hommes, dont Menandre a esté l'autheur et à l'imitation de laquelle nous avons faict les nostres. Les anciens avoyent encores une autre sorte de comedie qu'ils appeloyent mimus ou bastelerie, pourautant qu'elle estoit faicte de parolles ordes et villaines et de matiere [vi] assez deshonneste, laquelle aussi estoit representée par des basteleurs, voire le plus près du naturel qu'il estoit possible, comme tesmoigne Ciceron en son 2. de l'*Orateur* et Quintilian en son 2. livre.[g] De là sont venues les farces des François, comme nous pouvons facilement voir.

Or pourautant qu'en la comedie nouvelle (comme aussi en toutes tragedies) l'on propose les hommes demenants quelques affaires, on a divisé le tout par actes, que les Grecs ont appelé δράματα, ἀπὸ τοῦ δρᾷμ, qui est autant à dire que faire ou negotier. L'origine de la comedie, selon l'opinion de plusieurs, se donne aux Atheniens, lesquels voulants noter d'infamie les mal vivans venoyent d'une gayeté de cueur de rue en rue et, montez sur quelques chariots, les nommoyent par noms et par surnoms. Et quant à moy,

3. leur *1561*

f. Cited by Donatus, *Commentum Terenti* (ed. Wessner, Leipzig: Teubner, 1902, I, 22): "comoediam esse Cicero ait imitationem uitae, speculum consuetudinis, imaginem ueritatis." The passage is also incorporated by Badius Ascensius among the preliminary materials of his Terence (cf. ed. Lyon: Marion, 1517, fol. b ij). The passage may be a paraphrase of Cicero's *Pro Sexto Roscio Amerino*, xvi. 47.

g. Possibly Cicero, *De Oratore*, II, 241–44, and Quintilian, II.x.13, although both passages are doubtful.

je suis de ceste opinion que la comedie a pris son nom *ἀπὸ τῶν κωμῶν*, c'est-à-dire des rues par lesquelles de ce premier temps elles[4] estoyent jouées. Et semble qu'encore ceste coustume soit demeurée en Flandres et Païs Bas, où les joueurs de comedies se font trainer par les carrefours sur des chariots et là jouent leurs histoires, comedies, [vi *v*] et farces. De ces premiers a escript Horace en son *Art poëtique*:

> Ignotum tragicae genus invenisse Camenae
> dicitur et plaustris vexisse poemata Thespis.[h]

Et de là est venu le proverbe entre les Grecs *ἐξ ἁμάξης λοιδορεῖν*, c'est-à-dire injurier en chariot ou bien se moquer, comme le prend aussi Demosthene en son oraison *Pour la Couronne*.[i] Entre les premiers poëtes comiques on met Susarion, Rulle et Magnes, lesquels plustost par moquerie qu'autrement taxoyent appertement un chascun. Depuis vindrent Aristophane, Eupolis et Cratine, lesquels poursuivants et detestans les vices de leurs[5] princes composerent des comedies assez fortes, tant que Menandre et Philemon commencerent à les addoucir, ainsi que les voyons en Terence lequel a pris ses comedies de Menandre et Appollodore. Après Menandre et Philemon, aucteurs Grecs, vint le premier à Rome Andronique; puis Plaute et Terence, lesquels nous ont laissé leurs[5] comedies parfaictes de tous poincts et, comme dit Ciceron, pleines de choses ingenieuses, civiles, elegantes et facetieuses, comme les livres des philosophes Socratiques.[j]

Voylà [vij] l'origine et succès de la comedie, que j'estime avec Aristote avoir esté inventée du mesme temps que la tragedie.[k] Car comme ainsi soit que des hommes les uns soyent graves et severes, les autres gaillards et joyeux, il est advenu que les premiers se sont mis à escrire des tragedies graves et severes, les seconds se sont exercez en comedies gaillardes et joyeuses. Le profict que tu en peux recevoir est de te garder de pareilles adventures qui sont advenues en icelles par la mesgarde d'aucuns, par la simplicité des autres, par l'astuce des plus rusez; et cognoistre aussi la diverse maniere de vivre des divers estats. Car comme disoit Andronique, la comedie est le mirouer de la vie journaliere.[l] Ceste seule cause m'a esmeu

4. elle *1561* 5. leur *1561*

h. Horace, *Ars poetica*, ll. 275–76; cited by Diomedes, *Artis grammaticae*, Bk. III (ed. Keil, *Grammatici Latini*, Vol. I, Leipzig: Teubner, 1857), p. 487, and by Donatus *op. cit.*, V, 9. Cf. Badius, *op. cit.*, fol. b ij *v*.

i. *De Corona*, 122.

j. The reference in Cicero (*De Officiis*, I. xxix. 104) is to Plautus only: "alterum elegans, urbanum, ingeniosum, facetum. Quo genere non modo Plautus noster et Atticorum antiqua comoedia, sed etiam philosophorum Socraticorum libri referti sunt."

k. *Poetics* 1449*a*2 ff.

l. Cited by Donatus, *op. cit.*, I, 23: "et comoediam et tragoediam et togatam primus Liuius Andronicus repperit. aitque esse comoediam cotidianae uitae speculum." Cf. Badius, *op. cit.*, fol. b iij.

davantage à mettre celles-cy en avant, en la composition desquelles j'ay plustost ensuyvi la nayveté de nostre vulgaire et les communes manieres de parler que pris peine d'ensuyvre les anciens, encore que je ne m'en soy' du tout retiré, comme pourront appercevoir ceux qui seront un peu versez en l'Aristophane, Plaute et Terence. L'autre cause qui me l'a faict faire a esté voyant les lourdes fautes [vii *v*] lesquelles se commettent journellement ès jeux de l'Université de Paris, qui doit estre[6] comme un parangon de toute perfection de sciences; où nous voyons toutesfois mille fautes commises en cest endroict, lequel a esté tant recommandé des anciens Romains que plus souvent les empereurs et grands seigneurs, oultre la despence en telles affaires, s'employoyent à l'execution de leurs tragedies et comedies. Nous en avons encor pour tesmoignage aujourdhuy les ruines des amphitheatres somptueux et les livres des poëtes et historiographes. La faute que j'y voy, c'est que contre le commandement du bon precepteur Horace, ils font à la maniere des basteleurs un massacre sur un eschaffaut,[m] ou un discours de deux ou trois mois (et semble qu'en cest endroit ils ayent conjuré pour mal faire), et autres telles badineries que je laisse pour estre plus bref. Je ne mets pourtant en ce nombre quelques-uns qui en ont faict leur devoir; mais plustost je les prie au nom de tous amateurs des bonnes lettres de poursuyvre et aider à chasser ce monstre d'entre une tant docte compagnie, par devers laquelle accourent non seulement les Fran[viij]çois, mais aussi les estrangers des plus lointaines provinces. Et quant est de ma part, pourautant que plus grande estude m'a retiré par devers soy, j'en laisse la charge aux amateurs de l'antiquité; et te priray, lecteur, de prendre le tout plustost en bonne part que opiniastrement te bander contre la verité. A Dieu.

[43] AU LECTEUR

La liberté des poëtes comiques a tousjours esté telle que souventesfois ils ont usé de mots assez grossiers, de sentences et manieres de parler rejectées de la boutique des mieux disans ou de ceux qui pensent mieux dire; ce que paraventure l'on pourra trouver lisant mes comedies. Mais pourtant il ne se fault renfrongner, car il n'est pas icy question de farder la langue d'un mercadant, d'un serviteur ou d'une chambriere, et moins orner le langage du vulgaire, lequel a plustost dict un mot que pensé. Seulement le comique se propose de representer la verité et naïveté de sa langue, comme les mœurs, les conditions et les estats de ceux qu'il met en jeu; sans toutesfois faire tort à sa pureté, laquelle est plustost entre le vulgaire (je dy si l'on change quelques mots qui resentent leur terroir) qu'entre ces courtizans

6. stre *1561*

m. *Ars poetica*, ll. 185 ff.

qui pensent avoir faict un beau coup quand ils ont arraché la peau de quelque [44] mot Latin pour déguiser le François, qui n'ha aucune grace (disent-ils) s'il ne donne à songer aux femmes, comme s'ils prenoyent plaisir de n'estre point entendus. Tu ne trouveras donc estrange, lecteur, si en ces comedies tu ne trouves un langage recherché curieusement et enrichi des plumes d'autruy. Car je ne suis point de ceux qui font parler un cuisinier des choses celestes et descriptions des temps et des saisons, ou bien une simple chambriere Françoise des amours de Jupiter avec Leda et des vaillantises d'Alexandre le Grand. Je me contente seulement de donner aux François la comedie en telle pureté qu'anciennement l'ont baillée Aristophane aux Grecs, Plaute et Terence aux Romains. Ce que je me suis proposé tousjours en escrivant ce poëme, ainsi qu'ont peu appercevoir ceux qui ont veu *la Maubertine*, premiere comedie que je mis en jeu et que j'avoye bien deliberé te donner si elle ne m'eust esté desrobée. Toutesfois, celles-cy pourront suffire pour mon[45]strer le chemin à ceux qui viendront après nous. Tu peux donc maintenant, ami lecteur, adverti de ce poinct, te mettre à lire ce poëme; et si tu trouves quelque chose qui ne soit à ton goust, souvienne-toy que ce n'est chose estrange si ceux qui vont les premiers en un desert et pays incogneu se fourvoyent souventesfois de leur chemin.

[47] LA TRESORIERE

AVANT-JEU

Non, ce n'est pas de nous qu'il fault,
Pour accomplir cest eschaffault,
Attendre les farces prisées
Qu'on a tousjours moralisées;
Car ce n'est nostre intention
De mesler la religion
Dans le subject des choses feinctes.
Aussi jamais les lettres sainctes [48]
Ne furent données de Dieu
Pour en faire après quelque jeu.
Et puis tout' ces farces badines
Me semblent estre trop indignes
Pour estre mises au devant
Des yeux d'un homme plus sçavant.
Celuy donc qui vouldra complaire
Tant seulement au populaire,
Celuy choisira les erreurs
Des plus ignorans basteleurs.
Il introduira la Nature,

Le Genre humain, l'Agriculture,
Un Tout, un Rien, et un Chascun,
Le Faux-parler, le Bruict-commun,
Et telles choses qu'ignorance
Jadis mesla parmi la France.
  Que pourrons-nous donc inventer
Afin de chascun contenter?
Quoy? le badinage inutile
Par qui quelquefois Martinville[n]
Se feit escouter de son temps?
Quoy? demandez-vous ces romans
Jouer d'une aussi sotte grace
Que sotte est ceste populace
De qui tous seuls ils sont prisez?
Vous estes bien mieux avisez,
Comme je croy; vostre presence [49]
Merite avoir la joüissance
D'un discours qui soit mieux limé.
Aussi avons-nous estimé
Que la gentille poësie
Veult une matiere choisie
Digne d'estre mise aux escrits
De ceux qui ont meilleurs esprits,
Et non pour estre ainsi souillée
Ou en mille pars detaillée
Par ceux qui encor' ne l'ont pas
Saluée du premier pas,
Et qui pensent malgré Minerve
La retenir ainsi que serve
Ou dans l'escole la lier
Ainsi qu'un petit escolier.
Non, non, ce n'est pas sa nature
Qu'elle s'en voise à l'avanture
Vers celuy qui la veult avoir.
Il fault premierement sçavoir
Petit à petit sa pensée;
Car ell' ne veult estre forcée

n. Cf. Henry Lyonnet, *Dictionnaire des Comédiens français*, Geneva: Bibliothèque de la Revue Universelle Internationale Illustrée, II, 399: "Martainville, Nicolas, Michel dit.—Comédien qui faisait partie de la troupe Lepardonneur à Rouen en 1558. On croit même qu'il fût associé dans l'entreprise. Il est nommé par Noël du Fail à propos de la farce du *Bateleur*."

Ny traictée comme souvent
Nous l'avons veue auparavant
Au joug d'une plume marastre.
N'attendez donc en ce theatre
Ne farce ne moralité,
Mais seulement l'antiquité [50]
Qui d'une face plus hardie
Se represente en comedie.
Car onc je ne pourroy penser
Qu'aucun se voulut courroucer
Encontre nous, si pour mieux faire
Nous voulons aux doctes complaire.
Or sçachez qu'en tout ce discours
Nous representons les amours
Et la finesse coustumiere
D'une gentille tresoriere
Dont le mestier est descouvert
Non loing de la place Maubert.
Vray est que le protenotaire,
Principal de tout' ceste affaire,
Est de nostre université.
Mais j'ay un peu trop arresté;
Il vault mieux avec le silence
Vous en donner la joüissance.

[113] LES ESBAHIS

AVANT-JEU

Je ne suis pas icy venu
Pour vous conter par le menu
Le discours de la comedie;
Car ce seroit oster l'envie
Que chacun de vous doit avoir
De nous entendre et de nous voir,
Attendant qu'elle soit parfaicte.
Je vien de la part du poëte,
Lequel vous remonstre par moy
Ce qui plus le tient en esmoy. [114]
Le premier poinct, c'est qu'on endure
Ces estourdis, faisans Mercure
De chasque bois mal raboté
Pour servir l'Université.

Une grand' troupe mal choisie
Se joue de la poësie,
Et impudente rimassant
A cor-et-cry va pourchassant
Ceste deesse tant prisée,
Dont ils font naistre la risée.
Car comme nouveaux basteleurs,
Afin d'enrichir les fureurs
De leurs tragedies farcées
Ou leurs farces moralisées,
Pour la foiblesse de leurs reins,
A trompettes et tabourins
Et gros mots qu'on ne peult entendre,
Ils se sont essaiez de rendre
Et mouvoir au-dedans du cueur
Du plus attentif auditeur
Une pitié, une misere;
Au lieu qu'un bon vers le doit faire.
L'autre poinct qui m'a faict venir
Est pour vous faire souvenir
De ceste plaincte qui fut faicte
Naguere encontre le poëte [115]
Pour la rancune et le soucy
Des dames de ce quartier-cy;
Qui pour estre un peu trop friandes
Feront six plats de deux viandes,
Et alors qu'on n'y pense pas
D'un rien elles feront grand cas.
Car quand le poëte pense faire
Quelque chose pour vous complaire,
Elles prennent opinion
Que c'est à leur intention,
Et que tousjours on parle d'elles
Si aux comedies nouvelles
On a possible découvert
Un lieu de la place Maubert.
Et voylà, ce que je propose
Fait que froidement il dispose
Par ses vers le gentil discours
De ces tant heureuses amours,
Dont toutefois il eut envie
De composer la comedie

Que vous aurez presentement.
Mais il n'a pas tant seulement
Osé mettre en escript la rue
Où il a ceste affaire veue,
Craignant leur donner quelque ennuy.
Ce nonobstant j'ay sceu de luy, [116]
Comme une chose bien secrette,
Que ceste comedie est faicte
Sur le discours de quelque amour
Qui s'est conduit au carefour
De sainct Sevrin; mais je vous prie,
D'autant que vous avez envie
D'estre secrets, de tenir coy.
Car je voy cy derriere moy
Le sire Josse; que personne
Ne face que trop il soubçonne.
Car notez qu'il est fiancé,
Pourtant qu'il a tousjours pensé
Que madame Agnès estoit morte.
Mais il fera, avant qu'il sorte
De ce lieu, que sommairement
Vous cognoistrez tout son torment.

PIERRE DE RONSARD

Abbregé de l'Art Poëtique François

1565

TEXT:

Abbregé de l'Art poëtique françois. A Alphonce Delbene Abbé de Havtecombe en Savoye. *Scribendi rectè, sapere est, & principium & fons.* A Paris. Chez Gabriel Buon, au clos Bruneau, à l'enseigne S. Claude. 1565. Auec Priuilege du Roy. [B.N., Paris.]

[Cf. Brunet, IV, 1383; Tchemerzine, IX, 445; De Ricci, No. 57, p. 129.]

COLLATED:

(1567) Les Poemes de P. de Ronsard Gentilhomme Vandomois. Tome Troisiesme. A Paris, Chez Gabriel Buon au cloz Bruneau à l'enseigne S. Claude. 1567. Avec privilege dv Roy. [*Abrégé*, pp. 175 *v*-188 *r*. Library of Congress.]

(1571) Les Poemes de P. de Ronsard gentilhomme Vandomois, Tome Troisiesme. A Paris, Chez Gabriel Buon au cloz Bruneau, à l'enseigne S. Claude. 1571. Avec privilege dv Roy. [A separate section of the volume, with pages numbered 1–30, but without separate title page. Harvard College Library.]

(1573) Les Poemes de P. de Ronsard gentilhomme Vandomois, Tome Troisieme. A Paris, Chez Gabriel Buon au cloz Bruneau, à l'enseigne S. Claude. 1573. Avec privilege dv Roy. [*Abrégé*, pp. 495–524. Harvard College Library.]

(1592) Les Qvatre Premiers Livres de la Franciade. Av Roy Tres-Chrestien, Charles nevfiesme de ce nom. Plvs, Le Bocage Royal, à Henry III. Roy de France & de Polougne. Par Pierre de Ronsard Gentilhomme Vandomois. Tome III. A Lyon, Povr Thomas Sovbron. M.D. XCII. [*Abrégé*, pp. 399–424. Harvard College Library.]

[Brunet, IV, 1383, also lists separate editions of Paris: Guil. Linocier, 1585 and Avignon: Jac. Barro, 1586; cf. Tchemerzine, IX, 445. De Ricci, No. 59, p. 131, lists an edition of Rouen: Jean et Pierre Gaultier, 1566. None of these editions have been collated.]

In the opinion of Dom Edmond Bernardet (*Un Abbé de Hautecombe*, Grenoble, 1937, pp. 28–30), the immediate occasion for the writing of the *Abrégé* was the funeral of Adrien Turnèbe, who died in Paris on June 12, 1565. Alphonse Delbene, who had studied under Turnèbe at the Collège Royal, came to Paris for the rites and there renewed contact with Ronsard. The two friends discussed the art of poetry, and out of these discussions came the *Abrégé*, quickly completed and addressed to Delbene: "lequel," says Ronsard, "en faveur de toy a esté en trois heures commencé et achevé" (p. 209 below). It was published separately in the same year and subsequently incorporated in various editions of the complete works, undergoing frequent correction and modification. The major revision took place in the text of 1567, most of whose new readings persisted in later texts. There are some revisions in 1592 which may represent Ronsard's final corrections for the edition which he was preparing at the time of his death, although some of these give definitely inferior readings. Various modern editions are available, among them that of Gustave Cohen in the *Œuvres complètes*, Paris: Bibliothèque de la Pléiade, 1938, II, 997–1011, and that of the Cambridge *L'Art poétique*, Cambridge: University Press, 1930, pp. 1–24.*

[Aij] ABBREGÉ DE L'ART POËTIQUE FRANÇOIS

A ALPHONCE DELBENE,[a] ABBÉ DE HAUTECOMBE EN SAVOYE[1]

Combien que l'art de poësie ne se puisse par preceptes comprendre ny enseigner, pour estre plus mental que traditif, toutesfois d'autant que l'artifice humain, experience et labeur le peuvent permettre, j'ay bien voulu t'en donner quelques reigles icy,[2] afin qu'un jour tu puisses estre des premiers en la congnoissance d'un si aggreable metier, à l'exemple de moy qui confesse y estre assez passablement versé.[3]

Sur toutes choses tu auras les muses en reverence, voire en singuliere veneration, et ne les feras jamais servir à choses deshonnestes,[4] à risées, ny[5] à libelles injurieux, mais les tiendras cheres et sacrées comme les filles de Juppiter, c'est-à-dire de Dieu, qui de sa saincte grace [A ij *v*] a premierement par elles faict cognoistre aux peuples ignorans les excellences de sa majesté. Car la poësie n'estoit au premier aage qu'une theologie allegoricque, pour faire entrer au cerveau des hommes grossiers par fables plaisantes et colorées les secretz qu'ilz ne[6] pouvoyent comprendre quand trop ouvertement on leur[7] descouvroit la verité. On dict qu'Eumolpe[8] Cecropien, Line maistre d'Hercule, Orphée, Homere, Hesiode inventerent un si doux alechement.[9] Pour ceste cause ilz[10] sont appellez poëttes divins, non tant pour leur divin esprit qui les rendoit sur tous admirables et excellens,[11] que pour la conversation qu'ilz avoyent avecques les oracles, prophetes, devins, sybilles, interpretes de songes, desquelz ilz[12] avoyent apris la meilleure part

*The edition of Laumonier in Vol. XIV of the *Œuvres complètes* (Paris: Didier, 1949), pp. 1–38, reached me after this manuscript had already gone to the printer.

1. en Savoye *1565 only* 2. icy *1565 only* 3. enseigné *1567 ff.*
4. chose deshonneste *1573, 1592* 5. ny *1565 only* 6. ne *omitted 1567*
7. leur *1565 only* 8. On dict qu' *1565 only* 9. si excellent mestier *1567 ff.*
10. ilz *1565 only* 11. et excellens *1565 only* 12. il *1565*

a. On Alphonse Delbene, cf. Dom Edmond Bernardet, *Un Abbé d'Hautecombe Ami de Ronsard: Alphonse Delbene, Evêque d'Albi, 1538–1608*, Grenoble: Edition de la Revue "Les Alpes" 1937.

de ce qu'ilz sçavoyent. Car ce que les oracles disoyent en peu de motz, ces gentilz personnages l'emplifioyent, coloroyent et augmentoyent, estans envers[13] le peuple ce que les sybilles et devins estoyent en leur endroit. Longtemps après eulx[14] sont venuz d'un mesme païs les seconds poëtes, que j'appelle humains pour estre plus enflez d'artifice et labeur que de divinité. A l'exemple de ceux-cy,[15] les poëtes Romains ont foisonné en telle fourmiliere[16] qu'ilz ont apporté aux librairies[17] plus de charge que d'honneur, excepté cinq ou six, desquelz la doctrine accompagnée d'un parfaict artifice m'a tousjours tiré en admiration.

Or pource que les muses ne veulent [A iij] loger en une ame si elle n'est bonne, saincte, et vertueuse, tu seras de bonne nature, non meschant, renfrongné, ne chagrin; mais animé d'un gentil esprit, ne laisseras rien entrer en ton entendement qui ne soit surhumain et divin. Tu auras en premier lieu les conceptions hautes, grandes, belles, et non trainantes à terre. Car le principal poinct est l'invention, laquelle vient tant de la bonne nature que par[18] la leçon des bons et anciens autheurs. Et[19] si tu entreprens quelque grand œuvre, tu te montreras religieux et craignant Dieu, le commençant ou par son nom ou par un autre qui representera quelque effect de sa majesté, à l'exemple des poëtes Grecs, Μῆνιν ἄειδε, θεὰ;[b] Ἄνδρα μοι ἔννεπε, Μοῦσα;[c] Ἐκ Διὸς ἀρχώμεσθα;[d] Ἀρχόμενος σέο, Φοῖβε.[e] Et noz Romains, *Æneadum genitrix;*[f] *Musa, mihi causas memora.*[g] Car[20] les muses, Apollon, Mercure, Pallas[21] et autres telles deitez ne nous representent autre chose que les puissances de Dieu, auquel les premiers hommes avoyent donné plusieurs noms pour les divers effectz de son incomprehensible majesté. Et c'est aussi pour te montrer que rien ne peut estre ny bon ny parfaict si le commencement ne vient de Dieu.

Après tu seras studieux de la lecture des bons poëtes, et les apprendras par cœur autant que tu pourras. Tu seras laborieux à corriger et limer tes vers, et ne leur pardonneras non plus qu'un bon jardinier à son ante, quant il la voit chargée de branches inutiles ou de bien peu de prouffict. Tu converseras [A iij *v*] doucement et honnestement avecque les poëtes de ton temps. Tu honoreras les plus vieux comme tes peres, tes pareilz comme tes freres, les moindres comme tes enfans, et leur communiqueras tes escritz. Car tu ne dois jamais[22] rien mettre en lumiere qui n'ayt premierement esté

13. vers *1567 ff.* 14. eulx *1565 only* 15. de ces derniers *1567 ff.*
16. ont foisonné en l'abondance de tant de liures empoulez & fardez *1567 ff.*
17. Libraires *1571 ff.* 18. de *1567 ff.* 19. Et *1565 only*
20. Car *omitted 1571 ff.* 21. Pallas, Venus *1567 ff.* 22. jamais *1565 only*

b. *Iliad,* I, 1.
c. *Odyssey,* I, 1.
d. Aratus, *Phaenomena,* l. 1.
e. Apollonius of Rhodes, *Argonautica,* I, 1.
f. Lucretius, *De Rerum Natura,* I, 1.
g. *Aeneid,* I, 8.

veu et reveu de tes amis que tu estimeras les plus expers en ce mestier, afin que par telles conjonctions et familiaritez d'espritz, avecque les lettres et la bonne[23] nature que tu as, tu puisses facilement parvenir au comble de tout honneur, ayant pour exemple domestique les vertus de ton pere, qui non seulement a surpassé en sa langue Italienne les plus estimez de ce temps, mais encores a faict la victoire douteuse entre luy et ceux qui escrivent aujourdhuy le plus purement et doctement au vieil langage Romain.[h]

Or pource que tu as desja la congnoissance de la langue Grecque et Latine, et qu'il ne te reste plus que la Françoise, laquelle te doibt estre d'autant plus recommandée qu'elle t'est maternelle, je te diray en peu de paroles ce qu'il me semble le plus expedient, et sans t'esgarer par longues et facheuses forestz, je te meneray tout droict par le sentier que j'auray congneu le plus court, afin que aysément tu reguaignes ceux qui s'estans les premiers mis au chemin, te pourroyent avoir aucunement devancé.

Tout ainsi que les vers Latins ont leurs piedz, comme tu sçais, nous avons en nostre poësie Françoise, de laquelle je veux [A iv] traicter icy, une certaine mesure de syllabes selon le dessein des carmes que nous entreprenons composer, qui ne se peut outrepasser sans offencer la loy de nostre vers, desquelles mesures et nombre[24] de syllabes nous traiterons après plus amplement. Nous avons aussi une certaine cæsure de la voyelle *e*, laquelle se mange toutes les fois qu'elle est rencontrée d'une autre voyelle ou diftongue, pourveu que la voyelle qui suit *e* n'ait poinct la force de consonne. Après, à l'imitation de quelqu'un de ce temps,[25] tu feras tes vers masculins et fœminins tant qu'il te sera possible, pour estre plus propres à la musicque et accord des instrumens, en faveur desquelz il semble que la poësie soit née. Car la poësie sans les instrumens, ou sans la grace d'une seule ou plusieurs voix, n'est nullement aggreable, non plus que les instrumens sans estre animez de la melodie d'une plaisante voix. Si de fortune tu as composé les deux premiers vers masculins, tu feras les deux autres fœminins et paracheveras de mesme mesure le reste de ton elegie ou chanson, afin que les musiciens les puissent plus facilement accorder. Quant aux vers lyriques, tu feras le premier couplet à ta volonté, pourveu que les autres suyvent la trace du premier.

Si tu te sers des noms propres des Grecs et Romains, tu les tourneras à la terminaison Françoise autant que ton langage le permet; car il y en a beaucoup qui ne s'y peuvent nullement tourner. [A iv *v*] Tu ne rejetteras point[26] les vieux motz de noz romans,[27] ains les choisiras[28] avecques meure

23. bonne *1565 only* 24. nombres *1573, 1592* 25. à mon imitation *1567 ff.*
26. ne dois reietter *1567 ff.*
27. les mots de noz vieux Romains *1567, 1592* (Romans *1571, 1573*)
28. choisir *1567 ff.*

h. Bartolomeo Delbene, born ca. 1515, wrote poems in Italian and a Latin treatise, *De civitate veri seu morum* (published 1609). Cf. Bernardet, *op. cit.*, pp. 19–20.

et prudente election. Tu practiqueras bien souvent[29] les artisans de tous mestiers comme[30] de marine, vennerie, fauconnerie, et principalement les artisans de feu,[31] orfevres, fondeurs, mareschaux, minerailliers, et de là tireras[32] maintes belles et vives comparaisons, avecque les noms propres des mestiers,[33] pour enrichir ton œuvre et le rendre plus aggreable et parfaict.[34] Car tout ainsi qu'on ne peult veritablement[35] dire un corps humain beau, plaisant et accomply s'il n'est composé de sang, venes, arteres et tendons, et surtout d'une plaisante[36] couleur; ainsi la poësie ne peut estre plaisante ny parfaicte[37] sans belles inventions, descriptions, comparaisons, qui sont les ners et la vie du livre qui veult forcer les siecles pour demourer de toute memoire victorieux et maistre[38] du temps. Tu sçauras dextrement choisir et approprier à ton œuvre les mots[39] plus significatifs des dialectes de nostre France, quand mesmement tu n'en auras point de si bons ny de si propres en ta nation,[40] et [41] ne se fault soucier si les vocables[42] sont Gascons, Poitevins, Normans, Manceaux,[43] Lionnois, ou d'autre païs, pourveu qu'ilz soyent bons et que proprement ilz signifient[44] ce que tu veux dire, sans affecter par trop le parler de la court, lequel est quelquesfois très mauvais pour estre le langage de damoiselles et jeunes gentilzhommes qui font plus de[45] profession de bien combattre que [B] de bien parler. Et noteras que la langue Grecque n'eust jamais esté si faconde et abondante en dialectes et en motz comme elle est sans le grand nombre de republicques qui fleurissoyent en ce temps-là, lesquelles comme amoureuses de leur bien propre vouloyent que leurs doctes citoyens escrivissent au langage particulier de leur nation. Et de là sont venuz une infinité de dialectes, frases, et manieres de parler qui portent encores aujourd'huy sur le front la marque de leur païs naturel, lesquelles estoyent tenues indifferemment bonnes par les doctes plumes qui escrivoyent de ce temps-là. Car un païs ne peult jamais estre si parfaict en tout qu'il ne puisse encores quelquefois emprunter je ne sçay quoy de son voisin, et ne fais point de doute que si il y avoit encores en France des Ducs de Bourgongne, de Picardie, de Normandie, de Bretaigne, de Champaigne, de Gascongne,[46] qu'ilz ne desirassent pour l'honneur de leur altesse[47] que leurs subjectz escrivissent en la langue de[48] leur païs naturel. Car les princes ne doivent estre moins curieux d'agrandir

29. bien souvent *1565 only* 30. comme *1565 only*
31. principallement ceux qui doiuent la perfection de leurs ouurages aux fourneaux *1567 ff.* 32. tirer *1567 ff.* 33. outils *1567 ff.* 34. et parfaict *1565 only*
35. veritablement *1565 only* 36. nayue *1567 ff.*
37. plaisante, viue ne parfaitte *1567 ff.*; si plaisante, *etc. 1592*
38. et maistre *1565 only* 39. vocables *1567 ff.*
40. quand ceux de ta nation ne seront assez propres ne signifians *1567 ff.*
41. et *1565 only* 42. s'ils *1567 ff.* 43. Manceaux *omitted 1592*
44. expriment *1567 ff.* 45. de *1565 only*
46. de (*all five repetitions*) *1565 only* 47. pour vn extresme honneur *1567 ff.*
48. en la langue de *omitted 1567, 1571, 1573;* selon *1592*

les bornes de leur empire[49] que d'estendre leur langage[50] par toutes nations. Mais aujourdhuy, pource que nostre France n'obeist qu'à un seul roy, nous[51] sommes contraincts, si nous voulons parvenir à quelque honneur, de[52] parler son langage;[53] autrement nostre labeur, tant fust-il honorable et parfaict,[54] seroit estimé peu de chose ou (peult estre) totalement mesprisé.[55] [B *v*]

DE L'INVENTION

Pource qu'auparavant j'ay parlé de l'invention, il me semble estre bien à propos de t'en redire un mot.[56] L'invention n'est autre chose que le bon naturel d'une imagination concevant les idées et formes de toutes choses qui se peuvent imaginer, tant celestes que terrestres, animées ou inanimées,[57] pour après les representer, descrire, et imiter. Car tout ainsi que le but de l'orateur est de persuader, ainsi celuy du poëte est d'imiter, inventer, et representer les choses qui sont, qui peuvent estre, ou que les anciens ont estimé comme veritables.[58] Et ne fault poinct[59] douter qu'après avoir bien et hautement inventé, que la belle disposition de vers ne s'ensuyve, d'autant que la disposition suit l'invention, mere de toutes choses, comme l'ombre faict le corps. Quand je te dy que tu inventes choses belles et grandes, je n'entends toutesfois ces inventions fantasticques et melencoliques, qui ne se rapportent non plus l'une[60] à l'autre que les songes entrecoupez d'un frenetique, ou de quelque patient extremement tourmenté de la fievre, à l'imagination duquel, pour estre blessée, se representent mille formes monstrueuses sans ordre ny liayson. Mais tes inventions, desquelles je ne te puis donner regle pour estre spirituelles, seront bien ordonnées et disposées; et bien qu'elles semblent passer celles du vulgaire, elles[61] seront tou[B ij]tesfois telles qu'elles pourront estre facilement conceues et entendues d'un chascun.

DE LA DISPOSITION[62]

Tout ainsi que l'invention despend d'une gentille nature d'esprit, ainsi la disposition despend de la belle invention, laquelle consiste en une elegante et parfaicte collocation et ordre des choses inventées, et ne permet que ce

49. Seigneurie *1567 ff.*

50. estendre à l'imitation des Romains le langage de leur pays *1567 ff.*

51. nous *1565 only* 52. de *1565 only* 53. langage courtizan *1567 ff.*

54. tant docte qu'il soit *1567 ff.*

55. *Added 1567 ff.*: Et pour-ce que les biens & faueurs viennent de tel endroit, il faut bien souuent ployer sous le iugement d'vne damoyselle ou d'vn ieune courtizan, encores qu'ils se connoissent d'autant moins en la bonne & vraye Poësie qu'ils font exercice des armes & autres plus honorables mestiers.

56. t'en refraischir la memoire par vn petit mot *1567 ff.* 57. inanimes *1565*

58. qui sont, ou qui peuuent estre, vrai-semblables *1567 ff.*

59. poinct *1565 only* 60. l'vn *1571 ff.* 61. elles *1565 only*

62. LA DISPOSITION *1565*

qui appartient à un lieu soit mis en l'autre, mais se gouvernant par artifice, estude et labeur, ajance et ordonne dextrement toutes choses à son poinct. Tu en pouras tirer les exemples des autheurs anciens et de noz modernes qui ont illustré depuis quinze ans nostre langue, maintenant superbe par la diligence d'un si honorable labeur. Heureux et plus que heureux,[63] ceux qui cultivent leur propre terre sans se travailler après une estrangere, de laquelle on ne peult retirer que peine ingrate et malheureuse pour toute recompense et honneur. Quiconques furent les premiers qui oserent abandonner la langue des anciens[64] pour honorer celle de leur païs, ilz furent veritablement bons enfans et non ingratz citoyens, et dignes d'estre couronnez sur une statue publicque, et que d'aage en aage on face une perpetuelle memoire d'eux et de leurs vertus.[65] [B ij *v*]

DE L'ELOCUTION

Elocution n'est autre chose qu'une proprieté et splendeur de paroles bien choisies et ornées de graves et courtes sentences, qui font reluyre les vers comme les pierres precieuses bien enchassées les doigts de quelque grand seigneur. Soubs l'elocution se comprend l'election des paroles, que Vergile et Horace ont si curieusement observée. Pour ce tu te doibs travailler d'estre[66] copieux en vocables, et trier[67] les plus nobles[68] et signifians[69] pour servir de ners et de force à tes carmes, qui reluyront d'autant plus que les mots seront significatifs, propres[70] et choisis.[71] Tu n'oubliras les comparaisons, les descriptions des lieux, fleuves, forests, montaignes, de la nuict, du lever du soleil, du midy, des vents, de la mer, des dieux et déesses, avecques leurs propres metiers, habits, chars, et chevaux, te façonnant en cecy à l'imitation d'Homere, que tu observeras comme un divin exemple sur lequel tu tireras au vif les plus parfaictz lineamens de ton tableau.

DE LA POESIE EN GENERAL

Tu doibs sçavoir sur toutes choses que les grands poëmes ne se commencent jamais par la premiere occasion du faict, ny ne sont tellement ac-[B iij]complis que le lecteur, espris de plaisir, n'y puisse encores desirer une plus longue fin; mais les bons ouvriers le commencent par le milieu, et sçavent si bien joindre le commencement au milieu et le milieu à la fin,

63. Heureux & presques Dieux *1567 ff.* 64. anciens Grecs & Romains *1567 ff.*

65. *Added 1567 ff.*: non qu'il faille ignorer les langues estrangeres, ie te conseille de les sçauoir perfaictement, & d'elles comme d'vn vieil tresor trouué soubz terre enrichir ta propre nation: car il est fort malaisé de bien escrire en langue vulgaire si on n'est perfaictement, à tout le moins mediocrement instruit en celles des plus honorables & fameux estrangers. 66. d' *omitted 1567, 1571, 1573;* à *1592*

67. tirer *1592* 68. propres *1567 ff.* 69. signifians que tu pourras *1567 ff.*

70. propres *1565 only* 71. choisis auecques iugement *1567 ff.*

que de[72] telles pieces rapportées ilz[73] font un corps entier et parfaict. Tu ne commenceras jamais le discours d'un grand poësme s'il n'est esloigné de la memoire des hommes, et pour ce tu invoqueras la muse, qui se souvient de tout comme déesse, pour te chanter les choses dont les hommes ne se peuvent plus aucunement[74] souvenir. Les autres petitz poësmes veulent estre abruptement commencez, comme les odes lyriques, à la composition desquelz je te conseille premierement t'exerciter,[75] te donnant de garde surtout d'estre plus versificateur que poëte. Car la fable et fiction est le subject des bons poëtes, qui ont esté depuis toute memoire recommandez de la posterité; et les vers sont seulement le but de l'ignorant versificateur, lequel pense avoir faict un grand chef-d'œuvre quand il a composé beaucoup de carmes rymez, qui sentent tellement la prose que je suis esmerveillé comme noz François daignent imprimer telles drogueries, à la confusion des autheurs et de nostre nation. Je te dirois icy particulierement les propres subjectz d'un chascun poësme si tu n'avois desja veu l'*Art poëtique* d'Horace et d'Aristote, ausquelz je te cognois assez mediocrement versé. Je te veux advertir de fuir les epi[B iij *v*]thetes naturelz, qu'ilz[76] ne servent de rien à la sentence[77] de ce que tu veux dire, comme *la riviere coulante, la verde ramée.*[78] Tes epithetes seront recherchez pour signifier, et non pour remplir ton carme ou pour estre oyseux en ton vers: exemple, *Le ciel vouté encerne tout le monde.* J'ay dit "vouté," et non "ardant," "clair," ny "hault" ny "azeuré," d'autant qu'une voute est propre pour embrasser et encerner quelque chose. Tu pouras bien dire, *Le bateau va de sur l'onde coulante,* pource que le cours de l'eau faict couler le bateau. Les Romains ont esté très curieux observateurs de ceste regle, et entre les autres Virgile et Horace. Les Grecs, comme en toutes choses appartenantes aux vers, y ont esté plus libres et n'y ont advisé de si près. Tu fuiras aussi la maniere de composer des Italiens en ta langue, qui mettent ordinairement quatre ou cinq epithetes les uns après les autres en un mesme vers, comme *alma, bella, angelica e fortunata dona.* Tu vois que tels epithetes sont plus pour empouller et farder le[79] vers que pour besoing qu'il en soit. Bref, tu[80] te contenteras d'un epithete ou pour le moins de deux, si ce n'est quelquesfois par gaillardise en mettras cinq ou six; mais si tu m'en crois, cela t'aviendra le plus rarement que tu[81] pourras.

DE LA RYME

La ryme n'est autre chose qu'une consonance[82] et cadance de syllabes tombantes sur la fin des [B iv] vers, laquelle je veux que tu observes tant aux masculins qu'aux fœminins, de deux entieres et parfaites syllabes ou

72. de *omitted 1592* 73. ilz *1565 only* 74. peuuent nullement *1567 ff.*
75. te rompre & façonner *1567 ff.* 76. qui *1592* 77. la sentences *1565*
78. ramée, & infinis autres *1567 ff.* 79. les *1567* ff. 80. tu *omitted 1592*
81. tu *1565 only* 82. cosonance *1565*

pour le moins d'une aux masculins, pourveu qu'elle soit resonante et d'un son entier et parfaict. Exemple des fœminins: *France, esperance, despence, negligence, familiere, fourmiliere, premiere, chere, mere.* Exemple des masculins: *surmonter, monter, douter, sauter, Juppiter.* Toutesfois tu seras plus songneux de la belle invention et des motz que de la ryme, laquelle vient assez aisement d'elle-mesme après quelque peu d'exercitation.[83]

DE LA VOYELLE E

Toutes fois et quantes que la voyelle *e* est rencontrée d'un autre voyelle ou diftongue, elle est tousjours mangée, se perdant en la voyelle qui la suit sans faire syllabe par soy. Je dy rencontrée d'une voyelle ou d'une diftongue pure; autrement elle ne se peult manger quant l'*i* et *u* voyelles se tournent en consones, comme *Je, vive.* Exemple de *e* qui se mange: *cruelle et fiere et dure et facheuse amertume*; *Belle au cœur dur inexorable et fier.*[84] Davantaige *i* et *a* voyelles se peuvent elider et manger. Exemple d'*a*: *L'artillerie, l'amour,* pour *la artillerie, la amour.* Exemple de la voyelle *i*: *n'à ceux-cy, n'à ceux-là.*[85] Quant tu mangerois l'*o* et l'*u*, pour la necessité de tes vers, il n'y auroit point de mal, à la mode des Italiens ou [B iv *v*] plustost des Grecs, qui se servent des voyelles et diftongues comme il leur plaist et selon leur necessité.

*DE L'*H

L'*h* quelquesfois est note[86] d'aspiration, quelquesfois non; quand elle ne rend point la premiere syllable du mot aspirée,[87] elle se mange tout ainsi que faict *e* fœminin. Quand elle la rend aspirée,[88] elle ne se mange nullement. Exemple de *h* non aspirée: *Magnanime homme, humain, honneste et fort.* Exemple de celle qui rend la premiere syllabe du mot aspirée[89] et ne se mange point: *La belle femme hors d'icy s'en alla*; *le gentilhomme hautain alloit par tout.* Tu pourras voir par la lecture de noz poëtes[90] François l'*h* qui s'elide[91] ou non. Tu eviteras autant que la contraincte de ton vers le permettra les rencontres des voyelles et diftongues qui ne se mangent point. Car telles concurrences de voyelles sans estre elidées[92] font le[93] vers merveilleusement rude[94] en nostre langue, bien que les Grecs soyent coustumiers de ce faire comme par elegance. Exemple: *vostre beauté a envoyé amour.* Ce vers icy te servira de patron pour te garder de ne tomber en telle aspreté, qui escraze plustost l'oreille que[95] ne luy donne plaisir.

Tu doibs aussi noter que rien n'est si plaisant qu'un carme bien façonné,

83. d'exercice & labeur *1567 ff.* 84. Belle maitresse inexorable & fiere *1567 ff.*
85. *Added 1567 ff.*: pour dire *ny a ceux cy ny à ceux là* 86. marque *1567 ff.*
87. aspirée & rude à prononcer *1567 ff.* 88. aspirée & rude *1567 ff.*
89. dure *1567 ff.* 90. noz bons Poëtes *1567 ff.* 91. se mange *1567 ff.*
92. sans estre elidées *1565 only* 93. les *1573, 1592* 94. rudes *1573, 1592*
95. qu'elle *1567 ff.*

bien tourné, non entr'ouvert ny beant. Et pour ce, sauf le jugement de noz [C] Aristarques, tu doibs oster la derniere *e* fœminine, tant de[96] vocables singuliers que pluriers qui se finissent en *ée* et en *ées*,[97] quand de fortune ilz se rencontrent au milieu de ton[98] vers. Exemple du masculin plurier: *Rollant avoit deux espées en main.* Ne sens-tu pas que ces "deux espées en main"[99] offencent la delicatesse de l'oreille? Et pour ce tu doibs mettre: *Rollant avoit deux espés'*[100] *en la main* ou autre chose semblable. Exemple de l'*e* fœminine singuliere: *Contre la troupe*[101] *Ænée print sa picque.* Ne sens-tu pas comme derechef "Ænée" sonne très mal au milieu de ce vers? Pour ce tu mettras: *Contre la troupe*[102] *Æné' bransla sa picque.* Autant en est-il[103] des[104] vocables terminez en[105] *ouë* et *uë*, comme *rouë, jouë, nuë, venuë*, et mille autres qui doivent recevoir syncope[106] au milieu de ton vers. Si tu veux que ton poëme soit ensemble doux et savoureux, pour ce tu mettras *rou', jou', nu'*, contre l'opinion de tous noz maistres qui n'ont de si près advisé à la perfection de ce mestier.

Encores je te veux bien admonester d'une chose très necessaire. C'est quand tu trouveras des motz qui difficilement reçoyvent ryme, comme *or*, *char*, et mille autres, les rymer hardiment contre *fort, ort, acort, part, renart, art*, ostant par licence la derniere lettre, *t*, du mot "fort" et mettre "for' " simplement avec la marque de l'apostrophe. Autant en feras-tu de *far'* pour *fard*, pour le rymer contre *char*.[107] Je voy le plus[108] souvent mille belles sentences et mille beaux vers perdus par[109] faute de telle hardiesse, si [C *v*] bien que sur *or* je n'y voy jamais ryme[110] que *tresor* ou *or* (pour *ores*), *Nestor*, *Hector*, et sur *char*, *Cesar*. Tu sincoperas aussi hardiment ce mot de *comme*, et diras à ta necessité *com'*; car[111] je voy en quelle peine bien[112] souvent on se trouve par faute de destourner l'*e* finale de ce mot.[113] Et mesmes au commencement du vers.

Tu accourciras aussi (je dis en tant que tu[114] y seras contrainct) les verbes trop longs, comme *donra* pour *donnera*, *sautra* pour *sautera*, et non les verbes dont les infinitifz se terminent en *e*, lesquelz au contraire tu n'allongeras poinct; et ne diras *prendera* pour *prendra*, *mordera* pour *mordra*,

96. des *1592* 97. en ce et en ces *1573, 1592* 98. tous *1592*
99. en la main *1571 ff.* 100. espees *1592*
101. Contre Mezance *1567, 1571, 1573;* Contre de Mezance *1592*
102. Contre Mezance *1567 ff.* 103. il *1565 only* 104. de *1571 ff.*
105. en *1565 only* 106. syncope & apocope *1567 ff.*
107. *Added 1567 ff.*: Exemple:

Venus faisant atteler son beau char
Y fist monter son enfant plain de far'.

108. le plus *1565 only* 109. par *1565 only* 110. rymer *1567 ff.*
111. car *1565 only* 112. bien *1565 only*
113. se trouue faute de couper la lettre e finale de ce mot comme *1567 ff.*
114. tu *omitted 1592*

n'ayant en cela reigle plus parfaicte que ton oreille, laquelle ne te trompera jamais si tu veux prendre son conseil avec certain jugement et raison. Tu eviteras aussi l'abondance des monosyllabes en tes vers, pour estre rudes et mal plaisans à ouyr. Exemple: *Je vy le ciel si beau, si pur et net.* Au reste, je te conseille d'user de la lettre *ò*, marquée de ceste marque, pour signifier "avecques"[115] à la façon des anciens, comme *ò luy* pour *avecques luy*; car "avecques,"[116] composé de trois syllabes, donne grand empeschement au vers, mesmement quant il est court. Je m'asseure que telles permissions n'auront si tost lieu que tu cognoistras incontinent de quelle peine se voyront delivrez les plus jeunes, par le courage de ceux[117] qui auront si hardiment osé. Tu pourras aussi à la mode des Grecs, qui disent οὔνομα pour ὄνομα, adjouster un *u* après un *o* pour faire ta ryme plus ri[C ij]che et plus sonante, comme *troupe* pour *trope*, *Callioupe* pour *Calliope*.[118]

Tu n'oublieras jamais les articles et tiendras pour tout certain que rien ne peut tant deffigurer ton vers que les articles delaissez. Autant en est-il[119] des pronoms primitifz, comme *je, tu,* que tu n'oublieras non plus[120] si tu veux que tes carmes soyent parfaictz et de tous poinctz bien accomplis. Je te dirois encores beaucoup de regles et secretz de nostre poësie; mais j'ayme mieux en nous promenans te les apprendre de bouche, que les mettre par escrit pour fascher peult estre une bonne partie de ceux qui pensent estre grands maistres, dont à peine ont-ils encores touché les premiers oustilz de ce mestier.

DES VERS ALEXANDRINS

Les Alexandrins tiennent la place en nostre langue telle que les vers heroïques entre les Grecs et les[121] Latins; lesquelz sont composez de douze à treize syllabes, les masculins de douze, les fœminins de treize, et ont tousjours leur repos sur la sixiesme syllabe (comme les vers communs sur la quatriesme, dont nous parlerons après). Exemple des masculins: *Madame, baisez-moi, je meurs en vous baisant,* où tu vois manifestement le repos de ce vers estre sur la sixiesme syllabe. Exemple du fœminin: *O ma belle maistresse, as-tu pas bonne envie.* Tu doibs icy noter [C ij *v*] que tous noz[122] François qui se terminent en *es*, ou en *e* lente sans force et sans son, ou en *ent*,[123] sont fœminins. Tous les autres, de quelque terminaison qu'ilz puissent estre, sont masculins. Exemple de *e* fœminine singuliere: *femme,*[124] *beste, nasarde, livre, escritoire.* [Exemple des noms pluriers terminez en *es*:][125]

115. avecques *1565 only* 116. le mot auecques *1567 ff.* 117. des vieux *1567 ff.*
118. *Added 1567 ff.: espouse* pour *espose*, *chouse* pour *chose* 119. il *1565 only*
120. iamais *1567 ff.* 121. les *1565 only* 122. motz *1567 ff.*
123. es *1565*; ent, pluriers des verbes *1567 ff.*
124. e fœminin: *singuliere femme 1565*
125. *Text of 1567 ff.; 1565* escritoire, des livres, livres

livres, *escritoires*, *chantres*, etc.[126] Exemple des masculins: *donné*, *haut*, *chapeau*, *descendez*, *surmontez*.[127] Il fault aussi entendre que les pluriers des verbes qui se finissent en *ent* sont reputez fœminins, comme *ilz viennent*, *disent*, *souhaittent*, *parlent*, *marchent*, etc. La composition des Alexandrins doibt estre grave, hautaine, (et si fault ainsi parler) altiloque, d'autant qu'ilz sont plus longs que les autres et sentiroyent la prose si n'estoyent composez de motz esleus, graves, et resonnans, et d'une ryme assez riche, afin que telle richesse empesche le stille de la prose, et qu'elle se garde tousjours dans les oreilles jusques à la fin de l'autre vers.[128] Tu les feras donc les plus parfaictz que tu pourras, et ne te contenteras point comme la plus grand part de ceux de nostre temps qui pensent, comme j'ay dict, avoir accomply je ne sçay quoy de grand quand ilz ont rymé de la prose en vers. Tu as desja l'esprit assez bon pour descouvrir tels versificateurs par leurs miserables escritz, et par la congnoissance des mauvais faire jugement des bons; lesquelz je ne veux particulierement nommer pour estre en petit nombre, et de peur d'offencer ceux qui ne seroyent couchez en ce papier; aussi que je[129] desire[130] eviter l'im[C iij]pudence de telle maniere de gens. Car tu sçais bien que non seulement κεραμεὺς κεραμεῖ κοτέει καὶ τέκτονι τέκτων mais aussi ἀοιδὸς ἀοιδῷ.[131]

DES VERS COMMUNS

Les vers communs sont de dix à onze syllabes, les masculins de dix, les fœminins d'onze, et ont sur la quatriesme syllabe leur repos ou reprise d'aleine, ainsi que les vers Alexandrins sur la fin des six premieres syllabes. Or comme les Alexandrins sont propres pour les subjectz heroïques, ceux-cy sont proprement nez pour les amours, bien que les vers Alexandrins reçoyvent quelquesfois un subject amoureux, et mesmement en elegies et aiglogues, où ilz ont assez bonne grace quand ilz sont bien composez. Exemple des vers communs masculins: *Heureux le roy qui craint d'offencer Dieu.* Exemple du fœminin: *Pour ne dormir j'alume la bougie.* Telle maniere de carmes ont esté fort usitez entre les vieux poëtes François. Je te conseille de t'y amuser quelque peu de temps, avant que passer aux Alexandrins. Sur toute chose je te veux bien[132] advertir s'il est possible (car tousjours on ne faict pas ce qu'on propose) que les quatre premieres syllabes du vers commun ou les six premieres des Alexandrins soyent façonnez d'un sens

126. chantres, dances, &c. *1567 ff.* 127. *Sentence omitted 1567 ff.*

128. vers qui est long *1567 ff.* 129. aussi suyuant mon naturel ie *1567 ff.*

130. desire infiniment *1567 ff.*

131. *Added 1567 ff.*: Si ie n'ay commencé ma Franciade en vers Alexandrins, lesquels i'ay mis (comme tu sçais) en vogue & en honneur il s'en faut prendre à ceux qui ont puissance de me commander & non à ma volonté: car cela est fait contre mon gré, esperant vn iour la faire marcher à la cadance Alexandrine: mais pour cette fois il faut obeyr. 132. bien *1565 only*

aucunement parfaict, sans l'emprunter du mot suyvant. Exemple du sens par[C iij *v*]faict: *Jeune beauté maistresse de ma vie.* Exemple du vers qui a le sens imparfaict: *L'homme qui a esté de sur la mer.*

DES AUTRES VERS EN GENERAL

Les vers Alexandrins et les communs sont seulz entre touts qui reçoyvent cesure (sur la sixiesme et quatriesme syllabe). Car les autres marchent d'un pas licencieux, et se contentent seulement d'un certain nombre que tu pourras faire à plaisir, selon ta volonté, tantost de sept à huict syllabes, tantost de six à sept, tantost de cinq à six, tantost de quatre à trois, les masculins estans quelquesfois les plus longs,[133] quelquesfois les fœminins selon que la caprice te prendra. Telz vers sont merveilleusement propres pour la musique, la lyre et autres instrumens, et pour ce[134] quand tu les appelleras lyriques tu ne leur feras point de tort, tantost les allongeant, tantost les accoursissant, et après un grand vers un petit ou deux petitz, au choix de ton oreille, gardant tousjours le plus que tu[135] pouras une bonne cadence de vers propres (comme je t'ay dict auparavant) pour la musique et autres instrumens. Tu en pourras tirer les exemples en mille lieux de noz poëtes[136] François. Je te veux aussi bien advertir de hautement prononcer tes vers[137] quand tu les feras, ou plustost les chanter, quelque voix que puisses avoir, [C iv] car cela est bien une des principales parties que tu dois le plus curieusement observer.

DES PERSONNES DES VERBES FRANÇOIS ET DE L'ORTOGRAPHIE

Tu n'abuseras des personnes des verbes, mais les feras servir selon leur naturel, n'usurpant les unes pour les autres comme plusieurs de nostre temps. Exemple en la premiere personne, "J'alloy" en non "j'allois, il alloit"; si ce n'est aux verbes anomaux, desquels nous avons grand quantité en nostre langue comme en toutes autres. Et cela nous donne à cognoistre que le peuple ignorant a fait les langages et non les sçavans. Car les doctes n'eussent jamais tant creé de monstres en leur langue, qui se doibt si sainctement honorer. Ils n'eussent jamais dit *sum*, *es*, *est*, mais plustost *sum*, *sis*, *sit*; et n'eussent dit *bonus*, *melior*, *optimus*, ains *bonus*, *bonior*, *bonissimus*. Mais ayant trouvé desja les motz faictz par le peuple, ilz ont esté contrainctz d'en user pour donner à entendre plus facilement au vulgaire leurs conceptions, par un langage desja receu. Tu pourras avecques licence user de la seconde personne pour la premiere, pourveu que la personne se finisse par une voyelle ou diftongue et que le mot suyvant s'y commence, afin d'eviter un mauvais son qui te pourroit offencer, comme *j'allois à Tours* pour dire *j'alloy à Tours*, *je* [C iv *v*] *parlois à ma dame* pour

133. loings *1565* 134. et pour ce *1565 only* 135. tu *1565 only*
136. bons Poëtes *1567 ff.* 137. *Added 1571 ff.*: en ta chambre

je parloy à ma dame, et mille autres semblables qui te viendront à la plume en composant. Tu pourras aussi adjouster par licence une *s* à la premiere personne, pourveu que la ryme du premier vers le demande ainsi. Exemple:

> Puisque le Roy faict de si bonnes loix,
> Pour ton profit, ô France, je vouldrois
> Qu'on les gardast.

Tu ne rejecteras point les vieux verbes Picards, comme *voudroye* (pour *voudroy*), *aimeroye, diroye, feroye.* Car[138] plus nous aurons de motz en nostre langue, plus elle sera parfaicte et donnera moins de peine à celuy qui voudra pour passetemps s'y employer. Tu diras[139] selon la contrainte de ton vers *or, ore, ores,*[140] *adoncq, adoncque, adoncques, avecq, avecque, avecques,* et mille autres que sans crainte tu trancheras et alongeras ainsi qu'il te plaira,[141] gardant tousjours une certaine mesure consultée par ton oreille, laquelle est certain juge de la structure des vers comme l'œil de la peincture des tableaux.[142] Tu eviteras toute ortographie superflue et ne mettras aucunes lettres en telz motz si tu ne les proferes;[143] au moins tu en useras le plus sobrement que tu pourras. En attendant meilleure reformation, tu escriras *écrire* et non *escripre, cieus* et non *cieulx.*

Tu pardonneras encores à noz *z,* jusques à tant qu'elles soyent remises aux lieux où elles doivent servir, comme en *roze,*[144] *choze, espouze,* et mille autres.[145] Quant au *k,* il est très utile en nostre langue, comme en ces motz: *kar, kalité, kantité, kaquet, kabaret,*[146] et non le *c,* qui tantost occupe la force d'un *k,* [D] tantost d'un *ſ,* selon qu'il a pleu à nos predecesseurs ignorans de les escrire,[147] comme *France* pour *Franſe*; et si on te dit qu'on prononceroit *Franze,* tu respondras que la[148] lettre *ſ* ne se prononce jamais par un *z.* Autant en est-il[149] de nostre *g,* qui souventesfois occupe si miserablement le lieu de l'*i* consone, comme en *langage* pour *langaje.* Autant en est-il[149] de nostre *q* et du *c,* lesquelz il[149] faudroit totalement oster; d'autant que le *k,* qui est κ des Grecs, peut en nostre langue servir sans violence en lieu du *q* et du *c.* Il faudroit encores inventer des lettres doubles à l'imitation des Espagnolz, de *ill* et de[150] *gn,* pour bien prononcer *orgueilleux, Mon-*

138. Car *1565 only* 139. ne diras *1592* 140. ores *omitted 1592*
141. plaira bien *1592*
142. *Added 1567 ff.*: Tu feras pour vne reigle infalible tes carmes masculins & fœminins acheuant tousiours ton œuure par telle mesure estant en ton choix de commencer par les deux premiers masculins ou fœminins, et si tu commences par les deux fœminins, les deux ensuyuans seront masculins les autres apres fœminins les autres masculins en gardant ceste reigle iusques à la fin.
143. les prononces en les lisant *1567 ff.* 144. ruze *1592* 145. rutres *1565*
146. *Added 1567 ff.*: et mille autres 147. de le mettre *1567 ff.* 148. là la *1592*
149. il *1565 only* 150. d, *1565*

seigneur; et reformer en la plus grand part nostre a, b, c, lequel je n'ay entreprins pour le present, t'ouvrant par si peu d'escriture la cognoissance de la verité d'ortographie et de la poësie, que tu pourras plus amplement practiquer de toy-mesme, comme bien né, si tu comprens ce petit abbregé, lequel en faveur de toy[151] a esté en trois heures commencé et achevé. Joinct aussi que ceux qui sont si grands maistres de preceptes, comme Quintilian, ne sont jamais volontiers parfaicts en leur mestier.

Je te veux encores advertir de n'écorcher point le Latin, comme noz devanciers qui ont trop sottement tiré des Romains une infinité de vocables estrangers, veu qu'il y en avoit d'aussi bons en nostre propre langage.[152] Toutesfois tu ne les desdaigneras s'ilz sont desja receuz et usitez d'un chascun. Tu composeras hardiment des motz à l'imitation des Grecs [D *v*] et Latins, pourveu qu'ilz soyent gratieux et plaisans à l'oreille, et n'auras soucy de ce que le vulgaire dira de toy; d'autant que les poëtes, comme les plus hardis, ont les premiers forgé et composé les motz, lesquelz pour estre beaux et significatifz ont passé par la bouche des orateurs et du vulgaire, puis finablement ont esté receuz, louez, et admirez d'un chacun. J'ay entendu par plusieurs de mes amis que si ceux qui se mesloyent de la poësie (les plus estimez en ce mestier) du temps du feu roy François et Henry eussent voulu sans envie permettre aux nouveaux une telle liberté, que nostre langue en abondance se feust en peu de temps égallée à celle des Romains et des Grecs.

Tu tourneras les noms propres des anciens[153] à la terminaison de ta langue autant qu'il se peult faire, à l'imitation des Romains qui ont approprié ce qu'ilz ont peu des Grecs[154] à leur langue Latine, comme 'Οδυσεύς, *Ulysses*, *Ulysse*, ou par syncope *Ulyss*; 'Αχιλλεύς, *Achilles*, *Achille*; 'Ηρακλέης, *Hercules*, *Hercule*, ou *Hercul*; Μενέλαος, *Menelaus*, *Menelas*; Νικόλαος, *Nicolaus*, *Nicolas*. Les autres sont demeurez en leur premiere terminaison,[155] comme *Agamemnon*, *Hector*, *Paris*, et plusieurs autres que tu pouras par-cy par-là trouver en la lecture des auteurs.

Tu ne dedaigneras les vieux motz François, d'autant que je les estime tousjours en vigueur, quoy qu'on die, jusques à ce qu'ilz ayent faict renaistre en leur place, comme une vieille souche, un rejetton; et lors tu te serviras du rejetton et non de la souche, laquelle faict aller toute sa sub-[Dij]stance à son petit enfant, pour le faire croistre et finablement l'establir en son lieu. De tous vocables, quelz qu'ilz soyent, en usage ou hors d'usage, s'il reste encores quelque partie d'eux, soit en nom, verbe, adverbe, ou participe, tu le pourras par bonne et certaine analogie faire croistre et multiplier, d'autant que nostre langue est encores pauvre et qu'il fault

151. *Added 1567 ff.*: Alphonce d'Elbene 152. langue *1567 ff.*
153. des anciens *1565 only* 154. approprié les noms Grecs *1567 ff.*
155. *Added 1567 ff.*: d'autant qu'ils n'ont peu nullement se tourner

mettre peine, quoy que murmure le peuple, avec toute modestie de l'enrichir et cultiver. Exemple des vieux motz: puisque le nom de *verve* nous reste, tu pourras faire sur le nom le verbe *verver* et l'adverbe[156] *vervement*; sur le nom d'*essonie*, *essonier*, *essoniement*,[157] et mille autres telz. Et quant il n'y auroit que l'adverbe, tu pourras faire le verbe et le participe librement et hardiement. Au pis aller, tu le cotteras en la marge de ton livre, pour donner à entendre sa signification. Et sur les vocables receus en usage, comme *pays*, *eau*, *feu*, tu feras *payser*, *euer*, *fouer*, *éuenement*, *foüement*,[158] et mille autres tels vocables, qui ne voyent encores la lumiere faute d'un hardy et bienheureux entrepreneur.

Or si je congnois que cest abbregé te soit aggreable, et utile à la posterité, je te feray un plus long discours de nostre poësie, comme elle se doibt enrichir, de ses[159] parties plus necessaires, du jugement qu'on en doibt faire, si elle se peult regler aux[160] piedz des vers Latins et Grecz ou non, comme il fault composer des verbes frequentatifz, incoatifz, des noms comparatifz, superlatifz et autres telz ornements de nostre langage pauvre et manque de soy. [D ij *v*] Et ne se fault soucier, comme je l'ay dit tant de fois, de l'opinion que pourroit avoir le peuple de tes escris, tenant pour reigle toute asseurée qu'il vault mieux servir à la verité qu'à l'opinion du peuple, qui ne veut sçavoir sinon ce qu'il voit devant ses[161] yeux, et croyant à credit pense que noz devanciers estoyent plus saiges que nous, et qu'il les fault totalement suivir,[162] sans rien inventer de nouveau; en cecy faisant grand tort à la bonne nature, laquelle ilz pensent pour le jourd'huy estre brehaigne et infertile en bons esprits, et que dès le commencement elle a respandu toutes ses vertus sur les premiers hommes, sans avoir rien retenu en espargne pour donner comme mere très liberale à ses enfans qui devoyent naistre après[163] au monde par le cours de tant de siecles à venir.

Fin de l'Art Poëtique.[164]

156. abverbe *1565* 157. essoine, essoiner, essoinement *1567 ff.*
158. païser, eüer, foüer *1567, 1571, 1573; other words omitted 1567 ff.*
159. ces *1565* 160. au *1565* 161. ces *1565* 162. suiure *1567 ff.*
163. après *1565 only* 164. Fin des poemes *1567, 1571, 1573*

ANDRÉ DE RIVAUDEAU

DEDICATION AND PREFACE TO *Aman*

1566

TEXT:

Les Oevvres d'André de Rivavdeav Gentilhomme dv Bas Poitov. Aman. Tragedie Saincte, Tiree dv VII. Chapitre d'Esther, Livre de la Saincte Bible. A Ianne de Foix, Tres illustre & tres-vertueuse, Royne de Nauarre. Outre deux Liures du mesme autheur, Le premier, Contenant les Complaintes, Le second, Les Diuerses Poësies. A Poitiers, Par Nicolas Logeroys. M.D.LXVI. [Arsenal, Paris.]

[Cf. Brunet, IV, 1319.]

Although Rivaudeau's tragedy, *Aman,* was produced in 1561 (cf. Lanson, *Revue d'histoire littéraire,* X [1903], 200), the dedication to Jeanne de Foix and the "Avant-parler" were not written until the collected works were being prepared; the latter is dated May 1, 1565. Both of these selections are included in a reprint of the complete works by Mourain de Sourdeval, Paris: Aubry, 1859, pp. 37–52. This edition is inaccurate and does not give a satisfactory text of the selections; but some materials on Rivaudeau are presented in the introductory pages.

[¶2] A JANNE DE FOIX

TRÈS ILLUSTRE ET TRÈS VERTUEUSE ROYNE DE NAVARRE

Madame, tous ceux-là qui consacrent aux grans
Leurs escritz serieux, les sçavent ignorans;
Et si ne les font pas juges de leur doctrine.
Mais ilz pensent cecy, que la grandeur est digne
Des muses, ou plustost enseignent aux seigneurs
D'avancer les savans aux biens et aux honneurs;
Et en particulier atendent recompense
De leur docte labeur, d'une vaine esperance
Dont ilz restent trompés; et mieux il leur vaudroit
S'en adroisser à tel qui leur cause entendroit,
Et, bien que d'ailleurs fust sa puissance petite,
Certes peust dignement estimer leur merite.
L'honneur soustient les artz, le vertueux desir
De louange adoucist le travail en plaisir.
Mais quoy? la povreté, presque aux doctes commune,
Assise en leur fouyer les foule et importune,
Et très mal aisement maintz se peuvent sauver

De qui ce monstre laid fait les vertus couver.
Car de ce temps les mains des princes sont fermées
Aux savans, et sont peu les lettres estimées.
Barbare chicheté! les finances des rois
Servent aux carnevaux, aux lices et tournois.
Les mignons d'Apollon acroupis aux estudes [¶2 *v*]
Façonnent les leçons de leurs escholiers rudes,
Qu'on pourroit employer aux affaires d'estat
Ou celles qu'aux palais en justice on debat,
Ou grans ambassadeurs d'une grave eloquence
Discourir sur la guerre ou sur la patience.
Mais on avance là ceux qui sçavent un peu,
Gens qui ont bonne mine et souvent mauvais jeu.
  Je ne parle pour moy, qui par la providence
De Dieu me trouve hors de toute ceste dance.
Je ne suis souffreteux de ma condition,
Et n'ay besoin de mieux; puis franc d'ambition
Je mesprise la gloire et l'honorable peine
De monter aux honneurs d'une atendante aleine.
J'ay aprins les faveurs des rois et de la cour
Pratiquées longtemps se passer en un jour;
Quand elles dureroyent, qu'il est mal aisé suyvre
Tout ensemble la cour et ensemble bien vivre;
Que les conseilz des bons n'y sont si tost receus
Que des meschans par qui les princes sont deceus.
Et quand l'ame j'auray haute et ambitieuse,
Et quand j'auray la main très povre et disetteuse,
Neantmoins si j'estois un petit vertueux
J'auroy bien rencontré remede pour les deux
En vostre Royauté, qui du sceptre et couronne
Semblés les autres grans, et non de la personne;
Miroir des bonnes meurs et de la pieté,
Suyvant les pas d'Astrée et la droite equité; [¶3]
Très liberale aux bons, aux meschans rigoureuse,
Amie des savans, savante et vertueuse,
Vers qui ni les plaisans, les postes, ni flateurs,
Ni ces trouveurs d'argent, ni ces grans prometteurs
Ont favorable accès; mais ceux dont la justice
Vous est bien aperceuë, ennemie du vice.
Mais faut-il discourir si longuement un fait
Esprouvé par les bons, que tout le monde sçait?

Il suffit que cela m'a fait vouër mon livre
A vostre majesté pour plus seurement vivre
Soubz si digne faveur, qui sçavez estimer
Les escriptz saintz et bons, les louër et aimer.
  Qui taxe la bonté d'une fauce sagesse
Et l'estime souvent au prix de la vieillesse,
Comme les vieux escus les poëmes plus vieux
Il tient pour les meilleurs, plus chers et pretieux.
C'est tout; je veux pourtant vous advertir d'un cas:
Le jugement du peuple icy ne suyvés pas.
Il hait les nouveautés, et les plumes Gregeoises
Et Romaines il met au-dessus des Françoises.
Il faut en preferant les estrangers aux siens,
Et aux doctes nouveaux les resveurs anciens.
Je croy qu'il[1] y en a, dont la troupe est petite,
Qui de tous ces premiers esgalent le merite.
Je ne metz en ce ranc un monde d'escrivains
Qui de mille cayers nous barbouillent les mains,
Ne servent qu'aux beurriers et aux fripiers libraires, [¶3 *v*]
Aux merciers, aux grossiers, et aux apothicaires.
Mais certes il en est qui aux langues et artz
Nous rendent les espritz de ces divins vieillardz,
Soit, si je l'ose dire, en la theologie,
Ou en la medecine, ou la philosophie.
  Et de ma part je veux, tant que je puis tascher,
Quelques fautes fuïr où je voy trebucher
L'Euripide ancien, dont le grand Aristote,
Très severe censeur, le chastie et le cotte.[a]
Je ne veux suyvre Plaute en ce qu'Horace dit
Estre en luy vitieux, rabaissant son credit.[b]
Mais de ces repreneurs les plumes trop hardies
N'eussent peut-estre fait de bonnes tragedies;
Et aussi n'entrepren-je au langage estranger
A ce prince tragic de me comparager.
Bien que j'escrive en Græc et bien que je l'entende,
Je ne sçauroy pourtant faire une œuvre si grande.
Mais je veux en ma langue oser, audacieux,
Faire entendre qu'on peut tout autant que les vieux

1. qu'l *1566*

a. Cf. *Poetics* 1453*a*32, 1456*a*29, 1461*b*23, etc.
b. Possibly a reference to *Epistles*, II.i.170–76.

Lorsqu'ils ont le mieux fait, sans ensuyvir pour guide
En ce qu'ils ont failly Plaute ni Euripide.
Quoy! chacun dit ainsi, et chascun se promet,
Fauce temerité! d'ataindre le sommet.
Tous brouillent le papier, tous se meslent d'escrire,
Et des hommes cecy presque est la faute pire.
Moy-mesme, qui me di escrire point ou peu,
Avant l'aube du jour je demande du feu, [¶4]
Je demande une plume, et de fascheuse grace
Vint sujetz entrepris je renverse et retrace.
Je hurte le poupitre et mordille mes doitz.
Je tien la veuë basse, et haute quelque fois;
Je suis impatient, je rechigne et me ride.
Or je veux commenter l'*Electre* d'Euripide,[c]
Or je veux éclarcir les grans thesors des Græcz,
Ores des livres saintz les plus rares secretz.
Comment? un autre ouvrier ne prendra la boussole
Ni le cadran, craignant de mal joüer son role?
Celuy n'ordonne pas le cirop incognu
Au malade, qui est pour artizan tenu;
Car c'est aux medecins à composer les doses
De casse et d'agaric et de pareilles choses.
Chascun fait son mestier, mais les sages et fouz,
Les bons et les mauvais, escrivent presque tous.
Je ne veux pas toucher les humeurs des poëtes,
Leurs cerveaux esventés, leurs trop legeres testes,
Leur vie trop oisive, ou leur condition
Chetive et affamée, ou leur presomption.
Je diray seulement qu'on juge le poëte
Non pas tant par les vers que le sujet qu'il traite.
Empedocle se doit philosophe nommer,
Theögnis ne se doit poëte surnommer,
Ni Phocylide encor', Lucrece, ni Pontan,
Ni Candre, ni Lucan, ni mesmes Opian.
L'un traite la nature et un autre l'histoire, [¶4 *v*]
L'autre enseignant les meurs a[2] avancé sa gloire.
Autres sont les discours de la folle Sapphon,
De Stesichore, Ibyc, du chauve Anacreon.

2. à *1566*

c. Rivaudeau refers to his commentary on *Electra* at the beginning of the "Avant-parler" (p. 215 below).

Je veux de ces premiers surpasser le merite,
Non pas par mon sçavoir, car ma force est petite,
Mais par le puissant nom de ce très grand seigneur
Dont je chante les faitz, la victoire, et l'honneur.
Madame, ce nom-là m'aporte confiance
Que soubz vostre faveur la Navarre et la France
Recevront mon labeur et verront quelquefois
Mon livre bien venu aux familles des rois.

[¶¶] AVANT-PARLER D'ANDRÉ DE RIVAUDEAU

A MONSIEUR DE LA NOUE-CHAVAIGNE DE BRETAIGNE[d]

Mon bon seigneur et amy. C'est aux rois et aux princes à qui les tiltres magnifiques des livres se doyvent vouer, et mesmement à ceux qui aiment et favorisent les bonnes lettres. Mais quand l'on desire recommander sa cause et faire entendre son intention plus privément, il se faut adroisser à un amy, et non seulement cela, mais à un amy savant et avisé. Et est toutesfois cela si peu aisé que la plus grande povreté que nous ayons en ce monde est de telz amis. J'ay toute ma vie tasché par les moyens que Dieu m'a donnés d'en aquerir. Mais il ne me resouvient point d'en avoir jamais veu ni rencontré aucun de qui, pour l'avoir si peu hanté, je desirasse tant l'amitié que je fay la vostre, m'estant persuadé que ce me sera un singulier bien, honneur, et contentement d'esprit s'il vous plaist me tenir en vostre bonne grace comme le plus affectionné à vostre service et le plus grand admirateur de vostre vertu que vous sçauriez jamais rencontrer. Si je gagne ce point, je feray bien entendre à la posterité, Dieu aidant, que je m'en tiens fier et glorieux comme d'une très riche conqueste. Je viens maintenant à ce que je vous veux discourir et communiquer du fait qui s'offre.

Si la disposition des temps m'eust peu souffrir mettre au jour les amples commentaires que j'ay faitz y a bien six ans sur *Electre*, tragedie d'Euripide nouvellement née par le labeur de Pierre Victorius[e] et non encores exposée d'aucun, ilz me dispenseroyent dès ceste heure (comme encores enten-je qu'ils me dispensent à l'advenir, Dieu aidant) du travail, que j'eusse autrement pris au sueil de ceste œuvre, de donner plus grande clarté à ceste partie de la poësie. En laquelle depuis les premiers Græcz nul homme, à mon avis, a fidelement versé ni s'est composé au vray et naif artifice que Seneque seul, qui encores ne se est du tout formalizé ni à l'art ni à la façon

d. Cf. the edition of Sourdeval, the Errata at the end of the volume, for a note on François de la Noue-Chavaigne.

e. Pietro Vettori's edition of the Greek text of *Electra* appeared in 1545, his Latin translation in 1546.

des anciens. Vray est que ceux qui auront bien leu le petit traité d'Aristote n'auront pas grand besoin ni de tout ce que j'ay escript en mon livre ni de ce que j'en sçauroy enseigner icy. Parquoy je les renvoye là ce pendant, fors en ce [¶¶ *v*] qui n'est si bien raporté à l'estat de nostre temps, à l'humeur de nostre nation, et à la proprieté de nostre langue; sans quoy le plus abile Græc de Chrestienté, ni le Philosophe mesme qui en a escript, encores qu'ils entendeissent nostre langage, sçauroyent bien bastir une tragedie Françoise. Cela se cognoistra aux discours que j'en ay faict sur *Electre*. Maintenant je n'en ay rien à dire, fors que ceux qui font des tragedies ou comedies de plus d'un jour ou d'un tour de soleil (comme par l'Aristote)[f] faillent lourdement. Ce que je di hardiment, combien que Terence ait donné deux jours à son *Eautontimorumene* (c'est-à-dire à "Celuy qui se chastie soy-mesme") et d'autres de mesmes. Car en tout cas cela ne se peult sauver du vice; mais il est monstrueux d'y mettre beaucoup de mois ou d'ans, comme font quelques-uns. Mais ces tragedies sont bien bonnes et artificielles qui ne traitent rien plus que ce qui peut estre advenu en autant de temps que les spectateurs considerent l'ebat. Le vocable du Philosophe, ici poëte, est fort propre pour ce que je veux dire, et est traduit par Marc Ciceron au commencement de son livre des *Orateurs renommés* à un autre propos.[g]

Mais je ne mesle point de Græc parmi le François. Je conseille à ces songes de poëtes qui ont tant tiré à la courroye de l'escriture sainte sans faire un seul brodequin qui valust, que quand ilz voudront amener un messager sur l'eschafaut (qui ait en voyage de plus d'un jour affaire), qu'ilz le facent parler jà retourné. S'ilz veulent envelopper en leur farce une chose avenue devant, qu'ilz la facent conter sans la representer. Il y a mille autres moyens pour couvrir son jeu, que je veux bien croire qu'ils entendent.

Un moindre vice est de ce qu'ilz[3] apellent les machines, c'est-à-dire des moyens extraordinaires et surnaturelz pour deslier le nœud de la tragedie: un dieu fableux en campagne, un chariot porté par dragons en l'air, et mille autres grossieres subtilitez sans lesquelles les poëtes mal fournis d'inventions ou d'art, ou mesprisans ce dernier, ne peuvent venir à bout de leur fusée ni depestrer le nœud Gordien sinon de la façon du grand Alexandre, à coupz de baston. Aristote[4] marque ceste faute en la *Medée*,[h] et je l'ay cottée en *Electre* avec d'autres. Or il ne faut imiter leur licencieuse façon que nous pouvons blasmer comme Horace tenaille franchement celle de Plaute en son *Art Poëtique*,[i] où je renvoy aussi ceux qui voudront lire

3. ily *1566* 4. Aristoste *1566*

f. *Poetics* 1449*b*12.
g. Unidentified.
h. *Poetics* 1454*b*1.
i. *Ars poetica*, ll. 270 ff.

quelque chose de la tragedie, et à un gros volume qu'en a fait un Scaliger, dont je n'ay veu encores que le titre.[j]

[A long section on the Esther story is omitted here.] [¶¶3]

Pour le reste, je me suis rengé le plus reservement et estroitement que j'ay peu en escrivant ceste tragedie à l'art et au modelle des anciens Græcz, et n'ay esté ni trop superstitieux ni trop licentieux, ni en la rime ni ès autres parties de la poësie. Cela peux-je bien asseurer, et quelques-uns de mes familiers me sont fideles tesmoins que devant que me contenter de moy-mesmes en ce genre d'escrire, j'ay fait des tragedies en toutes les langues qu'on en list aujourd'huy. Quant à mon intention, ce n'a pas esté pour en raporter louange (que je ne chercheroy pas en si petit que quand j'en seroy desireux comme je ne le suis nullement) ni autre quelconque mentionnable. Car j'avoy presque fait devant qu'avoir pensé pourquoy je faisoy. Enfin je me suis resolu que l'ayant escripte en ma grande jeunesse en un stile si rare à nos François et argument si saint, elle pourroit estre leüe avec plaisir et contentement de ceux qui aiment les saintes lettres et ne sont ennemis des muses que Marc Ciceron appelle gratieuses.[k]

Et est encores ceste-cy la premiere besoigne à qui j'ay fait humer l'air et prendre le vent de beaucoup de choses que j'ay escriptes sur la langue Græcque et les saintes lettres, que j'ay laissé denteler aux ratz philosophes, craignant deux sortes d'hommes. La premiere est de ces superstitieux et [¶¶3 *v*] renfroignez qui veulent bannir du monde la plus gentile et polie part de la doctrine, voire de la vie humaine, et qui cuident tout le zele Chrestien consister en mines, morgues, rechignement, et incivilité, usure d'acoustremens malpropres, enfoncement d'yeux, en faces plombées et saturniennes, et pour ce qui touche ce propos, en un stile ni docte, ni gaillard, ni eveillé, mais qui sente son vieux trespassé et sa charoigne de trois sepmaines. L'autre est de ces[5] malins, refroignez et esventez censeurs de qui les bisarres jugemens et les troignes ont despesché et renvoyé en moins d'un quart d'heure ce qui a[6] esté elaboré en beaucoup d'ans. Une autre cause a[6] fait tomber mes livres sur l'esponge, qui est la tourbe espaisse de tant de millions d'escriptz, et de tant de sortes, que je croy la masse du monde en estre toute moulue et ennivrée. Outre, je n'esperoy pas les petites œuvres d'un nouveau né et fraichement ecloz des entre-mondes d'Epicure peussent[7] tenir quelque ranc parmi le faste de ces païs fortunés, où il ne faut que penser estre savant pour l'estre[8] incontinent, comme j'ay escript quelque part ailleurs en une epistre qui est au jour.[l] Et pour dire vray,

5. ses *1566* 6. à *1566* 7. penssent *1566* 8. astre *1566*

j. Scaliger's *Poetices libri septem* had appeared in Lyon in 1561.
k. Unidentified.
l. Unidentified.

il m'eust fasché que tant de livres indignes et pernitieux, comme les *Amadis*, *Tristans*, et autres de mesme farine—c'est-à-dire ou inutiles, ou indoctes, ou deshonnestes, tant en vers qu'en prose—eussent eu plus de credit et de vogue que telle chose que mes longues veilles et mon bien grand et bien long travail eussent taillé pour servir à la chose publique. Au reste, je me sentiray suffisamment satisfait et recompensé de mon labeur si vous et vos semblables l'aprouvez et prisés, le jugement et louange desquelz je recevray mieux que du demeurant de tous les hommes.

Je prie Dieu, monseigneur, qu'il augmente les graces qu'il vous a[9] largement departies.

A La Groizardiere, ce premier jour de may, 1565.

9. à *1566*

PIERRE DE RONSARD

FIRST PREFACE TO *La Franciade*

1572

TEXT:

Les Qvatre Premiers Livre de la Franciade. Av Roy. Tres-Chrestien, Charles, Nevfieme de ce nom. Par Pierre de Ronsard, gentilhomme Vandomois. A Paris, Chez Gabriel Buon, demeurant au Cloz bruneau, à l'enseigne sainct Claude. 1572. Avec Privilege dv Roy. [B.N., Paris.]

[Cf. Brunet, IV, 1383–84, and *Supplément*, II, 511; Tchemerzine, IX, 447; Cat. Rothschild, No. 678; De Ricci, No. 66, p. 145. The first preface was reprinted in the edition of Turin: Jean-François Pico, 1574, listed by the British Museum; this edition has not been collated.]

Ronsard's first preface to his *Franciade* was replaced in 1573 by a short paragraph to the reader; in 1587, by a longer preface which is also printed later in this collection. In Ronsard's time, this first preface was reprinted only in the Turin edition of 1574. In the modern period, it has been reprinted in the major editions of the poet, most recently in the *Œuvres complètes*, edited by Gustave Cohen (Paris: Bibliothèque de la Pléiade, 1938, II, 1012–16), from which both of the notes given below have been taken.

[ã ij] AU LECTEUR

Encore que l'histoire en beaucoup de sortes se conforme à la poësie, comme en vehemence de parler, harangues, descriptions de batailles, villes, fleuves, mers, montaignes, et autres semblables choses où le poëte ne doibt non plus que l'orateur falsifier le vray, si est-ce quand à leur sujet ils sont aussi eslongnez l'un de l'autre que le vraysemblable est eslongné de la verité. L'histoire reçoit seulement la chose comme elle est ou fut, sans desguisure ny fard, et le poëte s'arreste au vraysemblable, à ce qui peut estre, et à ce qui est desja receu en la commune opinion. Je ne veux conclure qu'on doive effacer du rang des poëtes un grand nombre de Grecs et Latins pour honnorer d'un si venerable tiltre Homere, Virgile, et quelques autres pareils d'invention et de sujet. J'ose seulement dire (si mon opinion a quelque poix) que le poëte qui escrit les choses com[ã ij *v*]me elles[1] sont ne merite tant que celuy qui les feint et se recule le plus qu'il luy est possible de l'historien—non toutefois pour feindre une poësie fantastique comme celle de l'Arioste, de laquelle les membres sont aucunement beaux mais le corps est tellement contrefaict et monstrueux qu'il ressemble mieux aux resveries d'un malade de fievre continue qu'aux inventions d'un homme bien sain. Il faut que l'historien de poinct en poinct, du commencement jusqu'à la

1. elle *1572*

fin, deduise son œuvre, où le poëte, s'acheminant vers la fin et redevidant le fuzeau au rebours de l'histoire, porté de fureur et d'art (sans toutesfois se soucier beaucoup des reigles de grammaire) et surtout favorisé d'une prevoyance et naturel jugement, face que la fin de son ouvrage par une bonne liaison se raporte au commencement.

Je dy cecy pource que la meilleure partie des nostres pense que la *Franciade* soit une histoire des rois de France, comme si j'avois entrepris d'estre historiographe et non poëte. Bref, ce livre est un roman comme l'*Iliade* et l'*Æneïde*, où par occasion le plus brefvement que je puis je traitte de nos princes, d'autant que mon but est d'escrire les faits de Francion et non de fil en fil, comme les historiens, les gestes de nos rois. Et si je parle de nos monarques plus longuement que l'art Virgilien ne le permet, tu dois sçavoir, lecteur, que Virgile (comme en toutes autres choses) en cette-cy est plus heureux que [ã iij] moy, qui[2] vivoit sous Auguste second empereur; tellement que n'estant chargé que de peu de rois et de Cesars, ne devoit beaucoup allonger le papier, où j'ay le faix de soixante et trois rois sur les bras. Et si tu me dis que d'un si grand nombre je ne devois eslire que les principaux, je te responds que Charles nostre seigneur et roy, par une genereuse et magnanime candeur, n'a voulu permettre que ses ayeulx fussent preferez les uns aux autres, à fin que la bonté des bons et la malice des mauvais luy fussent comme un exemple domestique, pour le retirer du vice et le pousser à la vertu.

Au reste, j'ay patronné mon œuvre (dont ces quatre premiers livres te serviront d'eschantillon) plustost sur la naïve facilité d'Homere que sur la curieuse diligence de Virgile, imitant toutesfois à mon possible de l'un et de l'autre l'artifice et l'argument plus basty sur la vraysemblance que sur la verité. Car pour ne dissimuler ce qu'il m'en semble, je ne sçaurois croire qu'une armée Grecque aye jamais combatu dix ans devant Troye. Le combat eust esté de trop longue[3] durée et les chevaliers y eussent perdu le courage, absents si longtemps de leurs femmes, enfans et maisons; aussi que la coustume de la guerre ne permet qu'on combate si longuement devant une forte ville en un païs estranger. Et davantage je ne sçaurois croire que Priam, Hector, Polydame, Alexandre, et mille autres[4] tels ayent jamais esté, qui ont [ã iij *v*] tous les noms Greqs inventez par Homere. Car si cela estoit vray, les chevaliers Troyens eussent porté le nom de leur païs Phrygien. Et est bien aisé à cognoistre par les mesmes noms que la guerre Troyenne a esté feinte par Homere, comme quelques graves auteurs ont fermement assuré. Les fables qui en sont sorties depuis sont toutes puisées de la source de cest Homere, lequel comme fils d'un dæmon, ayant l'esprit surnaturel, voulant s'insinuer en la faveur et bonne grace des Æacides, et

2. qui *for* qu'il? 3. longne *1572* 4. autre *1572*

aussi (peut estre) que le bruit de telle guerre estoit receu en la comune opinion des hommes de ce temps-là, entreprit une si divine et parfaite poësie pour se rendre et ensemble les Æacides par son labeur à jamais très honorez. Je sçay bien que la plus grande partie des historiens et poëtes sont du costé d'Homere, mais quand à moy je pense avoir dit la verité, me soumetant toujours à la correction de la meilleure opinion. Autant en faut estimer de Virgile, lequel lisant en Homere qu'Ænée ne devoit mourir à la guerre Troyenne et que sa posterité releveroit le nom Phrygien, et voyant que les vieilles annales de son temps portoyent qu'Ænée avoit fondé la ville d'Alba, où depuis fut Rome, pour gaigner la bonne grace des Cesars, qui se vantoyent estre sortis d'Iüle fils d'Ænée, conceut ceste divine *Æneide*, qu'aveq toute reverence nous tenons encores aujourd'huy entre les mains.

Suivant ces[5] deux grands personna[ã iv]ges, j'ay fait le semblable. Car voyant que le peuple François tient pour chose très assurée selon les annales que Francion fils d'Hector, suivy d'une compagnie de Troyens après le sac de Troye, aborda aux palus Mæotides et de là plus avant en Hongrie, j'ay allongé la toille et l'ay fait venir en Franconie, à laquelle il donna le nom, puis en Gaule fonder Páris en l'honneur de son oncle Pâris. Or' il est vraysemblable que Francion a fait tel voyage d'autant qu'il le pouvoit faire, et sur ce fondement de vraysemblance j'ay basti ma *Franciade* de son nom: les esprits conçoivent aussi bien que les corps. Ayant donc une extresme envie d'honorer la maison de France et par surtout le roy Charles neufiesme, mon prince, non seulement digne d'estre loué de moy mais des meilleurs escrivains du monde pour ses heroiques et divines vertus, et dont l'esperance ne promet rien de moins aux François que les heureuses victoires de Charlemaigne son ayeul, comme sçavent ceux qui ont cet honeur de le cognoistre de près, et ensemble desirant de perpetuer mon renom à l'immortalité; fondé sur le bruit commun et sur la vieille creance des *Chroniques de France*,[a] je n'ay sceu trouver un plus excellent sujet que cestui-cy. Or' comme les femmes qui sont prestes d'enfanter choisissent un bon air, une saine maison, un riche parrain pour tenir leur [ã iv *v*] enfant, ainsi j'ay choisi le plus riche argument, les plus beaux vers et le plus insigne parrain de l'Europe pour honorer mon livre et soutenir mon labeur.

Et si tu me dis, lecteur, que je devois composer mon ouvrage en vers Alexandrins, pource qu'ils sont pour le jourd'huy plus favorablement receuz de nos seigneurs et dames de la court et de toute la jeunesse Françoise, lesquels vers j'ay remis le premier en honeur, je te responds qu'il m'eust esté cent fois plus aisé d'escrire mon œuvre en vers Alexandrins qu'aux

5. ses *1572*

a. *Les Grandes Chroniques de France*, ed. Jules Viard, Paris: Société de l'Histoire de France, 1920, I, 9–12, relates the story of Francio's voyage to Thrace, etc.

autres, d'autant qu'ils sont plus longs et par consequent moins sujets, sans la honteuse conscience que j'ay qu'ils sentent trop leur prose. Or tout ainsi que je ne les aprouve du tout si ce n'est en tragedies ou versions, aussi je ne les veux du tout condamner. J'en laisse à chacun son libre jugement pour en user comme il voudra.

Je revien seulement à ce qui touche mon fait. Je ne doute qu'on ne m'accuse de peu d'artifice en ce que la harangue de Jupiter au commencement de mon premier livre est trop longue, et que je ne devois commencer par là. Tu dois sçavoir que trente lignes de Latin en vallent plus de soixante de nostre François, et aussi qu'il failloit que je me servisse de l'industrie des tragiques, où quand le poëte ne peut desmesler son dire et que la chose est douteuse, il fait tousjours comparoistre quelque dieu pour esclaircir l'obscur de la matiere. Les hom[ẽ]mes ne sçavoient comme Francion avoit esté sauvé du sac de Troye; un seul Jupiter le sçavoit. Pour ce j'ay esté contraint de l'introduire pour mieux desnouër la doute et donner à comprendre le fait. Et mesmes à Junon, laquelle est prinse icy comme presque en tous autres poëtes pour une maligne necessité qui contredit souvent aux vertueux, comme elle fit à Hercule; mais la prudence humaine est maitresse de telle violente fatalité. Si tu vois beaucoup de feintes en ce premier livre, comme la descente de Mercure, l'ombre d'Hector, la venüe de Cybele, Mars transformé, j'ay esté forcé d'en user pour persuader aux exilez de Troye que Francion estoit fils d'Hector, lesquels autrement ne l'eussent creu d'autant qu'ils pensoient que le vray fils d'Hector estoit mort, et aussi que Francion avoit tousjours esté assez pauvrement nourri, sans autorité royalle ny aucun degré de mediocre dignité.

Quelque autre curieux en l'œuvre d'autruy me reprendra de quoy je n'ay suivy la perfecte reigle de poësie, ne commenceant mon livre par la fin, comme faisant embarquer Francion[6] encore jeune et mal experimenté. Celuy doit entendre qu'Helenin son oncle l'avoit desja envoyé en plusieurs beaux voyages pratiquer les mœurs des peuples et des rois, et qu'à son retour en Cahonie où son oncle et sa mere habitoyent, fut pressé de partir par la con[ẽ *v*]trainte du destin, imitant en cecy plustost Apolloine Rhodien que Virgile, d'autant qu'il m'a semblé meilleur de le faire ainsi. Et si tu me dis qu'il combat trop tost et en trop bas aage le tyran Phovere, je te responds qu'Achille combatit en pareil aage et renversa les forteresses des alliez de Troye, ayant à peine laissé la robbe de femme qu'il portoit. Son fils Pyrrhe fit de mesme, et beaucoup davantage si nous voulons croire à Quinte Calabrois.[b]

6. Ftancion *1572*

b. Quintus of Smyrna, *The Fall of Troy*, VII, 172 ff. Pyrrhus was also called Neoptolemos; see Pauly-Wissowa, XVI², 2440 ff.

Or, lecteur, pour ne te vouloir trop vendre ma marchandise ny aussi pour la vouloir trop mepriser, je te dy qu'il ne se trouve point de livre parfait, et moins le mien, auquel je pourray, selon la longueur de ma vie, le jugement et la syncere opinion de mes amis, adjouter ou diminuer, comme celuy qui ne jure en l'amour de soy-mesmes ny en l'opiniastreté de ses inventions. Je te supliray seulement d'une chose, lecteur, de vouloir bien prononcer mes vers et accommoder ta voix à leur passion, et non comme quelques-uns les lisent, plustost à la façon d'une missive ou de quelques lettres royaux que d'un poëme bien prononcé; et te suplie encore derechef où tu verras cette merque "!" vouloir un peu eslever ta voix pour donner grace à ce que tu liras. Bref, quand tu auras acheté mon livre, je ne te pourray empescher de le lire ny d'en dire ce qu'il te plaira comme estant chose tienne, mais devant que [ẽ ij] me condamner tu pourras retenir ce quatrin par lequel j'ay fermé ce preface pour fermer la bouche à ceux qui de nature sont envieux du bien et de l'honneur d'autruy:

Un list ce livre pour aprendre,
L'autre le list comme envieux;
Il est aisé de me reprendre
Mais malaisé de faire mieux.

Tu excuseras les fautes de l'imprimeur, car tous les yeux d'Argus n'y verroient assez clair, mesme en la premiere impression.

JEAN DE LA TAILLE

De l'Art de la Tragédie

1572

TEXT:

Savl le Fvrievx, Tragedie prise de la Bible, Faicte selon l'art & à la mode des vieux Autheurs Tragiques. Plvs, Vne Remonstrance faicte pour le Roy Charles IX. à tous ses subiects, à fin de les encliner à la paix. Avec Hymnes, Cartels, Epitaphes, Anagrammatismes, & autres Oeuures d'vn mesme autheur. A Paris. Par Federic Morel Imprimeur du Roy. M.D. LXXII. Auec Priuilege dudit Seigneur. [B.N., Paris.]

[Cf. Brunet, III, 869; Tchemerzine, VII, 105; Cat. Rothschild, V, 3317 (1093a).]

On the basis of internal evidence, it is probable that Jean de la Taille wrote this preface to his *Saül le furieux* sometime between 1570 and 1572, the date of publication (cf. Frederick West's edition of the text, Manchester, 1939, p. 3). The tragedy itself was apparently complete in manuscript by May of 1562 (cf. A. Werner, *Jean de la Taille und sein Saül le furieux*, Leipzig, 1908, pp. xx–xxi). Both tragedy and preface were reprinted in 1598, 1601, and 1602. The text of the *Art de la Tragédie* was edited by Werner in 1908 and by Frederick West in 1939. The reader is referred to the latter edition for a study of the text and for the notes, a few of which have been incorporated into the present edition. Biographical details on Jean de la Taille may be found in T. A. Daley's biography, *Jean de la Taille (1533–1608): Etude historique et littéraire* (Paris: Gamber, 1934).

[A ij] DE L'ART DE LA TRAGEDIE

A TRÈS HAULTE PRINCESSE HENRIETTE DE CLEVES, DUCHESSE DE NEVERS, JAN DE LA TAILLE DE BONDAROY

Madame. Combien que les piteux desastres advenus nagueres en la France par nos guerres civilles fussent si grands, et que la mort du roy Henry, du roy son fils, et du roy de Navarre vostre oncle, avec celle de tant d'autres princes, seigneurs, chevaliers et gentilshommes, fust si pitoiable qu'il ne faudroit jà d'autre chose pour faire des tragedies; ce neantmoins, pour n'en estre du tout le proper subject, et pour ne remuer nos vieilles et nouvelles douleurs, volontiers je m'en deporte, aimant trop mieux descrire le malheur d'autruy que le nostre, qui m'a fait non seulement voir les deux rencheutes de nos folles guerres, mais [A ij *v*] y combattre et rudement y estre blessé. Je veux sans plus icy vous dedier une tragedie du plus miserable prince qui porta jamais couronne, le premier que jamais Dieu esleut pour commander sur son peuple, le premier aussi que j'ay esleu pour escrire; à fin qu'en vous faisant un tel present je puisse quant et quant monstrer à l'œil de tous un des plus merveilleux secrets de toute la Bible, un des plus estranges mysteres de ce grand Seigneur du monde, et une de ses plus terribles providences. Or à fin que du premier coup vous y rencontriez le plaisir que je desire, j'ay pensé de vous donner quelque ouverture et quelque goust d'une tragedie, et en dechifrant les principaux poincts vous en pourtraire seulement l'ombre et les premiers traicts.

La tragedie donc est une espece et un genre de poësie non vulgaire, mais autant elegant, beau et excellent qu'il est possible. Son vray subject ne traicte que de piteuses ruines des grands seigneurs, que des inconstances de fortune, que bannissements, guerres, pestes, famines, captivitez, execrables cruautez des tyrans, et bref que larmes et miseres extremes; et non point de choses qui arrivent tous les jours naturellement et par raison commune, comme d'un qui mourroit de sa propre mort, d'un qui seroit tué de son ennemy, ou d'un qui seroit condamné à mourir par les loix et pour ses demerites. Car tout cela n'esmouveroit pas aisément et à peine m'arracheroit-il une larme de l'œil, veu que la vraye et seule intention d'une tragedie est d'esmouvoir et de poindre merveilleusement les affections d'un chascun. Car il faut que le subject en soit si pitoyable [A iij] et poignant de soy qu' estant mesmes en bref et nument dit, engendre en nous quelque passion; comme qui vous conteroit d'un à qui l'on fit malheureusement manger ses propres fils, de sorte que le pere (sans le sçavoir) servit de sepulchre à ses enfans; et d'un autre qui ne pouvant trouver un bourreau pour finir ses jours et ses maux fut contraint de faire ce piteux office de sa propre main. Que le subject aussi ne soit de seigneurs extremement meschants et que pour leurs crimes horribles ils meritassent punition; n'aussi par mesme raison de ceux qui sont du tout bons, gents de bien et de saincte vie, comme d'un Socrates, bien qu'à tort empoisonné. Voilà pourquoy tous subjects n'estants tels seront tousjours froids et indignes du nom de tragedie, comme celuy du *Sacrifice d'Abraham* où ceste fainte de faire sacrifier Isaac, par laquelle Dieu esprouve Abraham, n'apporte rien de malheur à la fin;[a] et d'un autre où Goliath, ennemy d'Israël et de nostre religion, est tué par David son hayneux;[b] laquelle chose tant s'en faut qu'elle nous cause quelque compassion, que ce sera plustost un aise et contentement qu'elle nous baillera.

Il faut tousjours representer l'histoire ou le jeu en un mesme jour, en un mesme temps, et en un mesme lieu; aussi se garder de ne faire chose sur la scene qui ne s'y puisse commodément et honnestement faire, comme de

a. Théodore de Bèze, *Sacrifice d'Abraham*, 1550.

b. The trilogy of Des Masures, *David Combattant*, *David Fugitif*, and *David Triomphant*, 1563 and 1566.

n'y faire executer des meurtres et autres morts, et non par fainte ou autrement, car chascun verra bien tousjours que c'est, et que ce n'est tousjours que faintise, ainsi que fit quelqu'un qui avec trop peu de reverence et non selon l'art fit par fainte crucifier en plein thea[A iij *v*]tre ce grand Sauveur de nous tous. Quant à ceulx qui disent qu'il fault qu'une tragedie soit tousjours joyeuse au commencement et triste à la fin, et une comedie (qui luy est semblable quant à l'art et disposition et non du subject) soit au rebours,[c] je leur advise que cela n'advient pas tousjours, pour la diversité des subjects et bastiments de chascun de ces deux poëmes.

Or c'est le principal point d'une tragedie de la sçavoir bien disposer, bien bastir, et la deduire de sorte qu'elle change, transforme, manie et tourne l'esprit des escoutans deçà delà, et faire qu'ils voyent maintenant une joye tournée tout soudain en tristesse et maintenant au rebours, à l'exemple des choses humaines; qu'elle soit bien entrelassée, meslée, entrecouppée, reprise, et surtout à la fin rapportée à quelque resolution et but de ce qu'on avoit entrepris d'y traicter, qu'il n'y ait rien d'oisif, d'inutile, ny rien qui soit mal à propos. Et si c'est un subject qui appartienne aux lettres divines, qu'il n'y ait point un tas de discours de theologie, comme choses qui derogent au vray subject et qui seroient mieux seantes à un presche; et pour ceste cause se garder d'y faire parler des personnes qu'on appelle fainctes et qui ne furent jamais, comme la Mort, la Verité, l'Avarice, le Monde, et d'autres ainsi, car il faudroit qu'il y eust des personnes ainsi de mesmes contrefaittes qui y prinssent plaisir.

Voilà quant au subject. Mais quant à l'art qu'il fault pour la disposer et mettre par escript, c'est de la diviser en cinq actes et faire de sorte que la scene estant vuide de joueurs, un acte soit finy et le sens aucunement parfait.[d] Il fault qu'il y ait un chœur, c'est-à-[A iiij]dire une assemblée d'hommes ou de femmes qui à la fin de l'acte discourent sur ce qui aura esté dit devant; et surtout d'observer ceste maniere de taire et supplier ce que[1] facilement sans exprimer se pourroit entendre avoir esté fait en derriere;[e] et de ne commencer à deduire sa tragedie par le commencement de l'histoire ou du subject, ains vers le milieu ou la fin (ce qui est un des principaux secrets de l'art dont je vous parle), à la mode des meilleurs poëtes vieux et de ces grands œuvres heroiques; et ce à fin de ne l'ouir froidement, mais

1. que *for* qui?

c. This was a commonplace at the time. Cf. Badius Ascensius, *Praenotamenta* to Terence, ed. Lyon: Marion, 1517: "itaque tragedia principium letum et finem tristem habet. Comedia contra principium ambiguum et satis tristem continent: finem autem letissimum." (fol. [A v *v*]).

d. This sentence may be borrowed from Charles Estienne's preface to *Les Abusez*, 1548; cf. p. 137 above and *Modern Language Notes*, LXI (1946), 262–65.

e. Cf. Estienne, p. 136 above, and *MLN*, *loc. cit.*

avec ceste attente et ce plaisir d'en sçavoir le commencement et puis la fin après.

Mais je serois trop long à deduire par le menu ce propos que ce grand Aristote en ses *Poëtiques* et après luy Horace (mais non avec telle subtilité) ont continué plus amplement et mieux que moy, qui ne me suis accommodé qu'à vous et non aux difficiles et graves oreilles des plus sçavants. Seulement vous adviseray-je qu'autant de tragedies et comedies, de farces et moralitez (où bien souvent n'y a sens ny raison, mais des paroles ridicules avec quelque badinage)[f] et autres jeux qui ne sont faicts selon le vray art et au moule des vieux, comme d'un Sophocle, Euripide et Seneque, ne peuvent estre que choses ignorantes, mal faites, indignes d'en faire cas, et qui ne deussent servir de passetemps qu'aux varlets et menu populaire et non aux personnes graves. Et voudrois bien qu'on eust banny de France telles ameres espiceries qui gastent le goust de nostre langue, et qu'au lieu on y eust adopté et naturalisé la vraye tragedie et comedie, qui n'y sont point en[A iiij *v*]cor à grand' peine parvenues, et qui toutefois auroient aussi bonne grace en nostre langue Françoise qu'en la Grecque et Latine. Pleust à Dieu que les roys et les grands sceussent le plaisir que c'est de voir reciter et representer au vif une vraye tragedie ou comedie en un theatre tel que je le sçaurois bien deviser,[g] et qui jadis estoit en si grande estime pour le passetemps des Grecs et des Romains. Je m'oserois presque asseurer qu'icelles estans naifvement jouées par des personnes propres, qui par leurs gestes honestes, par leurs bons termes (non tirez à force du Latin), et par leur brave et hardie prononciation ne sentissent aucunement ny l'escolier, ny le pedante, ny surtout le badinage des farces, que les grands (dis-je) ne trouveroient passetemps (estans retirez au paisible repos d'une ville) plus plaisant que cestuy-ci, j'entens après l'esbat de leur exercice, après la chasse et le plaisir du vol des oiseaux.

Au reste je ne me soucie (en mettant ainsi par escript) d'encourir icy la dent outrageuse et l'opinion encor brutale d'aucuns qui, pour l'effect des armes, desestiment et dedaignent les hommes de lettres; comme si la science et la vertu, qui ne gist qu'en l'esprit, affoiblissoit le corps, le cœur et le bras, et que noblesse fust deshonorée d'une autre noblesse qui est la science. Que nos jeunes courtisans en haussent la teste tant qu'ils voudront, lesquels voulants honnestement dire quelqu'un fol ne le font qu'appeller poëte ou philosophe, soubs ombre qu'ils voient (peut estre) je ne sçay quelles tragedies ou comedies qui n'ont que le tiltre seulement sans le subject ny la disposition, et une infinité de rymes sans [A v] art ny science que font un tas d'ignorants qui—se meslants aujourd'huy de mettre en lumiere (à cause de

f. Cf. Estienne, p. 136 above, and *MLN*, *loc. cit.*

g. It is possible that Jean de la Taille's knowledge of the theater was derived from the Estienne preface quoted above, which contains a description of the ancient theater.

l'impression trop commune, dont je me plains à bon droit) tout ce qui distille de leur cerveau mal tymbré—font des choses si fades et malplaisantes qu'elles deussent faire rougir de honte les papiers mesmes; aux cerveaux desquels est entrée ceste sotte opinion de penser qu'on naisse et qu'on devienne naturellement excellent en cest art avec une fureur divine, sans suer, sans feuilleter, sans choisir l'invention, sans limer les vers, et sans noter en fin de compte qu'il y a beaucoup de rymeurs et peu de poëtes.

Mais je ne dois non plus avoir de honte de faire des tragedies que ce grand empereur Auguste, lequel nonobstant qu'il pouvoit tousjours estre empesché aux affaires du monde a bien pris quelquefois le plaisir de faire une tragedie nommée *Ajax*, qu'il effaça depuis pour ne luy sembler peut estre bien faitte;[h] mesmes que plusieurs ont pensé que ce vaillant Scipion avec son Lælius a fait les comedies que l'on attribue à Terence.[i] Non que je face mestier ny profession de poësie; car je veux bien qu'on sçache que je ne puis (à mon grand regret) y despendre autre temps (à fin qu'on ne me reproche que j'en perde de meilleur) que celuy que tels ignorants de cour employent coustumierement à passer le temps, à jouer et à ne rien faire, leur donnant congé de n'estimer non plus mes escripts que leurs passetemps, leurs jeux, et leur faineantise. Mais cependant qu'ils pensent que si l'on est fol en ryme, qu'ils ne le sont pas moins en prose, comme dit Du Bellay.[j] N'est-ce pas plus grande [A v *v*] mocquerie à eulx d'engager leur liberté et la rendre miserablement esclave, de laisser legerement le paisible repos de leur maison, de forcer leur naturel, bref de ne sçavoir faire autre chose que de contrefaire les grands, d'user sans propos de finesses frivoles, de prester des charitez, de faire vertu d'un vice, de reprendre à la mode des ignorants ce qu'ils n'entendent pas, et de faire en somme profession de ne sçavoir rien?

Pour conclusion, je n'ay des histoires fabuleuses mendié icy les fureurs d'un Athamant,[k] d'un Hercules,[l] ny d'un Roland,[m] mais celles que la verité

h. Cf. Suetonius, *Divus Augustus*, LXXXV, 2. Erasmus relates an anecdote connected with the tragedy; cf. *Apophthegmata*, Bk. IV (Cologne, 1553), p. 291, and the translation of Macault (Paris, 1549), p. 159 *v*.

i. Suetonius, *De Poetis: Vita Terenti*, III: "Non obscura fama est adiutum Terentium in scriptis a Laelio et Scipione." This life of Terence was a part of the Donatus commentary upon Terence and appeared with various sixteenth-century editions of the comedies, e.g. the *Praenotamenta* of Badius, ed. 1517, fol. [bij*v*]. Robert Estienne, in his *Dictionarium propriorum nominum* (Paris, 1542), pp. 502–3, also records the tradition.

j. I have not found the source for this statement.

k. Jacques de la Taille had written a tragedy called *Athamant*, which was never published.

l. Probably an allusion to Euripides' *Hercules furens*, which had not yet been translated into French, but of which an edition had appeared as early as 1503 and a Latin translation in 1562.

m. The *Orlando Furioso* of Ariosto had appeared in 1516.

mesme a dictées, et qui portent assez sur le front leur sauf-conduit partout. Et parce qu'il m'a esté force de faire revenir Samuël, je ne me suis trop amusé à regarder si ce devoit estre ou son esprit mesmes, ou bien quelque fantosme et corps fantastique, et s'il se peut faire que les esprits des morts reviennent ou non, laissant la curiosité de ceste dispute aux theologiens. Mais tant y a que j'ay leu quelque autheur qui, pensant que ce fust l'ame vraye de Samuël qui revint, ne trouve cela impossible, comme disant qu'on peult bien pour le moins faire revenir l'esprit mesmes d'un trespassé avant l'an revolu du trespas, et que c'est un secret de magie. Mais j'auray plus tost fait de coucher icy les propres mots Latins de cest autheur nommé Corneille Agrippe, qui sont tels en son livre *De la vanité des sciences*, alleguant Sainct Augustin mesmes:[2]

> In libris Regum legimus Phytonissam mulierem euocasse animam Samuëlis: licet plerique interpretentur non fuisse animam Prophetæ, sed malignum spiritum qui sumpserit illius imaginem: tamen Hebræorum magistri dicunt, quod etiam [A vi] Augustinus ad Simplicianum fieri potuisse non negat, quia fuerit verus spiritus Samuëlis, qui ante completum annum à dicessu ex corpore facile euocari potuit, prout docent Goetici.[n]

Combien qu'un autre en ses annotations Latines sur la Bible allegue Sainct Augustin au contraire, toutefois je trouve qu'Agrippe (homme au reste d'un merveilleux sçavoir) erre grandement (dont je m'esmerveille) de penser que Samuël revint dans l'an de sa mort, veu que Josephe en ses *Antiquitez*[3] dit notamment que Saul regna vivant Samuël dix-huit ans et vingt après sa mort, au bout desquels on fit revenir par enchantements l'ombre du prophete.[o] Sainct Paul aux Actes des Apostres,[4] adjoustant encor deux ans au regne de Saul plus que Josephe, raconte là qu'il regna XL. ans.[p] Je sçay que les Hebrieux et qu'aujourd'huy les plus subtils en la religion tiennent sans doubte que c'estoit un diable ou dæmon que fit venir la Phytonisse, et non l'esprit vray de Samuël. Mais d'autre part je voudrois bien qu'ils m'eussent interpreté ou accordé ce que dit Salomon en son Ecclesiastique, qui parlant de Samuël dit ainsi:[5] "Et après qu'il fut mort il prophetisa, et monstra au roy la fin de sa vie, et esleva sa voix de la terre en prophetie."[q]

2. Au lieu où il parle de Magie. *Margin 1572* 3. Liure 6. *Margin 1572*
4. Chap. 13. *Margin 1572* 5. Chap. 46. *Margin 1572*

n. The passage is from the chapter "De Goetia et Necromantia" of the *De incertitudine et vanitate scientiarum declamatio invectiva*; cf. the *Opera*, Lyon, [1531], II, 75 and the separate edition, Cologne, 1568, fol. L4 *v*.

o. Josephus, *Jewish Antiquities*, VI, 378, gives the period of reign after Samuel's death as twenty-two years.

p. Acts 13:18.

q. Ecclesiasticus 46:23.

Et si ma muse s'est (comme maugré moy) en s'esgayant quelque peu espaciée hors les bornes estroictes du texte, je prie ceulx-là qui le trouveront mauvais d'abbaisser en cela un peu leur sourcy plus que stoique, et de penser que je n'ay point tant desguisé l'histoire qu'on n'y recognoisse pour le moins quelques traicts ou quelque ombre de la verité, comme vraysemblablement la chose est advenue; m'estant prin[A vi *v*]cipalement aidé de la Bible, à sçavoir des Livres des Roys et des Chroniques d'icelle, et puis de Josephe et de Zonare Grec.[r]

Or parce que la France n'a point encor de vrayes tragedies, sinon possible traduittes, je mets ceste-cy en lumiere soubs la faveur du nom de vous, madame, comme de celle qui presque seule de nostre aage favorisez les arts et les sciences, qui seront tenues aussi pour ceste cause de vous publier à la posterité pour luy recommander vostre gentil esprit, sçavoir et courtoisie, à fin qu'elle entende que vous avez quelquefois fait cas de ceulx qui ont quelque chose oultre ce vulgaire ignorant et barbare. Car j'ay autrefois conclud que vous serez ma seule muse, mon Phœbus, mon Parnasse, et le seul but où je rapporteray mes escripts.

Mais il me semble qu'il ne me souvienne plus que je fais icy une epistre et non un livre. Pour donc faire fin, je supplie Dieu, madame, qu'il n'advienne à vous ny à vostre excellente maison chose dont on puisse faire tragedie.

r. Josephus, *Jewish Antiquities*, Bk. VI; Zonaras, *Annales*, Bk. I, Ch. XXVII ff.; cf. Migne, *Patrologia Graeca*, CXXXIV (1864), 127 ff. The *Annales* had been published in Greek and Latin by Heinrich Wolf (Basel: Oporinus, 1557) and in French translations by J. Millet (Lyon, 1560) and Jean de Maumont (Paris, 1561).

JEAN DE LA TAILLE

DEDICATION TO JACQUES DE LA TAILLE'S *Daire*

1573

TEXT:

Daire, Tragedie de feu Iacques de la Taille, du Pays de Beauce. A Paris. Par Federic Morel Imprimeur du Roy. M.D.LXXIII. Auec Priuilege dudit Seigneur. [B.N., Paris.]

[Cf. Brunet, III, 870; Tchemerzine, VII, 107; and Cat. Rothschild, Nos. 1094 and 3317 (1093a). The work was reprinted by Morel in 1574; the British Museum lists an edition of 1598.]

Jacques de la Taille, born in 1542, was a younger brother of Jean. He went to Paris in 1556 to study under Jean Dorat. There, in 1561, he wrote his tragedy of *Daire*; there, in 1562, he died of the plague. Later, when Jean was preparing an edition of his own works, he also published some of those of his brother. For the tragedy of *Daire* he wrote a dedication, dated "ce premier jour de l'an 1573."

[A ij] A FRANÇOIS DE DANGENES, CHEVALIER, SEIGNEUR DE MONLOUËT,[a] JEHAN DE LA TAILLE DE BONDAROY

Ayant ouy le recit de vos vertus et sceu l'alliance que vous faictes en vous des armes et des muses et le bon vouloir qu'il vous plaist me porter (sans m'avoir jamais veu), persuadé (possible) que j'ayme ce que vous aymez et qu'en moy j'ay allié ces mesmes choses, ayant fait preuve des unes et profession des autres, j'ay pensé que je ne pourrois choisir un meilleur curateur à ce pauvre orflin (dont le pere fut né gentilhomme) qu'à un si sçavant et courtois chevalier que vous, encore que ne soyez [A ij *v*] prince, duc, ny compte; aymant mieux l'addresser à un qui n'estant né prince merite de l'estre qu'à tel qui l'estant ne merite de l'estre. C'est, monsieur, la tragedie presente que feu mon frere fit en l'aage de dix-neuf ans, et qui le vintiéme de ses ans mourut à Paris de peste, avec un autre mien frere et un cousin germain, presque tous trois en un jour. Et si le souverain moteur de l'univers luy eust presté autant de vie et d'heur que de sçavoir, il eust bientost en la carriere des muses jecté la poussiere et le soleil en la veuë (ainsi que vous-mesme pourrez juger par ses vers) de nos poëtes François, voire des plus excellents, et non seulement de ceux qui si depiteusement déchirent et tirent au poil nostre pauvre poësie et n'y entendent rien; m'asseurant, monsieur, si vous l'eussiez cogneu autant par hantise comme vous pourrez faire par le peu de ses escripts abortifs, que

a. Unidentified.

vous eussiez jugé qu'il avoit desja en soy la gravité de Ronsard, la facilité de Du Bellay, et la promptitude de Jodelle. Il vous plaira donc en l'honneur de noblesse estre protecteur de ce *Daire*, où je m'asseure [A iij] que, voyant un si grand monarque trahy et bouleversé du haut en bas de son empire, avec la perte de sa vie et des siens, vous en pourrez au moins recueillir ce fruict, d'apprendre à supporter plus patiemment (par le malheur d'un plus grand) toutes nos adversitez, ensemble toutes les piteuses et sanglantes tragedies qu'on a depuis dix ou douze ans jouées sur l'eschaffault de France et durant le commun malheur de nos folles guerres civiles, où les uns et les autres avons porté les armes malheureuses, teinctes en nostre propre sang.

A Dieu, monsieur, lequel je supplie vous donner plus d'heur que n'eut celuy dont est faicte ceste tragedie, que je vous envoye de Bondaroy pour vos estrenes, ce premier jour de l'an 1573; attendant que je mette en lumiere et vous face voir ma *Geomance* et mes autres poëmes.

JEAN DE LA TAILLE

PROLOGUE TO *Les Corrivaux*

1573

TEXT:

La Famine, ou les Gabeonites, Tragedie prise de la Bible, & suiuant celle de Saül. Ensemble plusieurs autres Oeuures poëtiques de Iehan de la Taille de Bondaroy gentilhomme du pays de Beauce, & de feu Iaques de la Taille son Frere, desquels œuures l'ordre se void en la prochaine page. A Paris. Par Federic Morel Imprimeur du Roy. M.D.LXXIIII. Auec Priuilege dudit Seigneur. [Boston Public Library.]

[According to Tchemerzine, VII, 106, "L'édition de 1574 est identique à la précédente (1573); elle a le même titre et est aussi de 173 ff. et (3) ff." On the 1573 ed., see also Cat. Rothschild, V, 3317 (1093a), and Brunet, III, 870, who mentions 1574 as a separate edition.]

One year after the publication of *Saül le furieux*, Jean de la Taille published his tragedy of *La Famine*; like the former volume, this one contained other works of the author, and was really the second volume of his complete poetic works. *Les Corrivaux* was probably written about 1562, when both Jean and Jacques de la Taille were living in Paris and associating with members of the Pléiade group. The "Prologue" may have been written at the time of composition of the comedy, since it addresses the audience in the manner of the Terentian prologues; but it is also possible that it may have been written especially for the publication in 1573. The comedy itself was the only one of this period of the Renaissance written in prose (cf. T. A. Daley, *Jean de la Taille*, Paris: Gamber, 1934, pp. 182, 198, n.1). The "Prologue" was reprinted by René de Maulde in his *Œuvres de Jean de la Taille* (Paris: Willem, 1878–82, II, v–xi), and its theories were summarized by Daley (*op. cit.*, pp. 182–85).

[I] LE PROLOGUE

Il semble, messieurs, à vous voir ainsi assemblez en ce lieu, que vous y soyez venus pour ouir une comedie. Vrayement, vous ne serez point deceus de vostre intention. Une comedie pour certain vous y verrez, non point une farce ny une moralité; car nous ne nous amusons point en chose ne si basse ne si sotte, et qui ne monstre qu'une pure ignorance de nos vieus François. Vous y verrez jouer une comedie faite au patron, à la mode et au pourtrait des anciens Grecs, Latins, et quelques nouveaux Italiens qui premiers que nous ont enrichi le magnifique et ample cabinet de leur langue de ce beau joyau; une comedie, di-je, qui vous agreera plus (si vous estes au moins admirateurs des choses belles) que toutes (je le diray librement) les farces et moralitez qui furent oncques jouées en France. Aussi avons-nous grand desir de bannir de ce royaume telles badineries et sottises, qui com[I *v*]me ameres espiceries ne font que corrompre le goust de nostre langue, et vous monstrer au parangon d'icelles le plaisir et la douceur qu'a[1] une comedie faite selon l'art comme est ceste-cy, et qui n'a moins de grace en nostre vulgaire que les Latines et Italiennes au leur. Aussi me puis-je bien vanter que nostre langue pour le present n'est en rien inferieure à la leur, tant pour bien exprimer nos conceptions que pour enrichir et orner quelque chose par eloquence.[a]

Nous sçavons bien qu'il y aura quelques-uns qui avec un hochement de teste et froncement de sourcil ne feront pas cas de comedie, comme chose trop commune (ce leur semble) encor qu'elle soit rapportée à l'art d'un Terence; ajoustans que c'est afaire[2] à gens de basse et vile condicion que de faire des jeus pour donner passetemps aux autres. A ceux-là on respondra (si d'avanture ils meritent response) qu'ils ne sçavent que c'est d'une comedie faite selon l'art, et qu'on en jouë bien rarement en France de telle sorte, d'autant que les Plautes, les Terences, et les Ariostes y sont rares; lesquels, bien qu'ils fussent grands personnages, n'ont dedaigné de faire tels jeus. Et si on m'allegue qu'on jouë ordinairement assez de jeus qui ont ce nom de comedies et tragedies, je leur rediray encores que ces beaux tiltres sont mal assortis à telles sottises, lesquelles ne retiennent rien de la façon ny du style des anciens. Au moyen dequoy nous voudrions bien qu'on se desaccoustumast d'ouir et de faire telz jeus et telles malplaisantes farces et moralitez, qui sont de [Iij] nostre creu, et que cependant on prist la pacience d'ouir une comedie toute entiere, naïve, et faite à l'antique; et telle que si nous eussions sceu bonnement que c'estoit, et la recreation qu'il y a, je suis seur que nous l'eussions pieça faite nostre.

Apprenez donc desormais que c'est de l'art d'icelle, que mesmes ceux qu'on estime sçavans n'ont pas entendu et la pluspart de ceux qui s'en sont meslez ne l'ont pas pratiqué; et puis après la naturalisons en nostre langue comme ont desja fait les Italiens. Or est-il ainsi que nous avons appellé ceste comedie *Les Corrivaus* à cause qu'il y a en icelle deus jeunes hommes amoureux qui pretendent en un mesme endroit. Au reste elle vous representera comme en un miroir le naturel et la façon de faire d'un chascun du populaire, comme des vieillards, des jeunes gens, des serviteurs, des filles de bonne maison, et autres. Escoutez donc soigneusement tout ce qu'on y dira; car si vous faisiez autrement, vous perdriez à sçavoir l'histoire, et par ainsi vous auriez un maigre plaisir et passetemps. Mais à fin que vous ne ahaniez point tant à entendre le discours de ce qui est icy contenu, je vous vais faire quelque ouverture de l'argument. ... [A brief summary of the plot follows in the text.]

1. qu'à *1573* 2. à faire *1573*

a. This sentence is borrowed from Charles Estienne's preface to *Les Abusez*; cf. p. 136 above and *Modern Language Notes*, LXI (1946), 262–65.

ANTOINE DE HARSY

DEDICATION TO THE *Oeuvres Poëtiques* OF MELLIN DE SAINT-GELAIS

1574

TEXT:

Oevvres Poëtiqves De Mellin De S. Gelais. A Lyon, Par Antoine de Harsy, M.D.LXXIIII. Auec Priuilege du Roy. [B.N., Paris.]

[Cf. Brunet, V, 46, and *Supplément*, II, 557; Tchemerzine, X, 108; Le Petit, p. 84; Cat. Rothschild, No. 630. The copy at the Library of Congress, dated 1574, in reality belongs to the edition of Paris: Guillaume de Luyne, 1656, with the spurious title page found in most copies; cf. the above references. The edition of Lyon: Benoist Rigaud, 1582, has not been collated.]

The first edition of the poetic works of Mellin de Saint-Gelais appeared in 1547. But that edition was apparently already rare in the sixteenth century, since Harsy did not know it; he speaks only of the poems scattered in the works of other authors and calls his own edition "ce beau fruict postume." It was on the margins of a copy of this Harsy edition of 1574 that Bernard de la Monnoye made various annotations, which were first published in the edition of Prosper Blanchemain, Paris: Bibliothèque Elzévirienne, 1873.

[†2] À TRÈS DOCTE ET VERTUEUX SEIGNEUR, MONSEIGNEUR M. HIEROSME CHATILLON, CONSEILLER DU ROY, ET PRESIDENT EN LA COUR DE PARLEMENT DE DOMBES, ET EN LA SENESCHAUSSÉE ET SIEGE PRESIDIAL À LYON[a]

Que la poësie, monseigneur, soit une invention belle et gentile, voire grandement recreative et plaisante, il est assez notoire, et n'y a (comme j'estime) bon esprit qui aucunement en doute; mais de son efficace et vertu beaucoup en parlent diversement. Toutesfois, laissant l'opinion d'aucuns bijarres cerveaux qui l'ont en mauvaise reputation pource qu'elle engendre, disent-ils, beaucoup de lascivetés ès esprits de ceux qui s'y addonnent, prenans leur argument sur quelques nouvelles poësies, je m'arresteray à ce qu'en ont jugé nos bons anciens, lesquels vrayement l'ont estimée si excellente, et de telle utilité, force et vigueur, qu'ils en ont rapporté l'origine à leurs [†2 *v*] dieux, disans la poësie n'estre autre chose qu'un enthousiasme ou celeste fureur; bref que sur tous autres amateurs de sagesse on les devoit tenir pour saincts et sacrés; qui est la cause aussi que bien souvent en

a. Bernard de la Monnoye provides a note on Châtillon, who associated with various savants of the period, in his commentary on the poems of Saint-Gelais; cf. ed. Blanchemain, Paris: Bibliothèque Elzévirienne, 1873, I, 145–46.

leurs escrits nous trouvons de telles et semblables jactances:

> Dieu est en nous, et par luy poussés sommes,
> Nostre œuvre point ne procede des hommes;
> Ce que contient ceste machine basse
> Perira tout, nos vers demeureront;
> Bref, toute chose par le temps se fracasse,
> Mais nos escrits à jamais floriront.[b]

Il est donc à presumer qu'il y avoit de la deïté en eux, et que sans ce, ils ne se fussent de tant avancés; eux (dis-je) qui sur tous autres se monstrent modestes et fort religieux à observer ce qui est bien seant. Et de faict il ne faut estimer que toutes les fictions, inductions, et allegories qu'on trouve parmi leurs œuvres procedent d'ailleurs que d'un sens et science profonde. Ainsi Xenophon en sa *Cyripedie* a voulu pourtraire au vif l'office et devoir d'un bon et vray prince, et par tels utiles et certains enseignemens sous le nom de quelqu'un, instruire tout le monde, à fin que comme dans un miroir chacun avisast quel chemin il auroit à suyvre; le vertueux eust devant soy une reigle asseurée, suyvant laquelle il se guideroit par l'object de quelque magnifique seigneur depeint de toutes couleurs; le vicieux un exemple de son vice si au vif exprimé, avec la punition, qu'il eust occasion de s'en destourner et de choisir quelque autre chemin. Et pourtant ce grand [†3] philosophe Aristote fut bien advisé de persuader à son disciple Alexandre, homme ayant l'esprit bouillant, de s'addonner à lire les œuvres d'Homere, voire de les tenir ordinairement sous son chevet, pour la profondité du sçavoir et bons enseignements qu'elles contiennent.[c]

Disons d'Hesiode; il a escrit la genealogie des dieux. Qui ne diroit à lire cruement ce livre qu'il a abusé de son temps et loisir? Le sens neantmoins que les gens doctes en tirent, et où il a (je m'asseure) visé, est tel qu'on ne peut juger qu'il n'y ayt de la deïté, pource que par iceluy il nous a ouvert la source des vertus et vices. Orphée en ses hymnes s'est addonné à y declairer la divinité par semblable respect. Je laisse Callimach, Theocrite, quoy qu'il se soit addonné à la vie pastorale, Mosché, Musée, Theognis, Solon, Phocylide, et autres, desquels les escrits nous tesmoignent que leur but n'a esté autre que se declarer vrais censeurs et reformateurs des mœurs, et à laisser de bons et seurs enseignements à tout le genre humain. Et cuydez-vous qu'Aeschyle en descrivant un Promethée attaché au mont Caucase, un Xerxes venant en Grece avec une puissante armée, la mort d'Agamemnon et de sa femme,[d] et autres telles choses, n'ayt eu esgard qu'à

b. The passage is a free translation of Ovid, *Amores*, III.ix.17–20 and 28.

c. Cf. Plutarch, *Alexander*, VIII.

d. Allusions to the *Prometheus Bound*, *The Persians*, *Agamemnon*, and the *Choephoroi*, respectively.

l'histoire? Sophocle pareillement et Euripide en tous leurs escrits? Je ne le croy pas; autrement j'estimerois leurs œuvres de peu de proffit; et qui n'y voudroit autre chose considerer feroit contre leur vouloir et intention.

Quant aux poëtes comiques, quelques lascifs qu'ils soyent et pleins de propos dissolus, si bien on advise leurs comedies il n'y a celuy [†3 *v*] qui en juge autrement que des autres; non plus que des satyriques, qui encor sur tous les autres monstrent nostre dire estre très veritable, pour le grandissime soin qu'ils ont pris chascun à publier et par ce moyen chastier les vices de leur temps.

Je laisse à considerer en quelle autorité et credit chaque poëte de son temps a esté: Homere, pour la naissance duquel sept villes se sont prises à question, s'imputans à grandissime felicité de l'avoir pour leur citadin, luy cependant qui estoit yssu de si bas lieu et aveugle; Hesiode, l'autorité duquel a esté si grande, qu'il n'est besoin en faire plus long recit; tous les autres susdits, qui ont esté si bien cheris et aymés ès lieux de leur nativité que mesmes on proposoit grands sommes de deniers à qui vouloit expliquer et enseigner leurs escrits. Et que dirons-nous de Pindare, ce prince des lyriques? le renom duquel a esté tel qu'Alexandre le Grand, ruinant et saccageant Thebes, commanda qu'on pardonnast à sa maison et famille, usant en son endroit de mesme faveur qu'avoyent faict auparavant luy les Lacedemoniens.[e] Simonides vrayement, combien il a esté cheri des dieux Cicero et Valere le tesmoignent; car comme il eust veu un povre homme jetté sur le rivage de la mer et l'eust par compassion inhumé, adverti en songe de ne monter sur mer, evita le peril qu'encoururent ses compaignons, qui, ne le voulans croire, perirent tous le lendemain devant ses yeux.[f]

Je serois trop long, monseigneur, si je voulois deduire par le menu toutes les singularités qu'on peut observer ès escrits des divins poëtes. Concluant seulement je diray que c'est là où tout [†4] amateur de sagesse se doit arrester et conformer ses mœurs, sa vie, bref toutes ses actions; fuyant, au contraire, tous ceux qui s'amusans à follement rimer ne meritent rien moins que le nom de poëtes, le nom desquels emporte bien autre chose que de simplement bien rencontrer et ne faillir à la rime.

e. Cf. Plutarch, *Alexander*, XI; also L. G. Giraldi, *Historiae Poetarum* (Basel, 1545), Dialogue IX, pp. 998–99: "Nam cum Thebas Alexander, ut Arrianus & Plinius referunt, diriperet, Pindari uatis familiae penatibusque parci iusset: id quod & antea Lacedaemonios fecisse legimus..."

f. The story is told by Cicero, *De Divinatione*, I.xxvii. 56 and by Valerius Maximus, I.viii; cf. the edition of the latter of Paris: R. Estienne, 1544, p. 39. Harsy's direct source might well be L. G. Giraldi, *op. cit.*, p. 989: "Deis certè Simonidem gratum fuisse, ex ijs quae Cicero & Valerius tradunt colligimus. cum enim naufragum quendam in littore proiectum uidisset, & miseratione motus eum humasset, moneri se per somnum uisus est, ne crastino nauem conscendit: caeteri spreto hominis consilio cum soluissent, eo spectante, naufragio periere."

Je ne nieray toutesfois qu'il ne soit sorti de nostre temps un bon nombre de personnages qui, traictans ce mesme subject, ne se sont rendus indignes du rang des anciens; et en pourrois nommer quelques-uns qui se sont monstrés grandement louables et dignes d'admiration. Mais sur tous il me semble que je faudray si je ne mets Mellin de S. Gelais, poëte assez congnu de nativité et nom par la France; les œuvres duquel symbolizent si bien à ceste façon ancienne, estans fort doctes, gentiles et de bonne grace, qu'à mon advis il ne sera dit despriser sa vacation. Il avoit desja donné assez bon tesmoignage de son sçavoir en quelques petis fragments semés parmi les autres autheurs, qui aussi ont esté fort bien receus et grandement approuvés. Mais qui considerera tout l'œuvre qui maintenant se presente, et lequel jusques icy nous avoit esté caché, jugera (je m'asseure) avec moy qu'il est digne de singuliere recommandation, et que c'estoit dommage de le laisser ainsi esgaré. Et de faict qui prendra par le menu ses opuscules, ses elegies, ses epistres, sonnets, quadrains, sixains, huictains, dixains, onzains, douzains, epitaphes et epigrammes, les trouvera fort bien troussés et avec une merveilleuse dexterité d'esprit; resentans entierement ceste forme de composer ancienne et four[†4 *v*]nis de toute gentilesse et gaillardise.

Et pource que ce beau fruict postume, privé de son autheur, a besoin de faveur et ayde pour pouvoir subsister parmi tant d'envieux dont nostre France est peuplée, il vous plairra, monsieur, vous qui estes né en vertu, qui aymez et caressez ce qui en depend, le recevoir sous les esles de vostre protection, luy servir de garend, le maintenir et defendre contre tous ceux qui le voudroyent offenser. Vostre autorité est grande, vostre renom fort congnu, l'estude et plaisir singulier que prenez à la lecture des bons livres. Il ne sçauroit estre que bien asseuré et gardé sous vos mains et appuy. Je le sens desja comme resjouï de vostre bon traictement; plus il ne craindra à s'avancer s'il sent vostre support. Bien est vray qu'il est petit, mais bien troussé, rempli et accompli en tout ce qu'il luy faut. Je le rens donc entre vos mains et vous prie bien humblement le recevoir, ainsi que avez accoustumé recevoir toutes œuvres doctes et bien limées.

Que s'il y a trop de hardiesse de mon costé, je vous prie l'imputer au très humble et loyal service que j'ay envie de vous faire, comme à celuy qui par ses singulieres vertus le merite. Je prieray le createur, monseigneur, qu'il vous doint en santé heureuse et longue vie, à fin que longuement nous puissions jouïr de l'equité et droiture laquelle, comme bon et equitable chef de justice que vous estes, vous nous administrez tous les jours.

De Lyon, ce premier juillet, 1574.

Vostre humble et affectionné
serviteur, A. de Harsy.

PIERRE DE LARIVEY

DEDICATION AND PROLOGUES TO HIS *Comédies*

1579

TEXT:

Les Six Premieres Comedies facecievses, de Pierre de Larivey, Champenois. A l'imitation des anciens Grecs, Latins, & modernes Italiens. A sçavoir, Le Laqvais. La Vefve. Les Esprits. Le Morfondv. Les Ialovx. Les Escolliers. A Paris, Chez Abel l'Angelier, tenant sa boutique au premier pillier de la grand' salle du Palais. M.D.LXXIX. Avec privilege dv Roy. [Harvard College Library.]

[Cf. Brunet, III, 840, and *Supplément*, I, 781; Tchemerzine, VII, 30–31.]

COLLATED:

(1597) Les Comedies facecievses de Pierre de Larivey, Champenois... Seconde Edition. A Lyon, Par Benoist Rigavd. 1597. [Harvard College Library, Library of Congress.]

(1601) Les Comedies Facecievses de Pierre de L'Arivey, Champenois... Seconde Edition. A Roven, De l'Imprimerie, De Raphaël du Petit Val, Libraire & Imprimeur ordinaire du Roy. 1601. [University of Chicago Library.]

[Cf. Brunet, III, 840, and *Supplément*, I, 781; Tchemerzine, VII, 31–35. The 1601 edition is apparently the same as that of 1600, with a new t.p. The 1611 ed. has not been collated.]

Pierre de Larivey's comedies were not original; they were all translated or adapted from Italian plays which had been published earlier in the century. In the same way the prologues were for the most part borrowed from the Italian sources: that to *Le Laquais*, from Lodovico Dolce's *Il Ragazzo*; that to *La Veuve*, from Nicolò Buonaparte's *La Vedova*; that to *Les Jaloux*, from Vincenzo Gabiani's *I Gelosi*. However, the prologue to *Les Esprits* was apparently not borrowed from the original *Aridosio* of Lorenzino de' Medici. The plays as well as the prefaces are reprinted in Viollet Le Duc's *Ancien Théâtre françoys*, Vols. V–VII (Paris: P. Jannet, 1855–56); information on the sources is to be found in Volume V, pp. v-xxii. *Les Esprits* is also printed in Edouard Fournier's *Théâtre français au XVI*^e^ *et au XVII*^e^ *siècle* (Paris: Laplace, Sanchez et Cie, [n.d.]), I, 144–228. For a detailed bibliography of the comedies, see L. Morin, *Les Trois Pierre de Larivey* (Troyes: J.-L. Paton, 1937).

In spite of the fact that the majority of these prologues are not original, they are published here because of their close relationship to other statements on comedy during the century.

[aij] A MONSIEUR D'AMBOISE, ADVOCAT EN PARLEMENT[a]

Monsieur. J'ay tousjours pensé que ma nouvelle façon d'escrire en ce nouveau genre de comedie, qui n'a encores esté beaucoup praticqué entre noz François, ne sera tant bien receüe de quelques-uns trop severes comme je serois ayse me le pouvoir persuader: occasion qui m'a longtemps fait doubter si je devoy faire veoir le jour à ce mien petit ouvrage, basty à la moderne et sur le patron de plusieurs bons auteurs Italiens comme Laurens de Medicis, pere du Pape Leon dixieme, François Grassin, Vincent Gabian, Jherosme Razzi, Nicolas Bonnepart, Loys Dolce,[b] et autres qui [a ij *v*] ont autant acquis de reputation en leur vivant et esperé[1] de memoire après leur decès, s'esbatans en ces comedies morales et facecieuses comme s'exerceans en l'histoire ou en la filosofie, esquelles ils n'estoient pas moins versez qu'en toutes bonnes sciences. Toutesfois, considerant que la comedie, vray miroüer de noz œuvres, n'est qu'une morale filosofie, donnant lumiere à toute honneste discipline et par consequent à toute vertu (ainsi que le tesmoigne Andronique qui premier l'a faict veoir aux Latins),[c] j'en ay voulu jetter ces premiers fondemens, où j'ay mis comme en bloc divers enseignemens fort profitables, blasmant les vitieuses actions et louant les honnestes, affin de faire cognoistre combien le mal est à eviter et avec quel courage et affection la vertu doibt estre embrassée pour meriter louange, acquerir honneur en ceste vie, et esperer non seulement une gloire eternelle entre les hommes mais une celeste recompense après le trespas. Et voylà pourquoy mon intention a esté en ces populaires discours de representer quelque chose sentant sa verité, qui peust par [a iij] un honneste plaisir apporter, suyvant le precepte d'Horace, quelque profit et contentement ensemble.[d]

J'ay dict que j'en jette les premiers fondemens, non que par là je veulle inferer que je sois le premier qui faict veoir des comedies en prose; car je sçay qu'assez de bons ouvriers et qui meritent beaucoup pour la promptitude de leur esprit en ont traduict quelques-unes. Mais aussi puis-je dire

1. epseré *1579, 1597*

a. François d'Amboise, born in 1550. His literary works were published between 1572 and 1584, including a comedy, *Les Néapolitaines*, in 1584.

b. Cf. the prefatory note to this text for the original plays by these authors which Larivey translated. Francesco Grazzini's *Gelosia* had been used as a model for Larivey's *Le Morfondu*, and Girolamo Razzi's *La Zecca* for Larivey's *Les Escolliers*; prefaces to these comedies are not reproduced here.

c. Donatus, *De Comoedia et Tragoedia* (ed. Wessner), V, 5: "aitque [Liuius Andronicus] esse comoediam cotidianae uitae speculum, nec iniuria. nam ut intenti speculo ueritatis liniamenta facile per imaginem colligimus, ita lectione comoediae imitationem uitae consuetudinisque non aegerrime animaduertimus." Cf. also the Badius edition of Terence (ed. Lyon: Marion, 1517), fol. b iij.

d. *Ars poetica*, l. 343.

cecy sans arrogance, que je n'en ay encores veu de Françoises, j'enten qui ayent esté representées, comme advenues en France. Or si je n'ay voulu en ce peu, contre l'opinion de beaucoup, obliger la franchise de ma liberté de parler à la severité de la loy de ces critiques qui veullent que la comedie soit un poëme subject au nombre et mesure des vers (ce que sans me vanter j'eusse peu faire), je l'ay faict parce qu'il m'a semblé que le commun peuple, qui est le principal personnage de la scene, ne s'estudie tant à agencer ses paroles qu'à publier son affection, qu'il a plutost dicte que pensée. Il est bien vray que Plaute, Cecil, Terence, et tous les anciens ont embrassé, sinon le vray cors, à [a iij *v*] tout le moins l'ombre de la poesie, usans de quelques vers iambiques; mais avec telle liberté, licence, et dissolution que les orateurs mesmes sont le plus souvent mieux serrez en leurs periodes et cadances. Qui a donné occasion de rappeller en doubte s'il falloit mettre la comedie entre les poëmes parfaicts, bien qu'elle soit sœur germaine de la tragedie, issues toutes deux de mesmes parens, encor que ceste-cy comme puisnée n'ayt pas esté mariée en si haut lieu. Et comme vous sçavez, c'est l'opinion des meilleurs antiquaires que le *Querolus* de Plaute et plusieurs autres comedies qui sont peries par l'injure du temps ne furent jamais qu'en pure prose. Joint aussi que le Cardinal Bibiene, le Picolomini, et l'Aretin, tous les plus excellens de leur siecle, et les autres dont j'ay parlé cy-dessus et lesquels j'ay voulu principalement imiter et suyvre en ce que j'ay pensé m'estre possible et permis, n'ont jamais en leurs œuvres comiques (jaçoit qu'ils fussent des premiers en la poësie) voulu employer la rithme,[e] com-[a iiij]me n'estant requise en telle maniere d'escrire pour sa trop grande affectation et abondance de parolles superflues. Et ce sont les raisons desquelles vous et Monsieur Le Breton,[f] que j'honore beaucoup pour ses rares vertus, m'avez plus eguillonné de donner commancement à ces fables, qu'icy je vous offre et desdie comme au meilleur de mes meilleurs amys; affin que vous, qui estes mon auteur et garand formel, preniez s'il vous plaist la cause pour moy, et qu'au moyen des bonnes raisons que vous pourrez puiser en la vive source des bons livres qui sont entre voz mains, vous me serviez d'une levée et ferme rampart contre les inondations et torrens de quelques envieux qui me voudroient blasmer et calomnier la bonne et sincere affection que j'ay de profiter au public; me semblant, puisqu'avez mis entre mes mains la pierre dont j'ay faict ce coup, que me devez garantir envers et contre tous de l'offense qu'en cet endroit je pourrois

e. Bernardo Divizio da Bibiena, *La Calandria*, 1521; Alessandro Piccolomini, *Alessandro*, 1545, *L'Amor costante*, 1536, *Gli Ingannati*, 1531 (published 1537); Pietro Aretino, *Il Filosofo*, *La Cortigiana*, *Il Marescalco*, *Lo Hipocrito*, published in the 1530's and 1540's. All these comedies were in prose.

f. Guillaume Le Breton, a dramatic poet who died in 1578. His tragedy of *Adonis* was printed in 1579 by François d'Amboise.

avoir faicte. Et je vous en supplie, monsieur, d'aussi bon cueur que je desire e[a iiij *v*]stre recommandé à voz meilleures graces.

A Paris, ce premier jour de janvier, 1579.

Vostre affectionné serviteur et meilleur amy,
Pierre de Larivey.

[A vij] PROLOGUE TO *Le Laquais*

Messieurs. Il y a une sorte d'hommes lesquels, encor qu'ils soient du tout ignorans, veullent estre estimez plus sages que les autres, et faisans paroistre en leurs habits la sainctеté de Hilarion et en leurs propos l'eloquence de Ciceron, crient que le monde va de travers et que nous sommes au temps des miseres, calamitez et tribulations. Pour leur respondre avec toute patience, je dy qu'à la verité c'est un grand peché que tels personnages vivent, comme ceux qui ayans le cerveau gasté cherchent alterer celuy des autres; parce qu'il n'y eut jamais temps plus plaisant ny plus heureuse vie que celle du jourd'huy. Et qu'il soit vray, vous le voyez par ces bons peres à qui l'aage a desja mis un de leurs pieds en la fosse, lesquels voudroient estre rajeunis de trente ans pour vivre encores autant d'années avecques nous et oyr reciter tant de belles comedies que je sçay que noz François nous feront veoir cy-après, dressans un theatre autant magnifique, superbe et glorieux que nation qui soit au monde, affin de n'aller plus[2] chercher ailleurs qu'en [A vij *v*] noz propres maisons ces honnestes plaisirs et utiles recreations. Il y en a encores d'autres (mesdames) qui ventans par paroles la doctrine de Platon et suyvans par effect la vie d'Epicure vous fuyent comme on faict les bestes cruelles. Et combien que soyez l'ornement du monde, la consolation des hommes, la reparation du genre humain, et la doulceur de nostre vie, vous portent neantmoins une telle haine qu'il n'y a aucun d'eux qui veulle lever les yeux pour vous regarder au front. Et Dieu sçait si j'en suis fasché et en pren grande compassion.

Mais laissant pour ceste heure les temps, les influences, et les plaintes, je vous veux faire entendre que je suis icy envoyé pour vous supplier daigner escouter ceste comedie avec autant de patience qu'avez accoustumé veoir le bal, les festins et les mascarades qu'on faict en ceste ville non seulement aux jours gras mais tousjours generalement, sans mesmes en excepter le Caresme, et je m'asseure qu'on vous fournira de matiere non seulement pour rire mais pour aprendre, enseignant aux viellards à estre plus moderez et moins addonnez aux plaisirs de Venus, et conseillant les jeunes à laisser

2. plus *1579 only*

la trame amoureuse et suyvre la vertu; pource que le bois sec se convertyt incontinent en cendres et le verd se seiche au feu, puis enfin se consomme en sa braise. L'auteur l'a voulu intituler *le Laquais* non sans cause, d'autant qu'en un mesme tems vous verrez par trois diverses tromperies decevoir un viellard lequel, epris des beautez d'une jeune fille de laquelle son fils estoit amoureux, pensant la nuict estre couché avec elle, trouve entre [A viij] ses bras un laquais desguisé, cependant son fils joyt de ses amours, sa fille propre s'enfuyt avec son amy, et sa servante le desrobbe. Le faict se decouvre et le trouble est grand et brouillé. Enfin tout succede si bien que les amans sont espousez ensemble, le laquais recogneu pour frere de la fille amye du fils au viellard, et la servante rapporte son larcin, qui faict redoubler la feste. Mais quand j'y pense, je vous ay sans y penser dict l'argument de la comedie. S'il est advis à aucun que quelquefois on sorte les termes de l'honnesteté, je le prie penser que pour bien exprimer les façons et affections du jourdhuy il faudroit que les actes et paroles fussent entierement la mesme lasciveté. Or pource qu'il est temps de commancer, prenant vostre silence pour augure que nous vous serons agreables, je vas[3] trouver mes compagnons et leur dire qu'ils se hastent sans vous faire trop attendre. Mais voicy desja le viellard; escoutez-le.

[f vi *v*] PROLOGUE TO *La Vefve*

Affin de vous honorer (messieurs) nous vous representons ceste comedie, spectacle beaucoup plus plaisant et recommandable que les chasteaux, les chasses, les joustes, et autres tels passetemps qui recreent seulement la veue. Mais cestuy-cy delecte les yeux, les oreilles, et l'entendement: les yeux, par[4] la varieté des gestes et personnages y representez et par l'assemblée de tant honorables seigneurs et belles dames comme vous qui ravissez l'esprit d'un chacun en la contemplation du parfaict de voz perfections; les oreilles, par les plaisans et sentencieux discours qui y sont meslez; et l'entendement, parce que la comedie estant le mirouer de nostre vie, les vieillards aprennent à se garder de ce qui paroist ridicule en un homme d'aage, les jeunes à se gouverner en l'amour, les dames à conserver leur honesteté, et les peres et meres de famille à soigner aux affaires de leur mesnage. Bref, si les autres spectacles delectent et sont propres à la jeunesse, cestuy-cy delecte, enseigne, et est propre aux jeunes, aux vieux, et à un chacun. Et si les autres monstrent la dexterité du corps, cestuy-ci monstre la dexterité de l'esprit. Car comme une peinture est recommandée si representant une belle histoire elle est bien accommodée de couleurs, de beaux traits, lineamens, proportion, prospective, et finablement enrichie de festons, bordures, et vernis; ainsi est belle la comedie si premierement la

3. vay *1597, 1601* 4. per *1579*

fable est embellie par industrieuses tromperies [f vij] et gaillards et improveuz evenemens, puis tissue de graves et plaisans discours plains de sentences, comparaisons, metafores, railleries, et promptes et aigues responses —non d'inepties qui comme choses goffes et peu honnestes font rire les ignorans, mais d'une modeste gayeté et soigneuse prudence qui emeuvent encores les plus doctes. Or si ceste-cy n'a toutes ces perfections et n'est telle que meritez et comme l'auteur voudroit bien, il pense toutesfois que ne la blasmerez, ains excuserez sa bonne intention qui ne souhette autre chose que vous servir et doner une envye à noz François de faire mieux que luy.

Cependant (mesdames) n'attendez l'argument, parce que pour quelques occasions l'auteur n'en a point voulu faire. Quant à nous, nous vous le ferions volontiers, mais nous voudrions qu'il n'y eust tant d'yeux; car vous sçavez qu'en telles choses on ne demande pas si grande compagnie, de façon que vous vous en passerez s'il vous plaist pour ce coup, attendant meilleure occasion et lieu plus convenable. Toutesfois, si vous en enchargez et pensez qu'à ceste cause vos enfans en naistront[5] bossus ou[6] contrefaicts, pour obvier à ces inconveniens ceux-cy qui successivement se presenteront sur le theatre satisferont[7] à voz desirs; lesquels,[8] pour estre jà transformez[9] par les enchantemens de vos beautez en diverses personnes, et ayans jà dressé leurs pensées envers vous, feront ce qui leur sera possible, pourveu que les vouliez escouter. Et ils vous en supplient d'aussi bon cœur qu'ils desirent voz bonnes graces.

[l iij *v*] PROLOGUE TO *Les Esprits*

Que nostre aage se vante tant qu'il luy plaira de l'esprit et sçavoir de ses nourrissons, et se glorifie en son erreur et vaine persuasion, si est-ce que je diray tousjours que nos devanciers ont esté tant ingenieux en leurs estudes et sceu si bien dire et faire qu'il nous est impossible pouvoir parfaictement faire ou dire aucune chose sinon ce qui a esté dict ou faict par eux. Car tout ainsi qu'un sculpteur ou peintre ne peut graver ou pourtraire aucune figure dont il puisse acquerir honneur si premierement il ne void les medales et patrons antiques desquels il forme sa figure, ainsi nous ne pouvons faire aucune chose qui soit belle si comme en un mirouer nous ne nous representons ceste antiquité. Voylà pourquoy l'auteur pensant à toutes ces choses, mesmes que Plaute et Terence ont esté grands imitateurs (car l'un a[10] suivy Epicarme et l'autre Menandre), et que celuy seroit une trop grande presomption—voire expresse ignorance—si encor il ne suyvoit les traces de ceste sacrée antiquité, il a faict ceste comedie à l'imitation et de Plaute et de Terence ensemble. Or j'espere qu'elle vous plaira pour estre toute plaine

5. naistrot *1579* 6. où *1579* 7. satifferõt *1579* 8. desquels *1601*
9. trãformez *1579*; tranformez *1597* 10. à *1579*

de variables humeurs, affections, plaisirs, et passions. A ceste cause, messieurs et dames, vous nous ferez s'il vous plaist ceste faveur de vous tenir chacun en vos places et de ne parler d'encherir le pain, ny [l iiij] si ces prochaines vendanges nous aurons bonne vinée; de ne discourir aussi des armées qui se voyent en l'air, des monstres qui naissent sur la terre, ny si la Flandre sera bientost paisible, et si le nombre moindre commandera encor longtemps au plus grand; parce que demain matin, vous pourmenant en la Salle du Palais, vous en pourrez deviser plus commodement et à loisir. Au reste, l'autheur a pensé que ce seroit chose superflue vous reciter l'argument parce que d'acte en acte la comedie vous le declarera. A Dieu je me recommande.

[v x *v*] PROLOGUE TO *Les Jalous*

La comedie qu'ores nous vous representons est intitulée *les Jaloux* pource que les personnes qui interviennent en icelle, ou la pluspart, sont molestées de variables et diverses jalousies. Or comme elle est d'argument double, aussi la plus grande partie de son subject a esté prinse des deux premieres[11] de Terence, à sçavoir l'*Andrie* et l'*Eunuque*. Si en cela l'auteur s'est monstré trop licencieux, il vous supplie (messieurs) ne l'en vouloir blasmer, non plus qu'il n'a blasmé Terence d'avoir prins les siennes de Menandre. Aussi a-il pensé que marchant après les pas d'un tel personnage et sous son autorité, ce luy seroit suffisante deffense pour parer aux coups de ceux qui le voudroient accuser et reprendre de l'avoir desrobbé et suivy de trop près. Mais voicy qui le fasche davantage, c'est qu'il s'en trouve aucuns qui, avec aigres et fascheu[v xi]ses parolles, s'estudient vouloir rendre la comedie abominable à tout le monde, affermans que c'est un œuvre diabolique;[12] d'autant (disent-ils) qu'elle ne contient gueres autre chose que lascivetez, larcins, et toutes souillures, et qu'elle enseigne mille fois plus de mal que de bien. Helas! combien temeraires et indiscrets peuvent estre appellez ceux qui tant malicieusement donnent sentence diffinitive à l'encontre du labeur d'autruy! veu que l'advis des hommes est instable et trompeur, et leur renommée et gloire plus cheres que l'or et pierres precieuses! Semble-il donc à ceux-là que la comedie, qui tire son commencement des choses divines, soit tant à blasmer? Leur est-il advis qu'icelle, qui embrassant diverses coustumes et affections des affaires civiles et privées enseigne ce qui est utile à la vie, et comme il faut fuir les vices et se distraire de toute meschanceté, doive estre ainsi bannie d'un chacun? Quoy? La comedie (je parle de la nouvelle) n'a-elle pas dès [v xi *v*] son origine esté permise, louée, et aprouvée de tous hommes,[13] de tous temps, et en tous lieux? Où ces braves Quintils ont-ils[14] trouvé qu'elle enseigne plus de mal que de bien?

11. premiers *1597, 1601* 12. diabolibolique *1579*
13. de tous hommes *1579 only* 14. ont il *1579, 1597*

qu'elle soit deffenduë? et qu'elle doit estre reprouvée de tout homme de bon jugement? Je voudrois bien que pour probation de leur dire ils amenassent quelque passage de l'Escriture; sinon, je croiray avecques ceste noble assistance qui s'est icy assemblée pour nous escouter qu'ils ne sçavent qu'ils disent. Et de vouloir sofistiquer, allegans qu'elle doibt estre deffendue ne fust-ce que pource qu'elle scandalise beaucoup de personnes, cela n'a point de nez; car par mesme raison il faudroit dire que la justice est une tirannie parce que beaucoup se formalisent des executions qu'elle faict faire; que la misericorde est une lascheté de cœur parce que quelques cruels blasment sa douceur et clemence; et qu'il ne faut aller à l'eglise pour prier Dieu parce que assez d'ateistes pensent qu'on le faict par hipocrisie. O bon-[v xij]té divine! Helas! comme seroit traictée la verité et la diffinition des choses s'il falloit accorder que tant bonnes et sainctes œuvres fussent telles qu'aucuns les pensent! Mais c'est trop parlé de cecy, joint qu'il semble à l'auteur que tout ce qui n'est deffendu par aucune loy expresse s'entend devoir estre permis et qu'on en peut honnestement user. Voilà pourquoy (messieurs) il vous presente ceste comedie telle qu'elle est, vous priant luy donner autant d'audience qu'il est requis en choses semblables. Et en recompense *les Jaloux* vous donneront autant de plaisir qu'ils ont de martel en[15] teste. Il vous vouloit dire l'argument, mais parce qu'il a veu sortir ces deux jeunes hommes, il a pensé qu'ils vous le feront entendre; et puis la comedie est l'argument d'elle-mesme.

15. in *1579, 1597*

JEAN DE BEAUBREUIL

DEDICATION TO HIS *Regulus*

1582

TEXT:

Regvlvs, Tragedie Dressée sur vn faict des plus notables, qu'on puisse trouuer en toute l'Histoire Romaine. Par Iehan De Beavbrveil, Aduocat au Siege Presidial De Lymoges. A Lymoges. De L'Imprimerie de Hvgves Barbov. 1582. [B.N., Paris.]
[Cf. Brunet, I, 714–15.]

Various historians have cited the preface to Jean de Beaubreuil's *Regulus* as containing a highly interesting statement on the dramatic unities. Emile Faguet was the first of these: "Ce que j'y vois de plus intéressant est que l'auteur déclare dans sa préface avoir dû *'s'affranchir de la règle superstitieuse des unités,'* impossible à observer dans un *Régulus*" (*La Tragédie française au XVIe siècle*, Paris, 1883, p. 317). The same statement is quoted from Faguet by J. Dedieu in his edition of Pierre Delaudun's *Art poëtique français* (Toulouse, 1909), p. 164, and by W. F. Patterson in his *Three Centuries of French Poetic Theory* (Ann Arbor, Michigan, 1935), I, 693. No such statement appears in the original volume, but there is a passage in the note "Au Lecteur" to which Faguet may be alluding. But Faguet's statement is an interpretation, not a quotation, of the original text, and it goes far beyond the implications of the original. Beaubreuil states a point of view very similar to that of Pierre Delaudun (see above, Introduction, p. 42). The note "Au Lecteur" is printed here for the information of the reader.

[Ai *v*] AU LECTEUR

Amy lecteur, d'autant que les noms propres des Romains et plusieurs aultres ont plus de grace en la poësie Françoise estantz francifiés que demeurantz en leur langue, c'est pourquoy au lieu de Attilius, Regulus, et Manlius j'ay mis Attilie et Manlie; de laquelle licence je n'use escrivant en prose, comme appert par l'inscription de ceste tragedie et par l'argument d'icelle. Toutesfois, la douceur du son nous guide le plus souvent en escripvant les noms anciens Grecz ou Romains.

Au demeurant, pour cause des longs intervalles des temps qui sont en l'histoire de Regulus, tu ne trouveras estrange si pour la mieux faire entendre j'ay voulu que les cinq actes (qui parfont la tragedie) ne fussent estroictement compassés à la forme de quelques tragiques trop superstitieux, qui ont pensé qu'il ne falloit representer en la tragedie aultre chose que ce qui se pouvoit faire en un jour. Car j'ay recognu (premier qu'y mettre la main) qu'il ne se pouvoit aultrement faire, joinct que plusieurs doctes personnages de nostre temps versantz en pareil subject ont usé de mesme licence.

[A ij] A MONSIEUR DORAT, POETE DU ROY

Monsieur. Considerant l'humeur des hommes de nostre siecle, il me souvient de ce que raconte Strabo geographe estre advenu en Iassus, isle de Carie. En icelle, dict-il, se trouva jadis un excellent maistre joueur de luth, de tant plus admirable qu'il s'en trouvoit peu ou[1] point d'aultres en ce quartier. Or comme il estoit au milieu d'une grand' assemblée de ville, et que pour la contenter il animoit son luth à merveilles par un hardy tremblement de ses doigtz, incontinant qu'une certaine cloche sonna (qui estoit un signe pour les habitantz de l'heure qu'on vendoit le poisson) toute la troupe le quista, fors qu'un pauvre sourdaud qui ne l'avoit point ouye. Mesmes advint que ce joueur de luth, remerciant à haulte voix son fatal auditeur de l'honneur qu'il recevoit de sa companie, pour n'avoir couru au poisson comme les aultres, s'en veid bientost quité pour luy avoir donné conjecture que la cloche du poisson [A ij *v*] estoit sonnée. Tellement qu'il ne s'en trouva pas un en la ville qui tant estima un excellent maistre que je ne sçay quel poisson pourri.[a]

Mais quoy? Noz villes sont-elles aultres? A la verité les artz honnestes y sont encores à plus vil prix qu'en Iassus, si fort y commande l'avarice. J'en vois plusieurs (ausquelz je ne doibz rien) qui me feroient volontiers adjourner de ce que j'ayme la poësie, ne considerantz que j'estime plus ce gain de contenter mon esprit que d'estre fourni de trente balles de saffran, et que je me sens plus riche d'un escu qu'ilz ne sont de dix mille. J'en voys d'aultres qui font semblant au commencement, comme ceux de Iassus, de favoriser les nymphes de Parnasse et qui mesmes y sont tenuz, et toutesfois le gain d'un carolus leur feroit abandonner leur pere. De moy, je les estime ce qu'ilz vallent, et non plus, et me donne aultant de peine de tous ces[2] ragdenases que d'un enroué coaq de grenouilles. Mais au lieu de quister (quelque avarice qui regne) les muses qui m'ont pleu dès mon enfance, il me souvient tousjours des doctes remonstrances que j'ay sur ce faict quelque jour ouy de vostre bouche lorsque j'avois cest honeur d'estre vostre disciple.[b] Et si diray sans mentir que despuis que j'ay vestu la togue, ny le

1. où *1582* 2. ses *1582*

a. Strabo, *Geography*, XII.i.21–22. The story is told at length by Erasmus, *Apophthegmata*, Bk. VIII (Basel, 1539), p. 841.

b. Jean Dorat had been professor of Greek at the Collège Royale from 1556–1567. Charles IX gave him the title of *poeta regius*, which accounts for the "poete du roy" in the title of the dedication. Dorat died on Nov. 1, 1588.

gain ny l'object de plusieurs faisantz maison en mesprisant les muses n'ont tant peu sur moy que je les aye voulu quiter.

Au con[A iij]traire, par elles j'ay esté conduict despuis trois ans en ça sur les lieux qu'elles semblent avoir favorisé sur tous aultres, j'entendz les villes d'Italie, me plaisant principallement en celle-là qui leve aultant le chef sur ses voysines:

Quantum lenta solent inter viburna cupressi,[c]

dans laquelle je receus un grand contentement de voir nostre Muret en chaire, faisant sortir de sa bouche un tonnerre si aggreable que je fuz lors contrainct d'eschaper ce vers:

S'il escript bien, il dict encore mieux.

Et pouvez croire que ce ne fust poinct sans admirer la fortune de l'homme, le voyant passer par les rues de Romme dans un coche magnifique.[d] Mais obliroy-je les propos affables qui me recueillirent[3] en sa maison? "Je suis bien fort aise, disoit-il, de voir aujourdhuy le filz de ce Beaubrueil qui m'encouragea des premiers à l'amour des bonnes lettres, et me plaict aussi grandement de sçavoir des nouvelles de Dorat que tous deux avons heu pour maistre, et lequel j'estime avoir heu seul les delices de la langue Grecque." Voylà partie des propos que nous heusmes ensemble, et partie aussi du contentement que l'amour des lettres m'ha causé me conduisant par l'Italie.

Au demeurant, pour vous tesmoigner la souvenance que j'ay de vous, et combien je m'estime heureux d'estre au rang de ceux qui ont veu les muses en vo[A iij *v*]stre maison, je vous ay bien voulu faire present de mon *Regulus*, vous priant le recevoir comme avant-coureur de chose meilleure, l'acceptant non pour aultre valeur que seulement pour la bonne et entiere affection de celuy qui le vous presente.

De Lymoges ce 15. may. 1582.

3. recuillirent *1582*

c. Vergil, *Eclogues*, I, 25.

d. Marc Antoine Muret had fled from France to Italy in 1554, and had settled in Rome in 1559. He took holy orders in 1576 and died in Rome in 1585.

PIERRE DE RONSARD

THIRD PREFACE TO *La Franciade*

1587

TEXT:

Les Qvatre Premiers Livres de la Franciade. Av roy tres-Chrestien, Charles nevfieme de ce nom. Par Pierre de Ronsard gentil-homme Vandomois. Tome III. A Paris, Chez Gabriel Buon, au cloz Bruneau, à l'enseigne S. Claude. 1587. Avec privilege dv roy. [B.N., Paris.]

[Cf. Brunet, IV, 1375 and 1384, and *Supplément*, II, 503; Tchemerzine, IX, 477; De Ricci, No. 79, p. 171. The text is reprinted in the 1592 and 1597 editions of the *Œuvres*, both of which are available at Harvard; but since the 1587 edition is itself posthumous, these later editions represent only printers' or editors' changes. This conclusion is borne out by a collation of the texts; the results of the collation are not given here.]

The date of composition of Ronsard's last preface to *La Franciade* is not known, except that it was between 1572 and the time of his death in 1585. Meanwhile, the epic had been reprinted in 1573, with only a short epistle "Au Lecteur," and in the complete works of 1584, with no prefatory material. D. B. Wyndham Lewis, in his *Ronsard* (New York: Coward-McCann, 1944, p. 218), is of the opinion that the last preface was written "just before his death," and this seems to be a likely suggestion since it is known that at the time of his death Ronsard was at work on a revision of his writings. As in the case of the 1572 preface, that of 1587 has been reprinted in the major modern editions of the poet; some of the notes of the present edition are borrowed from Gustave Cohen's edition in the *Œuvres complètes* (Paris: Bibliothèque de la Pléiade, 1938, II, 1018–34).

[A iij] PREFACE SUR LA FRANCIADE, TOUCHANT LE POËME HEROÏQUE

AU LECTEUR APPRENTIF

Carmen reprehendite quod non
Multa dies et multa litura coercuit, atque
Perfectum decies non castigavit ad unguem.[a]

Il ne faut t'esmerveiller, lecteur, de quoy je n'ay composé ma *Franciade* en vers Alexandrins, qu'autrefois en ma jeunesse, par ignorance, je pensois tenir en nostre langue le rang des carmes heroiques, encores qu'ils respondent plus aux senaires des tragiques qu'aux magnanimes vers d'Homere et de Virgile, les estimant pour lors plus convenables aux

a. Horace, *Ars poetica*, ll. 292–94.

magnifiques argumens et aux plus excellentes conceptions de l'esprit que les autres vers communs. Depuis j'ay veu, cogneu, et pratiqué par longue experience que je m'estois abusé. Car ils sentent trop la prose très facile et sont trop enervez et flaques, si ce n'est pour les traductions, ausquelles à cause de leur longueur ils servent de beaucoup pour interpreter le sens de l'aucteur qu'on entreprend de traduire. Au reste, ils ont trop de caquet [A iij *v*] s'ils ne sont bastis de la main d'un bon artisan qui les face autant qu'il luy sera possible hausser (comme les peintures relevées) et quasi separer du langage commun, les ornant et enrichissant de figures, schemes, tropes, metaphores, phrases et periphrases eslongnées presque du tout, ou pour le moins separées, de la prose triviale et vulgaire (car le style prosaïque est ennemy capital de l'eloquence poëtique), et les illustrant de comparaisons bien adaptées, de descriptions florides (c'est-à-dire enrichies de passements, broderies, tapisseries, et entrelassements de fleurs poëtiques), tant pour representer la chose que pour l'ornement et splendeur des vers; comme ceste brave et très excellente description du sacerdote de Cybele Cloreus en l'onziesme livre des *Aeneides*, et le catalogue des capitaines envoyez à la guerre; puis la fin[1] du septiesme livre des *Aeneides* et cette inveterée querelle de ces deux bonnes dames Junon et Venus au dixiesme. Relisant telles belles conceptions, tu n'auras cheveu en teste qui ne se dresse d'admiration. Et encore davantage si tu lis attentivement le 8. du mesme autheur, quand Venus flatte et enjole son mary Vulcan pour le persuader de forger des armes à son fils Aenée:

> Dixerat et niveis hinc atque hinc diva lacertis,

jusques au vers

> Haec pater Aeoliis properat dum Lemnius oris.[b]

Et davantage si tu lis ceste oraison indignée et farouche de Iarbas à Jupiter son père, où tu [A iiij] verras un *femina*, un *litus arandum*, *Et nunc ille Paris cum semiviro comitatu*, et cette lamentation miserable de la pauvre vieille, mere d'Euriale, voyant la teste de son fils fichée sur le haut d'une lance, il n'y a cœur si dur qui se peust contenir de pleurer. Et cette brave vanterie de Numanus beau-frere de Turne, qui se commence *Is primam ante aciem*, jusques à ce vers *Talia iactantem dictis*; et la colere d'Hercule tuant Cacus; et ceste lamentable plainte de Mezance sur le corps mort

1. fiin *1587*

b. "Cybele Cloreus," *Æneid*, XI, 768 ff.; "catalogue des capitaines," VII, 641 ff.; "Junon et Venus," X, 16 ff.; "Dixerat, etc.," VIII, 387; "Haec pater, etc.," VIII, 454.

de son fils Lauzus;[c] et mille autres telles ecstatiques descriptions que tu liras en un si divin aucteur, lesquelles te feront poëte encores que tu fusses un rocher, t'imprimeront des verves, et t'irriteront les naifves et naturelles scintilles de l'ame que dès la naissance tu as receues, t'inclinans plustost à ce mestier que à cestuy-là. Car tout homme dès le naistre reçoit en l'ame je ne sçay quelles fatales impressions, qui le contraignent suivre plustost son destin que sa volonté.

Les excellens poëtes nomment peu souvent les choses par leur nom propre. Virgile, voulant descrire le jour ou la nuict, ne dit point simplement et en paroles nues, "Il estoit jour, il estoit nuict"; mais par belles circonlocutions,

> Postera Phoebea lustrabat lampade terras
> Umentemque Aurora polo dimoverat umbras.
>
> Nox erat, et placidum carpebant fessa soporem
> Corpora per terras, sylvaeque et saeva quierant [A iiij *v*]
> Aequora, cum medio volvuntur sidera lapsu,
> Cum tacet omnis ager, pecudes pictaeque volucres,[d]

et mille autres. Ceste Virgiliane description de la nuict est prise presque de mot à mot d'Apolloine Rhodien.[e] Voy comme il descrit le printemps:

> Vere novo, gelidus canis cum montibus umor
> Liquitur et Zephyro putris se glaeba resolvit.[f]

Labourer, *vertere terram*; filer, *tolerare vitam colo, tenuique Minerua*; le pain, *Dona laboratae cereris*; le vin, *Pocula Bacchi*: telles semblables choses sont plus belles par circonlocutions que par leurs propres noms. Mais il en fault sagement user, car autrement tu rendrois ton ouvrage plus enflé et boufi que plein de majesté.

Tu n'oubliras les descriptions du lever et coucher du soleil, les signes qui se levent et couchent avec luy, ni les serenitez, orages et tempestes.

> Ipse pater media nimborum in nocte corusca
> Fulmina molitur dextra,

---

c. "femina," IV, 211; "litus arandum," IV, 212; "Et nunc, etc.," IV, 215; "mere d'Euriale," IX, 481 ff.; "Is primam, etc.," IX, 595–620; "Talia iactantem, etc.," IX, 621; "Hercule tuant Cacus," VIII, 228 ff.; "plainte de Mezance," X, 846 ff.

d. IV, 6–7, and IV, 522–25.

e. Apollonius of Rhodes, *Argonautica*, III, 744 ff. Cf. A. S. Pease, *Publi Vergili Maronis Aeneidos Liber Quartus*, Cambridge: Harvard University Press, 1935, pp. 434–36.

f. *Georgics*, I, 43–44.

puis

> ... ille flagranti
> Aut Athon aut Rhodopen aut alta Ceraunia telo
> Deicit; ingeminant Austri et densissimus imber.[g]

Tu enrichiras ton poëme par[2] varietez prises de la nature, sans extravaguer comme un frenetique. Car pour vouloir trop eviter et du tout te bannir du parler vulgaire, si tu veux voler sans consideration par le travers des nues et faire des grotesques, chimeres et monstres [A v] et non une naifve et naturelle poesie, tu seras imitateur d'Ixion, qui engendra des phantosmes au lieu de legitimes et naturels enfans. Tu dois davantage, lecteur, illustrer ton œuvre de paroles recherchées et choisies et d'arguments renforcez tantost par fables, tantost par quelques vieilles histoires, pourveu qu'elles soient briefvement escrites et de peu de discours, l'enrichissant d'epithetes significatifs et non oisifs, c'est-à-dire qui servent à la substance des vers, et par excellentes et toutefois rares sentences. Car si les sentences sont trop frequentes en ton œuvre heroique, tu le rendras monstrueux, comme si tout ton corps n'estoit composé que d'yeux et non d'autres membres qui servent beaucoup au commerce de nostre vie; si ce n'estoit en la tragedie et comedie, lesquelles sont du tout didascaliques et enseignantes, et qu'il faut qu'en peu de paroles elles enseignent beaucoup, comme mirouers de la vie humaine; d'autant qu'elles sont bornées et limitées de peu d'espace, c'est-à-dire d'un jour entier. Les plus excellens maistres de ce mestier les commencent d'une minuict à l'autre et non du poinct du jour au soleil couchant, pour avoir plus d'estendue et de longueur de temps.

Le poëme heroïque, qui est tout guerrier, comprend seulement les actions d'une année entiere; et semble que Virgile y ait failli, selon que luy-mesme l'escrit:

> Annuus exactis completur mensibus orbis, [A v *v*]
> Ex quo reliquias divinique ossa parentis
> Condidimus terra.[h]

Il y avoit desja un an passé quand il feit les jeux funebres de son pere en Sicile, et toutefois il n'aborda de longtemps après en Italie.

Tous ceux qui escrivent en carmes, tant doctes puissent-ils estre, ne sont pas poëtes. Il y a autant de difference entre un poëte et un versificateur qu'entre un bidet et un genereux coursier de Naples, et pour mieux les accomparer, entre un venerable prophete et un charlatan vendeur de

2. per *1587*

g. *Georgics*, I, 328–29 and 331–33.
h. *Æneid*, V, 46–48.

triacles. Il me semble, quand je les voy armez de mesmes bastons que les bons maistres, c'est-à-dire des mesmes vers, des mesmes couleurs, des mesmes nombres et pieds dont se servent les bons autheurs, qu'ils ressemblent à ces Hercules desguisez ès tragedies, lesquels acheptent la peau d'un lion chez un peletier, une grosse massue chez un charpentier, et une fausse perruque chez un attiffeur; mais quand ce vient à combatre quelque monstre, la massue leur tombe de la main, et s'enfuient du combat comme couards et poltrons. Ces versificateurs se contentent[3] de faire des vers sans ornement, sans grace et sans art, et leur semble avoir beaucoup fait pour la republique quand ils ont composé de la prose rimée.

Au contraire, le poëte heroïque invente et forge argumens tous nouveaux, faict entreparler les dieux aux hommes et les hommes aux dieux, faict haranguer les capitaines comme il fault, [A vj] descrit les batailles et assaults, factions et entreprises de guerre, se mesle de conjecturer les augures et interpreter les songes, n'oublie les expiations et les sacrifices que l'on doit à la divinité. Tantost il est philosophe, tantost medecin, arboriste, anatomiste, et jurisconsulte, se servant de l'opinion de toutes sectes selon que son argument le demande. Bref, c'est un homme lequel comme une mousche à miel delibe et succe toutes fleurs, puis en fait du miel et son profit selon qu'il vient à propos. Il a pour maxime très necessaire en son art de ne suivre jamais pas à pas la verité, mais la vray-semblance et le possible; et sur le possible et sur ce qui se peut faire il bastit son ouvrage, laissant la veritable narration aux historiographes qui poursuivent de fil en esguille, comme on dit en proverbe, leur subject entrepris, du premier commencement jusques à la fin. Au contraire le poëte bien advisé, plein de laborieuse industrie, commence son œuvre par le milieu de l'argument et quelquefois par la fin. Puis il deduit, file et poursuit si bien son argument par le particulier accident et evenement de la matiere qu'il s'est proposé d'escrire, tantost par personnages parlans les uns aux autres, tantost par songes, propheties et peintures inserées contre le dos d'une muraille et des harnois et principalement des boucliers, ou par les dernieres paroles des hommes qui meurent, ou par augures et vol d'oiseaux et phantastiques visions de dieux et de demons, ou [A vj *v*] monstrueux langages des chevaux navrez à mort; tellement que le dernier acte de l'ouvrage se cole, se lie et s'enchesne si bien et si à propos l'un dedans l'autre que la fin se rapporte dextrement et artificiellement au premier poinct de l'argument. Telles façons d'escrire et tel art plus divin que humain est particulier aux poëtes, lequel de prime face est caché au lecteur s'il n'a l'esprit bien rusé pour comprendre un tel artifice.

Plusieurs croyent que le poëte et historien soient d'un mesme mestier; mais ils se trompent beaucoup. Car ce sont divers artisans qui n'ont rien

3. cotētēt *1587*

de commun l'un avecques l'autre sinon les descriptions des choses, comme batailles, assauts de montaignes, forests et rivieres, villes, assietes de camp, stratagemes, nombre des morts, conseils et pratiques de guerre; en cela il ne faut point que le poëte faille non plus que l'historien. Au reste, ils n'ont rien de commun (comme j'ay dict) sinon que l'un ne l'autre ne doit jamais mentir contre la verité de la chose, comme a failli Virgile au temps (c'est-à-dire en la chronique), lequel a faict Didon, fille de Belus, estre du temps d'Aenée, encore qu'elle fut cent ans devant pour le moins. Mais il inventa telle ruse pour gratifier Auguste et le peuple Romain vainqueur de Carthage, donnant par les imprecations de Didon commencement de haine et de discorde mortelle entre ces deux florissantes nations.

La plus grande partie de ceux qui escrivent de nostre temps [A vij] se trainent enervez à fleur de terre, comme foibles chenilles qui n'ont encore la force de grimper aux festes des arbres, lesquelles se contentent seulement de paistre la basse humeur de la terre, sans affecter la nourriture des hautes cimes ausquelles elles ne peuvent attaindre à cause de leur imbecillité. Les autres sont trop ampoulez et presque crevez d'enfleures comme hydropiques, lesquels pensent n'avoir rien fait d'excellent s'il n'est extravagant, crevé et bouffy, plein de songes monstrueux et paroles piafées qui resemblent plustost à un jargon de gueux ou de Boëmiens qu'aux paroles d'un citoyen honneste et bien appris. Si tu veux demembrer leurs carmes, tu n'en feras sortir que du vent, non plus que d'une vessie de pourceau pleine de pois que les petits enfans crevent pour leur servir de joüet.

Les autres, plus rusez, tiennent le milieu des deux, ny rampans trop bas ny s'eslevant trop haut au travers des nues; mais qui d'artifice et d'un esprit naturel elabouré par longues estudes, et principalement par la lecture des bons vieux poetes Grecs et Latins, descrivent leurs conceptions d'un style nombreux, plein d'une venerable majesté, comme a faict Virgile en sa divine *Aeneide*. Et n'en cherche plus d'autres, lecteur, en la langue Romaine, si ce n'estoit de fortune Lucrece; mais parce qu'il a escrit ses frenesies, lesquelles il pensoit estre vrayes selon sa secte, et qu'il n'a pas basti son [A vij *v*] œuvre sur la vray-semblance et sur le possible, je luy oste du tout le nom de poete, encore que quelques vers soient non seulement excellens mais divins. Au reste, les autres poetes Latins ne sont que naquets de ce brave Virgile, premier capitaine des muses; non pas Horace mesmes, si ce n'est en quelques-unes de ses odes, ny Catulle, Tibulle, et Properce, encore qu'ils soient très excellents en leur mestier; si ce n'est Catulle en son *Athis* et aux *Nopces de Peleus*: le reste ne vaut la chandelle. Stace a suivi la vray-semblance en sa *Thebaide*. De nostre temps Fracastor s'est monstré très excellent en sa *Syphillis*, bien que ses vers soient un peu rudes. Les autres vieils poetes Romains, comme Lucain et Silius Italicus, ont couvert l'histoire du manteau de poesie; ils eussent mieux fait, à mon advis, en quelques endroits d'escrire en prose. Claudian est poete en quelques endroits, comme au *Ravissement de Proserpine*; le reste de ses œuvres ne sont que histoires de son temps, lequel comme les autres s'est plus estudié à l'enflure qu'à la gravité. Car voyans qu'ils ne pouvoient egaler la majesté de Virgile, se sont tournez à l'enflure et à je ne sçay quelle poincte et argutie monstrueuse, estimants les vers estre les plus beaux, ceux qui avoient le visage plus fardé de telle curiosité. Il ne faut s'esmerveiller si j'estime Virgile plus excellent et plus rond, plus serré et plus parfaict que tous les autres, soit que dès ma jeunesse mon regent me le lisoit à l'escole, [A viij] soit que depuis je me sois fait une idée de ses conceptions en mon esprit (portant tousjours son livre en la main), ou soit que l'ayant appris par cœur dès mon enfance je ne le puisse oublier.

Au reste, lecteur, je te veux bien advertir que le bon poëte jette tousjours le fondement de son ouvrage sur quelques vieilles annales du temps passé, ou renommée inveterée laquelle a gaigné credit au cerveau des hommes; comme Virgile sur la commune renommée qu'un certain Troyen nommé Aenée, chanté par Homere, est venu aux bors Laviniens—luy, ses navires et son fils—où depuis Rome fut bastie, encores que ledict Aenée ne vint jamais en Italie; mais il n'estoit pas impossible qu'il n'y peust venir. Sur telle opinion desja receuë du peuple il bastit son livre de l'*Aeneide*. Homere auparavant luy en avoit fait de mesme, lequel fondé sur quelque vieil conte de son temps de la belle Heleine et de l'armée des Grecs à Troye (comme nous faisons des contes de Lancelot, de Tristan, de Gauvain et d'Artus) fonda là-dessus son *Iliade*. Car les propres noms des capitaines et soldats Troyens, qui parloient Phrygien et non Grec et avoient les noms de leur nation, monstrent bien comme evidemment ce n'est qu'une fiction de toute l'*Iliade*, et non verité; comme de Hector, Priam, Polydamas, Anthenor, Deiphœbus, Cassandre, Helenus, et presque tous les autres forgez au plaisir d'Homere. [A viij *v*]

Or imitant ces deux lumieres de poësie, fondé et appuyé sur nos vieilles annales, j'ay basti ma *Franciade*, sans me soucier si cela est vray ou non ou si nos roys sont Troyens ou Germains, Scythes ou Arabes; si Francus est venu en France ou non, car il y pouvoit venir; me servant du possible et non de la verité. C'est le faict d'un historiographe d'esplucher toutes ces considerations, et non aux poëtes qui ne cherchent que le possible, puis d'une petite scintille font naistre un grand brazier et d'une petite cassine font un magnifique palais qu'ils enrichissent, dorent et embellissent par le dehors de marbre, jaspe et porphire, de guillochis, ovalles, frontispices et pieds-destals, frises et chapiteaux; et par dedans de tableaux, tapisseries eslevées et bossées d'or et d'argent; et le dedans des tableaux cizelez et burinez, raboteux et difficile à tenir ès mains à cause de la rude engraveure des personnages qui semblent vivre dedans. Après ils adjoustent vergers et jardins, compartimens et larges allées, selon que les poëtes ont un bon esprit naturel et bien versé en toutes sciences et dignes de leur mestier; car la pluspart ne fait rien qui vaille, semblables à ces apprentifs qui ne sçavent que brayer les couleurs et non pas peindre.

Souvienne-toy, lecteur, de ne laisser passer soubs silence l'histoire ny la fable appartenant à la matiere, et la nature, force, et proprietez des arbres, fleurs, plantes et racines, principalement si elles sont anoblies [A ix] de quelques vertus non vulgaires et si elles servent à la medecine, aux incantations et magies, et en dire un mot en passant par quelque epithete ou pour le moins par un demi-vers. Nicandre, autheur Grec, t'en monstrera le chemin, et Columelle en son *Jardin*, ouvrage autant excellent que tu le sçaurois desirer. Tu n'oubliras aussi ny les montaignes, forests, rivieres, villes, republiques, havres et ports, cavernes et rochers, tant pour embellir ton œuvre par là et le faire grossir en un juste volume, que pour te donner reputation et servir de marque à la posterité. Quant aux capitaines et conducteurs d'armées et soldats, tu en diras les peres et les meres, ayeux, villes, et habillements, et leurs naissances, et feras une fable là-dessus s'il en est besoin, comme:

Hic Hammone satus, rapta Garamantide Nympha;

puis en un autre lieu parlant d'Hypolite:

... insignem quem mater Aricia misit,
Eductum Egeriae lucis umentia circum
Litora;

puis autre part, parlant d'Helenor qui estoit tombé de la tour demy bruslé:

... quorum primaevus Helenor,
Maeonio regi quem serva Licymnia furtim
Sustulerat vetitisque ad Troiam miserat armis.

Quant aux habillemens, tu les vestiras tantost de la peau d'un lion, tantost d'un ours, tantost: [A ix *v*]

Demissa ab laeva pantherae terga retorquens.

Tu n'oublieras à fortifier et asseurer ton esprit (s'il est en doute) ou par un augure ou par un oracle, comme:

At rex sollicitus monstris oracula Fauni,
Fatidici genitoris, adit...;

puis:

> Aspice bis senos laetantis agmine cycnos;

et en une autre part:

> Ecce levis summo de vertice visus Iuli
> Fundere lumen apex.

Il ne fault aussi oublier les admonestemens des Dieux transformez en vulgaires:

> ... Formam tum vertitur oris
> Antiquum in Buten. hic Dardanio Anchisae
> Armiger ante fuit.[i]

Tu ne transposeras jamais les paroles ny de ta prose ny de tes vers, car nostre langue ne le peult porter non plus que le Latin un solecisme. Il fault dire "Le roy alla coucher de Paris à Orleans" et non pas "A Orleans de Paris le roy coucher alla."

J'ay esté d'opinion en ma jeunesse que les vers qui enjambent l'un sur l'autre n'estoient pas bons en nostre poesie: toutefois, j'ay cognu depuis le contraire par la lecture des bons autheurs Grecs et Romains, comme:

> ... Laviniaque venit
> Litora.

J'avois aussi pensé que les mots finissans par [A x] voyeles et diphthongues et rencontrans après un autre vocable commençant par une voyele ou diphthongue, rendoit le vers rude. J'ay appris d'Homere et de Virgile que cela n'estoit point malseant, comme *sub Ilio alto*; *Ionio in magno.*[j] Homere en est tout plein. Je m'asseure que les envieux caqueteront de quoy j'allegue Virgile plus souvent qu'Homere qui estoit son maistre et son patron; mais je l'ay fait tout exprès, sçachant bien que nos François ont plus de cognoissance de Virgile que d'Homere et d'autres autheurs Grecs.

Je suis d'advis de permettre quelque licence à nos poetes François, pourveu qu'elle soit rarement prise. De là sont tant de belles figures que les poetes en leur fureur ont trouvées, franchissans la loy de grammaire, que depuis les orateurs de sens rassis ont illustrées et quasi baillé cours et credit, faisans leur profit de la folie d'autruy.

i. "Hic Hammone, etc.," *Æneid*, IV, 198; "insignem quem, etc.," VII, 762–64; "quorum primaevus, etc.," IX, 545–47; "Demissa, etc.," VIII, 460; "At rex, etc.," VII, 81–82; "Aspice, etc.," I, 393; "Ecce levis, etc.," II, 682; "Formam tum, etc.," IX, 646–48.

j. "Laviniaque venit Litora," I, 2–3; "sub Ilio alto," V, 261; "Ionio in magno," III, 211.

Quant aux comparaisons dont j'ay parlé au commencement assez briefvement, tu les chercheras des artisans de fer et des veneurs (comme Homere), pescheurs, architectes, massons, et brief de tous mestiers dont la nature honore les hommes. Il fault les bien mettre et les bien arranger aux lieux propres de ta poesie, car ce sont les nerfs et tendons des muses quand elles sont placées bien à propos et servantes à la matiere; sinon, elles sont du tout ridicules et dignes du foüet.

Ne sois jamais long en tes discours, si ce n'est que tu vueilles [A x *v*] faire un livre tout entier de ce mesme subjet. Car la poesie heroïque, qui est dramatique[4] et qui ne consiste qu'en action, ne peut longuement traicter un mesme subjet, mais passer de l'un à l'autre en cent sortes de varietez. Il ne faut oublier de faire à la mode des anciens des courtoisies aux estrangers, de magnifiques presens de capitaine à capitaine, de soldat à soldat, tant pour commencer amitié que pour renouveller l'ancienne et pour avoir de pere en fils logé les uns chez les autres. Tu embelliras de braves circonstances tes dons et ne les presenteras tout nuds ny sans ornement; comme le present du roy Latin à Aenée:

> (stabant ter centum nitidi in praesepibus altis);
> Omnibus extemplo Teucris iubet ordine duci
> Instratos ostro alipedes pictisque tapetis
> (aurea pectoribus demissa monilia pendent,
> Tecti auro fulvum mandunt sub dentibus aurum),
> Absenti Aeneae currum geminosque iugalis
> Semine ab aetherio, spirantis naribus ignem,
> Illorum de gente, patri quos daedala Circe
> Supposita de matre nothos furata creavit.

et au cinquiéme:

> Ipsis praecipuos ductoribus addit honores:
> Victori chlamydem auratam.

Un mediocre poëte se fust contenté de cela et n'eust pas adjousté: [A xi]

> Purpura Maeandro duplici Meliboea cucurrit;

encores moins:

> Intextusque puer frondosa regius Ida
> Velocis iaculo cervos cursuque fatigat,
> Acer, anhelanti similis.

Encore, jamais un mauvais poete ne se fust souvenu de ce divin hemistiche:

> ... saevitque canum latratus in auras.[k]

4. drauatique *1587*

k. "stabant ter, etc.," VII, 275 ff.; "Ipsis praecipuos, etc.," V, 249–50; "Purpura Maeandro, etc.," V, 251; "Intextusque, etc.," V, 252–54; "Saevitque, etc.," V, 257.

Tu n'oublieras à faire armer les capitaines, comme il faut, de toutes les pieces de leur harnois, soit que tu les appelles par leur nom propre ou par periphrases; car cela apporte grand ornement à la poesie heroique. Tu n'oublieras aussi la piste et battement de pied des chevaux, et representer en tes vers la lueur et la splendeur des armes frappées de la clarté du soleil, et à faire voler les tourbillons de poudre soubs le pied des soldats et des chevaux courants à la guerre, le cry des soldats, froissis de picques, brisement de lances, accrochement de haches, et le son diabolique des canons et harquebuses qui font trembler la terre, froisser l'air d'alentour. Si tu veux faire mourir sur le champ quelque capitaine ou soldat, il le faut navrer au plus mortel lieu du corps, comme le cerveau, le cœur, la gorge, les aines, le diafragme; et les autres que tu veux seulement blesser, ès parties qui sont les moins mortelles; et en cela tu dois estre bon anatomiste. [A xi *v*] Si quelque excellent homme meurt, tu n'oublieras son epitaphe en une demie ligne, ou une au plus, engravant dans tes vers les principaux oustils de son mestier, comme de Misene qui avoit esté trompette d'Hector puis avoit tiré la rame de bonne volonté soubs Aenée;[l] car c'estoit anciennement l'exercice de grands heroes et capitaines, et mesme de ces quarante chevaliers qui allerent avec Jason en Colchos.[m]

Tu seras industrieux à esmouvoir les passions et affections de l'ame, car c'est la meilleure partie de ton mestier, par des carmes qui t'esmouveront le premier soit à rire ou à pleurer, afin que les lecteurs en facent autant après toy.

Tu n'oublieras jamais de rendre le devoir qu'on doit à la divinité, oraisons, prieres, et sacrifices, commençant et finissant toutes tes actions par Dieu, auquel les hommes attribuent autant de noms qu'il a de puissances et de vertus, imitateur d'Homere et de Virgile qui n'y ont jamais failli.

Tu noteras encores, lecteur, ce poinct qui te menera tout droict au vray chemin des muses: c'est que le poete ne doit jamais prendre l'argument de son œuvre que trois ou quatre cens ans ne soient passez pour le moins, afin que personne ne vive plus de son temps qui le puisse de ses fictions et vrayes semblances convaincre, invoquant les muses qui se souviennent du passé et prophetisent l'advenir pour l'inspirer et conduire [A xij] plus par fureur divine que par invention humaine.

Tu imiteras les effects de la nature en toutes tes descriptions, suyvant Homere. Car s'il fait bouillir de l'eau en un chaudron, tu le verras premier fendre son bois, puis l'allumer et le soufler, puis la flame environner la panse du chaudron tout à l'entour, et l'escume de l'eau se blanchir et s'enfler à gros bouillons avec un grand bruit, et ainsi de toutes les autres choses. Car en telle peinture, ou plustost imitation de la nature, consiste toute l'ame de la poesie heroïque, laquelle n'est qu'un enthousiasme et

l. VI, 232–36.

m. Apollonius of Rhodes, *Argonautica*, e.g. I, 528–29.

fureur d'un jeune cerveau. Celuy qui devient vieil, matté d'un sang refroidy, peut bien dire adieu aux graces et aux muses.

Donc, lecteur, celuy qui pourra faire un tel ouvrage, et qui aura une bouche sonnant plus hautement que les autres, et toutesfois sans se perdre dans les nues, qui aura l'esprit plus plein de prudence et d'advis, et les conceptions plus divines, et les paroles plus rehaussées et recherchées, bien assises en leur lieu par art et non à la volée—donne-luy nom de poete, et non au versificateur, composeur d'epigrammes, sonnets, satyres, elegies, et autres tels menus fatras où l'artifice ne se peut estendre; la simple narration enrichie d'un beau langage est la seule perfection de telles compositions.

Veux-tu sçavoir, lecteur, quand les vers sont bons et dignes de la reputation d'un excellent ouvrier, suy le conseil d'Horace.[n] Il [A xij *v*] fault que tu les demembres et desassembles de leur nombre, mesure et pieds, et que tu les transportes, faisant les derniers mots les premiers et ceux du milieu les derniers. Si tu trouves, après tel desassemblement de la ruine du bastiment, de belles et excellentes paroles et phrases non vulgaires qui te contraignent d'enlever ton esprit oultre le parler commun, pense que tels vers sont bons et dignes d'un excellent poëte. Exemple des mauvais vers:

> Madame en bonne foy je vous donne mon cœur,
> N'usez point envers moy s'il vous plaist de rigueur.

Efface "cœur" et "rigueur," tu n'y trouveras un seul mot qui ne soit vulgaire ou trivial. Où si tu lis ceux-cy:

> Son harnois il endosse, et furieux aux armes
> Profendit par le fer un scadron de gensdarmes,

tu trouveras au desmembrement et deliaison de ces deux carmes, qui te servent d'exemple pour les autres, toutes belles et magnifiques paroles, "harnois, endosse, furieux, armes, profendit, fer, scadron, gensdarmes." Cela se doit faire tant que l'humain artifice le pourra; car bien souvent la matiere ny le sens ne desirent pas telle hausseure de voix, et principalement les narrations et pourparlers des capitaines, conseils et deliberations ès grandes affaires, lesquelles ne demandent que parole nue et simple et l'exposition du faict; car tantost il doit estre orné et tantost non, car c'est un extreme vice à un orfévre de plomber de l'or. Il fault imiter les bons mesnagers qui tapissent[5] bien [B] leurs sales, chambres et cabinets, et non les galetas où couchent les valets. Tu auras les conceptions grandes et hautes, comme je t'ay plusieurs fois adverti, et non monstrueuses ny

5. tapissant *1587*

n. Horace, *Satires*, I. iv. 53–62.

quintessencieuses comme sont celles des Espagnols. Il faudroit un Apollon pour les interpreter; encor il y seroit bien empesché avec tous ses oracles et trepieds.

Tu n'oublieras les noms propres des outils de tous mestiers, et prendras plaisir à t'en enquerre le plus que tu pourras, et principalement de la chasse. Homere a tiré toutes ses plus belles comparaisons de là.

Je veux bien t'advertir, lecteur, de prendre garde aux lettres, et feras jugement de celles qui ont plus de son et de celles qui en ont le moins. Car A, O, U, et les consones M, B, et les SS finissants les mots, et sur toutes les RR qui sont les vrayes lettres heroïques, font une grande sonnerie et baterie aux vers. Suy Virgile, qui est maistre passé en la composition et structure des carmes. Regarde un peu quel bruit font ces deux icy sur la fin du huictiesme de l'*Aeneide*:

> Una omnes ruere ac totum spumare reductis
> Convolsum remis rostrisque tridentibus aequor.

Tu en pourras faire en ta langue autant que tu pourras. Tu n'oublieras aussi d'inserer en tes vers ces lumieres, ou plutost petites ames de la poësie, comme *Italiam metire iacens*, qui est proprement un sarcasme, c'est-à-dire [B *v*] une moquerie que le vaincueur fait sur le corps navré à mort de son ennemy;

> "... et fratrem ne desere frater";
>
> ... et dulcis moriens reminiscitur Argos;
>
> Semianimesque micant digiti ferrumque retractant.[o]

Au reste, lecteur, si je te voulois instruire et t'informer de tous les preceptes qui appartiennent à la poësie heroïque, il me faudroit une rame de papier. Mais les principaux que tu as leu auparavant te conduiront facilement à la cognoissance des autres.

Or venons à nos vers communs de dix à unze syllabes, lesquels pour estre plus courts et pressez contraignent les poëtes de remascher et ruminer plus longuement; et telle contrainte en meditant et repensant fait le plus souvent inventer d'excellentes conceptions, riches paroles et phrases elabourées, tant vault la meditation qui par longueur de temps les engendre en un esprit melancholique, quand la bride de la contrainte arreste et refreint la premiere course impetueuse des fureurs et monstrueuses imaginations de l'esprit, à l'exemple des grandes rivieres qui bouillonnent, escument et fremissent à l'entour de leurs rempars, où quand elles courent la plaine sans contrainte, elles marchent lentement et paresseusement,

o. "Una omnes, etc.," *Æneid*, VIII, 689–90; "Italiam metire iacens," XII, 360; "et fratrem, etc.," X, 600; "et dulcis, etc.," X, 782; "Semianimesque, etc.," X, 396.

sans frapper les rivages ny d'escumes ny de bruit. Tu n'ignores pas, lecteur, qu'un poëte ne doit jamais estre mediocre en son mestier ny sçavoir sa leçon à demy, mais tout bon, tout excellent et [B ij] tout parfait. La mediocrité est un extréme vice en la poësie. Il vaudroit mieux ne s'en mesler jamais et apprendre un autre mestier.

Davantage je te veux bien encourager de prendre la sage hardiesse et d'inventer des vocables nouveaux, pourveu qu'ils soient moulez et façonnez sus un patron desja receu du peuple. Il est fort difficile d'escrire bien en nostre langue si elle n'est enrichie autrement qu'elle n'est pour le present de mots et de diverses manieres de parler. Ceux qui escrivent journellement en elle sçavent bien à quoy leur en tenir; car c'est une extreme geine de se servir tousjours d'un mot. Oultre, je t'advertis de ne faire conscience de remettre en usage les antiques vocables, et principalement ceux du langage Wallon et Picard, lequel nous reste par tant de siecles l'exemple naïf de la langue Françoise, j'entends de celle qui eut cours après que la Latine n'eut plus d'usage en nostre Gaule; et choisir les mots les plus preignants et significatifs, non seulement dudit langage mais de toutes les provinces de France, pour servir à la poësie lorsque tu en auras besoin. Malheureux est le debteur lequel n'a qu'une seule espece de monnoie pour payer son creancier. Oultre plus, si les vieux mots abolis par l'usage ont laissé quelque rejetton, comme les branches des arbres couppez le rajeunissent de nouveaux drageons, tu le pourras provigner, amender et cultiver, afin qu'il se repeuple de nouveau. Exemple de *lobbe*, qui est un vieil [B ij *v*] mot François qui signifie mocquerie et raillerie. Tu pourras faire sur le nom le verbe *lobber*, qui signifiera mocquer et gaudir, et mille autres de telle façon.

Tu te donneras de garde, si ce n'est par grande contrainte, de te servir des mots terminez en *ion* qui passent plus de trois ou quatre syllabes, comme *abomination*, *testification*; car tels mots sont languissants et ont une trainante voix, et qui plus est, occupent languidement la moictié d'un vers.

C'est autre chose d'escrire en une langue florissante qui est pour le present receüe du peuple, villes, bourgades et citez comme vive et naturelle, approuvée des roys, des princes, des senateurs, marchands et trafiqueurs, et de composer en une langue morte, muette et ensevelie sous le silence de tant d'espaces d'ans; laquelle ne s'apprend plus qu'à l'escole par le foüet et par la lecture des livres; ausquelles langues mortes il n'est licite de rien innover, disgraciées du temps, sans appuy d'empereurs, ny de roys, de magistrats ny de villes, comme chose morte laquelle s'est perdue par le fil des ans ainsi que font toutes choses humaines, qui perissent vieilles pour faire place aux autres suivantes et nouvelles. Car ce n'est la raison que la nature soit tousjours si prodigue de ses biens à deux ou trois nations qu'elle ne vueille conserver ses richesses aussi pour les derniers comme les premiers. En telles langues passées et defunctes (comme j'ay dit) il ne fault rien innover, comme ensevelies, ayant [B iij] resigné leur droict aux vivantes qui florissent en empereurs, princes et magistrats, qui parlent naturellement, sans maistre d'escole, l'usage le permettant ainsi; lequel usage le permet en la mesme façon que le commerce et trafic des monnoies pour quelque espace de temps. Ledict usage les descrie quand il veult. Pour ce il ne se fault estonner d'ouyr un mot nouveau non plus que de veoir quelque nouvelle jocondalle, nouveaux tallars, royales, ducats de sainct Estienne, et pistolets. Telle monnoie, soit d'or ou d'argent, semble estrange au commencement; puis l'usage l'adoucit et domestique, la faisant recevoir, luy donnant authorité, cours, et credit; et devient aussi commune que nos testons et nos escus au soleil.

Tu seras très advisé en la composition des vocables et ne les feras prodigieux; mais par bon jugement, lequel est la meilleure partie de l'homme quand il est clair et net, et non embabouiné ny corrompu de monstrueuses imaginations de ces robins de court qui veulent tout corriger.

Je te conseille d'user indifferemment de tous dialectes, comme j'ay desja dict; entre lesquels le courtisan est tousjours le plus beau à cause de la majesté du prince. Mais il ne peut estre parfaict sans l'aide des autres. Car chacun jardin a sa particuliere fleur, et toutes nations ont affaire les unes des autres; comme en nos havres et ports la marchandise bien loin cher[B iij *v*]chée en l'Amerique se debite partout. Toutes provinces, tant soient-elles maigres, servent aux plus fertiles de quelque chose, comme les plus foibles membres et les plus petits de l'homme servent aux plus nobles du corps.

Je te conseille d'apprendre diligemment la langue Grecque et Latine, voire Italienne et Françoise et Espagnole; puis, quand tu les sçauras parfaitement, te retirer en ton enseigne comme un bon soldat et composer en ta langue maternelle, comme a faict Homere, Hesiode, Platon, Aristote, et Theophraste, Virgile, Tite Live, Saluste, Lucrece, et mille autres qui parloient mesme langage que les laboureurs, valets et chambrieres. Car c'est un crime de leze majesté d'abandonner le langage de son pays, vivant et florissant, pour vouloir deterrer je ne sçay quelle cendre des anciens et abbayer les verves des trespassez, et encore opiniastrement se braver là-dessus et dire, "J'atteste les muses que je ne suis point ignorant, et ne crie point en langage vulgaire comme ces nouveaux venus qui veulent corriger le Magnificat";[p] encores que leurs escrits estrangers, tant soient-ils

p. "corriger le Magnificat" apparently means to make unfounded criticisms; cf. Henri Estienne, *Deux Dialogues du nouveau langage françáis italianizé*, ed. Ristelhuber, (Paris: Lemerre, 1855), I, 309, n. 1.

parfaits, ne sçauroient trouver lieu aux boutiques des apoticaires pour faire des cornets.

Comment veux-tu qu'on te lise, latineur, quand à peine lit-on Stace, Lucain, Seneque, Silius et Claudian, qui ne servent que d'ombre muette en une estude, ausquels on ne parle jamais que deux ou trois fois en la vie, encore [B iiij] qu'ils fussent grands maistres en leur langue maternelle? Et tu veux qu'on te lise, qui as appris en l'escole à coups de verges le langage estranger que sans peine et naturellement ces grands personnages parloient à leurs valets, nourrices et chambrieres? O quantesfois ay-je souhaité que les divines testes et sacrées aux muses de Josephe Scaliger, Daurat, Pimpont, Florent Chrestien, Passerat,[q] voulussent employer quelques heures à si honorable labeur:

Gallica se quantis attollet gloria verbis!

Je supplie très humblement ceux ausquels les muses ont inspiré leur faveur de n'estre plus latineurs ny grecaniseurs, comme ils sont plus par ostentation que par devoir; et prendre pitié, comme bons enfans, de leur pauvre mere naturelle. Ils en rapporteront plus d'honneur et de reputation à l'advenir que s'ils avoient, à l'imitation de Longueil, Sadolet, ou Bembe,[r] recousu ou rabobiné je ne sçay quelles vieilles rapetasseries de Virgile et de Ciceron, sans tant se tourmenter. Car quelque chose qu'ils puissent escrire, tant soit-elle excellente, ne semblera que le cry d'une oye au prix du chant de ces vieils cygnes, oiseaux dediez à Phebus Apollon. Après la premiere lecture de leurs escrits, on n'en tient non plus de compte que de sentir un bouquet fani. Encore vaudroit-il mieux, comme un bon bourgeois ou citoyen, rechercher et faire un lexicon des vieils mots d'Artus, Lancelot, et Gauvain, ou commenter le *Romant de la Rose*, [B iiij *v*] que s'amuser à je ne sçay quelle grammaire Latine qui a passé son temps. Davantage, qu'ils considerent comme le Turc en gaignant la Grece en a perdu la langue du tout. Ledit mesme seigneur Turc, occupant par armes la meilleure partie de l'Europe, où on souloit parler la langue Latine, l'a totalement abolie, reduisant la Chrestienté de si vaste et grande qu'elle estoit au petit pied, ne luy laissant presque que le nom, comme celle qui n'a plus que cinq ou six nations où la langue Romaine se debite. Et n'eust esté le chant de nos eglises, et psalmes chantez au leuthrin, longtemps y a que la langue Romaine se fust esvanouye, comme toutes choses humaines ont leur cours; et pour le jourd'huy vaut autant parler un bon gros Latin,

q. All these humanists (Joseph Justus Scaliger, Jean Dorat, Germain Vaillant de Guelis, abbé de Pimpont, Florent Chrestien, and Jean Passerat) wrote verse in Latin in addition to their scholarly activities.

r. Christophe de Longueil (Longolius), Jacopo Sadoleto, and Pietro Bembo were all celebrated humanists who had written prose and verse works in imitation of the Romans; Longueil and Bembo especially were noted Ciceronians.

pourveu que l'on soit entendu, qu'un affetté langage de Ciceron. Car on ne harangue plus devant empereurs ne senateurs Romains, et la langue Latine ne sert plus de rien que pour nous truchemanter en Allemaigne, Poloigne, Angleterre, et autres lieux de ces pays-là. D'une langue morte l'autre prend vie, ainsi qu'il plaist à l'arrest du destin et à Dieu qui commande, lequel ne veut souffrir que les choses mortelles soient eternelles comme luy; lequel je supplie très humblement, lecteur, te vouloir donner sa grace et le desir d'augmenter le langage de ta nation.

Quant à nostre escriture, elle est fort vicieuse et corrompue; et me semble qu'elle a grand besoin de reformation, et de remettre [B v] en son premier honneur le K et le Z, et faire des characteres nouveaux pour la double N à la mode des Espagnols, ñ, pour escrire *monseigneur*, et une L double pour escrire *orgueilleux*. Je t'en diray davantage quand j'en auray le loisir. A Dieu, candide lecteur.

JEAN VAUQUELIN DE LA FRESNAYE

PREFACE TO HIS *Satyres Françoises*

1605

TEXT:

Les Diverses Poesies dv Sievr de la Fresnaie Vavqvelin. Dont le contenu se void en la page suiuante. A Caen, Par Charles Macé Imprimeur du Roy. 1612. [Pierpont Morgan Library.]

[The 1612 edition is identical with the first edition of 1605 except for the t.p. and the preliminaries and the removal of the special t.p. for the "Satyres Françoises." Cf. Brunet, V, 1102, and *Supplément*, II, 848–49; Tchemerzine, X, 452–53; Le Petit, pp. 106–107; Cat. Rothschild, No. 725.]

There is some disagreement about the date of composition of Vauquelin de la Fresnaye's *Satires françaises*. Achille Genty, in his edition of Vauquelin's *Art poétique* (Paris: Poulet-Malassis, 1862, p. xii), indicated that they were written between 1581 and 1585; but Hugo Lichtenauer, *Jean Vauquelin ... der Schöpfer der klassischen Satire in Frankreich* (Dresden, 1889), pointed out that certain ones were written in 1588 or 1589, others after 1591. The preface is undated. It probably was written after the completion of the satires and just before their publication; Vauquelin speaks, in the final paragraph, of having published some of his verses "il y a près de cinquante ans," which must be a reference to the *Foresteries* of 1555. The preface was reprinted in a line-for-line transcription by Julien Travers in his edition of *Les Diverses Poésies de Jean Vauquelin* ... (Caen: Le Blanc-Hardel, 1869, I, 121–33). Travers also made a study of Vauquelin in the preliminary essay of his edition of the *Œuvres diverses* (Caen: Le Blanc-Hardel, 1872).

[I] DISCOURS POUR SERVIR DE PREFACE SUR LE SUJET DE LA SATYRE

La satyre estant une sorte de poësie qui n'est pas encores si commune en nostre France que les tragedies et comedies, j'ay bien voulu toucher quelque chose de l'antiquité de ce sujet pour en donner plus claire et facile intelligence, me persuadant que quand il sera connu il se pourra trouver autant utile et agreable en nostre langue que nul autre, quel qui puisse estre. Pour donc sçavoir d'où il a pris son origine et son commencement, il faut entendre qu'aux premiers temps que le monde sortoit de son enfance et que les gents estoient encores [I *v*] ignorants et grossiers, ayans plustost les mœurs simples et naturelles que fines et artificieuses, ils avoient accoutumé, comme bons et devotieux, de sacrifier à leurs dieux et d'acomplir leurs vœux avec grande feste et solennité; ce qu'ils faisoient en toutes saisons, mais beaucoup plus communement au temps de la moisson et des vendanges, d'autant que s'assemblans chacun en leurs champs, par diverses familles et compagnies, ils dressoient des autels de ramée, de branchages et de gazons, ausquels ils mettoient le feu en sacrifiant à Bacchus un bouc (qui s'apelle *Tragos* en Grec) et chantoient à qui mieux mieux une maniere de vers tous rustiques et mal polis; et de leur chant et de ce mot *Tragos* (comme qui eust dit "chanson du bouc") eut son origine la tragedie. Pour cette mesme cause on donnoit un bouc à celuy qui avoit le mieux chanté. Et la raison pourquoy ils immoloient plustost un bouc à Bacchus qu'un autre animal estoit que par son broust et viandis il nuisoit plus aux vignes que les autres animaux. A l'heure donc la tragedie n'estoit autre chose qu'un remerciment à Dieu de la bonne vendange et une louange de sa bonté, de sa largesse et de sa grandeur.

Mais pource que les hommes grands tyrans et puissants commencerent depuis à usurper les louanges qui appartenoient aux Dieux, il se trouva des personnes de gentil entendement qui commencerent [I iij] aussi à montrer par leurs vers combien la vie des hommes estoit fresle, debile, et infortunée, au respec de la bienheureuse felicité de Dieu. Ce que voulant faire voir par exemples, ils ramentevoient les calamitez des roys et des princes lesquels estoient tombez de leur grand et magnifique estat en misere et povreté. Qui fait croire que de là la tragedie, telle qu'elle est maintenant, eut son commencement. Au moyen de quoy les tragedies sont toutes fondées sur faits tous vertueux et pitoyables; et bien qu'elles soient à leurs entrées quelquefois pleines d'allegresse, toutefois à la fin elles sont toutes douloureuses; sinon celles d'Euripide, qui finissent en joye et contentement, comme l'*Alceste*, l'*Ifiginie*, l'*Ion*, etc. Ce qui a fait inventer aux modernes le mot de "tragicomedie," duquel les anciens Grecs et Latins n'usoient point.

La comedie, au contraire, est fondée sur faits tous vitieux, mais non de telle sorte que le vice ne s'en puisse bien amender et reparer. Et tout ainsi qu'en l'une ne sont introduits que roys et princes bien nourris et bien apris, aussi en l'autre ne se voyent que des personnes vulgaires et de moyenne condition, qui pour avoir debauché et suborné une fille ne font cas de l'épouser pour couvrir leur faute et eviter la punition du peché; et tousjours finit en noces ou autre contentement cette comedie, laquelle eut son origine en cette sorte: Devant que les Atheniens eussent basti leur cité, [I iij *v*] ils faisoient leur demeure en des tentes et pavillons, ils habitoient aux champs en des bordes et cabanes, et devant que sacrifier à leur Apolon Nomien, dieu des pasteurs et bergers, ils s'assembloient en grandes compagnies et grandes assemblées, et buvant et mengeant tous ensemble ils faisoient grand' chere, ils faisoient mile jeux, passoient le temps à divers plaisirs et chantoient une infinité de vers, toutefois goffes et mal faits, lesquels ils apeloient comedie de *Comos* ou *Comoï*, qui signifient en Grec "assemblée ou mengerie publique," comme qui diroit "chanson d'assemblée et de grand' chere." Et cette comedie ainsi faite ne contenoit autre chose que des vers et des chants qui principalement reprenoient les vices et les fautes d'autruy. D'où sortirent depuis les escriveurs de l'antique comedie, qui nottoient et découvroient, avec grande liberté, non seulement les vices des absents mais bien souvent aussi ceux des personnes presentes. Laquelle liberté de reprendre servit longtemps aux vertus et aux bonnes mœurs, pource que plusieurs, ayans crainte d'estre decouvers et diffamez pour leurs vicieuses actions et mauvais deportements, s'abstenoient de choses infames et deshonnestes et se gardoient de se faire remarquer de faute et de peché qui peust estre manifesté au public.

Mais afin que les poëtes de ce siecle-là peussent taxer plus librement les vices et les defauts voluptueux et lascifs de chacun, [I iiij] ils introduisoient devant tous quelques satyres, qui sont especes de dieux habitans les forests, ayans des cornes au front et des pieds de bouc, qui sont foletons, ehontez, et impudents, et qui surtout se recreent de paillardises et choses lascives. Et comme encore nos derniers majeurs, qui faisoient representer quelques jeux, farces, ou moralitez en public, mettoient quelquefois en avant un fol, un bouffon, un badin, pour parler en plus grande liberté; ainsi en ce temps-là ceux qui[1] n'avoient pas la hardiesse de dire les méchansetez et mauvaitiez d'alors, ils se couvroient de l'ombre et du nom de ces satyres. En cette maniere fut introduite la satyre antique et la comedie, lesquelles à peu près estoient semblables au vers et au sujet, mais elles differoient en ce qu'en la comedie on ne representoit point de satyres comme en la satyre. La satyre donc et la comedie sortirent incontinent après l'antique tragedie.

Mais depuis que les Grecs eurent usé par un long temps de cette façon d'escrire, ils commencerent à devenir un peu trop licentieux, parce qu' estant gaignez par prieres ou corrompus par presents, ils se mirent à diffamer et dire mal des plus gents de bien; qui fut occasion de faire la loy par laquelle il estoit deffendu de faire vers diffamatoires contre aucun homme vivant ne qui fust taxé par son nom. Pour cette raison Menandre trouva l'invention de la nouvelle comedie, et fut rejetée la liberté de dire [I iiij *v*] d'Aristophane. Finablement, Lucilius à Rome fut le premier inventeur de la nouvelle satyre. Il estoit né de la ville d'Aronce, homme docte, d'un sçavoir vehement et d'un courage franc et libre; lequel retint et conserva la vieille usance de reprendre les vices, mais il changea la maniere et façon des vers, moderant quelque peu la premiere liberté

1. qni *1605*

en consideration et consequence de la loy. Mais pource que ses vers alloient et sautoient d'un vice à l'autre, suivant la coutume des satyres, le nom de satyre demeura à ce genre d'escrire.

Or la satyre doit estre d'un stile simple et bas, entre celuy du tragic et du comic, imitant et representant surtout les choses naturelles, d'autant qu'il doit suffire au satyrique de reprendre ouvertement et sans artifice les fautes et les vanitez d'autruy. C'est pourquoy ceux-là ne meritent de louange qui, escrivant des satyres, usent d'un stile trop élevé; car ce seroit faire des vers heroïques, qui requierent un air haut et magnifique. Ce qui fait qu'au commencement de ces graves poësies on invoque quelque deité, quasi confessant que ce qu'on doit chanter surpasse les forces de l'entendement humain; chose qui n'avient point en la satyre, à raison qu'elle traite de choses basses, humbles et communes. Aussi les satyriques ne commencent leurs ouvrages avec invocation ou autre merveille, ains avec quelque dedain, quelque courroux ou autre telle façon de dire, comme s'ils e[I v]stoient provoquez et presque forcez[2] par l'abondance et multitude des vices à s'élever pour les reprendre, ne se pouvants taire estants piquez de l'eguillon d'un si juste depit. Davantage on introduit seulement des gents de moyenne qualité à discourir et parler en la satyre, comme flateurs, esclaves, serviteurs et autres telles gents; et par occasion on y entremesle des contes et des fables de choses pareilles et basses. Au contraire, aux poësies heroiques on ne met que des princes, des heros, et des grands et genereux capitaines, des gestes et exploits desquels le poete chantant embellit son œuvre et ses discours, comme aussi de mile fictions, de beaucoup de figures, de harangues et descriptions, de phrases et paroles esleues et choisies d'entre la naifveté du parler de sa nation. Mais la satyre ne demande que la verité simple et nue et des paroles du cru du pays de celuy qui escrit, sans s'élever ni rabaisser trop en son propos.

Telle est la maniere d'escrire d'Horace entre les satyriques, avec des vers si naifs et si bas que bien souvent il n'y a point autre difference entre eux et la prose que la mesure et la quantité, de sorte qu'à grand' peine ils semblent meriter le nom de poesie. Aussi il a compris ses satyres sous le nom de sermons, pris du mot Latin *Sermo*, qui n'est autre chose que le devis familier et commun d'entre un ou deux devisants ensemble. Et pour cette raison (et que pareillement Horace reprend les vices [I v *v*] en ses sermons) il est vraysemblable que l'usage a fait appeler de ce nom les predications de nos prescheurs.

Donc il ne faut douter que la satyre ne soit une espece de poesie qui sera merveilleusement plaisante et profitable en nostre François, pourveu qu'on s'abstienne de diffamer personne en particulier et qu'on ne se licentie par vengeance ou autrement à faire des vers pleins de medisance,

2. fotcez *1605*

d'injure et de menterie, tels que les cocqs-à-l'asne, lesquels prindrent pied et succederent aux sylvantez de nos poetes Walons et Provençauls qui avoient imité proprement en nostre langage les satyriques Latins. En quoy Marot (lequel regla le premier cette façon de cocqs-à-l'asne) se contint assez modestement, retenant la douceur et naifveté de nostre François (auquel il excelloit sur tous ceux de son âge). Il adoucissoit ses sornettes et brocards de tel jugement que ceux à qui il importoit de s'en resentir les comporterent doucement. Mais une infinité de rimeurs qui sont venus après, et qui chaque jour comme singes pensent contrefaire leur premier autheur, ont fait et font des cocqs-à-l'asne et des asnes-au-cocq qui sont vers injurieux et diffamatoires, plustost dignes d'estre bruslez avec leurs peres que d'estre veus d'aucun homme d'honneur.

Il faut donc fuir cette façon d'escrire, et retenir par ce que nous avons dit (et plus au long en nostre *Art poetique*)[a] qu'au sujet de la satyre ne sont requis l'ornement, [I vi] l'embellissement, ni la douceur de dire que requiert la matiere epique et heroique; mais y est requise une aigreur meslée de quelque sel poignant en general, adoucie de quelque trait joyeux et sentencieux. Les ignorants, tachez des vices communs aux vulgaires, se facheront de se voir depeints et remarquez en la satyre, comme si le poete avoit pensé à dechiffrer leurs mœurs et à les reprendre. Mais les sages et avisez se plairont de la lire, encores que leur naturel et leurs fautes y soient descrites et touchées; mesme par tel advertissement se corrigeront, et noteront les defauts que beaucoup n'aperçoivent point en eux. Que le sujet de la satyre soit donc pris d'une chose commune; en quoy faisant il ne faut que l'autheur luy-mesme se pardonne, ains qu'il depaigne le premier ses imperfections.

Quelques anciens ont remarqué que Lucilius estoit trop aspre et severe; mais Horace estoit plus doux et moderé en ses dedains, lesquels il cachoit davantage aux commencemens[3] de ses satyres. Juvenal, d'un stile entre les deux, les découvroit plus fort. Chacun avoit son stile particulier, comme Perse l'a different de tous les autres. C'est une chose aussi que j'ay notée, qu'il n'y a pas grande difference entre les epistres et les satyres d'Horace, fors que volontiers il escrit ses epistres à gents absents et à personnes élongnées, et qu'il semble qu'en ses satyres son intention ait esté d'arracher le vice du cœur des [I vi *v*] hommes, d'en defricher et deraciner les mauvaises herbes, pour en ses epistres y planter au lieu les vertus et y enter et greffer des fruits d'un bon ordre. Je di ceci d'autant qu'ayant en divers lieux imité Horace, tant en ses epistres qu'en ses satyres, j'ay diversement entremeslé les miennes soubs mesmes tiltres, comme a fait l'Arioste lequel j'ay pareillement suivi en quelques-unes.

3. *or* au commencement? *1605 reads* au commencemens

a. Vauquelin, *Art poëtique*, II, 726 ff. (ed. G. Pellissier, pp. 102–106).

Je ne diray rien de ma façon d'escrire, sinon que quelque imitation que j'aye faite et quelque liberté d'escrire que je me sois permise, j'ay tâché à ne sortir hors des limites qui doivent borner les affections d'un homme de bien et Chrestien, sans toutefois m'entremettre de parler des questions de la sainte theologie, dont je ne fay profession. Je confesseray en passant qu'encor que la simplicité requise en la satyre et la franchise de parler qu'on trouvera dans mes vers me deussent excuser en mon stile, que toutefois j'eusse bien desiré pouvoir contenter les hommes de cet[4] âge avec un langage plus net et poli que le mien et tel que je le voy aux ouvrages de beaucoup, qui l'ont non seulement adouci sur le meilleur idiome François, mais ont tellement naturalisé les manieres de parler Grecques, Romaines, Italiennes et Espagnoles qu'elles semblent avoir cru en nostre propre terroir. Ce que je n'enten pas du parler d'aujourdhuy quand il est tout confit en antitheses et contrarietez et dont userent quelques Latins soubs l'empire de [I vij] Neron; parler, di-je, que quelques Italiens font tenir aux pedants et aux docteurs introduits en leurs comedies, et duquel jamais le grave Virgile, Ciceron, et autres peres de la langue Romaine n'userent en leurs vers ni en leurs escrits. Je ne le di pas pour blamer du tout ces figures pointues, ni moins pour m'en formaliser autrement; j'en parle sans querelle, mais pour les prier de m'excuser en ma franchise et en ma façon d'escrire (que je reconnoy vraiment bien maigre et sterile) et considerer qu'ayant fait voir de mes vers à la France il y a près de cinquante ans,[b] il seroit trop tard de me deguiser desormais et bien dificile de changer mon stile et ma main. Toutefois je me ravise; les vers maintenant sont en peu d'estime. Lecteur, n'achette point les miens. Au moins je n'auray que faire, par ce moyen, que tu m'excuses; et toy, tu n'auras moindre contentement.

4. cét *1605*

b. *Les deux premiers livres des Foresteries*, 1555.

PIERRE DE LARIVEY

PROLOGUE TO *La Constance*

1611

TEXT:

Trois Comedies des six dernieres de Pierre de Lariuey Champenois. A l'imitation des ançiens Grecs Latins & Modernes Italiens. A Sçavoir: La Constance. Le Fidelle. Et les Tromperies. A Troyes, Par Pierre Chevillot, l'Imprimeur du Roy. M.DC.XI. [University of Pennsylvania Library.]

[Cf. Brunet, III, 840, and *Supplément,* I, 781; Tchemerzine, VII, 33, who points out the existence of a second edition of 1611.]

As in his earlier comedies, Pierre de Larivey again turned to Italian sources when he wrote the three comedies constituting the second volume of his works. *La Constance* was patterned after Girolamo Razzi's *La Gostanza,* and its prologue was adapted from that of the Italian author. For bibliography on Larivey and his works see the prefatory note to the excerpts from the 1579 volume, p. 241 above.

[A iij *v*] PROLOGUE TO *La Constance*

Quand il print envie à l'autheur de ceste comedie qu'il desire presentement vous faire veoir, il sembloit quasi que ce fust à regret, pource qu'il luy estoit advis qu'elle n'estoit bien parée ny agencée comme il desiroit affin de vous donner, messieurs et dames, quelque agreable contentement; encores qu'elle soit toute simple, ne dressant ses actions qu'à la constance du nom de laquelle il l'a[1] voulu nommer. Je sçay bien que plusieurs ne prennent goust qu'à l'antiquité, dont ils font si grande estime qu'ils la logeroient volontiers au ciel, blasmant tous ceux qui ne les ressemblent et ne sont de leur opinion. Autres veullent que com[A iiij]me les aages sont variables et different l'un de l'autre, et d'autant qu'aujourd'huy[2] l'on n'use des mesmes choses dont l'on usoit il y a vingt ans, qu'ainsi les modernes comedies ne doivent estre pareilles à celles qui estoient il y a mil six cens ans passez et plus, nostre vivre n'estant pareil au leur. Ceux-là disent qu'en Grece ou à Rome on usoit d'un autre langage, d'autre façon de vivre, d'autres coustumes, d'autres[3] loix, et—ce qui importe le plus—d'une religion toute contraire à la nostre Chrestienne et Catholique; et autres finalement ne s'en esloignent du tout, encores qu'ils se soient oubliez aux reigles, preceptes et usage qu'ont tenu les anciens recommandables comiques qui seront tousjours prisez et estimez d'un chacun. Mais quoy

1. l'à *1611* 2. qu'auioud'huy *1611* 3. d'aueres *1611*

qu'il en soit, il faut surtout que [A iiij *v*] les comedies soient faictes pour instruire et encor pour donner plaisir. Parquoy, pour revenir à nostre propos, il est malaisé que les hommes puissent faire chose qui agrée à un chacun, l'un ayant les aureilles sourdes, l'autre les yeux esbloüys, et cestui-cy l'esprit esgaré en ses fantastiques contemplations. C'est pourquoy nostre autheur, qui en cecy a voulu imiter les Latins, les Italiens, et autres comiques tant anciens que modernes, portera patiemment le blasme qui luy pourroit estre imputé par aucuns qui paraventure en ce recit penseront estre blasmez, à quoy il n'a jamais pensé. Je diray bien que si quelcun a[4] opinion n'estre vraysemblable ce qui est raconté de la bonté et fidelité des femmes et des hommes introduicts ès actes de la scene, peut estre parce que peu souvent se [A v] trouvent des femmes si chastes et fidelles et des hommes si rares en bonté. Ce neantmoins (recours aux histoires), s'en trouvent plusieurs de l'un et l'autre sexe qui ont esté, et en y a encores à present qui sont semblables aux nostres en amour, foy, et exemple de chasteté. Quoy qu'il en soit, l'autheur vous prie accepter sa bonne volonté, requerant un chacun prendre place et se disposer à entendre patiemment et sans bruit ce que veut commancer à dire Blaise, qui sort avec le pedant. Les voicy. Ouvrez les oreilles et vous orrez conter merveilles.

4. à *1611*

BIBLIOGRAPHY FOR THE GLOSSARY

Cot: Randle Cotgrave, *A Dictionarie of the French and English Tongves*. Compiled by Randle Cotgrave. London, Printed by Adam Islip. Anno 1611. [A few entries are from the edition of London: Islip, 1632.]

DP: [Robert Estienne], *Dictionarium puerorum...*, Apud Gullelmum Laemarium. M.D.LXXXVI.

DuC: Du Cange, *Glossarium Mediae et infimae Latinitatis*, Niort: L. Favre, 1883–87, 10 vols.

Dupuys: [Jacques Dupuys], *Dictionaire Francois-Latin*...Paris: J. Dupuys, 1573. [This second edition of Dupuys's dictionary is really a fourth (or fifth?) edition of Estienne's, with some additional material.]

Est: [Robert Estienne], *Dictionaire Francoislatin, contenant les motz & manieres de parler Francois, tournez en Latin*. A Paris. De l'imprimerie de Robert Estienne. M.D.XXXIX. Auec priuilege du Roy.

Est 2: Robert Estienne, *Dictionaire Francoislatin, avtrement dict Les mots Francois, auec les manieres dvser diceulx, tournez en Latin*. Corrigé & augmenté. A Paris: De l'imprimerie de Robert Estienne Imprimeur du Roy. M.D.XLIX. Par priuilege dudict Seigneur.

Gode: Frédéric Godefroy, *Dictionnaire de l'ancienne langue française*, Paris: Vieweg, 1880–1902, 10 vols.

Huguet: Edmond Huguet, *Dictionnaire de la langue française du seizième siècle*, Paris: Champion, 1925— [A-Fabrique only.]

Littré: Emile Littré, *Dictionnaire de la langue française*, Paris: Hachette, 1878, 5 vols.

MF: *Les Mots francois selon l'ordre des lettres, ainsi qu'il les faut escrire, tournez en Latin*. Par Guillaume de Laimarie. M.D.LXXXVI. [Definitions derived largely from Estienne's dictionary.]

Pals: Jean Palsgrave, *L'Eclaircissement de la langue française*, ed. F. Génin, Paris: Imprimerie nationale, 1852 ("Documents inédits sur l'histoire de France").

GLOSSARY

The glossary contains only words which are not listed in the *Dictionnaire général* of Hatzfeld, Darmesteter, and Thomas in the same or in a related meaning.

abbayer, *tr.* to cry out the merits of (Huguet: *Abbayer qqch.* Le crier très haut)

absolu, *past part.* completed (Huguet: Achevé, accompli, parfait)

adjourner, *tr.* to summon to court (Est 2: Citare, exhibere reum. Dupuys: *Fay moy adiourner*, Lege agito)

adombrer, *tr.* to approximate, imitate (Cot:...to pourtray, or draw a resemblance grossely, as Painters do in their first lines)

affierent, *intr.* are fitting (Est: *Affiert* = *conuient*, attinet)

altiloque, *adj.* lofty in style (Huguet: D'un langage élevé)

attrempance, *f.* temperance (Est 2: Modestia, Temperantia. Cot: *f.* Sobernesse, temperance, modestie, staiednesse, gouernment; moderation in behauiour, or humour)

badault, *m.* a fool (Cot: *m.* A foole, dolt, sot, fop, asse, coxcombe; gaping hoydon)

cetui, *adj.* this, that

chef, conduire à, mettre à, to bring about, to bring to completion (Est: *Mettre a chef quelque haulte entreprinse,* Consciscere facinus. Huguet: Accomplir, achever, mener à bonne fin)

clausule, *f.* a sentence (Huguet: Phrase, période)

comparager, *refl.* to compare (Est 2: *Comparer, ou Comparager. Se comparer a ung autre,* Conferre se alteri, vel cum altero)

conard, *m.* a fool (Huguet: Sot)

contemner, *tr.* to scorn, despise (Est 2: Temnere, Contemnere, Fastidire, Negligere, Despicere. Cot: To contemne, scorne, despise, neglect, make light of, set at nought)

contennement, *m.* scorn (Est: Fastidium, Neglectio. Est 2:...Contemptus, Contemptio)

contournement, *m.* turning up (Huguet: Action de tourner. Cot: *m.* A nimble turning, or winding)

cotter, *tr.* to make a marginal comment; to blame (Huguet: Marquer. Citer. Blâmer. Cot: To quote, or marke in the margent, to note by the way)

deliber, *tr.* to sip, taste (Huguet: Effleurer, goûter légèrement)

deputer, *tr.* to set aside, reserve (Gode: Fixer, choisir. Huguet: Affecter, assigner)

didascalique, *adj.* didactic, preceptive (*Thesaurus Linguae Latinae:* ad docendum idoneus, doctrinam continens. Huguet: Didactique)

ducat de sainct Estienne, *m.* a coin (Cot: [lists several kinds of ducats, not including this one] All forraine coynes; of whose value (often changed by the French Kings) no certaine interpretation can be giuen, other than that they hold a rate much about v or vj s. sterl. the peece)

duisant, *adj.* adapted, fitting (Est 2: *Il est bien duisant & conuenable,* Addecet. Cot: Apt, meet, conuenient, fitting: handsome, seemlie, becomming)

empouller, *tr.* to swell, inflate (Cot: *Empoulément,* Swellingly)

encharger, *intr.* to be or become pregnant (Cot: *Femme qui encharge.* That growes big on't; who burnishes, or whose bellie increases)

encheoir, *intr.* to fall (Huguet: Tomber)

enhorter, *tr.* to exhort (Est: Hortari, Adhortari, Cohortari, Exhortari, Vti hortatione)

entant que, *conj.* in so far as (Est 2: *Entant que a moy est,* Per me quidem, Mea quidem causa)

erre, *f.* a way, path; **reprendre ses erres,** to return to one's subject (Cot: To returne unto the way, or subiect from which he was diuerted. Dupuys:...reprendre son chemin qu'on auoit laissé: & par metaphore, Reprendre les erres de son propos, c'est retourner à l'endroict du propos dont on s'estoit diuerti)

escheoir, *impers.* to be necessary (Est 2: *S'il y eschet, Si mestier est,* Si res ita nata sit)

essonie, *f.* (also essoine, exoine) an excuse for not appearing in court (Pals: Excuse for nat apperyng before a judge)

estour, *m.* a battle (Pals: Tourney justes. Cot: *m.* A fight, combat, conflict, scuffling, shocke, incounter; also, the assault of a towne, or fortresse. Dupuys:...*c'est vn conflict & combat,* Conflictus)

feste, *m.* (= faîte) a top, summit (Est: *Le feste d'ung edifice,* Fastigium...Culmen)

force, *f.* necessity; **il est force,** it is necessary (Est: *C'estoit force de le faire,* Faciundum fuit, Necesse fuit hoc facere. Cot: *Ce que luy sera force.* Which he shall be faine, or forced, to do)

—— a great quantity (Est: *Vallee ou il y a force arbres,* Condensa arboribus vallis. Cot: *f.*...also, store, plentie, aboundance, many of...)

forclos, *adj.* prevented (Est 2: *Estre forclos,* Praescriptione temporis excludi. Cot: Excluded, reiected, expelled, shut out; dismissed, or debarred from)

grevance, *f.* inconvenience, difficulty (Dupuys: *grief, tort,* Damnum Iniuria. *Le mot est ancien, & vient de greuer lequel vient de ce mot Latin,* Grauis *prins pour* Molestus)

grossier, *m.* grocer, or wholesaler (Cot: A Grocer; or, as Marchant Grossier. *Marchant Grossier,* That sells only by Great, or utters his commodities by wholesale)

intermis, adj. interrupted (Est 2: *Intermettre, & discontinuer,* Intermittere, Desistere. Cot: Intermitted, discontinued, pawsed on, left off for a season, let passe for a while)

inveteré, *adj.* old, ancient (Cot: Inueterate, old, auncient, of long use, rooted by custome)

irrision, *f.* scornful laughter (Cot: *f.* Irrision, mocking, flowting, scoffing at; a deriding, or laughing to scorne)

jocondalle, *f.* a coin (Cot: A Daller; a peece of money worth about 3 s. sterl.)

labilité, *f.* inconstancy, instability (DuC: *Labilitas,* Levitas, inconstantia, instabilitas)

lays, *m.* (= legs) a legacy (Est: Legatum)

lubrique, *adj.* obscene; slippery (Cot: Lubricke; slipperie; deceitfull)

manciper, *refl.* to deliver oneself (Cot: To dispossesse himselfe, to deliuer the possession, or make liuerie and seisin, of; to sell, passe away, giue up)

manque, *adj.*, feeble, defective (Cot: Defectiue, lacking, wanting)

matté, *adj.* subdued, wearied (Est 2: Victus. Cot: Mated, amated, quelled, subdued, puld under, taken lower; tired, wearied)

mellificque, *adj.* producing honey

mercadant, *m.* a merchant (Cot: A poore marchant, paltrie tradesman; one that deales but for small, or sleight ware. Cf. H. Estienne, *Deux Dialogues du nouveau langage français italianizé,* ed. Ristelhuber, Paris: Lemerre, 1885, I, 170)

merir, *intr.* to acquire merit (Gode: v.a. mériter, gagner; abs., mériter, acquérir des mérites)

monopole, *m.* a debauch (Est 2: *Monopoler, ou Faire des monopoles,* Coire. *Monopoles & assemblees factieuses pour faire quelque menee,* Coitiones.)

naquet, *m.* a tennis court-keeper's boy (Cot: The boy that serues, or stops the ball after the first bound, to make a better chace, at Tennis; a Court-keeper, or Tennis Court-keepers boy)

noyse, *f.* a quarrel; a battle (Est: Altercatio, Concertatio, Contentio, Dissidium, Iurgium . . .)

obtemperer, *intr.* to obey (Est 2: Obtemperare. Cot: To obtemperate, obey; doe the will, follow the direction, be at the commaund of)

où, *conj.* whereas (Cot: . . . whereas)

oultrement, *adv.* excessively (Cot: *Oultréement.* Through and through; also, extreamely, excessiuely, exceedingly, beyond all measure)

palu, *m.* a marsh, swamp (Est: *Vng palu, & marescage,* Palus. Cot: A fenne, marsh; wet ground, or moore)

peregrin, *adj.* foreign (Est 2: Peregrinus. Cot: Peregrine, forraine, alien, stranger, outlandish)

piafé, *adj.* bombastic (Cot: *Piaffer.* To brag, or braue it fondly; to boast, or strout it vainely; to make a vaine-glorious, or foolish muster of himselfe)

poste, *m.* a courier, messenger (Dupuys: Larius vel Cursor, Alipedes nuntii, Pegasidae. Cot: A Poste, Currier, speedie messenger . . ., also, a rakehell, or Colledge-seruant, thats euer gadding, or ietting abroad)

pouraulant que, *conj.* because

precellant, *adj.* excellent, surpassing (Pals: *Je precelle,* . . . She precelleth all other in beaultye and good manners. Dupuys: *Preceller les autres en vertu,* Praecellere)

preignant, *adj.* rich in meaning, forceful (Cot: Pregnant, pithie, ripe, liuelie, forcible, strong)

premettre, *tr.* to place at the beginning (Gode: v.a., mettre en tête, exposer en premier lieu)

premis, *adj.* set aside (?) [L. praetermissus]

protenotaire, *m.* a protonotary (Cot: A Pregnotarie, principall Notarie, chiefe Scribe; [A title proper, and peculiar to the *Greffier civil de la Cour de Parlement de Paris*])

qui, *conj. pron.* = "si l'on" (Cot: *Ils se feront mal qui ne les departira,* They will mischieue one another if they be not parted)

quottation, *f.* a citation (Gode: citation)

ragdenase, *m.* a grumbler (?) (I have found no other trace of the word. But cf. Jaubert, *Glossaire du Centre de la France,* Paris, 1864, s.v. *Raguenasser,* v. n. Grogner; *Raguenassier,* s.m., Grognon. Also Mistral, *Dictionnaire provençal,* s.v. *Ragagnous, rangagnous, regagnous, regragnous...,* adj., Grognon, hargneux.)

rapetasserie, *f.* a patchwork (Cot: *Rapetacer.* To patch, peece, clowt, mend, botch)

recordation, *f.* remembrance (Est 2: *Recordation & souuenance,* Recordatio. Cot: A recordation, a remembrance)

refragant, *adj.* smelling (?)

rencheute, *f.* repetition (Est 2: *Rencheute de fiebures,* Recidiuae febres. Cot: A recidiuation, or new fall)

reprenable, *adj.* blamable

royale, *m.* a coin (Cot: An old coyne of gold, worth about 68 solz. *Royal de France.* Another of a later stampe, worth 68 solz Tourn. Cf. Sainéan, *La Langue de Rabelais,* I, 193)

scheme, *m.* a figure of speech (Littré: Nom générique des figures et de toutes les formes ou ornements du style)

sciamache, *m.* one who fights under cover (Laumonier, ed. Ronsard, STFM, I, 49; Foulet, *RHL,* 1907, p. 134; Mellerio, *Lexique de Ronsard,* s.v. *Sciamaches,* gens qui combattent des ombres)

senaire, *m.* a hexameter (Littré: Terme de versification ancienne. Se dit d'un vers iambique de six pieds, et du vers hexamètre ordinaire)

sentir de, *refl.* to feel (Est 2: *Je me sen bien souuent de ceste maladie quand le temps se change,* Admoneor saepe hoc morbo)

sophisticquement *adv.*, artificially

sotereau, *m.* a tumbler, buffoon (Cot: *Sautereaux, ou tombereaux de Verberie.* The boyes of that Burrough,tearmed so because they are woont, for the sport of passengers...to tumble from the top to the bottome of a hill that is there-by. Gode: Selon Escallier, dans les villages des environs de Valenciennes, on appelle *sauteriaus* ces joyeux compagnons, espèce de fous en titre d'office, qui sont attachés à quelques confrairies d'archers ou d'arbalétriers et qui ont mission de divertir le public par leurs intermèdes, leurs joyeusetés et leurs cabrioles)

spirant, *adj.* smelling

suppediter, *tr.* to take precedence over (Cot :...also, to vanquish, ouercome, subdue, tread or bring under)

supplier, *tr.* (= suppléer) to supply, make up for (Est : *Supplier & amender la faulte de quelque chose par une autre,* Supplere. So Dupuys. In MF, appears as *Suppleer.* Also *intr.*)

suppliment, *m.* a substitute

sus, *prep.* (= sur) on (Est : *Sus, ou sur,* Super)

sylvantez, *m. pl.* satirical poems; the Provençal *sirventés* (Vauquelin, *Art poëtique,* II, 718 : "Les Satyres qu'alors ils nommoient Syruentez." The present form is probably a result of false etymologizing, on the basis of *sylvan,* a synonym of *satyre*)

tallar, *m.* a coin (Cot : The coyne tearmed a Dollar)

traditif, *adj.* communicable (Cot : Traditiue, or of tradition, whence ; *Science traditive;* a Science deliuered by word of mouth from father to sonne ; or continued, or left unto posteritie, by tradition)

triacle, *m.* (= thériaque) treacle (Est : *Du thriacle,* Theriaca. Cot : *m.* Treacle)

trop, *adv.* much, a great deal (Cot :...also, much, greatly, mainly, mightily)

truchemanter, *tr.* to interpret, make understood (Cot : To interpret, or play the interpreter, to serue as an interpreter vnto, to meditate [*sic*] by interpretors, or by interpretation)

usurper, *tr.* to use (Est : *Vsurper, & souuent user de quelque chose, soit en parolles ou en faictz,* Vsurpare. Cot :...also, to use much, often to mention)

varie, *adj.* varied

verve, *f.* a caprice, fantasy (Cot :...also, an odd humor in a man ; a worme in the head, or brizze in the taile. Cf. H. Estienne, *Deux Dialogues du nouveau langage français italianizé,* ed. Ristelhuber, I, 170)

volatif, *adj.* of, or belonging to, flying

INDEX